Transcultural Italies

Mobility, Memory and Translation

Transnational Italian Cultures 4

Transnational Italian Cultures

Series editors:
Dr Emma Bond, University of St Andrews
Professor Derek Duncan, University of St Andrews

Transnational Italian Cultures will publish the best research in the expanding field of postcolonial, global and transnational Italian studies and aim to set a new agenda for academic research on what constitutes Italian culture today. As such, it will move beyond the physical borders of the peninsula as well as identifying existing or evolving transnational presences within the nation in order to reflect the vibrant and complex make-up of today's global Italy. Privileging a cultural studies perspective with an emphasis on the analysis of textual production, the series focuses primarily on the contemporary context but will also include work on earlier periods informed by current postcolonial/transnational methodology.

Transcultural Italies

Mobility, Memory and Translation

Edited by
Charles Burdett, Loredana Polezzi
and Barbara Spadaro

LIVERPOOL UNIVERSITY PRESS

First published 2020 by
Liverpool University Press
4 Cambridge Street
Liverpool
L69 7ZU

Copyright © 2020 Charles Burdett, Loredana Polezzi and Barbara Spadaro

The rights of Charles Burdett, Loredana Polezzi and Barbara Spadaro to be identified as the editors of this book has been asserted by them in accordance with the Copyright, Designs and Patents Act 1988.

All rights reserved. No part of this book may be reproduced, stored in a retrieval system, or transmitted, in any form or by any means, electronic, mechanical, photocopying, recording, or otherwise, without the prior written permission of the publisher.

British Library Cataloguing-in-Publication data
A British Library CIP record is available

ISBN 978-1-78962-255-3

Typeset by Carnegie Book Production, Lancaster
Printed and bound by CPI Group (UK) Ltd, Croydon CR0 4YY

Contents

List of Figures vii

List of Contributors xi

Introduction: Transcultural Italies 1
   Charles Burdett, Loredana Polezzi and Barbara Spadaro

Part 1: Traces

1. The Transnational Biography of 'British' Place: Local and Global Stories in the Built Environment 23
   Jennifer Burns

2. Porteña Identity and Italianità: Language, Materiality and Transcultural Memory in Valparaíso's Italian Community 47
   Naomi Wells

3. Italian Identity, Global Mediterranean: Tourism and Cultural Heritage in Post-Colonial Rhodes 75
   Valerie McGuire

4. Italy and Africa: Post-War Memories of Life in Eritrea and Ethiopia 101
   Charles Burdett

Part 2: Art, Objects and Artefacts

5. 'The Path that Leads Me Home': Eduardo Paolozzi and the Arts of Transnationalizing 127
   Derek Duncan

6. Moving Objects: Memory and Material Culture 155
   Margaret Hills de Zárate

7. Visualizing Spatialization at a Crossroads between Translation and Mobility: Italian Australian Artist Jon Cattapan's Cityscapes   179
Eliana Maestri

8. An Exhibition about Italian Identities: *Beyond Borders*   207
Viviana Gravano and Giulia Grechi

Part 3: Mobilities of Memory

9. Pitigliano, Maryland? Travelling Memories and Moments of Truth   227
Barbara Spadaro

10. Misplaced Plants: Migrant Gardens and Transculturation   253
Ilaria Vanni

11. The Chinese Community in Italy, the Italian Community in China: Economic Exchanges and Cultural Difference   275
Chiara Giuliani

12. Writing the Neighbourhood: Literary Representations of Language, Space and Mobility   297
Rita Wilson

13. From Substitution to Co-presence: Translation, Memory, Trace and the Visual Practices of Diasporic Italian Artists   317
Loredana Polezzi

Index   341

Figures

Fig. 1.1: Frontage of St Peter's Italian Church; Lonpicman. Own work, CC BY-SA 3.0, https://commons.wikimedia.org/w/index.php?curid=8543931 (downloaded 12 February 2020). 27

Fig. 1.2: Products at Terroni's. Author's own image. 31

Fig. 1.3: The Italian Hospital. Author's own image. 33

Fig. 1.4: Gazzano House. Author's own image. 35

Fig. 2.1: Statue of the Capitoline wolf in Valparaíso's Parque Italia. Author's own image. 53

Fig. 2.2: Bust of Giovanni Battista Pastene in Valparaíso's Parque Italia. Author's own image. 53

Fig. 2.3: Statue of Christopher Columbus, above the plaque marking 500 years since the 'discovery' of the Americas. Author's own image. 55

Fig. 2.4: Valparaíso's Scuola Italiana. Author's own image. 58

Fig. 2.5: An early photo, held by Renato, of the shop owned by his family. Author's own image. 65

Fig. 2.6: An image from inside the Almacén Naval, with a photo of the original Italian owners, above a sticker saying 'This is a heritage site of Playa Ancha [an area of Valparaíso]'. Author's own image. 69

Fig. 2.7: Renato believed this to be the site of one of the first Italian-owned shops established in the city. Author's own image. 70

Fig. 2.8: The Almacén & Botillería Garibaldi in Valparaíso. Author's own image. 72

Fig. 3.1: View of the medieval city gates after Italian renovation and reconstruction circa 1930. © Archive of the *Touring Club Italiano*. 82

Fig. 3.2: The Italian tourist waterfront of Rhodes circa 1930. © Archive of the *Touring Club Italiano*. 86

Fig. 3.3: Advertisement for a 1935 Crociera del Levante offered by the *Organizzazione Nazionale Dopolavoro*. © General State Archives of Greece. 90

Fig. 4.1: Asmara, food market and corn seed market, *Mai Taclì*, May–June 1993. 113

Fig. 4.2: View of Asmara, *Mai Taclì*, July–August 1997. 117

Fig. 4.3: View of Asmara, *Mai Taclì*, November–December 1997. 117

Fig. 5.1: Artwork from *Pop Paolozzi!* 134

Fig. 5.2: Slide from the *Pop Paolozzi!* presentation. 135

Fig. 5.3: *Print Generation*: the printing process. 136

Fig. 5.4: Making *BOLT!* 140

Fig. 5.5: Leonardo: the printing process. 146

Fig. 5.6: Leonardo: science and art. 146

Fig. 5.7: Enjoyment. 149

Fig. 5.8: 'The path that leads me home'. 150

Fig. 6.1: Italian dances, Feria de Las Colectividades, Morón, Buenos Aires Province, April 2015. Author's own image. 165

Fig. 6.2: Dancers, Feria de Las Colectividades, Morón, April 2015. Author's own image. 166

Fig. 6.3: Object Workshop, Morón, Buenos Aires Province, May 2015. Author's own image. 173

Fig. 7.1: *Untitled*, 1990 (From *Travel Suite* 1990–2015). Gouache and watercolor on paper, Collection National Gallery of Victoria; image courtesy the artist. 191

Figures

Fig. 7.2: *The Bookbuilder*, 1992. Oil on linen, Collection Artbank Australia; image courtesy the artist. — 193

Fig. 7.3: *Study after Endless* (Melbourne), 2014. Digital print and gouache on paper; image courtesy the artist and STATION. — 200

Fig. 8.1: Plan of the exhibition *Beyond Borders: Transnational Italy*, British School at Rome, 2016. Poster design by Carolina Farina. — 212

Fig. 8.2: The Passageway with photographs by Mario Badagliacca, 'Italy is Out', *Beyond Borders: Transnational Italy*, British School at Rome, 2016. Photo by Carolina Farina. — 215

Fig. 8.3: The Living Room, *Beyond Borders: Transnational Italy*, British School at Rome, 2016. Photo by Carolina Farina. — 219

Fig. 8.4: The Bedroom, *Beyond Borders: Transnational Italy*, British School at Rome, 2016. Photo by Carolina Farina. — 219

Fig. 8.5: The School, *Beyond Borders: Transnational Italy*, British School at Rome, 2016. Photo by Carolina Farina. — 221

Fig. 9.1: Fonte della Sapienza. Author's own photograph. — 241

Fig. 9.2: Paola in the classroom of aunt Clelia, Tripoli 1947. Courtesy of Paola Giuili. — 246

Fig. 9.3: Miriam and Elia Giuili (1920s). Photograph by Gaetano Nascia, Benghazi. Courtesy of Paola Giuili. — 248

Fig. 10.1: Front garden, some traces of the original Federation design and a copy of Michelangelo's David, Ilaria Vanni, 2017. — 254

Fig. 10.2: Planty transculturation in a front garden: flowers inspired by cottage garden design, a native fern tree, olive and mango trees, Ilaria Vanni, 2017. — 257

Fig. 10.3: Bananas and olive trees, Ilaria Vanni, 2018. — 261

Fig. 10.4: A backyard in Marrickville remixes tropical and Mediterranean plants, Ilaria Vanni, 2017. — 264

Fig. 10.5: Garden whimsy in Haberfield, Ilaria Vanni, 2018. — 267

Fig. 10.6: Mango and olive trees, Ilaria Vanni, 2017. 269

Fig. 10.7: A fence, prickly pear, gorse, and olive tree, Ilaria Vanni, 2018. 272

Fig. 13.1: B. Amore, *Great Grandmother's Ocean*. Dowry bedspread made by Giovannina Forte. Antique linen weaving, iron artefacts, fabric, Plexiglas, wood. 2′ × 8′ × 8′, 2004. Image courtesy of the artist; photograph by Christopher Burke. 328

Fig. 13.2: Luci Callipari-Marcuzzo, *Tracing Threads of the Past: Apron [Tracciando fili del passato: grembiule]*, live art performance, 27 October, *La Soffitta*, in *Beyond Borders: Transnational Italy/Oltre i confini: Italia transnazionale*, curated by Viviana Gravano and Giulia Grechi. The British School at Rome, Italy, 2016. Image courtesy of the artist; photograph by Carolina Farina (Routes Agency). 333

Fig. 13.3 and Fig. 13.4: Filomena Coppola, *Wallflower – Mirror, rorriM*. Pastel on paper, H 108 cm × W 216 cm. Mildura dirt and Murray River sand (approx 300 × 300 cm). Exhibited in Rio Vista Cellar Basement (original Chaffey home), Mildura Arts Centre (Australia), 2011. Images (before and after viewings) courtesy of the artist. 336

List of Contributors

Charles Burdett is Professor of Italian at the University of Durham. The principal areas of his research are literary culture under Fascism; travel writing; the Italian colonial presence in Libya and East Africa and its legacy; theories of inter-cultural contact; the representation of Islam and the Islamic world in recent Italian literature and culture. His books include *Journeys through Fascism: Italian Travel Writing between the Wars* (2007) and *Italy, Islam and the Islamic World: Representations and Reflections from 9/11 to the Arab Uprisings* (2016). He was principal investigator of the collaborative research project 'Transnationalizing Modern Languages: Mobility, Identity and Translation in Modern Italian Cultures' (2014–17). Developing from his work on colonial discourse under Fascism and on the aftermath of the Italian occupation of Ethiopia, he is currently working on a study of the memory of the Italian empire.

Jennifer Burns is Professor in Italian Studies at the University of Warwick. Her research engages with contemporary Italian literature and culture, primarily with narratives by migrant and mixed-ethnicity writers in the Italian language (*Migrant Imaginaries*, 2013). Underlying this research are questions of subjectivity, embodiment and affect, of language, and of the impacts of transnational upon 'national' literary cultures. Both independently and as co-investigator in the collaborative project 'Transnationalizing Modern Languages' (2014–17), her most recent work explores the shared spaces of language, creativity and everyday cultural practice that challenge the notion of discrete and bounded national cultures and reveal the extended relationality of human experience in subnational as well as transnational spaces and communities. This in turn has informed her engagement with initiatives to rethink the disciplinary framework and practices of research and teaching in Modern Languages for the present and future. She is also co-editor of *Transnational Modern Languages: A Handbook* (Liverpool University Press, forthcoming).

Derek Duncan is Professor of Italian at the University of St Andrews. He has published extensively on modern Italian culture, particularly on intersections of sexuality/gender and race/ethnicity in a transnational framework. He has been instrumental in the development of Italian Colonial and Postcolonial Studies and Italian Queer Studies. He was founding editor of the 'Cultural Studies' issue of *Italian Studies*, and edits Liverpool University Press's acclaimed series 'Transnational Italian Cultures'. He is also co-editor of *Transnational Modern Languages: A Handbook* (Liverpool University Press, forthcoming). He has organised numerous conferences in the UK and elsewhere. He is currently interested in exploring Italian cultural production as a set of vernacular material practices extending beyond the peninsula itself and in the multiple legacies of migration from Italy. He is increasingly engaged with developments in the Creative Humanities and in the fusion of academic research and creative practice.

Chiara Giuliani is Lecturer in Italian Studies at University College Cork (Ireland). Her research interests comprise postcolonial theories, memory and migration studies, material culture and geo-criticism. Such interests originate from her doctoral degree, which she obtained from the University of St Andrews on Italian postcolonial literature and home spaces. Her current research project investigates the ambiguities that shape the socio-economic relations between Italy and China and the role played by the Chinese community in Italy. She is particularly interested in examining the representation and self-representation of second and third generations of Chinese–Italians and the role they play in Sino-Italian dynamics. She has published articles on the representation of Chinese-Italian identities and on migration and public space; her monograph *Home, Memory and Belonging in Italian Postcolonial Literature* is forthcoming with Palgrave Macmillan.

Viviana Gravano is an art historian and a contemporary art curator. She is Associate Professor of Art History at the School of Fine Arts in Bologna, editor-in-chief, with Giulia Grechi, of the online journal *roots§routes – research on visual cultures* and member of the curatorial collective Routes Agency. Cura of Contemporary Art, based in Rome. She is director of the art gallery Attitudes_spazio alle arti in Bologna. At Routes Agency, she curated exhibitions and conferences in a range of cultural spaces (such as the MAXXI Museum and the Pigorini Ethnographic Museum in Rome). She has published numerous essays in catalogues, in books and in magazines. Her books include: *L'Arte fotografica. Fotografi da tutto il mondo nelle collezioni* *italiane* (1996); *L'immagine fotografica* (1997); *Crossing. Progetti fotografici di confine* (1998); *Paesaggi attivi. Saggio contro la contemplazione/L'attivismo paesaggistico nell'arte contemporanea* (2012); *Show, Milano 2015, una scommessa interculturale persa* (2016); and *Presente Imperfetto. Eredità coloniali e immaginari razziali contemporanei* (with Giulia Grechi) (2016).

Giulia Grechi is Professor of Cultural Anthropology at the Fine Arts School of Naples. Her research interests include cultural and post-colonial studies, migration and museology, with a focus on representations of the body, on 'italianità' and on how contemporary art practices can discuss and reshape these complex imaginaries. Since January 2015 she has been part of the EU 'MeLa – European Museums in the Age of Migrations' project. She is editor-in-chief, with Viviana Gravano, of the online journal *roots§routes – research on visual cultures* and founder of the cultural association Routes Agency. With Routes Agency she has curated exhibitions and conferences in a range of cultural spaces (such as the MAXXI Museum and the Pigorini Ethnographic Museum in Rome). Recent publications include *La Rappresentazione Incorporata. Una etnografia del corpo tra stereotipi coloniali e arte contemporanea* (2016); *The Ruined Archive* (with Iain Chambers and Mark Nash, 2014); and *Presente Imperfetto. Eredità coloniali e immaginari razziali contemporanei* (with Viviana Gravano, 2016).

Margaret Hills de Zárate is an Honorary Senior Lecturer at Queen Margaret University in Edinburgh. She studied at Goldsmith's College, Edinburgh University, The Scottish Institute of Human Relations and the University of Havana, Cuba. She has worked and taught in various countries including Taiwan, Spain, Argentina, Chile, Colombia, Mexico and Kenya, and latterly in Ukraine, where she was curator of the Art Psychotherapy training programme affiliated to the Ukrainian Psychotherapy Association from 2010 to 2014. Her research in collaboration with St Andrews, Bristol, Cardiff and Warwick Universities has been part of the international project 'Transnationalizing Modern Languages: Mobility, Identity and Translation in Modern Italian Cultures' (2014–17). Her work focuses on material culture, on our relationship with objects and on the practices and performances associated with them as a vehicle of cultural translation and personal discovery.

Eliana Maestri is Senior Lecturer in Translation Studies at the University of Exeter. Her research focuses on the interplay between gender, mobility, translation and the visual arts. She was the recipient of a British Academy

Rising Star Engagement Award to co-organise the 2019 Exeter Translation! Festival. She was a 2011–12 EUOSSIC Erasmus Mundus Post-Doctoral Fellow in European Studies at the University of Sydney, Australia. She was also the recipient of a 2014 MEEUC Research Fellowship at Monash University, Melbourne, working on Italian Australian second and third generations as self-translators. She has published on interpretations of Europe among Italian Australians and translations of mobile traditions into Italian Australian folk music (with Rita Wilson), as well as on Italian and French translations of contemporary autobiographical narratives in English. Her monograph *Translating the Female Self across Cultures* appeared in the John Benjamins Translation Library in 2018.

Valerie McGuire is Lecturer in Italian Studies and Comparative Literature at the University of St Andrews (Scotland). Her research focuses on Italian colonialism and postcolonialism and explores the entanglement of Italian migration with ideas of nation, race and Mediterranean-ness in Italian culture. Her book, *Italy's Sea: Empire and Nation in the Mediterranean, 1895–1945* (Liverpool University Press, forthcoming), investigates Italy's colonization of Rhodes and other islands in the Aegean, while also formulating an approach to the study of postcolonialism in Italian culture and of the Mediterranean as a regional unit, and showing how a transnational approach can enrich our understanding of Fascist imperialism. She received her PhD in Italian Studies from New York University and has held several research grants for Mediterranean history, including a Fulbright award to Greece, a Max Weber postdoctoral fellowship at the European University Institute in Florence and an Andrew Mellon multi-region Mediterranean research grant. She is also a co-founder of the Mediterranean insularities network, which critically examines the dynamics of space and power in sea-girt territories.

Loredana Polezzi is Alfonse M. D'Amato Chair in Italian American and Italian Studies in the Department of European Languages, Literatures and Cultures at Stony Brook University (USA). She previously held positions in Italian and in translation studies at the Universities of Warwick and Cardiff, in the UK. Her research interests combine translation studies and transnational Italian studies. She has written extensively on Italian travel writing, colonial and postcolonial literature, translingualism and migration. Her current work focuses on memory, mobility and translation in transatlantic Italian cultures. She has specialist interests in Italian American studies and in translation and the visual arts. With Rita Wilson, she is co-editor of leading international journal *The Translator* and she is the current President of the International Association for Translation and Intercultural Studies (IATIS). She was a co-investigator in the research projects 'Transnationalizing Modern Languages' and 'Transnationalizing Modern Languages: Global Challenges', funded by the UK's Arts and Humanities Research Council under the 'Translating Cultures' theme and Global Challenges Research Fund. She is one of the editors of the 'Transnational Modern Languages' book series, published by Liverpool University Press.

Barbara Spadaro is Lecturer in Italian History and Culture at the University of Liverpool, UK. The principal areas of her research are the history of Italians from North Africa, colonial and postcolonial migration, transcultural memory. Her recent research on memory and media focuses on comics and graphic narratives. She has published on these topics in the volume *Transnational Italian Studies*, ed. by Charles Burdett and Loredana Polezzi (Liverpool University Press, 2020) and in the article, 'The Transcultural Comics of Takoua Ben Mohamed: Memory and Translation a fumetti', *Modern Italy*, 25.2 (2020). Her previous publications include a monograph and articles on the history of women in the Italian empire, ideas of Italian whiteness, and the transcultural trajectories of Italian Jews from Libya. A member of the 'Transnationalizing Modern Languages' research project since 2014, she contributed with Takoua Ben Mohamed to the exhibition *Beyond Borders: Transnational Italy*, shown in Rome, London, New York, Melbourne and Addis Ababa. In 2018 she received an AHRC grant to take the exhibition to the Italian Cultural Institute of Tunis and La Manouba University. With Charles Forsdick, she is co-editor of 'Translating Cultures: Thematic Approaches to Translation', a special issue of the journal *The Translator* (25 April 2019), featuring a selection of research developed under the AHRC theme 'Translating Cultures'.

Ilaria Vanni, University of Technology Sydney, is Associate Professor in International Studies and Global Societies in the Faculty of Arts and Social Sciences. She researches the social, political and cultural dimensions of design and material culture using feminist and experimental methodologies drawn from ethnography, design research and archival research. She is the author of *Precarious Objects: Activism and Design in Italy* (Manchester University Press, 2020). She is the co-founder with Alexandra Crosby of Mapping Edges (www.mappingedges.org), a research studio with expertise in design research and ethnography focusing on recombinant and civic ecologies. Mapping Edges' latest publication is the special issue of the journal *Visual Communication* on

'Recombinant Ecologies in the City' (2020). Recent practice-led research projects include Home Gardens of Haberfield, an oral history project on collective planty heritage, and three participatory cartographies, *Marrickville Walks*, *The Planty Atlas of UTS* and *The Planty Atlas of Bankstown Biennale*, which remap three Sydney neighbourhoods following plants along the street edges.

Naomi Wells is a Postdoctoral Research Associate in Translingual Communities and Digital Humanities at the Institute of Modern Languages Research (School of Advanced Study, University of London) on the UK Arts and Humanities Research Council project 'Cross-Language Dynamics: Reshaping Community' (part of the Open World Research Initiative). Her current research focuses on London's Latin American communities and digital practices of communication and representation. She was previously a Research Fellow on the Arts and Humanities Research Council-funded 'Transnationalizing Modern Languages' project, where her work and recent publications focused on the linguistic and cultural practices of contemporary and historic migrant communities to and from Italy.

Rita Wilson is Professor in Translation Studies in the School of Languages, Literatures, Cultures and Linguistics at Monash University and Director of the Monash Intercultural Lab. Her current work contributes to the strand of research in Translation Studies that explores the connections between migrant cultural studies, translation, and intercultural studies. She has long-standing research interests in women's writing, Italian contemporary literature and transcultural narrative practices. Most recently, she has published on identity and culture in migratory contexts, on practices of self-translation and on narratives of mobility and place-making. With Loredana Polezzi she is co-editor of *The Translator*.

Introduction: Transcultural Italies

Charles Burdett, Loredana Polezzi and Barbara Spadaro

Mobility, Memory and Translation

The history of Italians and of Italian culture stems from multiple experiences of mobility and migration. While those experiences mark the history of the peninsula well before the formation of the Italian state, since the time of unification, in particular, a series of narratives about mobility and nation has been produced both inside and outside the boundaries of Italy by agents such as the Italian state, international organizations or migrant communities themselves. Statistical data, disciplinary canons and historical accounts are just some of the instruments that have been deployed to construct representations of what it means to be 'Italian'. Notions of citizenship and national borders have been variously constructed by essentializing conceptualizations of language, culture or heritage. Narratives may have converged or diverged over time, but they have all aimed to stabilize and fix the inherently dynamic and plural nature of Italian identities and cultures. And, while mobility is at the heart of all these narratives, the value attached to it can be positive or negative, and is often ambivalent.

At one level, Italy has acted as a point of origin for successive waves of emigration that, since the time of the country's unification in the 1870s, have seen more than 27 million Italians leaving the country and migrating to the US and other parts of the Anglophone world, to South America, to countries within Europe, and to what were Italy's main colonies – Libya,

Eritrea, Somalia and Ethiopia.[1] Today, the ongoing reconfiguration of such mobility mirrors changes happening at global level. More than 60 million people around the world currently identify as having Italian origins.[2] New streams of migration spring from the peninsula, which in turn has become a home, or a transit country, for migrants from a variety of national, linguistic and cultural backgrounds.[3] Such movements have given rise to narratives of Italy as an 'emigrant nation', an imperialist power and a European country facing the challenges of world system transformations.[4] At the other end of the scale, Italian mobility is made up of millions of individual and collective trajectories, traced through micro-processes of cultural translation, self-manifestation and acts of transmission and memory mediation. While, in fact, mobility and migration are deeply connected phenomena, they are not the same, nor are they co-extensive. What John Urry termed the new

---

1   The scholarship on these themes is extensive. On Italy and migration see, among others, Piero Bevilacqua, Andreina De Clementi, and Emilio Franzina, eds, *Storia dell'emigrazione italiana*, 2 vols (Rome: Donzelli, 2000–02); Paola Corti and Matteo Sanfilippo, *L'Italia e le migrazioni* (Bari: Laterza, 2012); Fernando Devoto, *Storia degli italiani in Argentina*, trans. by Federica Bertagna (Rome: Donzelli, 2007); Donna Gabaccia, *Italy's Many Diasporas* (London: UCL Press, 2000). For a history of Italian colonialism, see Nicola Labanca, *Oltremare: Storia dell'espansione coloniale italiana* (Bologna: il Mulino, 2002); Ruth Ben-Ghiat and Mia Fuller, eds, *Italian Colonialism* (New York: Palgrave Macmillan, 2005); Neelam Srivastava, *Italian Colonialism and Resistances to Empire, 1930–1970* (London: Palgrave MacMillan, 2018); and Roberta Pergher, *Mussolini's Nation-Empire: Sovereignty and Settlement in Italy's Borderlands, 1922–1943* (Cambridge: Cambridge University Press, 2017).

2   See Teresa Fiore, *Pre-Occupied Spaces: Remapping Italy's Transnational Migrations and Colonial Legacies* (New York: Fordham University Press, 2017), p. 3.

3   See, for instance, Maddalena Tirabassi and Alvise Del Pra', *La meglio Italia: Le mobilità italiane nel XXI secolo* (Turin: Accademia University Press, 2014); Michele Colucci, *Storia dell'immigrazione straniera in Italia: Dal 1945 ai nostri giorni* (Rome: Carocci, 2018); Graziella Parati, *Migration Italy: The Art of Talking Back in a Destination Culture* (Toronto: University of Toronto Press, 2005) and *Destination Italy: Representing Migration in Contemporary Media and Narrative*, ed. by Emma Bond, Guido Bonsaver and Federico Faloppa (Bern: Peter Lang, 2015). See also Luca Vullo's documentary on recent Italian migration to the UK, *Influx* (2016).

4   For a discussion and critique of this notion, see Mark Choate, *Emigrant Nation: The Making of Italy Abroad* (Cambridge, MA: Harvard University Press, 2008); see also Angelo Bolaffi and Guido Crainz, eds, *Calendario civile europeo: I nodi storici di una costruzione difficile* (Rome: Donzelli, 2019); Cristina Lombardi-Diop and Caterina Romeo, eds, *Postcolonial Italy: Challenging National Homogeneity* (New York: Palgrave Macmillan, 2012); Stephanie Malia Hom, *Empire's Mobius Strip: Historical Echoes in Italy's Crisis of Migration and Detention* (Ithaca, NY: Cornell University Press, 2019).

'mobilities paradigm' encompasses material as well as imaginative and communicative dimensions, thus extending beyond migration phenomena and also beyond the traditional boundaries of migration studies.[5] People move for different reasons and under radically different pressures. Yet we do not have to migrate in order to be mobile and cultural mobility is just as fundamental a phenomenon in the history of Italy as are the geographic trajectories of its peoples.

Researching Italian culture today means coming to terms with these different dimensions as well as with the global reach of Italian mobilities.[6] It also means asking how we can formulate notions of Italian culture that both eschew and exceed traditional geographic or linguistic boundaries, while at the same time retaining the ability to understand what it means to identify as 'Italian' in a globalized context, whether as an individual subject or as a community. How can we articulate a notion of Italian culture that is both distinctive and inclusive? What key notions and methodological tools will allow us to encompass cultural phenomena as varied and important as new and old Italian diasporas, the rise and fall of hyphenated identities, or the multilingual and multimodal nature of creative practices of cultural production in migrant contexts? How can we pluralize the concept of 'Italian cultures' in ways that acknowledge both this notion's reach outside the boundaries of the nation and its inherent transculturality? Whether we are dealing with local or global phenomena, we do not have to focus on migration to encounter the mobility of Italian cultures.

Mobility – whether geographic, social, linguistic or in any other form – produces change as well as resistance to change, and the history of Italian mobilities is inscribed with narratives of success and failure, punctuated with moments of friction as well as fruition. These encompass progressive tales of economic growth and transformation, creativity, innovation and social development or emancipation, as well as images of corruption, decadence, demographic decline or alien invasion. Over the 150 years of its existence the Italian state has negotiated the national and the transnational

---

[5] John Urry, *Mobilities* (Cambridge: Polity, 2007), p. 188; see also Kevin Hannam, Mimi Sheller and John Urry, 'Editorial: Mobilities, Immobilities, and Moorings', *Mobilities*, 1 (2006), 1–22. On mobilities and representation, see also Lynne Pearce, *Mobility, Memory, and Lifecourse in Twentieth-Century Literature* (London and New York: Palgrave Macmillan, 2019).
[6] See Ruth Ben-Ghiat and Stephanie Malia Hom, eds, *Italian Mobilities* (New York: Routledge, 2015); David Forgacs, *Italy's Margins: Social Exclusion and Nation Formation since 1861* (Cambridge: Cambridge University Press, 2016).

dimensions of such phenomena in its geopolitical ambitions, its history narratives and its regimes of citizenship. The social, cultural and human landscapes of Italian mobilities have reflected the tensions that are involved in these processes and have themselves been reflected in often contradictory narratives.

Transcultural Italies aims to explore these uneven territories and dynamic tensions by taking ideas of nation, migration and mobility and connecting them to those of memory and translation. This refocuses our gaze precisely on the dynamic and plural nature of processes of identification (rather than on static concepts of 'identity') and on their multimodal links to ideas of home, canon, citizenship or even humanity. The book thus also intends to acknowledge the intrinsic connection between the national and the transnational dimensions of all historical and cultural phenomena, their inescapable interdependency and their productive nature. While it does not replace or supersede the nation as a historical phenomenon, focusing on the transnational brings to the fore the porosity of cultures, their diversity, their dialogical nature and their constant state of flux. Adopting a transnational perspective allows us to consider how images of national and/or community belonging, for instance, are constantly mediated, translated and reactivated in the narratives of subjects whose material, affective and emotional trajectories transcend national boundaries. Contributors to this volume focus specifically on the fluidity of processes of identification and on the multiple tales of Italian belonging told by different agents and on different scales. Such tales are inherently transnational and transcultural, yet also distinctly localized in space and time, and they can be traced through a variety of material and imaginative practices, from food culture to the construction of urban spaces and personal archives. They also remind us of the intrinsic links between human mobility and the environment, a dimension which exceeds any political boundaries and inscribes social behaviour within ecosystemic logics.

The volume and the project from which it originates, 'Transnationalizing Modern Languages: Mobility, Identity and Translation in Modern Italian Cultures' (see below), thus aim to make a fundamental contribution to the 'transnational turn' in Italian Studies. As noted by Emma Bond in a seminal essay that calls for further investigation of the unique relationship between Italian culture and the transnational:

> The Italian case is, perhaps, at once peculiarly trans-national and transnationally peculiar: historically a space characterized by both internal

and external transit and movement, Italy itself can be imagined as a hyphenated, in-between space created by the multiple crossings that etch its geographical surfaces and cultural depths.[7]

Taking her move from Steven Vertovec's definition of transnational cultural production as closely associated with fluid forms such as syncretism, creolization, bricolage, cultural translation and hybridity, Bond stresses the 'fundamental sense of exchange that is inherent in the term' and 'the kinetic sense of flow and flexibility that characterizes the trans-national and which makes the use of the hyphenated trans- crucial in its ability to muddle notions of the national as fixed in time and space'.[8] The 'trans-' suffix, which Bond suggests hyphenating to stress the co-existence and imbrication between national and transnational dimensions, evokes notions of mobility, fluidity and change. It implies 'moving through', as well as ideas of productivity and transformation. The transnational, in this sense, is also closely linked to the notion of the transcultural: to those 'transcultural edges' of transformation, for instance, explored by Ilaria Vanni and Francesco Ricatti in their innovative approach to the history of Italians in Australia.[9]

Memory is another of the keywords highlighted in the present collection and, speaking specifically about transcultural memory, Astrid Erll has proposed that research should focus on processes 'unfolding *across* and *beyond*

---

[7] Emma Bond, 'Towards a Trans-national Turn in Italian Studies?', *Italian Studies*, 69 (2014), 415–24 (p. 421); see also Bond, *Writing Migration through the Body* (London and New York: Palgrave Macmillan, 2018). For further work that addresses issues relating to a transnational approach to Italian studies, see Jennifer Burns, 'Mapping Transnational Subjecthood: Space, Affects and Relationality in Recent Transnational Italian Fictions', *California Italian Studies*, 8 (2018), 1–17; Derek Duncan, 'Collaging Cultures: Curating Italian Studies', *Italian Culture*, 37 (2019), 3–25.

[8] Steven Vertovec, *Transnationalism* (New York: Routledge, 2009), p. 3 (cited in Bond, 'Towards a Transnational Turn' (2014), p. 416). See also Arjun Appadurai, *Modernity at Large: Cultural Dimensions of Globalization* (Minneapolis: University of Minnesota Press, 1996); Ulrich Beck, 'The Cosmopolitan State: Redefining Power in the Global Age', *International Journal of Politics, Culture, and Society*, 18 (2005), 143–59; Paul Jay, *Global Matters: The Transnational Turn in Literary Studies* (Ithaca, NY: Cornell University Press, 2014).

[9] Ilaria Vanni, 'The Transcultural Edge', *Journal of Multidisciplinary International Studies*, 13 (2016), 1–8, and the chapter in this volume; Francesco Ricatti, *Italians in Australia. History, Memory, Identity* (Cham: Palgrave, 2018); see also the contributions to the *Modern Italy* special issue 'Transcultural Exchanges and Encounters in Italy', ed. by Rita Wilson and Brigid Maher, 25 (2020).

cultures'.[10] This perspective shows the need for memory studies to open up beyond national perspectives, moving instead towards an understanding of what she terms 'travelling memory'. In a similar vein, Chiara De Cesari and Ann Rigney have noted that 'the time is ripe to move memory studies itself beyond methodological nationalism', leaving behind the assumption 'that the nation state is the natural container, curator, and telos of collective memory'.[11] Memory, with its emphasis on the temporal dimension, its persistencies and its transformations, thus becomes deeply enmeshed with spatial mobility within and across national perspectives (and therefore also with the history and the narratives of migration). In embracing the trans- prefix, memory studies recognizes the transnational and transcultural dimension of the processes of negotiation and renegotiation, mediation and remediation that are intrinsic to the mobility of cultures.

Memory, therefore, is also recognized as a profoundly translational process. And, like memory, translation is an inherently productive and transformative practice. Since its inception in the last few decades of the twentieth century, the field of translation studies has redefined the notion of translation, moving away from prescriptive paradigms based on a strictly linguistic model and on ideas such as faithfulness or equivalence. Instead, the emergence of descriptive translation studies has shifted attention towards the cultural dimension of translation and the key role it plays in the creation, circulation and consumption of cultural products.[12] Translation, as an inherently multimodal set of practices, has come to occupy a central position in the study of cultural transmission and transformation – so much so that

---

10   Astrid Erll, 'Travelling Memory', *Parallax*, 17 (2011), 4–18 (p. 9); like Wilson and Maher (2020), Erll's work refers to Wolfgang Welsch, 'Transculturality – the Puzzling Form of Cultures Today', in *Spaces of Culture: City, Nation, World*, ed. by Mike Featherstone and Scott Lash (London: Sage, 1999), pp. 194–213. On transculturality see also Mary Louise Pratt, *Imperial Eyes: Travel Writing and Transculturation* (New York: Routledge, 1992).

11   Chiara De Cesari and Ann Rigney, 'Introduction', in *Transnational Memory: Circulation, Articulation, Scales*, ed. by C. De Cesari and A. Rigney (Berlin/Boston: De Gruyter, 2013), pp. 1–25 (p. 2 and p. 1 respectively); see also Luisa Passerini, *Memoria e Utopia. Il primato dell'intersoggettività* (Turin: Bollati Boringhieri, 2003), English translation: *Memory and Utopia: The Primacy of Intersubjectivity* (London and Oakville: Equinox, 2007).

12   See, among others, Gideon Toury, *Descriptive Translation Studies and Beyond* (Amsterdam: John Benjamins, 1995); Susan Bassnett and André Lefevere, *Constructing Cultures: Essays on Literary Translation* (Clevedon: Multilingual Matters, 1998); Michael Cronin, *Translation and Globalization* (New York: Routledge, 2003).

in the 1990s scholars identified a 'translation turn' in cultural studies and the humanities.[13] At the same time, translation studies has itself undergone an 'outward turn', which acknowledges its intersection with fields such as adaptation studies, world literature or, indeed mobility, migration and memory studies.[14]

Mobility, memory and translation are creative forces in the production and transformation of Italian culture *across* and *beyond* borders. The present volume examines how the notion of 'Italianness' has been dynamically reformulated and performed by individual and collective subjects in relation both to models associated with the nation state at its geographical core and to those emerging from other localities. Chapters feature cases drawn from the geographic, historical and linguistic map of Italian mobilities: Italians in the US, Australia and South America; colonial settlement in Africa and across the Mediterranean; migrants within contemporary Italy; and the new circuits of global Italian mobility. In each case, people have been faced with different social policies and different language strategies, while the presence of Italian(s) has left site-specific linguistic and cultural traces. Processes of translation – whether directed to or emerging from the newcomers – have played an important role in such dynamic interactions and on related patterns of identification and self-identification. New forms of subjectivity and narration have emerged, shaping the relationship with local environments, while transcultural and polylingual mnemonic processes have produced creative understandings of present, past and future selves. Taken together, these many histories of 'being Italian' testify to the way in which multiple and distinct proximities mark processes of affective as well as political, private and public investment in cultural practices, relationships and localities.[15] Ultimately, examining cultural processes

---

13 See Susan Bassnett, 'The Translation Turn in Cultural Studies', in Bassnett and Lefevere, *Constructing Cultures*, pp. 123–40; Mary Snell-Hornby, *The Turns of Translation Studies* (Amsterdam: John Benjamins, 2006).

14 See Susan Bassnett and David Johnston, eds, 'The Outward Turn in Translation Studies', special issue of *The Translator*, 25 (2019). For an Italian Studies perspective see Charles Burdett, Nick Havely and Loredana Polezzi, 'The Transnational/Translational in Italian Studies', *Italian Studies*, 75 (2020), 223–36.

15 For a contemporary approach to the history of Italy that goes beyond the borders of the nation see Andrea Giardina (ed.), *Storia mondiale dell'Italia* (Rome-Bari: Laterza, 2017); for an at least partially similar approach relating to literary production see Luigi Bonaffini and Joseph Perricone, eds, *Poets of the Italian Diaspora: A Bilingual Anthology* (New York: Fordham University Press, 2014).

through a transnational and translational lens means concentrating not on what people are but on what they do.[16]

The transnational turn is therefore also a translational turn. Both moves have a powerful transformative effect not only on Italian studies but on modern languages, understood as a disciplinary field, as a whole. These new perspectives take us beyond the methodological nationalism embedded within the discipline and reflected in its established, institutionalized subdivision into 'French studies', 'German studies', and other such subject areas. Instead, a transnational and translational approach stresses processes of communication within and across linguistic and political boundaries, refuting the container model of national cultures. At the same time, the trans- prefix shared by translation, transnational and transcultural reminds us that all of these notions 'traverse disciplines, question assumptions, generate different ideas'.[17] The new approaches presented in this volume are therefore also inherently transdisciplinary in scope and nature. By adopting diverse and multiple perspectives on the history of Italian cultures and their mobility, the essays included in this volume redefine 'the disciplinary framework of modern languages, arguing that it should be seen as an expert mode of enquiry whose founding research question is how languages and cultures operate and interact across diverse axes of connection'.[18]

In establishing a substantial body of theoretical and applied research about Italian mobilities, the volume seeks to provide a model that can be adopted by other modern languages disciplines. In doing so, it aims to interact productively with the other volumes on this theme that are currently being prepared by Liverpool University Press (see below). While embracing the transnational turn in modern languages, the volume also engages with the trans-disciplinary and trans-methodological trends currently transforming the study of the human experience and its expanding forms of mediation. It does so by tackling the dynamism of human cultures, languages and subjectivities, by investigating their forms of narration, mediation and remediation, and by probing the global and local dimensions, the individual and collective

---

16 On these topics see Charles Burdett and Loredana Polezzi, 'Transnational Italian Studies: Introduction', in *Transnational Italian Studies*, ed. by Charles Burdett and Loredana Polezzi (Liverpool: Liverpool University Press, 2020), pp. 1–21.
17 Ilaria Vanni, 'The Transcultural Edge', p. 3, and also Vanni in this volume.
18 The quotation comes from the original outline of the TML project and is key to the series 'Transnational Modern Languages'. For further information, see <https://www.liverpooluniversitypress.co.uk/series/series-13275/> [accessed 3 December 2019].

Introduction 9

impact of human mobility. The volume thus takes up some of the key challenges in the contemporary refashioning of the study of the humanities.

From the TML Project to the Present Volume

As has been mentioned above, the present volume emerges from the work accomplished in the project 'Transnationalizing Modern Languages: Mobility, Identity and Translation in Modern Italian Cultures' (TML). Funded by the Arts and Humanities Research Council as part of its 'Translating Cultures' theme, the project ran from 2014 to 2017.[19] TML brought together a team of researchers with specialisms ranging across literary and cultural studies, translation, linguistics, history and art therapy, as well as an extensive range of project partners, who jointly set out to examine the forms of mobility that have defined the development of modern Italian cultures. Concentrating on exemplary cases, representative of the geographic, historical and linguistic map of Italian mobility, the project looked at the Italian communities established in the UK, the US, Australia, South America and Africa, and at the migrant communities of contemporary Italy. The focus was on cultural associations and the wealth of publications and visual media connected to them – journals, life stories, photographs, collections of memorabilia and other forms of representation. The aim was to investigate the processes of translation evident at every level of the communities in question and that characterize all the textual/visual material associated with them. The project thus attempted to explore how notions of cultural belonging are dynamically reformulated and performed in relation both to models associated with the nation state and to those emerging from specific local contexts. The overall intention was to broaden the frame in which we think of Italian cultures.

A further element that characterized the nature of TML was its focus (reflected in the project's title) on the nature and status of modern languages. Together with the other two large projects of the 'Translating Cultures' AHRC theme,[20] TML was explicitly intended to act as a focal

---

19 For detailed information, see the project website <https://www.transnationalmodernlanguages.ac.uk/> [accessed 3 January 2020].

20 These were 'Translation and Translanguaging: Investigating Linguistic and Cultural Transformations in Superdiverse Wards in Four UK Cities' and 'Researching Multilingually at the Borders of Language: The Body, Law and the State'. For more information, see <http://translatingcultures.org.uk/> [accessed 3 January 2020] and

point, attracting the interest and the energies present across this wider disciplinary field. Thus, in all the initiatives that it pursued, it sought to encourage discussion around – and creative engagement in – the themes that lay at the field's core. This was very much the case in the two large conferences that were organized towards the end of 2016 – 'Transnational Italies: Mobility, Subjectivities and Modern Italian Cultures' at the British School at Rome in October 2016 and 'Transnational Modern Languages' at the Italian Cultural Institute in London in December 2016 – as well as in a range of workshops and other public events which took place during the whole span of the initiative.[21] The present volume reflects the collaborative environment of the project as a whole and the breadth of ideas and approaches that it succeeded in bringing together. In common with all the publications of TML, the volume includes contributions by core members of the research team and by the much larger group of researchers who have played an active part in furthering its collective ambitions. It is thus the case that some of the chapters refer explicitly to work on strands that were integral to the development of TML while other chapters do not mention the project directly but bear strong links to its research initiatives, methodological approach and thematic focus.

Before introducing the structure of the book and the chapters that belong to each of its sections, it is useful to outline here some of the initiatives and activities that were central to TML and that are reflected (more or less explicitly) in individual contributions. A major output was the exhibition *Beyond Borders: Transnational Italy/Oltre i confini: Italia transnazionale*, shown at the British School at Rome (October–November 2016) and then, in different formats (from 2017 to 2018), in London, New York, Melbourne, Addis Ababa and Tunis. The exhibition brought together the work of the researchers on the project, their engagement with the partners of the grant and the photography of the project's artist in residence, Mario Badagliacca. *Beyond Borders* took the form of a series of installations incorporating material objects and virtual reality. It was intended to demonstrate how the most basic features of cultural and linguistic identities are always in movement and in translation, and how what we refer to as Italian language and Italian culture exceed geographical/

Barbara Spadaro, Charles Burdett, Angela Creese, Charles Forsdick and Alison Phipps, 'In conversation: Translating Cultures', *The Translator*, 25 (2020), 420–33.
21 Recordings of the conferences and workshops of the project, as well as the trailer for the project exhibition, are available in the media collection of the project website <https://www.transnationalmodernlanguages.ac.uk/> [accessed 3 January 2020].

territorial confines and operate through constant processes of rewriting and reworking of familiar ideas of tradition, nation and narration.[22]

Though initiatives such as *Beyond Borders* were concerned with the meanings of Italian culture (seen as instances of cultural production, circulation and consumption in a global frame), one of the aims of the project – as noted above – was to reflect on the range, purpose and object of study of modern languages as a disciplinary field and to suggest ways in which some of the insights of the project can inform collective thinking on the framework of the subject area and how research findings can be translated into pedagogical practice.[23] One important initiative in this area is the book series 'Transnational Modern Languages', which promotes a pedagogical model of modern languages seen not as the inquiry into separate national traditions but as the study of languages, cultures and their interactions (see above).[24]

A publishing initiative of this kind needed to be strongly connected with developments beyond higher education (in the UK and elsewhere) and part of the work of TML was to encourage thinking concerning cultural translation both within the wider community and at various stages within the educational process. The project organized a series of creative writing workshops in the West Midlands aimed at those writing and living between languages and cultures and led by translingual writer Shirin Ramzanali Fazel.[25] It also co-produced research with Drummond and Castlebrae Community High Schools in Edinburgh. The aim throughout was to embed the awareness of linguistic and cultural diversity within educational practices, from primary to higher and adult education.[26] It was this element of

---

22 For further information on the development of the exhibition see the chapters by Derek Duncan and by Viviana Gravano and Giulia Grechi in this volume, as well as the articles 'Transnationalizing Modern Languages: the Project Exhibition' by Duncan; 'Exhibiting Transnational Identities and Belongings: Italian Culture Beyond Borders' by Grechi; and 'Work, Concepts, Processes, Situations, Information' by Gravano, published together as a section entitled 'Beyond Borders: Transnational Italies', *Italian Studies*, 74 (2019), 381–96.

23 See Burdett, Havely and Polezzi, 'The Transnational/Translational in Italian Studies'.

24 For details of the series, see Liverpool University Press <https://www.liverpooluniversitypress.co.uk/series/series-13275/> [accessed 3 December 2019].

25 One of the outcomes of the workshops was a volume of original poetry published by Shirin Ramzanali Fazel in English and Italian as *Wings* (Middletown, DE: Createspace, 2017) and *Ali spezzate* (Italy: Createspace, 2018).

26 For a short video on the work that TML has accomplished in schools, see <http://www.transnationalmodernlanguages.ac.uk/2017/03/21/tml-work-with-drummond-and-castlebraech-schools/> [accessed 3 January 2020].

the project that was carried further (2016–18) through a Global Challenges follow-on grant.

'TML: Global Challenges' was a project involving Cardiff University's Phoenix Project and the University of Namibia (UNAM). The aim of the project was to examine how multilingualism can be developed in both the British and Namibian education systems. One of the key objectives of the cooperation was to examine the current educational practices in Namibia in relation to the country's language policies and language needs. Since achieving independence in 1990, Namibia has aimed to sustain its diverse linguistic and cultural heritage, which encompasses both indigenous and ex-colonial languages, while at the same time adopting and promoting English as the official language and main instrument of education. As a country characterized by a superdiverse linguistic environment,[27] Namibia faces the challenge of creating a sustainable linguistic and cultural ecology that will prevent the loss of its heritage while also ensuring the country's continuing development, economic growth, social cohesion and wellbeing. Through co-research and co-production, the project investigated the role of multilingualism across the full spectrum of education, focusing on primary schools on the one hand and, on the other, on higher education programmes for health professionals.[28] The links developed through this initiative enabled both sides to share experiences and learn from each other's methodologies.[29]

---

[27] Jan Blommaert and Ben Rampton, 'Language and Superdiversity', *Diversities*, 13 (2001), 1–21; Angela Creese and Adrian Blackledge, eds, *The Routledge Handbook of Language and Superdiversity* (Abingdon: Routledge, 2018).

[28] The recommendations that have emerged from the work that TML and TML: Global Challenges have pursued with their project partners were set out in the policy report 'Transnationalizing Modern Languages: Reframing Language Education for a Global Future', presented at the British Academy on 9 November 2018. The policy report is available at <http://www.bristol.ac.uk/policybristol/policy-briefings/transnationalizing-modern-languages/> [accessed 3 January 2020].

[29] The collaboration with colleagues at the University of Namibia has resulted, among other things, in co-teaching on the MOOC (Massive Open Online Course) 'Working with Translation: Theory and Practice' (https://www.futurelearn.com/courses/working-with-translation) and in the publication of the poetry anthology *My Heart in Your Hands: Poems from Namibia*, ed. by Naitsikile Iizyenda and Jill Kinahan (Windhoek: University of Namibia Press, 2020). The anthology originated from creative writing workshops held at UNAM by Shirin Ramzanali Fazel and by members of the TML team. A further result that originated from the collaboration with UNAM is the special issue of *Forum for Modern Language Studies*, 'Transnational African Literatures', ed. by Derek Duncan and Nelson Mlambo, 56 (2020).

While not aiming to present a comprehensive map of the project and of its initiatives, the present volume addresses the range of research questions that were central to the work of TML and which, more broadly, are at the base of the current move within the academy to address human experience in a transnational, transcultural and translational perspective. Similarly, the volume as a whole does not seek to provide a narrative history of the Italian diasporic experience: it seeks, rather, to sample and examine processes of cultural and linguistic translation in different contexts. Through its analysis of a multiplicity of instances of translation, the collection aims to explore how cultural and linguistic dislocation associated with migration and mobility inflects the constitution over time of communities marked by experiences of transnationality, while also allowing a continuing investment in notions of national identity. Chapters ask how processes of negotiation, contrast and transposition impact upon individual and collective performances of cultural identity. They aim, in other words, to analyse the subjectivities and processes of identification of people living in a globalizing, mobile and interconnected world. Despite all their differences, the life stories that are examined in each contribution are characterized by everyday practices of multilingualism, by diverse investments in ideas of national identity and by bodily, material and linguistic processes of cultural translation.

By investigating the many kinds of representation – visual, written, oral and digital – produced by mobile subjects through an expanding body of media, chapters also aim to acknowledge the multimodal nature of the experience of transculturality. Collectively, the volume seeks to address the way in which people negotiate their experiences and the multiplicity of media in which they represent and reflect upon their life trajectories, their self-perceptions and their subjectivities. The emphasis of each essay is different, so that the volume as a whole can capture the truly multifaceted nature of transnational and transcultural lives and their inherent tensions. Essays approach differently the question of how people make sense of their lives, how they relate to their communities and the broader environment, how they tell stories and how they think about the complex of practices in which they are involved. In some essays, the emphasis is on the intricacies of textual or visual communication, while others concentrate on the objects that people have created or on the nature of transnational spaces; other contributions focus more on the significance of linguistic transference.

Rather than being arranged in terms of geographical sites, the volume is organized according to the ways in which individual essays investigate the human experience of the transnational and according to the media of representation on which they concentrate. Thus, the collection is loosely divided into three parts, all of which to some degree overlap: the first, 'Traces', concentrates on the presence that communities establish over time in different global contexts; the second, 'Art, Objects, Artefacts', contains essays in which the emphasis is on the interpretation, reception or display of the realities of mobility; the third, 'Mobilities of Memory', focuses on the nature, expression and movement of memory and its practices.

In the opening essay of the first part Jennifer Burns examines how diasporic communities create a presence in space that exceeds the duration and the physical locality of the community's material residence in a given place. Observing the spaces of the everyday in a community in the UK identified as bearing Italian heritage – London's 'Little Italy' – her chapter explores how traces of Italianness are present in the fabric of the built environment and how they make meaning in relation to the area's 'Italian' past. Her chapter offers first a close reading of architectural features and usage in the present, and then places this into dialogue with the narrative practices of observer–residents from within the historic community, contained in textual and photographic life histories. Together, these elements assemble the collective biography of a community and of a place, and reveal that within the form of heterotopic relationality characterizing a global city – London – where multiple languages, cultures, locations and histories intersect, traces of a specifically but inclusively Italian habitation persist and provoke a retelling of national and transnational histories.

Following on from Burns' exploration of the architectural traces of the Italian community in London, the essay by Naomi Wells concentrates on language. Drawing primarily on the personal narratives of two self-identifying Italo-Chileans, Wells investigates the tangible and intangible traces of Italianness in the city of Valparaíso. As a community now made up of predominantly third- and fourth-generation Italians, and with a recent history of geographic and political isolation from Italy, regular use of Italian or Italian regional varieties is increasingly rare. Her chapter aims, however, to go beyond an isolated focus on language loss or maintenance, to explore instead the ways the cultural memory of language is interwoven with the embodied and material life of the city and its residents. By combining the analysis of public representations of Italianness with an ethnographic attention to more quotidian practices, the chapter illustrates how Italianness has permeated a broader transcultural sense of porteña identity and heritage.

The final chapters in this section look at the traces, evident in the present, of the development of Italian colonialism throughout the early part of the twentieth century. Valerie McGuire examines how the construction of a 'Mediterranean' resort aesthetic on Rhodes during Italian imperial rule of the island (1912–43) endures in contemporary postcolonial legacies and today supports new local demands for greater European inclusion and post-national identities. The chapter sets these demands into the larger context of the persistence of conflictual histories about the island's minority communities – that is, an invisible Turkish minority and a tiny post-Holocaust Jewish minority – and on the concurrent bleaching of all reference to Italian Fascism or the imperialist state that led to the Italian collaboration with the expulsion and destruction of these minority communities. The chapter suggests that Rhodes survives into the twenty-first century as both an example of the selective memory of the Italian colonial past and an example of the transnational dimensions of modern Italian culture. In his essay, Charles Burdett addresses the representation of the Italian presence in East Africa in the decades following the Second World War, the demise of Fascism and the end of Italian colonialism. Looking in depth at the publications of the former Italian residents of Eritrea and Ethiopia, the chapter considers, in particular, the journal *Mai Taclì*, which, since the 1970s, has published written memories of life in Africa, commentaries on current events, works of fiction and an extensive collection of photographs. The chapter argues that our ability to see written and visual representations not simply as straightforward narrations or as transparent reproductions of people's experiences but as complex evocations of multifaceted psychic realities, intimately bound up with unseen temporal processes, is enhanced if this kind of cultural production is seen as a means of discovering how the past can return to trouble the present and reveal the individual's unknowing participation in some of the most deeply layered practices of society.

The central part of the volume concentrates on art, objects and artefacts. Two of the chapters, one written by Derek Duncan and the other by Viviana Gravano and Giulia Grechi, concentrate on initiatives that were an essential part of TML. Duncan's chapter examines how the life and work of Eduardo Paolozzi were the inspiration for a series of research-based art projects carried out at Drummond and Castlebrae Community High Schools in Edinburgh. Paolozzi was born and grew up in Edinburgh and his parents were part of the large Italian community living there. His bi-cultural background is often said to have influenced his creative practice, although the link between nationality or ethnicity and artistic expression remains unspecified. The aim of the projects pursued at Drummond and Castlebrae was to investigate TML's core research questions about language, mobility and cultural identity through the medium of art as a means of exploring ways in which skills and competencies normally associated with language acquisition might be extended to other areas of the school curriculum. The projects drew on ideas and practices of intercultural translation to respond creatively to Paolozzi's life-long fascination with popular culture, found and waste materials, and innovation. The chapter gives an account of the different media and techniques used, each of which sheds new light on cross-cultural mobility. These accounts are mediated by the reflective commentary of participants and the work of cultural theorists such as Mieke Bal, Eve Sedgwick and Doris Sommer, as well as Paolozzi himself.

Margaret Hills de Zárate's chapter focuses on participatory ethnographic research and the role of objects as a vehicle of translation in relation to the transmission of Italian transgenerational identity in the Argentine province of Buenos Aires. It considers a series of objects, the narratives they embody and those they evoke within the context of events, discussion groups and individual interviews with narrators/participants who self-identified as being of Italian descent. These objects are referred to as 'moving objects' to include the performative and emphasize their shifting meanings through space and time, as well as their affective potential. Hills de Zárate charts how, as one thing or object leads to another in a chain of unfolding memories and associations, it would seem that the past merges with the present, and, in the case of the objects discussed, with a sense of what is Italian. In her chapter Eliana Maestri looks at how Italian experiences of migration to Australia inform artistic practices and, at the same time, how Italian Australian artworks visually translate mobility and migrant routes across the world. She focuses on the artistic career and productions of Melbourne-based second-generation migrant Jon Cattapan. Her analysis shows how his visual artwork can be read as a diasporic narrative and optical reflection on the added value provided by migration to the physiognomy and morphology of the city's linguistic landscape. It asks how his art displays imaginary journeys across generations, ethnicities and boundaries, and how it translates discourses of mobility and movement. The chapter aims to respond to the need to study constructions of Italianness in the face of constant reshaping of transcultural spaces and multimodal connections.

The concluding chapter of this section, written by Viviana Gravano and Giulia Grechi, presents *Beyond Borders: Transnational Italy/Oltre i Confini: Italia Transnazionale*, the exhibition that was the result of a close collaboration between TML's research team and Routes Agency: Cura of Contemporary Art, a contemporary art curatorial collective founded by art historian Gravano and visual anthropologist Grechi. Assuming the form of a usable 'object', the exhibition sought to represent not only the research material but also – crucially – the innovative methodology proposed by the TML team. The essay aims to explain the theoretical framework informing the organization of the exhibition from a curatorial perspective and presents the process of sharing and negotiation in which the curators and the TML researchers were engaged. The exhibition was not intended to provide answers but to generate questions, offering up the material on 'display' for continual reinterpretation or translation through an immersive and interactive experience.

The chapters in the third and final part concentrate on the connection between mobility and memory. They aim to shed new light on the history of Italian citizenship and cultural mobility, highlighting the fluidity of memory in tension with the politics of history. They acknowledge the polylingual, transcultural and relational nature of memory, exploring tensions within narratives of individual and collective selves. They consider the material, imaginative and discursive nature of memory practices, and they interrogate the relationship between mediation and translation of memory. The story told in Barbara Spadaro's chapter begins in Pitigliano, an Etruscan hill town in Tuscany known as 'La piccola Gerusalemme' (Little Jerusalem) because of the long history of its Jewish community. Pitigliano is the birthplace of Giannetto Paggi (1852–1916), a Jewish teacher who opened the first Italian school in Tripoli and was celebrated as 'the pioneer of Italian civilization in Libya' in the colonial and Fascist decades. His story sheds light on a series of tensions and fractures – including the occupation of Tripoli, the anti-Semitic laws introduced under Fascism and the expulsion of Italians from independent Libya in 1967 – that shaped notions of Italianness as much as individual and collective trajectories. Spadaro explores these trajectories in dialogue with members of the Paggi family, who were 'repatriated' to Italy in 1967, and with the founder of the Jewish Institute of Pitigliano in Maryland, a scholar of Sephardic history and culture. The chapter considers the mobility of memory as a series of intersubjective and translational processes. It draws on Luisa Passerini's concept of intersubjectivity, Naomi Leite's ethnography of affinity and Francesco Ricatti's 'emotion of truth' to engage with the processes of identification and knowledge exchange that emerged through the fieldwork. Spadaro explores the webs of imaginative and emotional interconnections linking her interviewees with the stories of Giannetto Paggi and Pitigliano, and, by extension, with narratives of Italianness and Jewishness.

Gardens have been identified as significant locations of place-making and environmental negotiation for migrant communities in Australia, as sites where people can recreate cultural and aesthetic practices and at the same time add to the cultural diversity of the urban landscape. Yet more nuanced understandings of Italian gardens and their place in diasporic cultures still need to be developed. Ilaria Vanni's chapter explores ways in which we can think about gardening practices from a transcultural point of view, as contact zones between different orders of things. It asks the questions: what happens when plants travel from one country to another? What cultural and social practices do they carry, and what cultural and social practices do they engender in their travels? It explores these questions, presenting examples of Italian gardening practices from contemporary documentaries and oral histories, arguing that diaspora gardens need to be considered as a practice of constant negotiation and reinvention, where plants, as well as humans, play a key role.

Chiara Giuliani's essay analyses the representation of Sino-Italian economic relationships as articulated in a selection of literary texts (both fictional and autobiographical) about the Chinese community in Italy and the expat community of Italians in China. It considers texts such as Edoardo Nesi's *Storia della mia gente* [Story of My People] (2010), Hu Lanbo's *Petali d'orchidea* [Orchid's Petals] (2012), TomcatUSA's *Te la do io la Cina* [I'll Give You China] (2008), Antonella Moretti's *Prezzemolo & cilantro* [Parsley & Cilantro] (2016) and MartinoExpress's *Lǎowài, un pratese in Cina* [Lǎowài, a Man from Prato in China] (2017). By focusing on the representation of the interactions between Italian and Chinese populations, both in Italy and in China, and by unpacking the recurrent idea of 'cultural difference', the chapter aims to investigate the extent to which these works belong to the wider discourse underpinning the complex relationship between Italy and China and Italy's resident Chinese community.

The last two contributions in the volume focus on translation as a key concept and methodological tool in our approach to questions of memory and migration. The complex intermingling of languages and cultures resulting from transnational migration has given rise to an increased interest in how patterns of mobility affect cultural orientations, sensibilities and, consequentially, creative expressions. In recent decades, translingual and transcultural literary narratives have brought to the fore the ways in which geographic and linguistic mobility are connected, and how the interplay of languages within superdiverse urban spaces contributes to an individual's experience of the city. This has led, in turn, to a new engagement with the interrelated issues of linguistic and cultural diversity and the spatial construction of identity and otherness in relation to a 'sense of place' that merges global influences with localized place meanings. Combining insights from cultural geography and translation studies, Rita Wilson's chapter examines recent literary texts that focus on multi-ethnic urban scenarios in Italy. It argues that literary representations of specific linguistic practices in everyday transcultural encounters concretely contribute to understanding the central role of translation in the discursive negotiation of social and cultural identities in global multilingual landscapes. The notion of translation is also central to Loredana Polezzi's analysis of the production of visual artists working in the context of Italian American and Italian Australian communities. The essay, which emerges from collaborations developed as part of the TML project, examines how female artists from the Italian diaspora use gendered practices, images and objects to construct a visual genealogy of migration that reminds us of its roots not just in trauma but also in desire. Their work embraces metaphorical as well as material forms of translation to invoke the double-edged nature of migration and of its memory: the ability to look towards the future while maintaining the threads that link us to our past. Their creative practices, Polezzi argues, substantiate a vision of translation which refutes fixed binary models based on notions of substitution and replacement, pointing instead towards the dynamic processes that allow us to travel, migrate, self-translate, while actively constructing individual and collective narratives that insist on continuity and co-presence. Translation, then, acts not as a form of erasure but as a trace, testifying to and making visible the tension between continuity and discontinuity that lies at the heart of transnational experiences and transcultural narratives.

The transnational and the transcultural ultimately call for a transdisciplinary approach and all the chapters of this volume indicate the range of theoretical tools upon which their analysis relies. The overall aim, in other words, has been to reflect not only on the way in which people have led and continue to lead transnational lives but also on how we can come to know about their experiences. Every chapter in the collection aims to engage with dynamic conceptualizations of subjectivity and belonging, seeking to challenge established categorizations regarding language, geography, temporality, gender and the human. The essays examine how notions of cultural identity are continually being reformulated and translated depending on place, context or generation (among other factors). Concentrating on a specific narrative, theme or representational strategy, they illustrate the way in which people make sense of their experiences and how their understanding not only of the present but also of the past – and indeed of the future – is inflected by the movement across more or less porous linguistic, social and cultural boundaries. Collectively, the chapters investigate how transcultural frameworks of memory are constructed and how alternative models of community are in dialogue within transnational spaces. The volume thus builds on pioneering historical research on the transnational experiences of Italy's many diasporas,[30] on the investigation of traces of colonial involvement and on a substantial body of theoretical and applied transdisciplinary research to develop a transcultural perspective that aims to overcome the methodological nationalism embedded in the study of the experiences of Italian mobility when these are considered as separate phenomena. Above all, the collection aims to show the interdependency of national and transnational, global and local, individual and community, and their impact on how we experience and narrate our lives.

Acknowledgements

We would like to thank the AHRC, the 'Translating Cultures' theme leader, Charles Forsdick, and all members of the project's Advisory Board for their support at every stage. From the very start, TML depended on the principles of co-research and co-production and we are deeply grateful to all of the many partners of the project and to other institutions, groups and individuals who have diversely engaged with us for their work in supporting the core aims of TML. We would also like to thank Kirsty Adegboro for the preparation of the index of this volume.

30 The allusion is to Gabaccia, *Italy's Many Diasporas*.

Part 1

Traces

Part 1

Traces

CHAPTER ONE

The Transnational Biography of 'British' Place: Local and Global Stories in the Built Environment

Jennifer Burns

Commenting on how humans in the digital age leave marks of their presence, John Urry notes that 'individuals [...] exist beyond their private bodies, leaving traces of their selves in space'.[1] This chapter elaborates upon Urry's emphasis on individual traces to examine how diasporic communities create a presence in space that exceeds the duration and the physical locality of the community's material residence in a given place. Observing the spaces of the everyday in a community in the UK identified as bearing Italian heritage – London's 'Little Italy' – the discussion explores how traces of Italianness are present in the fabric of the urban built environment and in the commercial and community activity of the everyday in these locations. It will examine in particular how the site articulates a notion of belonging or connecting to Italian culture within the complex visual and experiential matrix of ethnic and cultural performances that characterizes contemporary community in a global city such as London. In the context of the histories of Italian migration that pre-date population movements – largely post-imperial – into the UK from a global range of countries and cultures since the 1950s, the discussion pays particular attention to the ways in which city space negotiates the layered memory of transnational communities.[2] It will consider first present-day urban

---

1 John Urry, *Mobilities* (Cambridge: Polity Press, 2007), p. 15.
2 See Nancy Stieber, 'Microhistory of the Modern City: Urban Space, Its Use and Representation', *Journal of the Society of Architectural Historians*, 58 (1999), 382–91. The

space and practice, identified through a reading of architectural features and usage, and then place this into dialogue with the narrative practices of observer–residents from within the historic community, contained in a selection of textual and photographic life histories. Together these elements assemble the collective biography of a community and of a place.

The area of Clerkenwell in Holborn, east–central London, was known as 'Little Italy', from the mid-nineteenth century to the 1970s and 1980s, and housed one of the highest concentrations of Italian population in London over that period.[3] It is quite conceivable that someone living in, working in or passing through Clerkenwell now would be unaware of this presence of a transnational Italian history in the area. The traces of Italian presence that persist in the urban environment are materially and undeniably there, but could go unnoticed as isolated examples of migrant or transnational heritage, which exist in almost all cities and provincial towns of the UK. To some degree, the historical Italian community of this part of London is now hidden in plain sight: visible, but apparently unremarkable. This scarce visibility of a community that once dominated the area is easily explained by a catalogue of factors: changing patterns of migration from Italy to the UK; changing patterns of global migration, especially in the postcolonial era; new urban planning priorities; the upward economic and social mobility of city-centre areas formerly characterized as 'slums'; the ethnic diversity of London as a global city; and the ways in which economic, commercial, cultural and aesthetic priorities combine to reinvent the urban identity of particular postcodes. That the Italian community in Clerkenwell seems all but gone is thus not a surprise. What is interesting, though, is to look at the traces

---

method I adopt recalls Stieber's discussion – something of a manifesto – of microhistory in relation to architectural history: she calls for 'the close reading of evidence in case studies, fulfilling the promise of microhistory to describe thickly the complex and multivalent ways that urban form takes shape, engenders experience, creates identity, expresses ideology, and operates independently as a product of architectural knowledge' (p. 389).

3   The main historiographic sources on Italian migration to the UK are Terri Colpi, *The Italian Factor* (Edinburgh: Mainstream, 1991) and Lucio Sponza, *The Italian Immigrants in Nineteenth-Century Britain: Realities and Images* (Leicester: Leicester University Press, 1988) and *Divided Loyalties: Italians in Britain During the Second World War* (Bern: Peter Lang, 2000). For historical and cultural analysis of the London Italian communities see also Alessandro Forte, *La Londra degli italiani* (Rome: Aliberti, 2012); Anne-Marie Fortier, *Migrant Belongings: Memory, Space, Identity* (Oxford, New York: Berg, 2000); Margherita Sprio, *Migrant Memories: Cultural History, Cinema and the Italian Post-War Diaspora in Britain* (Oxford: Peter Lang, 2013).

that remain and to think about what they might mean, both to an observer connected to that past and to one who stumbles upon apparently dislocated signs of Italianness.

The hub of 'Little Italy' in Clerkenwell was historically St Peter's Italian Church on Clerkenwell Road, inaugurated in 1863.[4] The church remains active on this site and remains a focal point for many Italians in London (tourists included), who, even though much more widely dispersed across the city than in the past, still choose to worship there.[5] The church itself, as a monument and as a community space, speaks to a wider public of the memory and the sense of common values and purposes that are understood to define the multigenerational population of Italians in London. A memorial plaque in the entrance and a larger panel in the interior, listing names, both record the sinking of the *Arandora Star* in 1940, the single most striking wound borne collectively by Italians who inhabited all parts of the UK during and after the Second World War.[6] At the level of the everyday (and an everyday construed in continuity with the past), publications available to buy, such as a history of the church and a calendar, both record and state the currency of established practices that bridge the religious and the cultural, depicting events such as first communion as well as church-organized trips and pilgrimages. The calendar is a particularly eloquent artefact of temporality, its annual collection of new photographs stating the timelessness of traditional events and practices and marking the regularity of their recurrence, while also repopulating the images with new (often young) faces, so staking a claim to perpetuity into the future. Publications embedded entirely within the community – the newspaper *Londra Sera* [*London Evening News*], for example[7] – are also available alongside the specifically ecclesiastical ones, underscoring the function of the church as a hub not only of a faith community but also of a (trans)national one.

The peculiarities of the prominence of St Peter's Church come to light if the material form of the building itself is considered. The interior of the

---

4 See <https://www.italianchurch.org.uk/home> (all online references in this essay were last accessed on 12 February 2020).
5 The website states that St Peter's Church represents 'The biggest Catholic Italian Community in London' (see n. 4).
6 The SS Arandora Star was torpedoed by a German U-boat in July 1940 while carrying German and Italian civilian internees, as well as prisoners of war, from the UK to Canada. Of the total death toll of 865, 446 were Italian nationals.
7 *Londra Sera*, 'The Central Point for the Italians in England' (print and online). See <http://www.londrasera.com/default.htm>.

church commands significant space both vertically and horizontally, is richly decorated and accommodates a large congregation. It makes a statement about the presence and pride of an Italian Roman Catholic community in London: this is not a makeshift place of worship adapted from an existing building in order for a migrant community to be able to sustain religious practice, but rather a bespoke building, involving the intervention of an influential Roman priest, San Vincenzo Pallotti, significant investment, high-quality design and support from local urban planning authorities.[8] It signals that the Italian community has a permanent and dominant place in the locality and, celebrated as 'Chiesa di San Pietro per tutte le nazioni' [Church of St Peter for all nations], leads a wider global Roman Catholic population. From the outside, however, the impact of the building is different (Figure 1.1). It has an imposing neo-classical façade with twin columned archway entrances and marble steps rising directly, behind iron gates, from the pavement. However, the elevation facing Clerkenwell Road is no more than about eight metres in width, and sits squarely within the extended terrace of nineteenth-century buildings. It is clearly taller, more ornate and more colourfully decorated than the shops, offices and flats that flank it, but above the first storey it is brick-faced and has windows that match the architecture of the surrounding, more utilitarian, buildings. Architecturally and visually, then, the church as seen from the street is distinctive and majestic, but slots into its immediate urban architectural context rather than imposing upon it.

Until the mid-twentieth century St Peter's Church would have its presence on Clerkenwell Road and in the network of streets making up 'Little Italy' complemented by a range of landmark properties, including workshops, shops and cafés, and several large tenement buildings heavily populated by Italian nationals, along with other migrant groups, including those identifying as Irish. In this sense, it would topographically and spatially have been a hub: the centrepiece of a collection of buildings identifiable by names and by usage as part of the Italian community. For someone walking in this area, a series of signs of Italian habitation, commerce and culture would combine through a grammar of urban relations to signify that this area recreated Italy in a foreign context ('Little Italy') and that its primary reference point was the church. In the twenty-first century much of this evidence of Italian presence in the locality has gone, following the dispersal of the community to a wider range of localities in and around London and the entry into the area of businesses

---

8   See the section of the Church's website entitled 'La Storia': <https://www.italian church.org.uk/chiesa/la-storia>.

Fig. 1.1: Frontage of St Peter's Italian Church; Lonpicman. Own work, CC BY-SA 3.0, https://commons.wikimedia.org/w/index.php?curid=8543931 (downloaded 12 February 2020).

associated with newer migrant communities, particularly visible in terms of food outlets.[9] The refurbishment or replacement of low-cost housing with more expensive residential properties and high-quality office and retail space has also seen Clerkenwell attract design and media companies and develop a more mobile and mixed community in terms of social class and ethnicity.

The ways in which Italianness remains visible in the urban fabric of Clerkenwell are suggestive of the mechanisms by which a community sustains presence in a locality even when it has physically dispersed. In other words, they indicate how the past continues to figure in the present. Two elements are striking about buildings recognizable somehow as 'Italian' now, two decades into the twenty-first century: their spatial concentration and their anachronism. The former is evident in the fact that the frontage of St Peter's Church on Clerkenwell Road is flanked immediately to the left by the Casa Italiana San Vincenzo Pallotti (visible in Figure 1.1), housing the community organization related to the church, and, immediately to the left of this again, by Terroni's Italian delicatessen and café, a business existing in this location since 1878.[10] To the right is the central London office of ACLI.[11] This concentration suggests that, while the community has chosen to reside and do business elsewhere, they will still return to this place of 'origin' in London to worship and to access the solidarity, services and social opportunities historically furnished by the Italian community as represented by its apparently 'essential' components of shared creed, cultural practices, work ethic and foodways. Within this combined frontage of around thirty metres on Clerkenwell Road, the history and insistent presence of an Italian community that would once have been actively present along the full half-kilometre stretch of the road and through its connecting streets is stamped into the built environment.

The anachronism of this set of remaining buildings of 'Little Italy' is closely related to their tight concentration within a relatively confined space,

---

9   London's 'Little Italy' in this respect mirrors those in the USA, Canada and Australia. See Donna Gabaccia, 'Global Geography of "Little Italy": Italian Neighbourhoods in Comparative Perspective', *Modern Italy*, 11 (2006), 9–24; also Elisabeth Becker, 'Little of Italy? Assumed Ethnicity in a New York City Neighbourhood', *Ethnic and Racial Studies*, 38 (2015), 109–24. Becker notes the comparable emptying of New York's 'Little Italy' of Italian residents and workers, though their replacement with a constructed experience of Italian-ness – 'a pseudo-Italian fantasyland' (p. 121) – which is the object of her analysis is not a phenomenon affecting London's 'Little Italy'.
10   See <https://terroni.co.uk>.
11   ACLI, Associazioni Cristiane Lavoratori Italiani; Italian Christian Workers' Associations <https://www.acli.it>.

in that they present a perhaps counter-intuitively consistent presence in a road now populated by quite anonymous, dispersed buildings. In an urban setting without a coherent narrative they present to an observer who looks closely a tight micro-narrative of a community. Denis Byrne establishes the concept of 'heritage corridors' to express the two-way influence of built environments associated with diasporic communities. To set the context, he points out that:

> The sheer weight and groundedness of migration-associated built heritage may seem to resist our efforts to depict it in transnational terms. At face value, it appears rooted in the terrain of distinct nation-states: buildings sink their foundations in the very soil and 'geo-body' (Thongchai 1994) of the nation, while in-ground archaeological traces of migration are buried in that soil. Beyond this, however, modern nation-states have strategically finessed an abiding and almost religious conflation of themselves with the material past lying within their borders, however ancient that material past, however recent the borders (Gellner 1983; Handler 1988; Silberman 1982).[12]

In order to challenge this single 'ownership' of all forms and provenances of built heritage within the nation, Byrne notes that: 'Attention has also been given to the agency of migrants in reworking destination landscapes (Silvey and Lawson 1999, 124). The migrant is now seen as co-constituting these landscapes rather than being a mere guest in them (Hewage and Rigg 2011, 204)'.[13] St Peter's Church and the buildings that surround it are usefully interpreted in this light, as elements of 'English' and London built heritage that emphatically assert their transnational heritage as well as their significant presence in a national architectural history, and so open up a 'heritage corridor'.

While this suggests that these buildings and the community they represent are very much in place, they appear in many ways out of time. They represent a history still embedded in this locality and yet not actively and presently belonging in it any longer; a powerful reference point for a form of sociality and relationality that is sustained in modified ways and yet no longer viable in the context of the twenty-first-century diasporic Italian community in London. This temporal mismatch is announced by an interesting form

---

12 Denis Byrne, 'Heritage Corridors: Transnational Flows and the Built Environment of Migration', *Journal of Ethnic and Migration Studies*, 42 (2016), 2360–78 (p. 2361).
13 Byrne, p. 2364.

of anachronism in the outward presentation of the buildings themselves. The church is, of course, a historic and unchanging piece of monumental architecture. Next door, the Casa Italiana San Vincenzo Pallotti has an extensive shop window on to Clerkenwell Road that displays notices for the community: an array of photocopied sheets, posters and newspaper cuttings in both English and Italian. Amid the darkened glass office frontages or curated displays of design companies along the road, this unassuming display of improvised information and publicity looks old-fashioned and suggests a community speaking to itself, rather than to a wider world. The sign above the shop window is strikingly 'out of time' too, with the colours of the *tricolore* (the Italian flag) overlain with thick black lettering in an old-fashioned font (see Figure 1.1).

Terroni's delicatessen and café next door similarly creates a sense of elsewhere in time and place. A visitor or resident in London is now likely to have a very full experience of Italian cafés and restaurants, marked by carefully chosen representations of 'authenticity'. In this context, Terroni's stands out for its simplicity and functionality, as a place to buy and consume Italian products rather than an 'experience'. A range of Italian products, unfashionable and fashionable, is available (tins of tuna as well as fresh olives) (Figure 1.2). Lighting, décor, furniture and product display are functional rather than 'designed' and customers either visit for one specific item and spend minutes in the store or spend hours there, meeting friends or alone, consuming sporadically. In other words, it is a serviceable retail space, doing what it appears it has always done, with consumer demand adapting to (and attracted to) the business as it is, rather than the business adapting to meet changing demand.

None of this suggests that these three core locations of Italian community in Clerkenwell are necessarily on a path to extinction; rather, in the concentrated persistence of their presence and continued operation in this area they demonstrate that, though times have changed, as have the forms of Italian community in London, there remains a demand for that reproduction of key elements of community identity established in the past. They appear 'out of time' in that they bespeak tradition and positive conservatism in a zone that otherwise tends to style itself in terms of change, mobility and innovation.

I referred above to the 'narrative' – a clearly historical narrative – that the adjacent buildings discussed together assemble. Functioning metonymically to signify a large population, an influential commercial, social and cultural presence, religious and moral leadership, political impact – all extended over more than a century – these buildings *mean* something by virtue of

Fig. 1.2: Products at Terroni's. Author's own image.

the clear and direct relationality between them.[14] More isolated buildings associated with the London Italian community draw attention to how this

14 The architectural style of nearby Farringdon Road contributes incidentally to this 'narrative' of Italian cultural heritage, thanks to a nineteenth-century planning strategy: 'early development of Farringdon Road coincided with the vogue for Venetian Gothic as a suitable style for commercial buildings, given its mercantile associations'. BHO British

concentration affords meaning, suggesting that, without it, it is difficult to make sense of traces of Italianness. An example is the Italian Hospital in Queen Square Gardens, less than a kilometre north-west of the western end of Clerkenwell Road. It was established in 1884 by an Italian businessman in London, Giovanni Ortelli, who donated two adjacent houses he owned in Queen Square to offer bespoke medical care to Italians in London (though other nationalities were not excluded) at a time when living conditions in 'Little Italy' were poor and medical care difficult to access for Italians in the community, for financial, linguistic and cultural reasons.[15] The houses were demolished fifteen years later and a purpose-built hospital building erected in their place (Figure 1.3). This is an elegant, imposing building occupying one side of the square, and it fulfilled its function of providing medical care for the Italian community for almost a hundred years, closing in 1990. In this sense, it is a landmark building, marking Italians in London as a significant community capable of self-organizing and self-funding in order to establish public spaces and facilities both adequate to their needs and appropriate to the enhancement of the local built heritage in the destination environment: it creates a 'heritage corridor'. Like St Peter's Church and the buildings around it, it makes a statement of permanence on behalf of the Italian community. Whether that permanence is compromised by the closure of the Italian Hospital and the repurposing of the building is an important question. On the one hand, the building was bought by Great Ormond Street Hospital, whose other buildings surround it, and so it remains fit for purpose and functional, though for an undifferentiated body of users. For its intended original users, the foundation of the Italian Hospital retains its functionality and now runs as the Italian Medical Charity, offering financial support to Italians and 'those of Italian descent' in order to access medical care beyond that offered by the UK National Health Service.[16] On the other hand, the

History Online, 'Commercial architecture in Farringdon Road, 1860s–90s', <https://www.british-history.ac.uk/survey-london/vol46/pp358-384#p129>.
15   See Olive Besagni, *A Better Life: A History of London's Italian Immigrant Families in Clerkenwell's Little Italy in the 19th and 20th Centuries* (London: Camden History Society and Olive Besagni, 2011), p. 15, for a story of Ortelli recognizing the need for a dedicated Italian Hospital after witnessing the difficulties experienced by an Italian worker in communicating with hospital staff. See also chapter 7, 'Housing and Sanitary Conditions of the "Italian Quarter"' in Sponza, *Italian Immigrants in Nineteenth-Century Britain* (pp. 195–230) for an account of health risks emerging in 'Little Italy' and the responses of the British public and institutions.
16   <http://www.italianmedicalcharity.co.uk>.

Fig. 1.3: The Italian Hospital. Author's own image.

Italian Medical Charity is largely invisible at a public level: it provides an important support structure, but does not make the kind of statement of civic presence that a major building in respectable Bloomsbury would have made throughout the twentieth century. However, the building remains, is well maintained, and still bears the name 'The Italian Hospital' in elegant red lettering high up across its façade, as well as the original plaque detailing its Italian origins. These are important but easily overlooked markers of Italian history and, out of context in this immediate locality, may serve as an indecipherable sign of Italianness. Coincidentally, an archival narrative is also missing: the University College London (UCL) Bloomsbury Project, charting the history of buildings in the area, has a webpage dedicated to the Italian Hospital which notes that 'Most of its records are apparently lost' and that the only book charting its early history is missing from the British Library.[17]

A different kind of story of architectural repurposing attaches to the premises of the Gazzano café and delicatessen (Figure 1.4), which, like Terroni's, was a long-standing supplier of Italian food and related social space in 'Little Italy', established in 1911. Its shop on Farringdon Road was, at the start of the current century, bought and radically redeveloped to incorporate the original ground-floor business within a five-storey residential development above. This was an award-winning architectural project (2005 RIBA award) by Amin Taha Architects, completed in 2004 and creating a statement building that stands out among the Victorian and more recent office buildings of Farringdon Road, with its asymmetric window pattern and distinctive steel cladding (see Figure 1.4). The new and emphatically twenty-first-century development did not erase the original delicatessen and its history – instead, as well as maintaining the space for the business, it amplified its presence by naming the new building Gazzano House. This offers an interesting example of the folding of the Italian cultural history of the area into the new and future-facing architectural fabric of Clerkenwell, and a celebration of part of its social and commercial heritage retaining purpose and value for the future.[18]

This discussion so far has adopted the perspective of an observer external to the 'Little Italy' community experiencing in the present day the traces and signs of Italian presence in Clerkenwell. In order to understand this better

---

17 See UCL Bloomsbury Project, <https://www.ucl.ac.uk/bloomsbury-project/institutions/italian_hospital.htm>. The book referred to has no author attribution: *History of the Italian Hospital in London, 1884–1906* (London, 1906).

18 See <https://akt-uk.com/projects/gazzano%20house> for details of the project and photographs. A further sign of the importance of the Gazzano business in London is an obituary written by former food writer at the *Guardian* newspaper, Matthew Fort, for Joe Gazzano, who ran the business until his death in 2010: <https://www.theguardian.com/theguardian/2010/oct/25/joe-gazzano-obituary>.

Fig. 1.4: Gazzano House. Author's own image.

in relation to the meaning the surrounding built environment held for its residents and visitors in the twentieth century, when the Italian community was more visible, it is helpful to look at the accounts of individuals who lived there. Olive Besagni published in 2011 and 2017 two volumes of biographical accounts, oral histories and photographs.[19] These twin volumes look back at the life of 'Little Italy' from a position in the 2010s that acknowledges that 'Little Italy' is now barely visible. Besagni collects and publishes photographs, stories and multi-sourced forms of evidence of a community developing over around 150 years, and does so from the explicit position of an insider who inhabited the area (though she records her own move out to suburban London in later life) and knew its histories intimately.

An arresting element of the accounts that Besagni gathers, whether authored by others or by herself, is the emphasis on place. People are undoubtedly important, and the materials are ordered according to individuals or families, but these people are deeply and definitively emplaced, locked into their material environment with an emphasis that suggests that it constitutes them as much as they constitute it. The inside cover of both volumes bears a map of 'Little Italy', and the streets that make up this triangle are then regarded in the volumes as familiar, named routinely as the essential coordinates within which to interpret the events and characters recounted. Besagni thus – and in the titles of the volumes – claims the name of the area with conviction and pride, taking ownership of what is at root an exclusionary toponym that Donna Gabaccia demonstrates to be an invention of the English-speaking host culture:

> It was the efforts of natives to understand and to interpret the significance of the arrival and clustering of Italians that first generated the label Little Italy. But only in the US, at first, then the UK and somewhat later in Canada and much later still in Australia, did this occur, and only after long years of referring to emerging clusters of immigrants in very different terms.[20]

As Gabaccia also points out, 'The term *piccola Italia* [little Italy] was not part of Italian nationalist discourse of the early twentieth century. On the contrary, Italian nationalists of both imperialist and liberal tendencies instead developed alternative visions of *la più grande Italia* (a larger Italy)'.[21] In this vision, communities of Italians overseas are identified as *colonie* [colonies], extending Italian labour and commercial (as well as political) dominion into

---

19 Besagni, *A Better Life*; Besagni, *Changing Lives. More Stories from London's Little Italy* (London: Camden History Society and the Estate of Olive Besagni, 2017).
20 Gabaccia, 'Global Geography of "Little Italy"', p. 19.
21 Gabaccia, 'Global Geography of "Little Italy"', p. 17.

other nations.[22] This term is vividly in evidence in St Peter's Church, where the external plaque commemorating Italian soldiers lost in the First World War self-identifies the community as the 'colonia italiana di Londra'. The formal statement of national solidarity in the face of the effects of global conflict uses the language of 'greater Italy', while Besagni, elaborating a micronarrative of community life, adopts the nomenclature of the host/home nation.

Within Besagni's map of the area specific buildings are routinely cited, relying upon either the informed reader's established knowledge of the area or the uninformed reader's incipient understanding of what these buildings mean. A long account of the Terroni family (original owners of the delicatessen) describes the partial dispersal of Italian families from Clerkenwell following the internment of Italian adult males as enemy aliens once Italy entered the Second World War in 1940, and also the severe bombing of Clerkenwell. Looking then at the early 1950s, the same account reinstates the importance of the area according to the community's attachment to specific buildings:

> Many of the former residents who had moved into the surrounding areas constantly returned to the Hill to meet in the Coach and Horses. [...] There was also plenty going on at St Peter's Church, where the Children of Mary and various other groups still met. The large tenements: Victoria Dwellings, Cavendish Mansions, Farringdon Buildings, Griffin Mansions and Corporation Buildings, were still inhabited by a mixture of Italians, Irish and Cockneys. Many of the younger married couples, second and third generation Italians, and Irish, lived on the Bourne Estate, a massive council block with a large entrance in Clerkenwell Road and bordering Leather Lane. On Sunday mornings after Mass old friends would go for a chat in Terroni's, which would be packed with ex-residents of the Hill all buying their wine, pastas, salamis, olives, Italian hams, cheeses etc.[23]

This short and practical description speaks volumes about changes in the social and geographical constitution of the community, while also underscoring its recourse to the same social and spatial coordinates: the key dwellings, the church, and Terroni's. The mention of 'Italians, Irish and Cockneys' notes

22   For discussion of the 'double use' of this term, see also Teresa Fiore, 'The Emigrant Post-"Colonia" in Contemporary Immigrant Italy', in *Postcolonial Italy: Challenging National Homogeneity*, ed. by Cristina Lombardi-Diop and Caterina Romeo (New York: Palgrave Macmillan, 2012), pp. 71–82 (p. 71).
23   Besagni, *A Better Life*, p. 110.

the mixed cultural make-up of the community, and generational shift is indicated by the move from the 'tenements' of the nineteenth century to the 'massive council block' of the mid-twentieth century. However, the naming of these key places of residence serves as a reminder that this diaspora within a diaspora – the now less-concentrated 'Little Italy' community – still defines itself in terms of long-familiar buildings known as 'belonging' in large part to the Italian community. The accounts in Besagni's two volumes almost all refer principally to place and date to establish the family or individual whose history is to be offered. Place is often initially place of departure in Italy, defined as a village or locality, followed swiftly by a specific address in Clerkenwell, usually one of the buildings listed above. Place, in this sense, locks the individual or family to an identity in 'Little Italy' and to belonging within that community.

The passage quoted above draws attention to the porosity of a community sometimes characterized as homogeneously Italian in Clerkenwell in the early to mid-twentieth century. Irish migrants and their families in fact made up a significant proportion of the population in this period, with a shared commitment to labour and the Roman Catholic faith providing the cultural context for the shared living spaces in the same buildings that Besagni lists above. Her first volume, *Changing Lives*, includes an account from an Irish man born and raised in Clerkenwell who also attended St Peter's Italian School from 1928 to 1937. She notes that this man, A. W. Kibble, 'preferred to be called Victor because it felt Italian'.[24] His memoir begins, as do those that Besagni authors, with an address – 39 Bowling Green Lane – and a description of the building he inhabited there: 'a two-up, two-down drab brick dwelling with a communal lavatory and wash house out in the back yard'.[25] His account, sent to the *Backhill* newspaper in 1988, some fifty years after he had left the area, picks out home, school, Italian friends and the Finsbury mortuary, built among residential buildings on the edge of Clerkenwell, as the coordinates of his memory of that place and time.[26] Albeit filtered through memory, this child's-eye view of place offers a striking perception of the

---

24   Becker notes the 'instrumental employment of ethnicity in presenting identity' (p. 110). That Kibble deploys an anglicized version of a presumed Italian name in order to '[feel] Italian' is indicative of the cultural and identitarian transactions underlying community cohesion in a mixed neighbourhood constructed as dominantly Italian.
25   Besagni, *Changing Lives*, p. 27.
26   *Backhill* was established in the early 1970s as the newspaper of the 'Little Italy' community, now existing as a web journal, *Backhill online*, <http://www.backhillonline.com>. The title refers to Back Hill, a central street within 'Little Italy'.

everyday as a child inhabiting this relatively small urban area. Photographs of Clerkenwell by the celebrated photographer of London Colin O'Brien bring to life an analogous perspective reproducing a child's-eye view, since he began taking these photographs as a child himself. O'Brien has something in common with 'Victor' Kibble, being of Irish descent and born and raised in Clerkenwell with Italian neighbours and friends, albeit a generation later. His photographs of the area in the 1950s and 1960s, many sold to newspapers, give a powerful sense of a shared transnational and transcultural place populated by Italian, Irish and Jewish migrants and refugees whose presence bespeaks the trauma not only of displacement but also of persecution. The photographs do not search for or sentimentalize these histories, but rather, as snapshots of the everyday, accompanied in a neighbourly and familiar way by individual names, communicate a fragile domesticity built on the hope for 'a better life' that Besagni foregrounds.[27]

Putting O'Brien's photographs into the context of social research and social history in Britain from the 1940s to the 1960s helps to both elucidate their mechanisms of making meaning – and making place – and expose the ways in which they speak to the construction of transcultural experience and belonging in Besagni's volumes. Joe Moran has explored the imaginary of street life in early post-war Britain that emerged from the combined work of sociologists, photographers and architects to create 'a homegrown anthropology'.[28] Moran refers particularly to the work of photographers Nigel Henderson and Roger Mayne in the context of a more widespread commitment of middle-class social researchers to engage, through close and extended proximity, with the experience of the urban street.[29] Their work, Moran notes, 'combined social concern with a certain aesthetic attraction to working-class street life'; 'Mayne admired the "unfettered physicality" of children playing outdoors and the "decaying splendour" of the streets themselves'.[30] Work of this kind, albeit compromised by the experiential

---

27 See <http://www.colinobrien.co.uk> and/or O'Brien's book collecting selected photographs from 1948 to 2014: Colin O'Brien, *London Life* (London: Spitalfields Life Books, 2015).

28 Joe Moran, 'Imagining the Street in Post-War Britain', *Urban History*, 39 (2012), 166–86 (p. 167).

29 See *Streets: Nigel Henderson's Photographs of London's East End 1949–53*, ed. by Clive Coward (London: Tate Publishing, 2017); *Roger Mayne's Street Photographs*, ed. by Richard Cork (London: South Bank Centre, 1987); and Martin Harrison, *Young Meteors: British Photojournalism: 1957–1965* (London: Jonathan Cape, 1998).

30 Moran, pp. 168, 169.

distance between subject and object of observation that Moran spotlights, informed post-war social research and urban policy in substantive ways – ways that are echoed in Besagni's comments above on changes to the housing stock and gradual suburbanization. It also sheds light on O'Brien's photographic practice in London and in Clerkenwell in particular: he is doing much the same, and is attracted in similar ways by the aesthetics of everyday life, but he does so from a position of absolute embeddedness, as someone for whom this environment is home.

As well as bringing to light the layered histories of transnational belonging in Clerkenwell in this period through people, O'Brien's photos give a strong sense of place for place's sake. Living in a flat on the top storey of Victoria Dwellings (one of the Clerkenwell residential developments mentioned frequently by Besagni), his photographs articulate a child's curiosity at quite simply looking at the world through the window, and from a striking vertical vantage point. In contrast with the gaze of the post-war photographers discussed by Moran, these early photographs have a child's eye behind the lens. A thought-provoking series of his photographs records the traffic at the busy junction below his home, and particularly the car accidents.[31] Wet tarmac, overhead power cables, advertising hoardings and overturned or damaged vehicles say nothing particular about Italian or transnational communities in this area but serve emphatically to contextualize what other narratives of those communities tell, and to attach that knowledge to urban space. Whereas the vast collection of photographs that appears in Besagni's volumes of course emphasizes Italianness – family groups, costumes, religious events and ceremonies, buildings marked as 'Italian' – O'Brien's photos remind the reader/viewer that all of this activity takes place within a tight configuration of urban space in which other lives and other cultural histories are intersecting and 'changing', to cite Besagni's title.[32] The speed, urgency, distraction and possibly aggression denoted by the accident photographs suggest the friction of new forms of relationality in this already, historically, relational urban space. This is not to suggest that Besagni's and other accounts of 'Little Italy'

---

31   O'Brien, pp. 36–38 (1960), p. 41 (early 1960s), pp. 42–44 (1962). The caption to the latter poignantly notes, 'I read later that a child died in this accident' (p. 44), prompting the viewer to look back at the scene and identify a child lying on the pavement surrounded by adult passers-by and a nurse.
32   For photographic records of Italians in the UK see also Terri Colpi, *Italians Forward. A Visual History of the Italian Community in Great Britain* (Edinburgh and London: Mainstream Publishing, 1991).

deny the tensions and violence that emerge within the Italian community and with others: she records fights, gang rivalries and interventions by the police, as well as the direct and indirect impact of the violence of war.[33] O'Brien's photos complement this, however, by exposing the more heterogeneous relationality of London in the decades after the war. Furthermore, their snapshot quality – bespeaking 'street photography's interest in the unexpected social encounter, the fleeting instant, the captured moment'[34] – as well as the specific subject of traffic collisions, underlines the notion of accident: things simply happen that challenge the routines, practices and continuities by which any one diasporic community may seek to establish security and stability in the neighbourhood to which it stakes a claim. 'Little Italy' is, ultimately, 'little' in its concentration, easily dislodged by changing forms of urban interaction.

O'Brien's observational photographic records of moments in the life of this part of London serve as a useful prompt to re-view visual, topographical and written accounts of Italians in Clerkenwell less through the celebratory frame that histories of little Italy inevitably set and with more attention to trauma. As noted above, Besagni's volumes refer to intra-community tensions, but using a discourse that codes these events according to stereotypes of young masculinity, and particularly 'Latin' masculinity. Similarly, references to wartime deaths owed to action in the military field, bombings in Clerkenwell or the fundamental trauma of the sinking of the *Arandora Star* deploy a discourse of familial and community tragedy that contains the pain of these losses within a mutually recognized cultural process. In drawing attention to what goes wrong and causes pain in everyday life, O'Brien's photographs inform a different reading of Besagni's anecdotal community history, and one which speaks of struggle. The celebratory narrative of the migrant who leaves home with nothing and, through hard work and perseverance, makes good in a challenging destination environment is thus tinted with a darker emphasis on the difficulty of sustaining endurance, particularly within a culture of mutual responsibility for the collective 'success' of family and community as evaluated within both destination and departure cultures. The trauma of migration for Italians in London in the post-war period is perhaps reopened by the trauma of war and of rejection (as enemy aliens) within the destination culture. Viewed from this perspective, the dogged resistance of

---

33   See Besagni, *Changing Lives*, p. 52; also chapter 8, 'The Italian Immigrants and the Law', in Sponza, *Italian Immigrants in Nineteenth-Century Britain*, pp. 231–65.
34   Moran, p. 172.

the 'Little Italy' community and the concentration of its key buildings on Clerkenwell Road articulate resilience. Recalling Gabaccia's core argument and my comments above on the term *colonia*, this resilience seems at once a response to the mission for Italians to be proudly present and influential in overseas locations ('greater Italy') and an expression of the burden of surviving under the oppressive forces of the politics and economics of both departure and destination cultures ('Little Italy'). 'Little Italy', in this light, looks to be doubly colonized.

The discourse of resilience that threads through both Besagni's and O'Brien's accounts of Clerkenwell in the post-war decades does not envisage an indefinite endurance of the 'London Life' that they each, differently, narrate. The title of Besagni's second volume, *Changing Lives*, gives a hint of impermanence and of the inevitability of the community that her books define adapting to new conditions. In collecting and publishing in twin volumes the visual, written and spoken evidence of a community developing over around 150 years, as author/editor she memorializes that community and its physical spaces, and acknowledges that its time has passed: she offers 'a snapshot, and a somewhat idealized one, of a very specific moment in the history of Italian migration and settlement'.[35] This element is underlined by the fact that the second volume appeared posthumously, one year after Besagni's death at the age of ninety-one, with the effect that the volume becomes a memorial to her as well as to the community as she knew it. Her 'Afterword' to the *Changing Lives* volume reads:

> This year, 2015, my husband Bruno and I will both be celebrating our 90th birthdays. It is my belief that Bruno, the oldest son of the Besagni family, is one of the few remaining Italians who were born and grew up 'down the Hill'. We now have three children, Anita, Tony and Nicolette, seven grandsons and a granddaughter, Leah, who recently presented us with our first great-grandchild, a girl, Gaby. Time to conclude my story. Ciao![36]

The author's closing comment points to continuity into a future that will be shaped by others, while at the same time confirming an ending to one particular way of life. Her husband, she suggests, is one of the last surviving traces of the community that her books have chronicled. The values that have been celebrated in those accounts are restated by her own emphasis on

---

35 Gabaccia, 'Global Geography of "Little Italy"', p. 12.
36 Besagni, *Changing Lives*, p. 64.

intergenerational continuity, but the question of whether those values are shared and perpetuated by those she names is one left emphatically open.

O'Brien's photographs, when viewed in the retrospective collection making up the *London Life* volume, have a similarly strong autobiographical frame, dating from 1948 (O'Brien was born in 1940) to 2014, with, as noted above, a large proportion taken during his childhood and teenage years.[37] While the subjects and scenes photographed connote past-ness, they tend to communicate present-ness and vitality through O'Brien's photo-journalistic practice of capturing a moment. Interestingly, as in Besagni's volumes, it is the act of curating and collecting these images for publication that installs the 'sense of an ending' to the narrative that they offer.[38] Captions added by O'Brien, and longer verbal contextualizations, stress finality. For example, a photograph taken in 1952 of a cinema in Skinner Street, Clerkenwell, is accompanied by the comment, 'Long since demolished, the Rio Cinema was where we used to go as kids and watch films over and over again until we got bored.'[39] The erasure of the buildings that defined childhood and community experience figures again, in a still more personal way, in a photograph titled, 'Clerkenwell Road, Seventies', which shows the demolition of Victoria Dwellings, one of the key built coordinates of the history of Little Italy.[40] Community and individual are placed in direct correspondence in the caption, which notes that: 'After more than a century of use by hundreds of families, Victoria Dwellings was demolished and we moved into a flat on the twenty-third floor of the newly-built Michael Cliffe House in Skinner Street on the other side of Clerkenwell'. High-rise building, 'newly-built' and located on 'the other side' are signals of definitive change. Moving to other areas of London in more recent photographs, the emphasis in captions is often again on ending: a shoe repair shop 'closed recently' (p. 253); 'The shop closed on October 2nd 2010, shortly after I took this photograph' (p. 261); smokers in a pub on 'the final day of legal smoking in public places' (p. 248). A late photo returns to what was 'Little Italy', with the following comment: 'When Clerkenwell Fire Station closed on January

---

37 O'Brien, like Besagni, died in 2016.
38 See Frank Kermode, *The Sense of an Ending: Studies in the Theory of Fiction* (Oxford: Oxford University Press, 1967). Kermode famously argues that human beings need to identify a structure to their life in order for it to have meaning, and hence strive to establish a narrative of beginning, middle and (constructed) ending in order to allay discomfort at not knowing how their own story will end.
39 O'Brien, p. 105.
40 O'Brien, p. 151.

8th 2014, after one hundred and forty-two years of service, I photographed the firefighters on their last day at Britain's oldest operating fire station' (p. 281). Like Besagni's books, O'Brien's collection speaks of an impetus to record and memorialize a form of 'London Life' that appears to be passing, while nevertheless documenting its very live-ness.

Besagni's and O'Brien's books, though presented differently and populated by different kinds of material, all offer biographies of a built environment and of the communities that inhabit it. Besagni's focus on 'Little Italy' as a community reproducing a 'homeland' with sharply characterized practices and values does not exclude the presence in Clerkenwell of other, largely migrant, populations, and particularly those of Irish heritage. O'Brien's collection complements this by, through his own heritage in part, stressing the shared agency of the Irish community in particular in constituting the urban reality of Clerkenwell in the twentieth century. His early photographs feature the annual procession to the church in honour of Our Lady of Mount Carmel (early 1950s) and his friends of Italian descent ('Raymond Scallione and Joe Bacuzzi, outside the premises of Pastorelli and Rapkin Ltd in Hatton Garden, 1948').[41] As a photographer, O'Brien's very literal point of view on what is known as 'Little Italy' brings to attention a heterogeneous community, noted also by Besagni above as 'a mixture of Italians, Irish and Cockneys'.[42] Besagni's formulation is interesting in drawing together diasporic populations with indigenous Londoners, but also in highlighting social class: these are not affluent, middle-class British nationals but a subnational community defined, like Italians and Irish in Clerkenwell, by urban location, class and accent. O'Brien's photographs do similar work in making visible the overlayered quality of urban communities in the twentieth century and beyond, in which intersections of ethnicity, culture, faith, economic and social circumstances and, crucially, everyday experience may connect different populations within a shared space. These intersections may be systematic (shared religious practice and space) or coincidental (encounters in shared space, accidents).

Returning to the present-day experience, on the street, of Clerkenwell, this overlayered quality is immediately evident. Thinking about it specifically in terms of the biography of an Italian community and an Italian 'place' in London, the built environment of Clerkenwell indicates, firstly, the co-presence of times in terms of the traces in the present of the 'Little Italy' of the past, and, as discussed above, these are substantive traces articulated

---

41   O'Brien, pp. 6–7 and 53.
42   Besagni, *A Better Life*, p. 110.

through architectural statements and visible community practices that take place in the present whilst also referring to enduring traditions surviving from the past. The co-presence of global spaces is indicated also by the layered and diverse use of commercial buildings in particular: businesses presenting as Italian (such as Terroni's) remain, while Gazzano's delicatessen was enfolded into a new building celebrating the historical name of Gazzano but in a radically new-looking architectural form created by the practice of an architect, Amin Taha, born in East Berlin of Iraqi and Sudanese parents, living since childhood in the UK and now dwelling in Clerkenwell. A clear marker of changing axes of transnational connection over time is that the street sign at the Clerkenwell Road end of Back Hill, the street perhaps most regarded as the icon of the 'Little Italy' community, sits directly above the frontage of Ngon Ngon, a Vietnamese food and drink outlet. Lastly, the co-presence not only of diverse ethnicities but of diverse social groups comes to the surface of the built environment in terms of the mix of old retail businesses, new and expensively styled professional and commercial locations and routine, mid-range service providers, such as gyms or printing outlets. Amin Taha lives in the neighbourhood in a controversial building designed by himself, metres away from the significantly refurbished but original Cavendish Mansions, formerly identified as 'tenements' and inhabited by Italian and Irish migrants.[43]

This social inclusivity is in many ways nothing like that which emerges from Besagni's or O'Brien's narratives of literally shared living space, where inclusion is a factor of necessity rather than of choice, and is underpinned by a sense of mutual endeavour towards 'a better life'. Clerkenwell now, in common with comparable redeveloped urban spaces, is an environment in which some users of its spaces and services will be resident and many not, and where some residents may have chosen to make this area their base while others are there through accident of opportunity, cost or convenience. The buildings and practices of present-day 'Little Italy' bespeak a form of heterotopic relationality making both elective and accidental connections between languages, cultures and places across the globe. Present – in both spatial and temporal terms – within that matrix are traces of a specifically but inclusively Italian habitation. This is not only a passive residence, however, but also an active participation in and contribution to constructing the lived

---

43 Dominic Lutyens, 'Amin Taha: London's Most Controversial Architect', in *Financial Times*, 10 January 2019 <https://www.ft.com/content/a0d0ea3e-1033-11e9-b2f2-f4c566a4fc5f>.

environment, structural and social, of the area. While Italian communities in and around London now relate and communicate probably more along digital than material 'corridors', to borrow Byrne's formula, these newer forms of relationality and of transnational self-expression can be traced back to the substantive and extended place-making activity that the material biography of 'Little Italy' continues to tell, discreetly.[44]

---

44 See Sara Marino, 'Making Space, Making Place: Digital Togetherness and the Redefinition of Migrant Identities Online', *Social Media and Society*, July–December 2015, 1–9.

CHAPTER TWO

Porteña Identity[1] and Italianità: Language, Materiality and Transcultural Memory in Valparaíso's Italian Community

Naomi Wells

The empowering paradox of diaspora is that dwelling *here* assumes a solidarity and connection *there*. But *there* is not necessarily a single place or an exclusivist nation.[2]

James Clifford

Introduction

Outside of the country, Chile's Italian community remains overlooked, receiving little more than a brief mention in broader studies of Italian migration. While having a smaller demographic impact than in other countries, particularly in contrast to neighbouring Argentina, tangible and intangible traces of the Italian presence remain in both the physical landscape and in collective and individual narratives of experience and memory. This is evident in the case of Valparaíso, the city of arrival of many Italian migrants and a city whose identity is defined by its history of immigration. At the same time, as an urban port city of movement and multiple migrations these traces of Italianness,[3]

---

1 'Porteña/o' refers to residents of a port city, and is commonly used to describe residents of Valparaíso.
2 James Clifford, *Routes: Travel and Translation in the Late Twentieth Century* (Cambridge, MA: Harvard University Press, 1997), p. 269.
3 Across the article I use Italianness, italianidad and italianità as partially equivalent concepts, but maintaining all three terms is intended to draw attention to the fact that

beyond self-consciously memorializing monuments, are less easily identified than in more concentrated communities.

The geographical and political isolation of Chile further accentuates the inadequacy of an idea of italianidad based on 'la árida definición que la explica como el conjunto de las manifestaciones culturales producidas en territorio italiano' [the dry definition which understands it as the totality of cultural manifestations developed within the Italian territory].[4] Instead, following Clifford, it is essential to go beyond an axis of origin and return, to focus instead on specific local interactions that reveal how 'the connection (elsewhere) that makes a difference (here) [is] remembered and rearticulated'.[5] Drawing primarily on the narratives of experience and memory by two self-identifying Italo-Chileans, and with particular attention to language, this chapter explores the role of both institutional and more everyday representations and practices associated with Italianness within this contemporary urban context shaped by a complex history of transnational flows and transcultural influences.

Valparaíso's Italian Community

As Valparaíso grew rapidly to become a major industrial port in the nineteenth century, it became the focus of both internal and European migration,[6] with immigration often represented as a constitutive part of the city's identity.[7] In contrast to Brazil and Argentina, owing to the greater selectivity of the

this research is a product of both my own and others' practices of cultural and linguistic translation.
4 Gabriela Castillo, 'Preámbulo/Preambolo', in *La herencia italiana en la región de Valparaíso/L'eredità italiana nella regione di Valparaíso*, ed. by Gabriella Castillo Raga (Santiago: Consiglio della Comunità Italiana Regione Valparaíso and Escuela de Diseño Universidad Nacional Andrés Bello, 2011–12), pp. 22–39 (p. 30).
5 Clifford, p. 269.
6 Baldomero Estrada, 'Redes socioeconómicas y mercados urbanos: La colectividad italiana en Valparaíso, en el cambio de siglo/Reti socio-economiche e mercati urbani: La comunità italiana di Valparaíso a cavallo del secolo', in *La herencia italiana*, ed. by Castillo Raga, pp. 96–145 (pp. 104–05); Davide Piacenti, 'Los emigrantes italianos en la ciudad-puerto de Valparaíso (1880–1920)/Gli immigranti italiani nella città-porto di Valparaíso (1880–1920)', in *La herencia italiana*, ed. by Castillo Raga, pp. 78–95 (pp. 82–83).
7 Leonardo Carrera Airola, *Italianos en Chile: un proceso de inmigración y retorno* (Valparaíso: Pontificia Universidad Católica de Valparaíso, 2015), p. 29.

Chilean government's migration policies immigration from Italy was initially low. However, by the end of the nineteenth century the Italian community formed the largest foreign-born population in the city,[8] with around 70 per cent of those who arrived between 1880 and 1920 estimated to originate from the region of Liguria.[9]

The lack of formal cooperation with Italian state powers, in contrast to the English and German populations,[10] meant that most Italians went into the small business and tertiary sector.[11] Italians became particularly well known for running the corner shops or grocery stores known as 'emporios' or 'almacenes', which were dispersed across the city and which facilitated the community's integration into the economic, social and cultural life of the city.[12] Despite often starting with fairly limited economic means, this concentration in small businesses led to the development of a rapidly mobile middle class. Within the city the community established a number of explicitly Italian institutions early on, including the Societá di Beneficenza Italiana, founded as early as 1856, the newspaper *L'Italia*, founded in 1890, the Banco Italiano, founded in 1905, and the Scuola Italiana, founded in 1941.[13] At the same time, as Valparaíso's role in trade decreased, many members of the Italian community relocated to other areas, particularly Santiago, which by 1930 had become the preferred destination for Italians.[14]

Nevertheless, there remains a significant Italian community within the city, now predominantly made up of third- and fourth-generation Italo-Chileans. It is, however, a community noted for its high level of integration with the local population. This integration has also had linguistic consequences, with a fairly rapid shift to Spanish and limited use of Italian.[15]

8   Piacenti, p. 86.
9   René Salinas Meza, 'Perfil demográfico de la inmigración italiana a Chile', in *Presencia italiana en Chile*, ed. by Baldomero Estrada (Valparaíso: Instituto de Historia Universidad Católica de Valparaíso), pp. 11–24 (p. 19).
10 Estrada, 'Redes socioeconómicas', p. 107.
11 Baldomero Estrada, 'Participación italiana en la industrialización de Chile. Orígenes y evolución hasta 1930', in *Presencia italiana*, ed. by Estrada, pp. 89–124 (p. 105).
12 Piacenti, pp. 90–91.
13 Luigi Follegati, Juan Carlos Jeldes and Javier Iglesias, 'Una escuela erigida por todos/Una scuola costruita da tutti', in *La herencia italiana*, ed. by Castillo Raga, pp. 178–97 (pp. 181–82).
14 Salinas Meza, p. 19.
15 Carla Bagna, 'America Latina', in *Storia linguistica dell'emigrazione italiana nel mondo*, ed. by Massimo Vedovelli (Roma: Carocci, 2011), pp. 305–58 (p. 355).

While the concentration of Ligurian migrants may have initially created circumstances that encouraged widespread use of the Ligurian language variety – commonly referred to in Valparaíso as the Genovese dialect – its knowledge and use is increasingly rare. At the same time, even if the regular use of Italian or Italian regional languages is far from widespread, as Samata establishes, the influence of languages is not limited to those with complete fluency and, as will be explored, they may remain 'imbricate in the wider cultural patterns within which the community and the individual interact'.[16]

Uncovering Transcultural Memory and Heritage

In the context of a heavily integrated community that has remained isolated from contemporary Italy, from a methodological perspective it is not easy to trace and identify specifically 'Italian' features or practices. As Fox asks, how does one go about uncovering '¿Cuánto de este "ser Valparaíso" se le debe al aporte de los inmigrantes de la bota itálica?' [How much of this 'being Valparaíso' is indebted to the contribution of immigrants from the boot of Italy?].[17] Although there remain recognizable institutional aspects of Italianness, a more intangible and transcultural heritage is less easily identified. In relation to language, for example, as Samata notes, the felt absence or lack of a language presents 'little or no analysable form or function'.[18]

Following Samata, while starting out from a sociolinguistic perspective, in order to go beyond noting the scarcity of Italian languages in contemporary Valparaíso it was necessary to look to wider disciplinary perspectives, including cultural memory studies. While interviews were often focused on individual family histories as a starting point for discussion, the focus of my analysis was less on the specific details of these histories and instead on 'the selectivity and perspectivity inherent in the creation of versions of the past according to present knowledge and needs'.[19] In this sense, and as Ballinger establishes, Italianness should be understood not as a definitive list of easily

---

16 Susan Samata, *The Cultural Memory of Language* (London, New York: Bloomsbury, 2014), p. ix.
17 Alan Fox, 'Prefacio/Prefazione', in *La herencia italiana*, ed. by Castillo Raga, pp. 14–21 (p. 17).
18 Samata, *The Cultural Memory of Language*, p. viii.
19 Astrid Erll, 'Cultural Memory Studies: An Introduction', in *Cultural Memory Studies: An International and Interdisciplinary Handbook*, ed. by Astrid Erll and Ansgar Nünning (Berlin: De Gruyter, 2008), pp. 1–18 (p. 5).

identifiable features or practices but rather as a discursive 'configuration of meanings' established over time.[20] This approach is connected to critical heritage studies, which understands heritage not as merely the possession of a series of material objects or cultural artefacts, but instead as 'a process of appropriation and delineation' whereby specific aspects of the past 'are actively taken up and claimed, in a particular time-space context and by particular people'.[21]

Both Erll and Deumert recognize the coexistence of more public and official narratives of heritage and memory, alongside more private ones and what Erll describes as 'implicit ways of cultural remembering [...] or of inherently non-narrative, for example visual or bodily, forms of memory'.[22] As Erll notes, cultural memory research has focused primarily on the former, which may reflect the fact that, as their public nature suggests, these are more easily identified and consequently subjected to analysis. Equally, Deumert points to the challenge of keeping 'the multivocality of heritage, its haunted nature and multiple temporalities in focus', suggesting ethnographic approaches as the epistemology of choice for understanding 'the sociocultural complexities of the everyday'.[23] This is reflected in my research in Valparaíso, which involved a month-long period of fieldwork in the city in April 2016. The research relied primarily on extended interviews with individuals with some form of familial migration history connected to Italy, with an emphasis on narratives of experience and memory. Drawing, however, on ethnographic praxis, fieldwork also involved attendance at community-related events and other forms of emplaced engagement with the material landscape of the city, both at my own and research participants' prompting. In particular, through a process of what Pink describes as 'shared walking' with two research participants, I was able to be 'similarly emplaced' in ways that allowed me to better understand 'how others remember and imagine through their own immediate embodied experiences'.[24] This attention to materiality and embodiment also drew my analytical attention away from a more isolated focus on language to

---

20 Pamela Ballinger, *History in Exile: Memory and Identity at the Borders of the Balkans* (Princeton, NJ: Princeton University Press, 2003), pp. 31–32.
21 Ana Deumert, 'The Multivocality of Heritage – Moments, Encounters and Mobilities', in *The Routledge Handbook of Language and Superdiversity*, ed. by Angela Creese and Adrian Blackledge, 1st edn (Routledge, 2018), pp. 149–64 (p. 151).
22 Erll, 'Cultural Memory Studies', p. 3.
23 Deumert, p. 153.
24 Sarah Pink, 'An Urban Tour: The Sensory Sociality of Ethnographic Place-Making', *Ethnography*, 9 (2008), 175–96.

instead explore how it was 'interwoven with the rest of the action, the dynamic relations between semiotic resources, activities, artefacts and space'.[25]

This chapter is consequently informed by this broader ethnographic engagement. Interviews focused primarily on individual life narratives were complemented by more 'institutional' interviews with, for example, the current director of the Scuola Italiana and the head of Valparaíso's Council of the Italian Community. This chapter focuses, however, on the narratives of two specific individuals, Renato and Victor, who do not have a specific institutional role in the community. Renato, in his late fifties, is a third-generation Italo-Chilean, with three of his grandparents originally from Italy, two from Liguria and one from Tuscany. Victor, in his early fifties, is also a third-generation Italo-Chilean, although it was only one of his grandparents who came from Italy. In contrast to the majority, his grandfather came from the Friuli region and, after leaving Italy at a young age, spent most of his childhood in Argentina, before moving to Chile in his late teens. While not aiming to be comprehensive or generalizable, Renato and Victor's different family trajectories of migration, and very different relations to the 'institutions of italianità', provide partial insight into the internal heterogeneity and multiplicity of perspectives of those affiliated in distinct ways to some form of Italianness. At the same time, across their narratives there emerge connections that point to shared local understandings of what it means to be Italian in Valparaíso.

Monuments, Symbols and Institutions of Italianità

As a newcomer to Valparaíso, the most immediately identifiable signs of Italianness were the monuments that assert an Italian presence over the city's landscape. In the city's Parque Italia I was confronted immediately by the Capitoline wolf statue atop a high column (Figure 2.1). Although there are no clear records of the origin of the statue,[26] perhaps intentionally, the column is

---

25 Alastair Pennycook, 'Translanguaging and Semiotic Assemblages', *International Journal of Multilingualism*, 14 (2017), 269–82 (p. 273).
26 Journalistic accounts suggest Mussolini gifted similar statues to sites across the globe, including two others in Chile. See, for example, Jaime Liencura, 'Desde una obra regalada por Mussolini hasta un caballo tamaño real: las otras obras que están perdidas en Chile', *Publimetro*, 29 November 2018, <https://www.publimetro.cl/cl/noticias/2018/11/29/mussolini-talca-cabalo-obras-perdidas-chile.html> [accessed 10 May 2019].

Fig. 2.1: Statue of the Capitoline wolf in Valparaíso's Parque Italia. Author's own image.

Fig. 2.2: Bust of Giovanni Battista Pastene in Valparaíso's Parque Italia. Author's own image.

engraved with the year 1937 in Roman numerals, followed by 'XV EF' (15th year of the Fascist Era), and it is undoubtedly connected to Fascist Italy's more aggressive efforts to continue Liberal Italy's attempts to forge a form of 'emigrant colonialism'.[27] The use of Spanish in the barely legible engraved column points to the desire to project 'Italy's glories' outwards, and contrasts with the Italian engraved on the other Italian statue in the park, a bust of the Genoese admiral Giovanni Battista Pastene (Figure 2.2). A gift from the city of Genoa to Valparaíso in 1961, Pastene represents a more traditional colonial mission, having played a central role in the colonization of Chile and going on to become the first governor of Valparaíso.[28] Although, like Columbus, he was employed by the Spanish crown, his Genoese origins have been drawn on to establish an almost mythical connection to the individuals who arrived much later in the nineteenth and twentieth centuries.

27   Mark I. Choate, *Emigrant Nation: The Making of Italy Abroad* (Cambridge, MA: Harvard University Press, 2008).
28   Gabriele Mariano, 'Pastene, Giovanni Battista', *Dizionario Biografico degli Italiani*, Volume 81 (2014), http://www.treccani.it/enciclopedia/giovanni-battista-pastene_(Dizionario-Biografico)/ [accessed 10 May 2019].

The Columbus statue in the city (Figure 2.3) sees a similar attempt to establish direct connections with those who first colonized the Americas, with the striking description of him as the 'primo immigrante in terra americana' [first immigrant on American land] in a plaque added to the statue in 1992 by the Italian community to mark the 500th anniversary of the 'discovery' of the Americas. This description highlights how the Italian notion of 'emigrant colonialism' creates this unusual blurring of the role of immigrant and colonizer. This statue also has an unusual history, in that it was originally commissioned by the city governor, with seemingly no direct connection to the Italian community, but has since been repeatedly appropriated by the community with the addition of further plaques: in 1892, in 1986 to mark 450 years since the city's founding, in 1992 as previously mentioned, and in 2000 to mark the Catholic Jubilee.[29] While these other plaques are in Spanish, the use of Italian to mark the 'discovery' of the Americas and for the bust of Pastene suggests an attempt to 'reclaim' the colonization of Chile and the Americas as part of a specifically Italian history.

These monuments create a foundational myth for the Italian presence in Chile, in ways that, as is common in European narratives of the colonization of the Americas, erase the existing indigenous populations already present on the land. What is unique to the Italian case is an attempt to reclaim these figures as part of an Italian 'national' mission, despite their being employed by the Spanish crown. The fact that Italy as a state and Italian as a truly national language did not exist for these individuals who first arrived to colonize Chile accentuates the artificiality of monuments that project the idea of an Italian nation back on to those for whom it was at most an abstract reality.

The individual nature of these colonial figures, as well as the limited connection of later arrivals to state powers, seems to have allowed Italy to largely evade scholarly attention in relation to the colonization of Latin America, and potentially also allowed Italians in Valparaíso to occupy a more ambivalent, and more integrated, role than those affiliated more closely to colonial state powers. These monuments are, in contrast, aimed at narrating a history of Italianness in Chile associated more explicitly with ideas of

---

29 Ricardo Saavedra Foppiani, 'Cristobal Colón y su arribo a Valparaíso', in *La imagen de Cristóbal Colón en el arte latinoamericano del siglo XIX a través de la pintura y la escultura*, ed. by Nanda Leonardini (Lima: Facultad de Letras y Ciencias Humanas Universidad Nacional Mayor de San Marcos, 2008), pp. 50–55.

Fig. 2.3: Statue of Christopher Columbus, above the plaque marking 500 years since the 'discovery' of the Americas. Author's own image.

national 'glories' and an Italian colonial mission. I begin by highlighting them, not to suggest that they are the most important representations of Italianness, but rather as representative of the local legacies of 'emigrant colonialism' which continues to function as 'an enduring interpretive nexus'.[30]

The 'didactic logic'[31] of these monuments makes the rigidly nationalist narratives they attempt to impose a point of division between those who consider themselves members or not of an explicitly Italian community. Renato, for example, echoes this colonial narrative of a continuous Italian presence, responding when asked about Italianness in Valparaíso that it existed 'Bueno, desde prácticamente los primeros días de Valparaíso, con el Almirante Giovanni Battista Pastene' [Well, since practically the first days of Valparaíso, with the Admiral Giovanni Battista Pastene]. In contrast, it is this legacy that appears to create a need in Victor to distance himself from this 'official' history. He did so repeatedly across the interview, warning before recounting his own family history that:

> Victor: Es que en mi caso, y yo creo en el caso de- de mi familia, eh, no ha habido ta- hay más bien una historia familiar, sí. Una historia familiar que tiene una raíz que incluso en algunos momentos fue (..) no investigada en términos académicos, sino que en términos, eh, biográficos, emocionales. Eh, y por lo tanto hay algún conocimiento de- de esa historia, y de como se produce etcétera. Pero hay poco vínculo con la, eh, con la comunidad y con las asociaciones aquí en Valparaíso.[32]

> [Victor: The thing is in my case, and I believe in the case of- of my family, eh, there hasn't been- there is more of a family history, yes. A family history which has a root that even at some points was (..) not investigated in academic terms, but in, eh, biographical, emotional terms. Eh, and so there is some knowledge of- of this history, and of how it came about etcetera. But there's little connection with the, eh, with the community, and with the associations here in Valparaíso.]

While Victor's experiences and memories reveal closer connections to the community than initially suggested, we see his desire to establish a clear separation between his personal family history and the 'official' history of

---

30 Mark I. Choate, 'From Territorial to Ethnographic Colonies and Back Again: The Politics of Italian Expansion, 1890–1912', *Modern Italy*, 8 (2003), 65–75 (p. 66).

31 James E. Young, 'The Texture of Memory: Holocaust Memorials in History', in *Cultural Memory Studies*, ed. by Erll and Nünning, pp. 357–66 (p. 359).

32 Transcription conventions: - cut off; (..) significant pause; _____ emphasis.

the community. In particular, it is this 'official' history, connected to the explicitly Italian organizations in the city, that appears to demarcate clear community boundaries, in common with traditional narratives of national belonging.

Although the associations Victor mentions often originated as externally 'subsidized and somewhat artificial' attempts to 'brand emigrants as Italian',[33] this is not, however, to deny that they became a meaningful way for some migrants and their descendants to express a 'sentido de pertenencia' [sense of belonging] to Italy.[34] For the children and grandchildren of Italian migrants, these organizations and associated national celebrations have also gone on to serve new functions beyond purely 'political' purposes. For example, 2 June, the Festa della Repubblica, is the most important community celebration. At the same time, the head of Valparaíso's Council of the Italian Community positions this as a locally important celebration:

> Paolo: Oltre a- all'omaggio all'Italia come nazione, come alle nostre radici, ne- nell'inconscio nostro ci rendiamo conto che stiamo anche rendendo l'omaggio ai nostri- ai nostri nonni, una maniera di dire in forma incosc- incosciente, di dire senza parole ai nostri nonni, uh, grazie, grazie per tutto quello che ci avete legato, che ci avete dato, che ci permette di arrivare ai giorni di oggi come siamo, come comunità, come famiglie.

> [Paolo: Beyond a- a tribute to Italy as a nation, to our roots so to speak, in our- our subconscious we realize that we're also paying tribute to our- to our grandparents, a way of saying subconsc- subconsciously, of saying without words to our grandparents, uh, thank you, thank you for everything that you've handed down to us, that you've given us, that has allowed us to arrive where we are now as we are, as a community, as families.]

This explicitly 'national' celebration is resignified here as a way of commemorating the specific histories and experiences of community members' own parents and grandparents who first arrived in Chile, and the continuation of these Italian institutions can be understood as an attempt to pay tribute to the work of those who first created and sustained them.

33 Choate, *Emigrant Nation*, p. 101.
34 Carrera Airola, p. 43.

Fig. 2.4: Valparaíso's Scuola Italiana. Author's own image.

Inarguably, the most important of these institutions is Valparaíso's Scuola Italiana (Figure 2.4). The Scuola was opened in 1941, although plans for its construction date back to 1896,[35] at the peak of Liberal Italy's policy of emigrant colonialism.[36] However, its construction relied primarily on the organization and fundraising capabilities of the local Italian community in Valparaíso.[37] The imposing school building has come to stand as the primary physical representation of the community in the city, described in a 2008 book of photographs of the School as 'la traducción al espacio físico de un legado inmaterial' [the translation into the physical space of an immaterial legacy].[38] This points to an aim to make seemingly more solid the more widespread intangible Italian presence in the city. The School also occupies this dual position of both functioning as 'el lugar de la Italia lejana en Chile'

---

35 Follegati et al., p. 181.
36 Choate, 'From Territorial to Ethnographic Colonies'.
37 Follegati et al., p. 182.
38 Introductory text written by Oscar Acuña in the 2007 photobook *Scuola Mia* by Maite Larregui, cited in Follegati et al., p. 195.

[the site of distant Italy in Chile][39] while also, as its director emphasized in a 1983 speech, remaining closely identified with the city: 'Somos todos porteños de corazón' [We are all porteños at heart].[40]

This dual role is not without its tensions. For Victor, having not attended the School, it is seen as representative of a clearly bounded 'official' Italian community. As Carrera Airola explains, 'el haber estudiado en la *Scuola Italiana* se convirtió en un requisito tácito para ser considerado parte de la colectividad misma' [having studied in the *Scuola Italiana* became a tacit requirement for being considered part of the collectivity itself].[41] This was particularly true in the early decades of the School, when there was a requirement for children to have two Italian-origin surnames.[42] It is unclear when this policy ended, and, in the present day, the School actively encourages attendance even by those with no family connection to Italy. This early policy does, however, highlight the role of these institutions in attempting to maintain ideas of national purity, even in the face of inevitable transcultural influences. For, as Fiore notes, the diaspora is 'a community that is invariably implicated with motion and yet is constantly pulled toward a definition: The nation knocks at the door of the diaspora.'[43]

These tensions come to the fore in relation to the teaching of Italian, the primary function of Italian Schools in contexts of migration. Owing to the fact most migrants arrived speaking predominantly regional dialects, the Italian language risked remaining 'sterile' and 'artificial'.[44] The Scuola Italiana in Valparaíso faced the challenge of introducing its pupils to a largely unfamiliar language while operating within a predominantly Spanish-speaking environment. During the time Renato attended, this was achieved through immersion in Italian in the early years, alongside the prohibition of dialect. In Renato's case, the School did, however, succeed in creating strong affective ties to the language:

Me: ¿Y son importantes estas instituciones, asociaciones que quedan ahora en Valparaíso para reunir la colectividad y enseñar italiano y todo esto?

39   Follegati et al., p. 191.
40   Albino Misseroni's speech recorded in the *Diario El Mercurio de Valparaíso* on 21 April 1983, cited in Follegati et al., p. 194.
41   Carrera Airola, p. 57.
42   Carrera Airola, p. 57.
43   Teresa Fiore, *Pre-Occupied Spaces: Remapping Italy's Transnational Migrations and Colonial Legacies* (New York: Fordham University Press, 2017), p. 184.
44   Choate, *Emigrant Nation*, p. 108.

Renato: O sea, para mí fundamentales. O sea, si no hay Scuola, no es fácil que estudien italiano. O sea, cruzamos la calle y en el cuarto piso dice italiano, ruso, francés, inglés, portugués. Pero no es lo mismo, no es lo mismo tomar un curso rápido y aprender one two three four five, que vivir durante doce o trece o catorce años en un ambiente que es la segunda casa. Creo yo.

[Me: And are they important these institutions, associations that are still here now in Valparaíso to bring together the community and teach Italian and all of these things?
Renato: I mean, for me essential. I mean, if there isn't Scuola it's not easy for them to study Italian. I mean, we can cross the road and on the fourth floor it says Italian, Russian, French, English, Portuguese. But it isn't the same, it isn't the same to take a quick course and learn one two three four five, as living for twelve or thirteen or fourteen years in an environment which is a second home. That's what I think.]

The description of the Scuola as a 'second home', and the explicit comparison with more neutral language-learning environments, points to the importance of the physical environments in which languages are learnt and used. Despite the more institutional associations of the Italian language and its limited use outside of the Scuola, Renato's affective associations with the school environment – associations that both reinforce and are reinforced by his strong sense of belonging to the Italian community – allow him to appropriate the language and imbue it with 'affective resonances'[45] that go beyond a 'sterile' national language.

This was not the case for Victor, even if he did later go on to study Italian for a brief time as an adult after applying for Italian citizenship. He applied for citizenship not for reasons of national identity, but because his father was advised by the Italian consul in Valparaíso that it could offer him greater protection after he was detained during Pinochet's dictatorship. Despite these more practical motivations, the process of applying for citizenship provoked a sudden interest in exploring other aspects of Italianness:

Victor: El vínculo estaba digamos emocionalmente en términos de- de la historia duro. Pero uno nunca lo había pensado en términos formales, ah,

---

45 Claire Kramsch, *The Multilingual Subject* (Oxford: Oxford University Press, 2013), p. 2.

de la nacionalidad formal. Cuando aparece esa posibilidad, empiezan a aparecer además también las otras posibilidades. A mí antes no se me había ocurrido aprender italiano por ejemplo, eh, y a mi hermano tampoco.

[Victor: The connection was let's say emotionally in terms of- of that hard history. But it was never thought of in formal terms, ah, of formal nationality. When that possibility presents itself, other possibilities start to present themselves too. For me, it hadn't occurred to me before to learn Italian for example, eh, and not to my brother either.]

Although language learning was by no means a requirement of gaining citizenship, the learning of Italian is here intertwined with the formal elements of Italian national identity.

However, Victor did not go beyond a few classes in learning Italian, nor continue to use it later. Even Renato described using Italian as 'una sfida' [a challenge], as he does not have the daily opportunity to use it. As a result, usage of Italian remains highly marked as a self-conscious expression of Italian national identity, as illustrated by the way Victor's interest in learning the language was provoked only by the official process of gaining Italian citizenship. This explains the fragility of diasporic attempts to (re)produce a sense of national consciousness, in that the symbols of the nation, which include a standard national language, are not sufficiently embedded in daily life in ways that can allow them to become taken-for-granted or 'banal' forms of nationalism, or what Billig describes as 'invented permanencies'.[46] This appears to be heightened in the case of Italians in Chile because of the specific isolation of Chile from the peninsula in the post-war period, when the language and other national symbols began to seem less marked or artificial identity markers through their embeddedness in daily life within Italy.

In contrast with Victor's specific experience under Pinochet's dictatorship, for the wider community this period heightened an already significant geographical isolation, with Italy one of the few countries to cut off diplomatic relations.[47] Since the end of the dictatorship there have been attempts to re-establish closer connections with contemporary Italy. The Scuola Italiana, for example, established what is described as a 'paritary' education system, which means the Scuola now follows the Italian national

---

46 Michael Billig, *Banal Nationalism* (London, Thousand Oaks, CA: Sage, 1995), p. 29.
47 Heraldo Muñoz, *Las relaciones exteriores del Gobierno Militar Chileno* (Santiago: PROSPEL-CERC, 1986).

curriculum, although primarily via the medium of Spanish. Far from presenting a solution, however, this period of reconnection appears to have highlighted the profound differences between the development of the local Italian community and of contemporary Italian society. This was evident when talking with the current director of the Scuola, who had come from Italy rather than the local community, and who commented on the need to reconnect Chile's Italian Schools 'con l'Italia di oggi, con l'Italia vera' [with the Italy of today, with the real Italy']. This illustrates how institutions that carry an explicit identification with Italian culture and the language will inevitably find only their absence within the contemporary Italo-Chilean community, when measured against the imagined bearers of that language and culture from within the peninsula. This thus contributes to the sense expressed by Renato that Italianness is becoming 'diluted':

> Me: Y queda todavía este- italianità bastante fuerte aquí-
> Renato: Hay harto, hay mucho, hay bastante. Eh, a mí, me parece que es algo que se va como <u>diluyendo</u>. Pero mientras haya Scuola, mientras haya Stadio, mientras haya Società Canottieri Italiani, mientras haya Società Sportiva Italiana, mientras haya todas estas- Società Italiana di Beneficenza, todas estas instituciones, esto todavía se mantiene.

> [Me: And is there still this- quite strong italianità here-
> Renato: There's plenty, there's a lot, there's a fair amount. Eh, to me, it seems like it's something that is becoming <u>diluted</u>. But as long as there's Scuola, as long as there's Stadio, as long as there's Società Canottieri Italiani, as long as there's Società Sportiva Italiana, as long as there's all of these- Società Italiana di Beneficenza, all of these institutions, this is still maintained.]

The dominance of significantly older generations in these organizations, and the seeming lack of interest of younger generations repeatedly mentioned across interviews, suggests that their future is far from guaranteed. If we are to follow Renato's logic, this suggests the imminent disappearance of Italianness from the city. It is, however, important to note how my own use of the Italian term 'italianità' probably played a role in Renato's connecting my question to the presence of the more formal institutions associated with the Italian nation, rather than more locally defined conceptions and practices associated with Italianness.

Transcultural Italianidad: Language, Embodiment and Materiality

Beyond a straightforward narrative of total assimilation of the Italian community over time, there remain less marked forms of Italianness in both the landscape and contemporary practices of Valparaíso's residents, including those without an explicit Italian connection. In relation to these less overt forms of Italianness, it was notable that interviewees were often keen to go beyond the traditional interview and saw it as essential for me to engage 'with the material and sensorial qualities of the things they describe'.[48] This illustrated the struggle to express a less tangible Italian presence in the city through purely verbal narratives.

Even within verbal narratives of memory, the material world was interwoven as inseparable from linguistic resources. Renato, for example, was known within the community as one of the few people who still spoke Genovese, despite the prohibition of the language within Valparaíso's Scuola Italiana. His mother was, in fact, explicitly advised by a teacher not to use the language at home for fear it would cause confusion. Renato's mother, however, rejected this advice, even going on to explicitly teach the language to her children:

> Renato: Y mi madre, mi madre, nos enseñaba. Estaba la tabla para hacer la pasta. Que la tengo en casa y es de mi abuela, la mamá de mi mamá. Está media vieja, pero está, allí está en la cocina. Entonces mi madre, me parece verla, esta es la tabla, mi madre al medio, mi hermano acá a la derecha y yo aquí a la izquierda. Entonces pongan harina, una taza de harina. Pongan otra taza de harina. Ábranlo un poquito. Echen una tacita de agua. Después pongan el huevo, vamos aceite. Y allí nos aprovechaba de enseñar un poco la pronunciación.

> [Renato: And my mother, my mother, she taught us. There was the board for making pasta. Which I have at home and it's from my grandmother, my mum's mum. It's very old, but it's there, it's there in the kitchen. And so my mother, I can almost see her, this is the board, my mother in the middle, my brother there on the right and me here on the left. And so add the flour, a cup of flour. Add another cup of flour. Open it up a little. Add a little cup of water. Then add the egg, in goes the oil. And there she used the time to teach us some of the pronunciation.]

---

48   Sarah Pink, *Doing Sensory Ethnography* (London, Thousand Oaks, CA: Sage Publications, 2015), p. 79.

For Renato, the desire to continue speaking Genovese is tied to powerful affective associations of the language with his mother. However, the extract above also draws attention not just to the people and the words they speak but to the ways 'the semiotic and the material constantly cross-cut and convert into each other'.[49] Speaking Genovese is interwoven with the act of preparing pasta, which is also connected to the object of the board for making the pasta within the specific environment of the kitchen, an object that, importantly, Renato has kept, in parallel to the language he has made efforts to maintain.

From this perspective, the material surrounds can be understood not just as a context in which interactions take place but as 'part of an interactive whole that includes people, objects and space'.[50] This is further emphasized elsewhere in Renato's interview, where he highlights that, outside the home, he also associates the dialect with his parent's shop (Figure 2.5) and the other Italian-owned shops in the neighbourhood:

> Renato: ¿Y por qué? Por qué, esta es la pregunta. ¿Por qué llegábamos a hablar, y con mi mamá? Porque estábamos en el negocio. Se mantenía en el antiguo negocio.
> [...]
> Ahora, si tú quisieras en este preciso instante, caminamos las cuatro cinco cuadras y llegamos donde hay aún hijos de italianos, están trabajando en emporio, en el negocio. Y un poco más allá, otros hijos de italianos también, están en un negocio donde venden vasos, tazas, cucharas.
>
> [Renato: And why? Why, that's the question. Why did we end up speaking, and with my mum? Because we were in the shop. It was kept up in the old shop.
> [...]
> Now, if you wanted in this precise moment, we can walk four five blocks across and we'll arrive where there are still children of Italians, they're working in the emporio, in the shop. A little further on, other children of Italians too, they're in a shop where they sell glasses, cups, spoons.]

---

49 David Sutton, 'Cooking Skills, the Senses, and Memory: The Fate of Practical Knowledge', in *Food and Culture: A Reader*, ed. by Carole Counihan and Penny Van Esterik (New York: Routledge, 2013), pp. 299–319 (p. 303).
50 Pennycook, p. 277.

Porteña Identity and Italianità 65

Fig. 2.5: An early photo, held by Renato, of the shop owned by his family. Author's own image.

The objects Renato lists at the end of this extract illustrate how the material surrounds are inseparable from his memories of speaking Genovese and the opportunities he has to continue using it. Following Pennycook, we can see this as an example of how a specific 'semiotic assemblage' has become sedimented over time,[51] with the use of Genovese interwoven not only with the people but with the wider artefactual and spatial resources of these shops.

These shops, or emporios, are recognized across the city as particularly representative of this everyday form of Italian heritage in Valparaíso. The image of the Italian shopkeeper on the corner has become what Carrera Airola describes as a 'figura emblemática' [emblematic figure] in the economic and social life of the city.[52] A book on the Italian presence in Valparaíso refers to the 'grandes anaqueles perfumados por la añosa madera' [large shelves perfumed by ancient wood][53] surrounding this figure, highlighting the significance of material and sensory elements of cultural memory. At the same time, this figure of 'Don Giuseppe de la esquina' [Don Giuseppe on the corner] has come to function for some as a stereotype or even caricature in relation to local representations of Italianness,[54] and inevitably does not reflect the trajectories of all Italian migrants. Nevertheless, the emporios illustrate the way assemblages of people, spaces, objects and languages come to be organized along specific and recognizable trajectories[55] in ways that have contributed to the Italian community's sense of local rootedness in the city.

This does not mean the elements of the assemblage are fixed and remain stable over time. For example, while there are a handful of shops where Genovese is still spoken, this is by no means the case across the city. Many of these originally Italian-owned emporios are in fact either closed or now run and owned by individuals with less-direct connections to Italy. In relation to language, this means that use of either Genovese or Italian is increasingly rare, and the ways in which these emporios were embedded in neighbourhoods across the city, rather than in specifically Italian enclaves, contributed to the much greater integration of the community[56] in ways that probably also contributed to the fairly rapid learning and use of Spanish.

Nevertheless, despite the fact that use of Genovese or Italian is now fairly rare within these shops, they remain locally important sites of Italianness, including for Victor, who speaks neither Genovese nor the language of Friuli, from where his own grandfather originates:

51 Pennycook, p. 280.
52 Carrera Airola, p. 33 and p. 55.
53 Fox, p. 20.
54 Castillo, p. 25.
55 Pennycook, p. 271.
56 Carrera Airola, p. 55.

Me: ¿Pero aquí en Valparaíso se puede decir que hay una italianidad que no es sólo la- las asociaciones, la Scuola? ¿Hay algo más (..) sutil? Algo más-
Victor: Sí, sí sí sí. O sea, te doy por ejemplo el hábito que uno tiene, está vinculado con ese, el hábito que uno tiene, ehm, desde varias cosas. Una es lo que tiene que ver por ejemplo con este tema de los- de los comercios, de los mercados, de los almacenes. Eso. Y eso que tiene que ver al mismo tiempo con los oficios. Eso no es solamente de la colonia italiana en todo caso, pero en algunos- en algunos tiene que ver con la colonia italiana, en otros casos tiene que ver con la colonia árabe, etcétera. Pero que tiene que ver con la gente que tiene ese vínculo, ese aprecio por esa- esa forma digamos y por esa herencia.
[...]
Y todo lo compro allí, es un lugar donde la manera de relacionarse con la gente es distinta. Y ese hábito por ejemplo que es más o menos fuerte. Otro hábito que yo creo que proviene de allí, tiene que ver con todo lo que tiene que ver con una cuestión familiar y gastronómica. Es muy fuerte.
[...]
Entonces la comida, por ejemplo, eh, y la comida hecha, qué sé yo, yo lo hago aquí. Mi viejo lo hacía también etcétera. Yo hago el pan que consumo, no solamente hago el pan, hago la harina.

[Me: But here in Valparaíso is it possible to talk of an Italianness that isn't just th- the associations, the Scuola? Is there something more (..) subtle? Something more-
Victor: Yes, yes yes yes. I mean, I'll give you the example of the habit one has, which is linked to this, the habit one has, ehm, in relation to a number of things. One of them has to do for example with this subject of the- of the shops, the markets, the grocery stores. This. And this at the same time is connected to trade. This is not just for the Italian community in any case, but in some- in some cases it has to do with the Italian community, in others with the Arab community, etcetera. But it is linked to people that have this connection, this appreciation for this- this way, let's say, and for this inheritance.
[...]
And I buy everything there, in a place where the way of relating to people is different. And this habit for example is fairly strong. Another habit that I think originates from there, has to do with everything linked to the question of family and food. It's very strong.
[...]

So the food, for example, eh, and the homemade food, whatever, I make it here. My old man did the same too etcetera. I make the bread I eat, I don't just make the bread, I make the flour.]

Despite the lack of attention to language, there are clear connections with Renato's reflections in relation to the importance of the material environment of the emporios. In relation to food, Victor also emphasizes habitual embodied practices. While food is often identified as a marker of Italianness, significant here is the fact that Victor highlights not specifically Italian ingredients or recipes but instead the embodied process of preparing food from raw ingredients, echoing Renato's description of his mother's preparation of the pasta.

These processes are what Giard refers to as 'the invisible everyday', where 'there piles up a subtle montage of gestures, rites, and codes, of rhythms and choices, of received usage and practiced customs'.[57] This montage is also connected to Diana Taylor's notion of the 'embodied repertoire', which she argues is an alternative form of knowledge transmission to the more static archive associated with writing and more formal institutions: 'Multiple forms of embodied acts are always present, though in a constant state of againness. They reconstitute themselves, transmitting communal memories, histories, and values from one group/generation to the next.'[58] As Taylor emphasizes, unlike the stable objects of the archive, this 'state of againness' does not prevent the actions or elements of the repertoire from changing, even if 'the meaning might very well remain the same'.[59] For example, inevitably the ingredients that go into these recipes will change over time and, particularly in contexts of migration, will differ both from those originally used by those who migrated and those now used within Italy. This is particularly true in the case of Valparaíso's Italian community, and yet the emphasis on embodied processes rather than ingredients or the final product provides a way of recognizing the continuation of local practices associated with Italianness.

---

57 Michel de Certeau, Luce Giard and Pierre Mayol, *The Practice of Everyday Life. Volume 2: Living and Cooking* (Minneapolis: University of Minnesota Press, 1998), p. 171.
58 Diana Taylor, *The Archive and the Repertoire: Performing Cultural Memory in the Americas* (Durham, NC: Duke University Press, 2003), pp. 20–21. It is important to note that Taylor developed this concept in relation to Latin America and the erased histories of indigenous communities. The fact that European migrant communities to Latin America are still able to rely on an 'official' national archive clearly contributes to their greater visibility in the histories of cities such as Valparaíso.
59 Taylor, p. 20.

Fig. 2.6: An image from inside the Almacén Naval, with a photo of the original Italian owners, above a sticker saying 'This is a heritage site of Playa Ancha [an area of Valparaíso]'. Author's own image.

Returning to the emporios, these continue to signal Italianness across the generations through embodied actions connected to the material surrounds, even if the regular use of Genovese or any form of Italian language may be increasingly uncommon, and even if some of these stores are no longer owned by a family originating from Italy. In particular, as a meeting point for the whole neighbourhood, the emporios now function as a form of shared heritage across the city's residents.[60] When walking the city with Renato, for example, we visited one of the older shops he had not visited for some time to find it had changed ownership. Despite the new owner having no specific connection to the original owners or any Italian family, he had gone

60 Emilio Toro Canessa, 'El emporio italiano, como espacio de sociabilidad. Valparaíso 1900–1930', *Archivum: Revista del Archivo Histórico Patrimonial de Viña del Mar*, 11 (2013), 278–303 (p. 284).

Fig. 2.7: Renato believed this to be the site of one of the first Italian-owned shops established in the city. Author's own image.

to great efforts to maintain the traditional layout of the shop, while also proudly displaying a photo of the original Italian owners (Figure 2.6). This illustrates the 'multivocal' nature of heritage, and its potential to 'be claimed by different groups for different purposes and be imbued with different meanings'.[61]

The 'multivocality' of heritage is echoed earlier in Victor's hesitancy in designating specific practices, such as those associated with the emporios, as specifically 'Italian' and how in other cases they might be connected to other communities. Victor's hesitancy points to the challenges of separating out the cultural origins of practices that have developed over time in a context of multiple transcultural influences. Walking the city with interviewees drew attention more widely to the presence of a more transitory and transcultural Italianness within the palimpsestic and less self-consciously memorializing landscape. Renato, in particular, highlighted continuities, but also absences and changes (Figure 2.7), or what de Certeau describes as 'the invisible identities of the visible: it is the very definition of a place, in fact, that it is composed by these series of displacements and effects among the fragmented strata that form it and that it plays on these moving layers.'[62]

These inevitable displacements may explain the desire to sustain more stable representations of Italianness through, for example, monuments or designated Italian institutions or languages, associated with Taylor's notion of the official, static archive. At the same time, these less-explicit forms of Italianness permeate everyday life in the city, occupying the 'hollow places' of objects and material worlds, and 'concealed in gestures and bodies in motion'.[63]

Conclusion

While initially appearing to be a marginal or even 'artificial' presence, a powerful sense of Italianness remains in what Gabaccia describes as 'the humble details of everyday life' in Valparaíso.[64] At the same time, as Ballinger warns, we should be wary of drawing clear divisions between more official 'state-sponsored histories' and supposedly more 'authentic' forms of collective memory or individual life histories, and should instead recognize the inevitable 'discursive conjuctures' between them.[65] As illustrated by the local

---

61 Deumert, p. 161.
62 Michel de Certeau, *The Practice of Everyday Life. Volume 1* (Berkeley, CA: University of California Press, 2013), p. 108.
63 Certeau, pp. 108 and 105.
64 Donna R. Gabaccia, *Italy's Many Diasporas* (London: UCL Press, 2000), p. 177.
65 Ballinger, p. 26.

Fig. 2.8: The Almacén & Botillería Garibaldi in Valparaíso. Author's own image.

resignification of the 2 June celebration and Renato's affective associations with Italian, it is possible for explicitly 'national' symbols to be appropriated in locally meaningful ways. Equally, with many emporios bearing names associated with 'la patria distante' [the distant homeland],[66] we see attempts to project onto these more ordinary sites and histories a sense of the 'greatness' associated with Italian national heroes and traditions (see Figure 2.8).

Nevertheless, what we might describe as the 'official' archive of Italianness in Valparaíso is undoubtedly associated with attempts to delimit, and inevitably to purify, a heritage defined by movement and hybridity. A national language and identity are projected back onto earlier individuals and communities, perhaps to reassure later generations with the myth that, even if now 'diluted', they did once exist in a more complete form. Monuments or institutions associated with homogenizing nation-state discourses seek to fix and solidify, to sharpen the edges of an identity that is, in practice, 'plural, fragile, and debated'.[67] This is true of all national discourses, but in diasporic

66   Piacenti, p. 86.
67   Gabaccia, p. 175.

contexts, and particularly those marked by fragile connections to a country of origin, the artificiality of attempts to impose a monolithic national identity is heightened. For, as Clifford explains, 'Whatever their ideologies of purity, diasporic cultural forms can never, in practice, be exclusively nationalist. They are deployed in transnational networks built from multiple attachments.'[68]

Particularly as Italianness in Valparaíso has undergone multiple transcultural permeations across the generations, largely in isolation from developments within the peninsula, this may explain why these more static national narratives and symbols, including the language, are less meaningful for younger generations. At the same time, it is undoubtedly easier to construct a narrative based on easily recognizable national symbols and traditions than to attempt to isolate specifically Italian elements of more everyday practices and sites in the city shot through with a multiplicity of other influences. The ways in which Italianness has become entangled within a broader transcultural idea of porteña identity contributes to a sense of loss, reflected most visibly in the perceived absence of Italian national or regional languages. However, to avoid reinforcing false ideals of clearly bounded communities and associated cultures and languages that remain static over time, it is vital to go beyond straightforward narratives of cultural assimilation and language loss. Instead, we must find ways to excavate and narrate the 'haunted' nature of an Italian heritage[69] – 'the presences of diverse absences'[70] – which is interwoven in the verbal, embodied and material life of the city and its residents.

---

68 Clifford, p. 269.
69 Deumert, p. 153.
70 Certeau, p. 108.

CHAPTER THREE

Italian Identity, Global Mediterranean: Tourism and Cultural Heritage in Post-Colonial Rhodes

Valerie McGuire

In 2017 Rhodes made an unsuccessful bid to become a European cultural capital. Winning would have brought the island 1.5 million euros of investment in local business and development.[1] The designation might also have helped the island to jettison its reputation for high-season tourism and the sale of tchotchkes. A booming tourism industry has made Rhodes into one of Greece's most popular destinations – the island remains a top pick among international travellers and is accessed by Greek ferries, Mediterranean cruises, charter flights and, most recently, budget airlines such as Ryanair. But it is less often linked to heritage and culture. Offbeat British film comedies such as *High Season* (1985), which features Kenneth Branagh and Jacqueline Bisset as stereotypical Britons in Greece in search of Byronic romance, have solidified Rhodes' global reputation as a place overrun by sunburnt British and German tourists ripe for casual sex. The cultural capital designation, on the other hand, would have foregrounded the island's cultural heritage. A fortified medieval city first built by Knights Crusaders in the thirteenth century and restored by the Italian state during its rule of the island (1912–43) is an UNESCO world heritage site. The island is also home to a significant collection of antiquities and monuments from the Byzantine

---

1 The European Cultural Capital Programme is available on the EU Commission website <https://ec.europa.eu/programmes/creative-europe/actions/capitals-culture_en> [accessed 9 June 2019].

and Ottoman eras. The cultural capital project is an EU scheme meant to help put underprivileged European cities 'on the world map' and to boost a wider appreciation for European cultural heritage; it was initially pioneered by Greek actor and politician Melina Mercouri, who is perhaps most famous for advocating the return of the Elgin marbles from the British Museum in London to the Acropolis. The programme leads scores of small cities to compete on a triennial basis. Surpassing Rhodes the year that it competed were Matera in Italy and Plodviv in Bulgaria.

Had the island won the seed funding, the municipality would probably have used it to support further conservation in the medieval city centre. Since the passage of Greece into the European Union, the regional government has regularly solicited EU funds to repair the Italian-era colonial buildings that strikingly define its shorelines. The buildings comprise a dramatic urban intervention and testament to European architectural modernism and visually unify all the port towns of the fourteen islands in the Dodecanese prefecture. Recent efforts to conserve Italian-era architecture have not intensified debate about the period of Italian rule in the islands but, rather, have coincided with increasing European integration and efforts to position Rhodes as a global destination. If in the immediate post-war period calls to restore Italian-era architecture were criticized on the grounds that these were signs of the Italian state's authoritarian rule and suppression of Greek national and ethnic identity, the island's Italian colonial architecture has come to represent a new ethos of cosmopolitanism in the contemporary period. The revival of the Italian colonial past helps to fulfil new demands to assimilate Greece and the Dodecanese into the larger project of an increasingly federalist European Union.

In the presentation of the island's bid for cultural candidacy, the mayor of Rhodes described the cultural merit of the island in terms that were remarkably reminiscent of the interwar Italian idealization of the island:[2]

> Many cultures and civilizations have cohabited the island in peace and harmony through the years. The medieval structures, the slated streets and alleys, the mosques, the synagogue, the Orthodox churches, the Muslim library, the fountains, the squares and the parks, the traditional shops and businesses, all of them bring memories of the past closer to our colorful contemporary times.

2 The island's unsuccessful application for cultural capital candidacy remains available online.

The idea that Rhodes' 'multicultural' past is important to the 'modern' identity of the island was a prominent feature of Italians' discourse about Rhodes in the interwar period. In the same way that in Libya Mussolini laid claim to be ruling over a vast population of Turks, Muslims and Bedouins – and claimed to have acquired the 'sword of Islam' by invading Ethiopia – the appearance of maintaining the ethnic diversity of the local population was at the core of Italy's colonial renewal of the island.[3] In fact, were an Italian able to experience time travel and to catapult backwards by eighty or so years, he or she might find the mayor's description of Rhodes to be uncannily similar to those that once embellished Italian touring books. As described by Franco Ciarlantini during his 1936 tour of the island, the local ethnic diversity recalled a marvellous cross-cultural harmony benefiting from the presence of the 'strong' Italian state:

> Rodi è un esempio perfetto, molto in piccolo si capisce, della pacifica convivenza di razze e di civiltà diverse. Nella sua ristretta cerchia si parlano le più svariate favelle: l'italiano dai metropolitani, il turco dai mussulmani, il greco dagli ortodossi, un gergo spagnolo dagli ebrei; e tutti questi cittadini di lingua e di costume così diversi, vivono nei loro rispettivi quartieri animati e puliti, in perfetta concordia, in vicendevole rispetto delle costumanze e delle religioni cui sono attaccatissimi. I musulmani festeggiano il venerdì, gli israeliti il sabato, i cristiani la domenica; frequentando la moschea, la sinagoga, la chiesa ortodossa o cattolica, a seconda della confessione, ognuno ha un suo statuto civile e personale, e la vita si svolge in piena armonia, si sarebbe tentati di dire idillicamente.[4]

> [Rhodes is a perfect example, on a small scale of course, of the peaceful cohabitation of different races and civilizations. In its closed circle a variety of languages are spoken: Italian among metropolitans, Turkish among the Muslims, Greek among the Orthodox, and a Spanish dialect among the Jews; and all these citizens, of different languages and customs, live in their respective quarters, which are animated and clean, in perfect harmony, in mutual respect of traditions and religions, to which they are extremely attached. The Muslims celebrate on Friday, the

---

3   See John Wright, 'Mussolini, Libya, and the Sword of Islam', in *Italian Colonialism*, ed. by Ruth Ben-Ghiat and Mia Fuller (New York: Palgrave MacMillan, 2005), pp. 121–30.
4   Franco Ciarlantini, *Viaggio nell'Oriente Mediterraneo* (Milan: Mondadori, 1936), p. 114. The translation is my own.

Israelites on Saturday, the Christians on Sunday; attending the mosque, the synagogue, the Orthodox and Catholic churches, according to their confession, each one has his own civil and personal status and life carries on in full harmony, one would be tempted to say idyllically.]

Ciarlantini is better known for his involvement in the Fascist state and his support for the politics and projects of Fascist culture, including his founding of nationalist literary journal *Augustea* and his collaboration with the journal *Il grido della stirpe*. If his description of Rhodes here does not overtly convey colonial discourses of race, it is to do with the way the Italian state positioned the island's local diversity as inherent to the Italian state's 'multicultural' and 'Mediterranean' colonial modernity. Italian imperialists regularly insisted that Italy was renewing a *'pax romana'* in its rule of the islands.

Nowhere in the presentation of Rhodes' candidacy for cultural capital does the mayor mention local resistance to Italian rule. This omission is all the more striking given the ardently nationalist perspective that typically has characterized the history of modern Greece. As one of the last regions in Europe to be integrated into the nation-state (second only to Cyprus), Rhodes and the other Dodecanese islands have frequently presented historians and anthropologists with questions about the status of the 'national' at the margins of Europe.[5] Yet, to those familiar with studies of the Italian colonial empire, popular memory of Italian rule also seems to participate in an active redefining of Italy's colonial past that critics have observed troubles contemporary Italian culture. It is not just that there have been silences or a *'rimozione'* (repression) of the Italian empire, but rather that memories and traces of the Italian colonial past persist stubbornly and may have been redefined in the post-war era – whitewashed and bleached of their martial and Fascist underpinnings and in turn put to work in narratives of Italians as 'soft' imperialists, *brava gente*, or 'good people', more apt to make love than war. This phenomenon – this careful rewriting of the Italian colonial past – is not confined to Italy but is also felt in some of Italy's ex-colonies. As Mia Fuller has noted about postcolonial Asmara, where much of the Italian-era built environment stands intact, one is tempted to speculate about forms of 'colonial inertia' and to wonder about the ways that 'past colonial traces are being converted into currently useful forms of political, cultural, social, and

---

5 See Nicholas Doumanis, *Myth and Memory in the Mediterranean* (New York: St Martin's Press, 1997), as well as David Sutton, *Memories Cast in Stone: The Relevance of the Past in Everyday Life* (Oxford: Berg, 2000).

financial capital'.[6] The post-war fate of Italian architecture and restoration, as well as the broader cultural landscape of Rhodes, has followed the same route as postcolonial Asmara, and the tendency in urban planning has been toward preservation of Italian-era buildings as well as – to no small degree – the conservation of the touristic itinerary of Rhodes as it was organized by the Italian state. Recently, there have been calls for a complete conservation of the Italian architectural intervention, including not just the highly visible buildings of the tourist waterfront but also industrial architecture.[7] These renovations occur against the social backdrop of ongoing legends of Italians and Greeks playing the mandolin together during the Fascist era and the evergreen stereotype of 'una faccia, una razza' or 'one face, one race'. The cry for additional EU funding has also come amid new pressure on the islands, which make up an important part of the perimeter of Europe in the south-east Aegean, to help absorb and manage illegal migration in the Mediterranean.

If Italian postcolonial legacies may have a transcultural dimension, as appears to be the case with Rhodes, can such legacies intersect with contemporary dilemmas and doubts about the viability of the nation-state? This chapter aims to open up such a question. The premise that Rhodes is at once a destination for modern mass tourism and a repository for memories of the 'multi-ethnic' or multi-religious Mediterranean replicates the Italian project to reinvent the island as not only an emblem of Italian modernity but also a site for a new corporatist empire that curated leisure for a prosperous working class. Italy's annexation of Rhodes in 1923 was a hallmark of Mussolini's compromise with the radical nationalists and the island, along with Libya, was to become one of the major emblems of rapid modernization during the Fascist dictatorship. However, the transformation of the island into a 'modern' and 'global' tourist destination that advertised the empire pivoted on programmes of cultural heritage that 'preserved' the exotic, old-world Ottoman Orient. If tourism under the Italian administration served a very different purpose than it does today – advertising at home the success of the empire – such imaginative geographies of East/West, or Orient/Italy, persist in the contemporary geographies of the island, which celebrate the local/global binary, and help to promote the island as a 'multicultural'

---

6   Mia Fuller, 'Italy's Colonial Futures: Colonial Inertia and Postcolonial Capital in Asmara', *California Italian Studies*, 2 (2011). Article available at <https://escholarship.org/uc/item/4mb1z7f8> [accessed 17 November 2019].
7   Petition to save the Samica Flour Mill, <http://savesamica.blogspot.gr> [accessed 17 November 2019].

destination, at once European and Mediterranean. Although the average visitor is unlikely to encounter extensive information on the island's history during the twentieth century, the Italian state's colonial geography is still present in today's touristic cultural landscape. Indeed, post-war choices about heritage by the Greek state have consolidated a sense of the 'picturesque' setting while deliberately eliding complex and uncomfortable debates about minority identities in the island. A crowded assemblage of signposts of Italian 'authenticity' continue to denude the island of all sense of history and instead – in an almost postmodern fashion – make contemporary Rhodes into a touristic sign of itself.

Preservation in the Walled City of Rhodes

Although Rhodes' status as an official territory of the overseas empire was achieved thanks to the rise of the Fascist state, cultural heritage projects in Rhodes were central to the consolidation of Italy's unofficial sovereignty during the Liberal era. When the outspoken nationalist Enrico Corradini landed in Rhodes, for example, he described the medieval city as a '*borgo levantino*' abandoned by time, a backwater of modernity, 'but all the same a sovereign seat of poetry' with traces of Italian medieval history. The panorama of the medieval city reminded him of the towers of San Gimignano in Tuscany; and he likened the louvered windows and stone alleyways of the medieval city of Rhodes to a new Pompei. Corradini concluded that Rhodes' beauty depended partly on the fact that the island had not 'fallen into the hands of either the French or British empires' and therefore still maintained a uniquely emblematic expression of its Mediterranean identity. Corradini also affirmed that Italy should aim not to 'deform' Rhodes with an overly enthusiastic modernization, but that it should reunite Rhodes with its historic role at the crossroads of the Mediterranean through a project of preservation.[8]

8 'Rodi, così rimasta indietro nel tempo, era pure una sede sovrana di poesia, un'inaspettata meraviglia nel Mediterraneo. Ma noi italiani saremo il popolo che saprà il meno possibile deformare Rodi, rinnovandola, restituendole una missione, nel Mediterraneo, tra Europa, Asia e Africa, a cui è congiunta'. Enrico Corradini, *Sopra le vie del nuovo impero: Dall'emigrazione di Tunisi alla guerra nell'Egeo* (Milan: Fratelli Treves, 1912), p. 106. For Corradini, and other nationalists like him, the capture of Rhodes was very much tied into efforts to change the status of Italian diaspora communities residing in the Mediterranean, especially in Tunisia, where a community of over 100,000 people of Italian origin was under the flag of the French empire.

Within a year of its 1912 takeover Italy began to restore the island's impressive moated medieval city, a monument to both the Christian Crusader presence in the eastern Mediterranean and the Ottoman expansion in the Aegean. Since their 1522 capture of the island, the Ottoman Turks had continuously inhabited the medieval city until the Italian arrival. Their four centuries of rule had brought many Islamic additions to the medieval masonry as well as the conversion of Byzantine era churches into mosques. It was, indeed, this sense of overlapping imperial histories that the Italian state intended to 'valorize' in its full reconstruction of the medieval city. Between 1912 and 1915 the Italian administration first refurbished the Hospital of the Knights, one of the oldest original buildings of the medieval period, before beginning a project to rebuild entirely the medieval palace that had once loomed above the port. The reconstruction of the medieval city's multifaceted history included intervention in and reconstruction of both the medieval Christian and Ottoman phases of the walled city's development.

In the 1920s, alongside increasing efforts to establish the Italianness of the island, restoration efforts attempted to link Rhodes with medieval counterparts in Italy (Figure 3.1). Ottoman additions to the city were removed and replaced with what archaeologists argued were the 'original' design for buildings in the historic centre. Architects created a fake sandstone called *finta pietra* to help patch missing parts of the medieval masonry. The process was similar to the *sventramento* that occurred in Rome, where later 'accretions' were removed from buildings in the city's centre. In fact, much of the emphasis on the Crusader past of the island was because there was little Roman heritage to excavate. In comparison with Libya, where the colonial programme focused heavily on the archaeology of antiquities, most of the ancient heritage in the island was not Roman but Greek, and excavating Greek antiquities risked encouraging Greek nationalism and ultimately Greek claims on the islands.[9] The *finta pietra* sandstone was used to enhance the medieval quality of the city and was poured over a central street in the medieval area, the Avenue of the Knights, running from the old Palace at the summit down into a central plaza near the port. The Bank of Rome opened a branch in this plaza. The freshly restored stone building closely replicated a building from the medieval historic centre of Viterbo.[10]

9 On the difference between the archaeological projects in Libya and Rhodes see Stephen Dyson, *In Pursuit of Ancient Pasts: A History of Classical Archaeology in the Nineteenth and Twentieth Centuries* (New Haven, CT: Yale University Press, 2006), pp. 183–84.
10 Vasilis Kolonas, *Italian Architecture in the Dodecanese Islands* (Athens: Olkos, 2002).

Fig. 3.1: View of the medieval city gates after Italian renovation and reconstruction, circa 1930. © Archive of the *Touring Club Italiano*.

Meanwhile, the Italian preservation of Ottoman monuments emphasized the island as a place of cultural contrasts and multiple temporalities. Hermes Balducci, an engineer commissioned to assist with archaeological heritage, came to Rhodes and, between 1930 and 1934, surveyed the monuments of Islamic and Ottoman heritage.[11] His monograph, *Architettura turca in Rodi*, reflected the typical sentiment of moral superiority that the Italian state claimed over the Turkish inhabitants. But it also showed a remarkable attention to the Ottoman heritage of the island—one that contrasted strongly with a view, expressed elsewhere, that the Byzantine heritage was scarcely important.[12] Preservation efforts retained the 'picturesque' and Oriental tableau of strangeness that could make Rhodes a desirable touring destination. In a central part of the medieval city, for example, the local government undertook a full restoration of the Mosque of Soliman so as to put the building into active operation as an *hammam*, or Turkish bathhouse. The governor of the islands at the time even went so far as to order from Turkey special 'carpets' and uniforms that could ensure the 'preservation of Oriental costume for persons employed at the Bath'. The Italian governor of Rhodes, Mario Lago, asked that there always be on hand at least 'due bagni-masseur di età superiore ai venti e inferiore ai 50 anni, moralmente e fisicamente sani e provetti nella tecnica del bagno turco' [two bath masseuses who are at least 20 and less than 50 years old, morally and physically healthy, and experienced in the techniques of the Turkish Bath].[13]

As a symbol of continuity, the Italian state's commitment to restoring the medieval city continued unabated until Italy's entrance into the Second World War. During the administration of Cesare de Vecchi, a second major renovation to the medieval city of Rhodes took place, with the aim of reinforcing the presence of the Crusader heritage. De Vecchi – one of the original quadrumvirate who had marched on Rome – insisted on revising the urban landscape to emphasize an aesthetic quality of *romanità*, or Roman-ness.

---

11 Luca Orlandi, 'An Italian Pioneer on Ottoman Architecture Studies in the Dodecanese Islands: Hermes Balducci (1904–1938)', in *Proceedings of the 14th International Congress of Turkish Art*, ed. by Frédéric Hitzel (Paris: Collège de France, 2013), pp. 531–38.

12 The architectural historian Hermes Balducci completed a survey of all the mosques on the island in 1932; Hermes Balducci, *Architettura turca in Rodi* (Milan: Ulrico Hoepli, 1932). In comparison, Italian touring books demurred over the significance of the Byzantine architecture: 'Il periodo bizantino ha scarsa importanza per Rodi per quanto duri otto secoli. È un periodo oscuro. [...] Solamente qualche chiesetta dalla caratteristica cupola a tamburo, qualche mosaico e qualche cadente muro di torri costiere attestano la lunga dominazione di Bisanzio.' Touring Club Italiano, *Rodi: Guida del turista* (Milan: Bestetti e Tumelli, 1928), p. 12.

13 Department of Rhodes, General State Archives of Greece, hereafter GAK DOD, 1926/121/4.

Under his direction, many more of the Ottoman interventions were removed from throughout the walled city. The *finta pietra* composite was added to new masonry to give the city a fully medieval character. When stationed on Rhodes during transitional British rule of the island from 1945 to 1947, the novelist Lawrence Durrell described the Italian renovation as 'hideous archness' and a brash statement of the Fascist ideology that had dominated the final phase of Italian colonial rule.[14] But the stale and arguably phony quality of the medieval city was also a result of the way Italian designers had restored and appropriated the Ottoman and Oriental heritage of the walled city in the previous decade. During the four centuries of Ottoman rule (1522–1922) the Turkish and Jewish minorities had mainly inhabited the old city, while the Greek community lived outside the city's fortifications. In the early 1920s Italian zoning laws had placed the Jewish and Turkish areas of the medieval city of Rhodes inside a monumental zone, or green belt, within which the Ottoman character of the city was preserved and Turkish additions to medieval houses were left unrenovated. The contrast between the crusader masonry and the Ottoman atmosphere was frequently commented upon by travellers. Even in the late 1930s, as De Vecchi enforced the Fascist regime's anti-semitic laws, the Jewish and Turkish quarters were still considered an essential part of the Italian heritage tour of the island. The neighbourhood was inevitably indicated in Italian guidebooks and celebrated as offering a counterpoint to the 'modernizing' presence of the Fascist state. For what could be more colonial – and representative of Italian ambitions at the time – than the story of the Christian Crusaders' journey to recapture the Holy Land from the Muslim infidel? Preservation programmes in the medieval city reflected subtle colonial hierarchies of difference that were to be written into policy after the adoption of policies of race in 1937–38.

Rhodes: Pearl in a Global Mediterranean

'Here is Rhodes and from here we jump' (*Qui è Rodi e di qui salta*, in Latin, *Hic Rhodus, hic salta*), wrote the author of a 1912 article, quoting Aesop.[15] The

---

14 Lawrence Durrell, *Reflections on a Marine Venus* (London: Faber and Faber, 1963), p. 28. Or, as Mia Fuller suggests, by the end of Italian rule Rhodes was 'like an open-air museum', *Moderns Abroad: Architecture, Cities and Italian Imperialism* (New York: Routledge, 2007), p. 79.

15 'Rodi: L'isola delle rose', *Rivista mensile del Touring Club Italiano*, 6 (1912), 297–313.

island's geographic proximity to areas of Italian imperial interest sustained narratives and temporalities linked to the idea of returning Italy to its former glory in the Mediterranean. 'Rhodes is no more than a fragment of a system of mountains that at one time must have joined the three continents of Europe, Asia, and Africa.' Such prosaic descriptions of the island could be found in guidebooks published by the *Touring Club Italiano*. These guidebooks ambivalently located the island as part of the nation, and yet apart from it.[16] As a point of connection, a miniature bridge, it was logical that the island would become a hub and point of reference for both international tourism and Italians in the eastern Mediterranean:

> Under the Italian regime Rhodes is reborn and flourishes again with a thousand civil works; it becomes one of the great destinations of international tourism and regains for the third time its function as an intermediary between Orient and Occident, a center of collection and diffusion of every Italian activity in the eastern basin of the Mediterranean.[17]

The project to capitalize on Rhodes as a symbol of new Italian economies of empire was also accomplished through the development of a waterfront meant to accommodate organized tourism (Figure 3.2). That project eventually inspired a large-scale renovation of the island in the 1920s and 1930s to make Rhodes into a modern-day *stazione balneare* (seaside resort).[18] These new constructions centred on highlighting Rhodes' historical diversity at the crossroads of East and West. The journey to Rhodes – and by extension, the Orient – was envisioned as a journey that allowed visitors, especially Italian ones, to rehearse what it meant to be a traveller in an Ottoman land. Rhodes also happened to be an Italian colony at the time and therefore an advertisement for Italian state-building projects under Mussolini: the

---

16 This institution had been invested in the project of Italian nationalism since its inception. See Stephanie Malia Hom, *Beautiful Country: Tourism and the State of Destination Italy* (Toronto: Toronto University Press, 2015).

17 Draft for a guidebook. Greek National Archives of the Dodecanese Prefecture (GAK DOD), 1043/1931.

18 At the time of the Italian conquest of the Dodecanese the islands were under the Ottoman Empire. With the exception of Rhodes and Kos, which had Turkish and Sephardic Jewish minorities, the other islands were entirely populated by ethnic Greeks. Although there had been some uprisings in the Dodecanese against the Ottoman rulers at the time of the original 1821 Greek revolution, the nascent Greek state had ultimately traded the Dodecanese for the much larger island of Euboea.

Fig. 3.2: The Italian tourist waterfront of Rhodes circa 1930.
© Archive of the *Touring Club Italiano*.

'industrious energies' employed in state building at home went hand in hand with opportunities for leisure and relaxation in the empire. The local colonial government eventually curated every aspect of the experience of the island – from the creation of a new Italian colonial city adjacent to the walled medieval city of the Knights-Hospitaller to the design on the cocktail napkins used at the luxurious *Albergo delle Rose*.[19]

Some of the most inspired and original buildings of touristic Rhodes brought together 'local' Ottoman elements and references to 'global' Italian empire. Italian architects at the time suggested that the island's new, predominantly modernist architecture should be dressed in 'Muslim attire' and include autochthonous forms in the new urban landscape.[20] But the incorporation of Ottoman motifs was usually bound into the highlighting of the island as a space of (national) regeneration. The Baths of Kalithea are a wonderful example of how new Italian designs regrafted an imaginary of the Ottoman past onto a new Italian global empire of leisure travellers.

19 See Leonardo Ciacci, *Rodi: Come si inventa una città* (Venice: Marsilio, 1991).
20 Anthony Antoniades, 'Italian Architecture in the Dodecanese: A Preliminary Assessment,' *Journal of Architectural Education* 38 (1984), 18–25.

The multi-level site includes a double-chambered bathing pool, adjacent semicircular building and an entrance gazebo on the upper level. Set into a scenic bay in the location of the 1912 Italian landing, about 25 kilometres outside the main town of Rhodes, the baths were promoted in the 1930s as a resort and hotel where visitors would undergo spa treatments using the mineral water from the nearby spring. Arabic decorative elements at the base of a large cupola over a bathing pool intimate a Turkish *hammam*. Not a *hammam* – but clearly inspired by one – the Baths of Kalithea point to the Ottoman empire and suggest the overlapping imaginaries and cross-cultural fertilizations of the Mediterranean.

These architectural plans led to an unresolvable and yet highly productive paradox relating to the island's identity: the picturesque and Oriental strangeness of the local environment, and its inhabitants, was 'valorized' at the same time that the island was 'upgraded' to reinforce the picture of Italian modernization programmes under the Fascist state. In many important cases, the embrace of this paradox resulted in highly original architecture, such as the new Governor's Palace – today the city hall of the island – which closely reproduces the Doge's Palace in Venice's Piazza San Marco. In following the Venetian practice of incorporating elements of Islamic decoration (in this case, chamfered arches), the building also refers back to the Ottoman history of the island. Both the Governor's Palace and the Baths of Kalithea have recently been restored and are used to encourage visitors to remain in Rhodes for a longer stay that involves heritage and cultural tourism.

Similarly, while there has been some recent discussion about rebuilding a giant Colossus across the harbour of Rhodes, a plan of this kind has never been approved. However, the harbour still boasts the two columns the Italian administration installed where the Colossus might have stood; the sculptures of the wolf and the deer, symbols of Rome and Rhodes, respectively, that once adorned these columns have long since been removed, yet there still stands a lingering trace of the ways in which the Italian state created a new sense of 'historic' Rhodes in order to shape a sense of the island's importance within imperial histories. The sculptures of the wolf and deer signified the double identity that the regime planned to shape for the Dodecanese archipelago, as both Italian and Oriental, simultaneously modern and a signpost of the Ottoman past. As one Italian traveller of that period observed: 'Italian Rhodes does not need a Colossus anymore. Now it is grace and prosperity that call, that collect the ships that come from the Orient and Occident. The ships entering the port pass under an ideal arch made of ancient suggestion and very new power.'[21] In underscoring Italy's longstanding cultural and economic ties with the Orient, the local administration subtly reframed the issue of Italian emigration: the empire was not just about the resettlement of unemployed peasants in Africa, but about the recalling of Italy's history of exploration and the remaking of Italians into a globetrotting nation.[22]

Precedent for Italy's mandate in Rhodes dated from at least the late nineteenth century, when hundreds of thousands of Italian emigrants had migrated into Ottoman territories. Alongside the famous Italian communities in Galata, the Italian quarter of Constantinople first founded by the Genoese, the Italian language could be heard spoken among the Greek, Jewish and Turkish communities spread throughout the Balkans and Mediterranean, in areas that had gradually come under European influence with the decline of the Ottoman empire.[23] As Barbara Spackman has recently written, Italians were 'accidental Orientalists', and most of them arrived in Ottoman areas through experiences of displacement and migration.[24] The 1923 annexation of Rhodes to Italy represented an official anchor in an Ottoman world that, while remaining invisible within Italy, and to a certain degree, the Ottoman empire, had long been an important part of Italian culture overseas.

Eventually, the Italian state leveraged the island to promote the larger nationalist rhetoric according to which the colonial empire would restore

---

21 'Rodi italiana non ha più bisogno di colossi. Ora sono la sua grazia e la sua prosperità a chiamare, ad accogliere le navi che vengono d'Oriente e d'Occidente, e le navi entrando nel porto passano sotto un arco ideale fatto di antica suggestione e di nuovissima potenza.' Franco Ciarlantini, *Viaggio nell'Oriente Mediterraneo*, p. 118.

22 On the relationship between Italian migration and African colonization, see Mark Choate, *Emigrant Nation: The Making of Italy Abroad* (Cambridge, MA: Harvard University Press, 2008), pp. 17–56.

23 For an animated example of nineteenth-century Italian descriptions of Galata in Constantinople see Edmondo de Amicis, who described the tower of Galata thus: 'a monument crowned with Genoese glory, and no Italian can look upon it without proudly remembering that small band of merchants, sailors and soldiers, haughty and bold and heroically stubborn, who for centuries held the banner of their republic aloft and negotiated on equal terms with the emperors of the East'. Edmondo de Amicis, *Constantinople*, trans. by Stephen Parkin (London: Hesperus Classics, 2005), p. 38.

24 Spackman shows precisely how the indeterminacy of the Italian nation-state during this period of time made the 'Orient' into a tableau for defining Italian identity. Barbara Spackman, *Accidental Orientalists: Modern Italian Travelers in Ottoman Lands* (Liverpool: Liverpool University Press, 2017). The same pattern was to be articulated in the occupation of Rhodes and the Dodecanese, though with increasing concern that the Italian state was not vigilant enough about ethnic difference.

Italy to its former glory. These imaginative geographies of unity and prosperity were closely tied to the idea of the Mediterranean. While the rhetoric of Mediterranean empire would reach a fever pitch during the Fascist rule of the islands, it was present in subtle ways within the mobilization of tourism throughout the 1920s and early 1930s. Organized tourism in Rhodes activated a much larger apparatus at home, which vied to reinvent Italians as travellers, amateur ethnographers and Orientalists. Since the late nineteenth century the institutions of archaeology and cartography, as well as centres for research and Oriental studies, had supported and paved the way for Italian colonial projects from the Mediterranean to East Africa. Especially during the years that followed the Italian defeat in Ethiopia in 1896, when the Italian state abandoned its colonial programme and emigration to North and South America intensified, the mapping and exploration of Africa had maintained enthusiasm for a colonial adventure.[25] By the mid-1920s a number of organizations were offering ordinary Italian citizens luxury cruise tours from Italy through to the eastern Mediterranean, or 'Levant', as it was still known at the time. The National Geographic Society, the Naval League, the Italian Tourism Company, the Society of Italian Navigation and the numerous *Dopolavoro* organizations active throughout Italy, as well as the Fascist Colonial Institute itself, eventually all sponsored cruises that included a stop in Rhodes (Figure 3.3).

Cruise itineraries followed epic routes and directed tourists to take in the historic sites of an 'Italian' cultural patrimony – that is, the monuments of Roman and Venetian rule that could be found scattered throughout the Mediterranean. Yachts sailed first along the coasts of southern Italy and then to the Aegean, an itinerary that mirrored the expansionist programme that Italy had inaugurated with the invasion of Libya and the Dodecanese in 1911–12. Fascist metaphors of national regeneration – and claims that the average citizen would be transformed by the state – were also visible in advertising for cruises across the Mediterranean. As a brochure for the 1935 cruise offered by the Italian Naval League explained, 'everyone will have the opportunity to complete a maritime experience and to learn about the reality of the great life at sea.'[26] Fortuitously situated between Zara (Zadar in modern-day Croatia), also an Italian territory at the time, and the legendary

---

25 See Giancarlo Monina, *Il consenso coloniale: Le società geografiche e l'istituto coloniale italiano, 1896–1914* (Rome: Carocci, 2002).
26 This epigraph introduced the brochure for the 1935 *Ferragosto* cruise led by the Italian Naval League. GAK DOD, 216/1935.

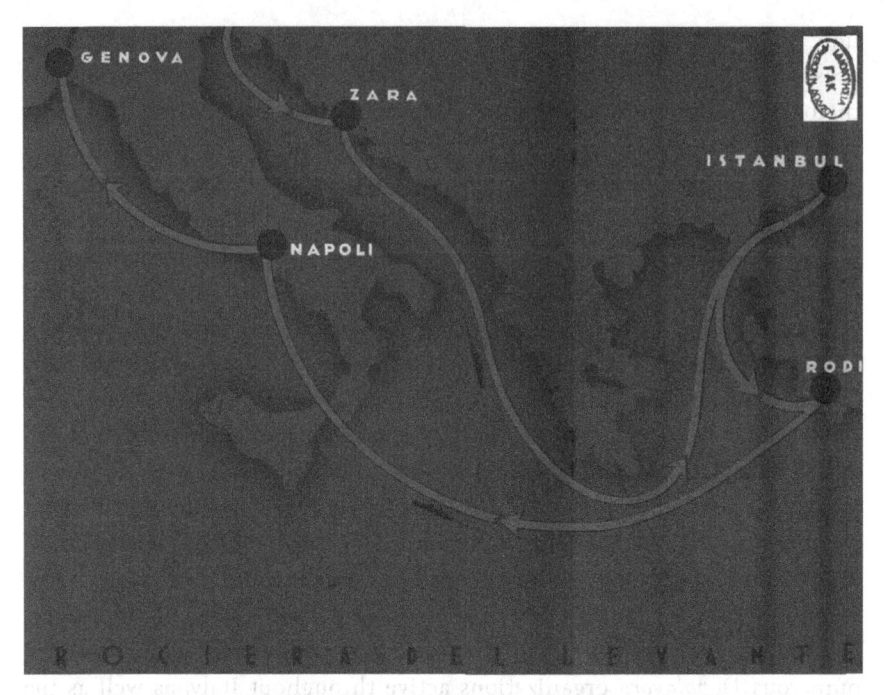

Fig. 3.3: Advertisement for a 1935 Crociera del Levante offered by the *Organizzazione Nazionale Dopolavoro*. © General State Archives of Greece.

Constantinople, Rhodes remained a central pivot of typical Mediterranean cruise itineraries.

If this formulation of Rhodes as both emblematic of the Italian empire and a site of exoticizing memories of the Levant worked from the perspective of Italian colonial discourses, it eventually had to be revised for foreign audiences. In a diplomatic cable to a public relations agency in Milan, the secretary in the office of propaganda and tourism lamented that German tourists viewed Rhodes as one of Italy's colonies and were therefore unwilling to visit it. Believing that it was a colony, travellers anticipated lower prices, a fact that local state actors understood as a slight to Italy's prestige and a lack of appreciation for the enormous investment the country had made in new public works to upgrade the island and bring it up to 'European' standards.[27] The Italian state thus came increasingly to

27 'Il fatto che la Germania considera Rodi come colonia e non come Italia e perciò la priva del beneficio concesso all'Italia di un maggiore assegno mensile ai turisti (anche in questi giorni abbiamo avuto una Principessa con la sua dama di compagnia costretta

promote the view that Rhodes was in fact a provincial extension of Italy. When Italian cruise companies deviated from the typical itinerary, and stayed away from Rhodes, the state intervened to discourage this.[28] Local state actors in Rhodes corresponded with publicity firms in Italy and around the world to promote the view that Rhodes drew not just Italian visitors but an international jet set – calling it a 'pearl' in the Mediterranean and comparing it to other European spa resorts, such as Carlsbad and Montecatini. But even as the local administration went to great efforts to ensure them of the high standards of modernity and accommodation that they would find, foreign diplomats and members of royal families regularly declined invitations to visit Rhodes. With the invasion of Ethiopia and rumours that sanctions against Italy had led to an outbreak of malaria, international tourism declined sharply. Nevertheless, even after Italy had entered the Second World War and the Mediterranean had become a theatre for major international hostilities, the local administration continued to promote tourism and kept careful records of the number of visitors for each season until 1942.

Organized tourism helped to bring Rhodes into an economics of colonial representation. By framing the island's Ottoman past, new constructions highlighted the authority and modernity of the Italian colonizers. For local state actors, it was not incongruent to maintain that the island was Italian, even *italianissima*, and at the same time to exalt the 'local' as it was manifest in the historical centre's numerous monuments and the continuing presence of the multi-ethnic society of the Ottoman Empire. Indeed, it was precisely because the Italian state had intervened to upgrade the island and provide accommodation of European standard that the former Ottoman state could be experienced as a source of exotic fascination.[29] Ironically, foreign visitors

---

a viaggiare in seconda classe ed ad alloggiare in un albergo di secondo ordine per la suddetta ragione)' [The fact is that Germany considers Rhodes a colony and not part of Italy and therefore deprives the island of the benefit conceded to Italy of a greater monthly allowance to its tourists who travel there (for this reason we recently had a [German] Princess whose lady-in-waiting was forced to travel in second class and stay in a second-class hotel)]. GAK, 1486/1935.

28   Mario Lago inveighed against a cruise sponsored by the Italian Navigation Association that was to travel instead to the island of Patmos, which was 'certainly notable as a curiosity, but in any case, not comparable to Rhodes'. GAK DOD, 216/1935.

29   On tourism as a cultural practice that reinforces a sense of modernity see Dean MacCannell, *The Tourist: A New Theory of the Leisure Class* (Berkeley: University of California Press, 2013).

did not always see it this way, and Italy's reputation as a minor empire (and nation-state) impacted the success of the tourism project. In ways that foreshadowed the post-war notion that the Italian empire was never significant, the island drew Italian tourists above all, and never obtained the international fame that the local government imagined it would gain in the early 1920s, when it broke ground on the 'master plan' to reinvent the city of Rhodes as a tourist destination.

Restoration, new architecture and tourism programmes navigated a dilemma that was at the core of Italian colonialism. To make a claim for an empire that could rival the French and the British in the Mediterranean meant that Italy should leverage colonial settings to prove it was an advanced industrial nation-state, one capable of aggressive modernization in its overseas territories. And yet, to ensure that its own population should also benefit from this enterprise – that it should also obtain a sense of its own 'modernity' when visiting these colonial settings – it was simultaneously necessary to retain a sense of the exotic and local environment. The quixotic mission to highlight the island's 'multicultural' history through restoration, architecture and the construction of new tourist sites disguised this dilemma. The emphasis on the overlapping Christian and Ottoman histories of the island provided the basis for a wholesale reinvention of the idea of the 'local' in the built environment. In many ways, the resulting cultural landscape anticipated the island's post-war identity. Rhodes is a place where visitors do not experience the island's cultural heritage so much as the colonial geographies that underpin contemporary tourist practices.

Longing for Empire: Postcolonial Rhodes

As scholars examine the Italian colonial empire more critically, they wrestle with the fact that, for many Italians, empire has only ever been a latent experience, one never fully discussed in textbooks or in politics. Because Italy lost all of its overseas colonies during the Second World War, without experiencing wars of independence or undergoing a process of decolonization (as the French and British empires did), there has been little impetus to recognize that the empire was, in fact, a meaningful part of the country's modern history. As Cristina Lombardi Diop and Caterina Romeo remark, 'the lack of a clear-cut distinction between colonization and postcolonization has produced the idea, still persistent in the Italian imagination, that colonialism was not so detrimental after all.'[30] Imperialism was not only a part of Italy's unitary, post-unitary and then Fascist politics, but it has also played a part in Italy's post-war politics, with the gradual recognition of the empire coinciding with Italy's transition to Europe's southern frontier. The 'rediscovery' of Italian imperialism that has occurred since the 1970s has supplied an important rethinking of Italy's history as a nation-state in a period of European integration. This period has also been one of transition from being a country that sends immigrants to one that mainly receives them. Indeed, it is no exaggeration to assert that the project of recovering Italy's colonial past has happened alongside and in response to Italian culture's entrance into European postcolonial conditions.[31]

While Italian and Anglophone scholars have debunked the notion of a colonially innocent Italian nation-state, elsewhere the myth of *Italiani brava gente* seems to live on – if for very different reasons. In the six decades since the end of the war, the Dodecanese prefecture has restored the Italian colonial buildings in the tourist harbour of Rhodes, next to the walled city, as well as others that have a touristic purpose (as is the case with the Baths of Kalithea). It might be understandable that the restoration of tourist infrastructure does not produce much critical debate, as tourism is the bread and butter of the local economy. But the tourism argument has been extended to justify the restoration of further Italian-era architecture in neighbouring islands apart from Rhodes – so that not only are Italian buildings designed for tourism worthy of restoring, but Italian architecture is in itself worthy of tourism and display.

On the nearby island of Leros, for example, there has been a large-scale restoration of Lakkhi, a model rationalist city built in the late 1930s for the purpose of housing members of the Italian navy and their families.[32] Funded mainly by the EU, the restoration of Lakkhi has been framed as a project of international architectural heritage. Revealingly, arguments in favour of

---

30 Cristina Lombardi-Diop and Caterina Romeo, 'Italy's Postcolonial "Question": Views from the Southern Frontier of Europe', *Postcolonial Studies* 18 (2015), 367–83.
31 For example, the recognition that the Fascist dictatorship had a 'racist phase' in the late 1930s, one that implicated not only Italian Jews but also natives of East Africa and the Bedouin populations in North Africa, has been an important milestone in understanding and documenting how the empire, however latent or redefined, may in subtle but important ways impact social and cultural responses to the reception of immigrants in Italy.
32 The island of Leros was the centre of Italian naval operations for the eastern Mediterranean.

restoration revive the rhetoric of Italian cosmopolitanism and the 'European' quality of the buildings. They also tend to disavow the links between Italian urbanism and Fascism. As an Italian architect described in the online edition of the English-language Greek daily *Ekathimerini*:

> Until recently, there were some reservations about all that in Italy because these buildings were constructed during Fascist rule. However, these buildings were never symbols of the party, while Rationalism, although originating in Italy, became an international style. Lakki is precious to Leros. It is a jewel which could, under proper management, attract quality tourism to the island.[33]

If such statements replicate the Italian state's commitment to 'valorize' the Aegean during the interwar period for global recognition, their implied suggestion today that the Italian cultural patrimony of the islands is so rich and important – for Europe – that it should not be left for the Greek state to manage has an implicit colonial mentality. This point of view persists with regard to Greek antiquities, and has been used to justify, for example, the British museum's continuing possession of the Elgin marbles. Thus, the desire to claim an important cultural heritage in the islands would seem to be permanently at odds with a more honest appraisal of the period of Italian colonial rule there.

Local preservation efforts by and large strive to insist that Rhodes and the Dodecanese islands be included in a wider European cultural heritage. The medieval city, today an UNESCO world heritage site, claims in local signage to be 'the largest medieval city in all of Europe'. But post-war conservation of the medieval city reproduces Italian choices about it, and with little comment on this fact. After being severely bombed during the Second World War, the Palace of the Knights-St. John was reconstructed according to the Italian designs. It is today home to the Rhodes Archeological Museum – just as it was during the era of Italian rule. Until recently, the hammam at the Mosque of Soliman was also available for use by tourists as a Turkish bath and, though the central cupola designed to intimate the Mediterranean world remains in disrepair, the Baths of Kalithea have also undergone partial restoration and the surrounding landscape and entrance gazebo are open to the public. Some of the medieval city's Ottoman monuments that were part of the Italian

---

33 Giorgos Lialios, 'Lakki: Architectural Gem on Island of Leros, Finally Gets Due Attention', *Ekathimerini*, 19 September 2014.

commitment to retain the exotic and 'Oriental' aspect of the heritage landscape have undergone restoration in the post-war period. This includes several minarets and ablution fountains frequently depicted in Italian postcards of the islands in the 1930s.[34] Meanwhile, the actual Ottoman heritage as it was prior to the Italian state's arrival is under siege. Since 1947, many of the Turkish mosques in the islands have disappeared under the direction of the Greek state, with the local municipality of Rhodes committing to restore the original character of Byzantine churches that had been made into mosques by the Turkish rulers.[35] Under the aegis of restoration, then, the trace of the Ottoman past is being slowly wiped away on the island.[36]

The islands of Rhodes and Kos comprise one of two areas in Greece, alongside Thrace, with a recognized Turkish minority. Following the end of the First World War and the sectarian violence in the Aegean that culminated in the Greco-Turkish War, the British government orchestrated the exchange of almost 1.5 million Greek and Turkish minority populations in the Aegean region. The population exchange is widely viewed as a watershed event in Greek history, a moment of a collective trauma that still influences Greek national identity today.[37] A little commented fact, however, is that Rhodes and Kos, with their large Turkish and Jewish minority populations, were exempted from the population exchange because of the islands' annexation to the Italian empire. The islands of Rhodes and Kos hence became the last bastion of multi-ethnic Ottoman cosmopolitanism in a region otherwise divided along ethno-religious lines.[38]

In order to shore up the Italian sovereignty assigned to the Dodecanese according to the Lausanne convention, the Italian government further

[34] Emma Maglio, 'The Changing Role of Historic Town of Rhodes in the Scenario of Ottoman and Italian Rules in the Light of the Iconographic Sources', *Eikonocity*, 1 (2016), 75–88.

[35] Georgios Karatzas, 'Representing Historical Narratives in the Urban Space: The Making of a Heritage Space in Urban Rhodes, 1912–1950', paper presented at the Mediated City Conference, London, 1–3 April 2014.

[36] See Mia Fuller, 'Utopia Europe: Making Rhodes Greek', *Traditional Dwellings and Settlements Review*, 22 (2010), 15.

[37] See Bruce Clark, *Twice a Stranger: The Mass Expulsions that Forged Modern Greece and Turkey* (Cambridge, MA: Harvard University Press, 2009); Huw Halstead, *Greek without Greece: Local Homelands, National Belonging, and Transnational Histories amongst the Expatriated Greeks of Turkey* (Milton: Routledge, 2018).

[38] Renée Hirschon, 'Un-mixing Peoples in the Aegean Region', in *Crossing the Aegean: An Appraisal of the 1923 Population Exchange between Greece and Turkey*, ed. by Renée Hirschon (New York: Berghahn Books, 2008), pp. 3–12.

developed a special form of local Italian citizenship, exclusive of and inferior to Italian national identity and eventually written into law as 'Italian Aegean Citizenship', which enabled persons not currently living on the islands, but with property or family there, to assume Italian nationality. In the first decades of its rule, the local colonial government chose to embrace a relatively liberal attitude toward Greek and Jewish refugees from the Ottoman collapse – especially those from the so-called 'Asia Minor catastrophe' (the destruction of Smyrna) – and accepted almost all legitimate applications for residency as well as some clearly falsified ones. This renewal of Ottoman multiculturalism, in fact, coalesced with nationalist propaganda and the idea that the Italian empire embodied the renewal of previous eras of multiculturalism in the Mediterranean – from an age of Venetian commercial dominance to a *pax romana* in the Mediterranean. If in the interwar period a fantasy of 'Mediterranean-ness' helped to disguise dilemmas about Italian colonial identities as well as the often-brutal nature of the Fascist occupation, today it may be helping to distract from choices that the Greek state is making about Ottoman cultural heritage in the Aegean.

Although the Italian administration took a favourable attitude toward minority communities in the first decade of its rule, the hardline policies of race that defined Italy's colonization of Africa eventually did reach the Dodecanese. By the late 1930s the Italian state affirmed the view that the Turkish minority no longer had the same rights, owing to its not belonging to the ethnic Greek majority in the region. The result of this Italian policy shift was to force many Turks to migrate. The Italian state's rule over the islands in the interwar period therefore reflects an important, if little remarked, transition from the Ottoman empire to an ethnically homogeneous Greek nation-state.

While there has been a gradual return of the Turkish community since the end of the war, and official statistics place its membership at almost 5,000 people, it remains an almost invisible minority, with the Turkish language rarely to be heard. Most Turkish 'residents' probably spend most of the year on the nearby Turkish mainland. There have been recent calls for the Turkish community's greater visibility, for instance through instruction in Turkish language in local schools and greater openness around public displays of worship.[39] But monuments held to be important examples of Ottoman architecture found outside of Istanbul remain closed to the general public.

---

39   Kira Kaurinkoski, 'The Muslim Communities in Kos and Rhodes: Reflections on Social Identities in Contemporary Greece', *Slavica Helsingiensia*, 41 (2012), 47–78.

The Turkish quarter of Rhodes is but a ghost town of radically transformed Ottoman heritage. Nevertheless, Rhodes still advertises its Turkish heritage and promises visitors that they will be able to behold Ottoman history while on a Greek island holiday.

By the same token, although the Second World War marked the end of a resident Jewish minority – the *Djuderia* – the Jewish neighbourhoods of Rhodes and Kos have experienced a touristic revival in recent years. The neighbourhood is visited annually by the islands' Jewish diaspora, also known as the Rhodesli community, on the anniversary of the Jewish communities' deportation in mid-July. Thanks to the opening of archives that remained closed for six decades after the war, Italian collaboration with the Nazi deportations has recently been established.[40] Yet the period of Italian rule, from 1912 until 1936, is still sometimes registered as a 'golden age' in the community's history, as both the last period in which the community was resident in Rhodes and one in which the community prospered under the control of the Italian state.[41] Nevertheless, De Vecchi interpreted the 1938 *Leggi per la difesa della razza*, or the anti-semitic race laws, as a sentence of expulsion for all non-natives Jews residing in Rhodes and Kos, and, under his direction, the local administration committed to expelling almost 500 individuals – many of whom had naturalized thanks to Italy's earlier position that welcomed Jewish refugees of Ottoman collapse.[42] At this time, many more emigrated, correctly anticipating that worse scenarios lay ahead. Within a couple of years the Jewish community was halved. The remaining Jewish community of around 1,800 people was deported in 1944 during the Nazi occupation of Greece.

Paradoxically, then, much of the Rhodesli community was saved thanks to earlier emigration. Some of the community's emigration was encouraged by Italian anti-semitism after 1938, but much of it had begun at the turn

---

40 Marco Clementi and Ireni Toliou, *Gli ultimi ebrei di Rodi: Leggi raziali e deportazioni nel Dodecaneso italiano, 1938–1948* (Rome: DerriveApprodi, 2015).
41 On Italian patronage toward the Jewish community (and vice versa) see Aron Rodrigue, 'The Rabbinical Seminary in Italian Rhodes, 1928–38: An Italian Fascist Project', *Jewish Social Studies* 25 (2019), 1–19.
42 The Italian Anti-Semitic Racial Laws stripped Italian citizenship or permanent residency status from all Jewish subjects who had naturalized to Italy or any of its colonial territories after 1919, or the end of the First World War. In the Dodecanese, De Vecchi interpreted this as cause for stripping of this citizenship and expulsion of all 'non-native' Jewish residents. Given that the islands' Jewish communities were considered part of Italy's Jewry, the ordinance was protested and there were petitions for clemency by many.

of the century, when the era of open borders drew many immigrants from south-eastern Europe. Many descendants of Rhodesli Jews today continue to hold and even acquire Italian citizenship on the basis of heritage, but they may use their Italian citizenship to migrate more broadly – for example, from ex-colonial nations, such as South Africa and Zimbabwe, to the EU. Because the islands were part of the Italian state during the Second World War, UN reparations for Jewish victims of the Holocaust in Greece have never applied in Rhodes and Kos.[43] It is therefore unlikely that the *Djuderia* will be inhabited again by year-round residents (there are currently just 20 Jewish residents in Rhodes), but new global contexts reactivate Rhodesli links to the islands as well as to Italian postcolonial identities. Tourist practices certainly can be included in these global contexts, as they both supplement and consolidate the Rhodesli community's uniquely Mediterranean Jewish identity.

Rhodes has finally come to act synecdochally for a disappeared 'multi-ethnic' Mediterranean. While the island's history as a film location in the post-war period is long and illustrious, it is noticeable that films shot on Rhodes in recent history, such as *Pascali's Island* (1988), turn the island into a setting for a melancholic elegy about a world of Greeks, Turks and Jews that no longer exists. In *Pascali's Island*, a story about the rise of the Young Turks and the decline of the Ottoman and – to no small extent – British empires in the Mediterranean, colonial nostalgia is linked to the rediscovery of Greek antiquity and to the recovery of the roots of European culture. Alternatively, the island stands in for the possibility of overcoming the bitter conflicts between religious and ethnic communities that have defined the post-war eastern Mediterranean, as is the case in the 2006 historical epic *O Jerusalem*, about the 1948 establishment of the State of Israel. In *O Jerusalem* the old medieval city of the Knights of Rhodes – as it was painstakingly reconstructed by the Italian state in the interwar period and then modified to highlight the contrast between medieval Christian masonry and exotic Ottoman additions – offers an ersatz version of the old city of Jerusalem, one that provides the viewer with a sense of both what might have been and what could still also be. Today, the ways in which such fantasies of postcolonial multiculturalism draw upon choices the Italian state made in order to leverage the island's multi-ethnic identity for its own nationalist agenda may be entirely hidden. However, it is also reasonable to conclude that, without Italy and its interwar transformation of the island, Rhodes would not be tasked with the role of

---

43 Alexis Rappas, 'Memorial Soliloquies in Post-Colonial Rhodes and the Ghost of Mediterranean Cosmopolitanism', *Mediterranean Historical Review*, 33 (2018), 89–110.

holding the dream of both an ideal Europe and an ideal Middle East within its contemporary representation.

Postcolonial Rhodes affirms what many scholars have demonstrated to be broadly true about Italian colonialism: that even though Italy does not register and remember its empire in the ways that France and Britain do, prior colonial formations still have important consequences for contemporary national culture. Rhodes shows that this is true not only for Italy but also for Europe more broadly. If the more brutal and contentious aspects of the Italian colonial past in the islands seems willfully ignored today, one cannot help but ask what such ignorance does for the contemporary construction of Rhodes as both a Greek and a 'European' destination in the Mediterranean. It was precisely the a-temporal and even anachronistic confluence of Levantine 'multicultural' and Italian 'modern' amenities that placed Rhodes at the nexus of both providing 'local' or 'Oriental' colour and being worthy of modern touristic consumption. This sentiment seems to be echoed in today's *Lonely Planet* promise that, in Rhodes, 'Whether you're here on a culture-vulture journey through past civilizations, or simply for some laidback beach time, buzzing nightlife, or diving in crystal-clear waters, it's all here.'[44]

Perhaps the strongest legacy of the Italian era, if also the least commented part of its history, is Rhodes' enduring potential at once to be a local gem and to exert an international appeal. As the mayor of Rhodes concludes in his opening bid for the island's designation as a European cultural capital, 'Apart from a globally known high-profile destination, Rhodes is a place that stays in the hearts of the people.'[45]

---

44   'Welcome to Rhodes', *Lonely Planet* online edition <https://www.lonelyplanet.com/greece/dodecanese/rhodes> [accessed 5 January 2020].
45   The mayor's presentation of the island's candidacy for a European cultural capital may be viewed online at <http://www.rhodes2021.eu/v1/index.php/candidacy/mayor-message> [accessed 5 February 2019].

CHAPTER FOUR

Italy and Africa: Post-War Memories of Life in Eritrea and Ethiopia

Charles Burdett

Introduction

Among the aims of this volume is to contribute to a body of research that sees Italian culture as a current within world culture – as a complex, in other words, of related practices which within Italy itself reflects the movements (whether social, political, religious or other) that have, over centuries, traversed the peninsula and which, through time, has extended – largely though not exclusively through migration – to various parts of the globe, changing continually as it has come into contact with other modes of thought, behaviour and belief. One of the difficulties of this kind of approach, as is made clear in the Introduction, is that its reach has to be extremely extensive if it is, in some measure, to reflect the impact and legacy of one of the largest diasporas in human history. Another difficulty is that a volume of this kind cannot make a simple distinction between the consequences that flow from migration (both from and to Italy) and the lasting effects of colonialism. It is necessary to consider, to put this point differently, the kind of transnational realities that are created not only by the migratory flow of people over centuries but also by the legacies of imperial projects that originated in the late nineteenth and early twentieth centuries and which were to reach their climax under Fascism. Alongside the inquiry into the development of communities in Buenos Aires, Melbourne or New York, there should, in other words, be analysis of the troubled and multifaceted history of the Italian presence in towns and cities that were once under Italy's control during the period when the country was a colonial power.

This volume, as is indicated early on, does not attempt to reconstruct the stages either of migration from Italy or of expansionism from unification onwards.[1] Over the last two decades there has been a very significant increase in work that has reconstructed the stages of Italian colonial involvement and interrogated its effects in the longer term.[2] What this volume attempts to do, much more specifically, is to concentrate on the variety of ways in which it is possible to see the reality and legacies of mobility in the present and in the more recent past. Its emphasis is on the ways – whether through memory, creative writing, photography or other forms of visual culture – in which individuals have represented, or continue to represent, their participation within the mobility of Italian cultures and their sense of the fluidity of a notion of selfhood that is characterized, at the most profound level, by the intermingling of cultural practices and associations. Rather, therefore, than seeking to recount the phases of Italian colonial involvement overseas, what follows concentrates on the period following the Second World War; in the wake, that is, of the end of Italian colonialism. It centres on the types of narration that have characterized how people have looked back at lives spent in Eritrea and Ethiopia.

There are many pathways that one can follow to delve deeper into the East Africa that Italians inhabited in the wake of the Second World War and the collapse of colonial rule. Perhaps the most direct, though by no means the simplest, mode of accessing the life stories of those who have lived through these decades in the history of Eritrea and Ethiopia is to gather together their testimonies. It is this kind of initiative that lies behind the volumes of memories that Irma Taddia published in the 1980s and 1990s[3] and which has animated more recent research projects such as 'Returning and Sharing Memories' or 'Coloni senza colonie' [Colonists without colonies].[4]

---

1   For a history of Italian migration see Donna Gabaccia, *Italy's Many Diasporas* (London: UCL Press, 2000) and Mark Choate, *Emigrant Nation: The Making of Italy Abroad* (Cambridge, MA: Harvard University Press, 2008).
2   For a history of Italian colonialism see Nicola Labanca, *Oltremare: Storia dell'espansione coloniale italiana* (Bologna: il Mulino, 2002). Examples of recent additions to this body of work include Neelam Srivastava, *Italian Colonialism and Resistances to Empire, 1930–1970* (London: Palgrave Macmillan, 2018) and Rhiannon Welch, *Vital Subjects: Race and Biopolitics in Italy 1860–1920* (Liverpool: Liverpool University Press, 2016).
3   Irma Taddia, *La memoria dell'impero: Autobiografie d'Africa orientale* (Manduria: Lacaita, 1988) and *Autobiografie africane: Il colonialismo nelle memorie orali* (Milan: Franco Angeli, 1996).
4   For information on the research project 'Returning and Sharing Memories', see <www.memorie coloniali.org> [accessed December 2019]. For the project 'Coloni senza

The life histories that these projects have collected reveal the intensity and complexity of the events in which people, at whatever level, have participated. Part of my own research for TML was to explore the spaces of the Italian community in Addis Ababa and to speak to members of the community about their experiences of living within and between languages and cultures.[5]

Another means of gaining access to the post-war Italian experience in Africa is, of course, to investigate the forms of literary production that have sought to give expression to the interior world of people living through the aftermath of colonialism, through the turmoil of Eritrea's struggle for independence and through the memory of violence that past generations have suffered. Unsurprisingly, many of the writers who have used literature as a means of delving into some of the most tragic and unresolved episodes of the past have grown up in those parts of East Africa that were witness to the arc of Italian colonialism and/or individuals whose parents are both African and Italian.[6] Texts as important as Gabriella Ghermandi's *Regina di fiori e di perle* [Queen of Flowers and Pearls] or Igiaba Scego's *Adua* have relied on complex literary frameworks to expose the transgenerational nature of the experience of colonialism and the power that it retains to continue to haunt the present.[7] The work of writers such as Ghermandi or

---

colonie', see Alessandro Pes, 'Colonialismo di ritorno: i rimpatriati dalle ex colonie italiane e la questione del lavoro', in *Europa in movimento. Mobilità e migrazioni tra integrazione europea e decolonizzazione 1945–1992*, ed. by Giuliana Laschi, Valeria Deplano and Alessandro Pes (Bologna: il Mulino, 2017), pp. 171–208.

5   I undertook, together with Gianmarco Mancosu, two research trips to Addis Ababa, the first in October 2015, the second in March 2016. I am very grateful to Francesca Amendola and the staff of the Italian Cultural Institute for facilitating the research in every way possible and to the members of the Italian community for their generosity in sharing their experiences. The research, together with the photographs of Gianmarco Mancosu, formed part of the exhibition *Beyond Borders: Transnational Italy/Oltre i confini: Italia transnazionale*, staged between 2016 and 2018 at various sites worldwide. For a presentation of the exhibition see the chapter by Viviana Gravano and Giulia Grechi in this volume.

6   See Daniele Comberiati, *La quarta sponda. Scrittrici in viaggio dall'Africa coloniale all'Italia di oggi* (Rome: Pigreco, 2007) and Cristina Lombardi-Diop, 'Filial Descent: The African Roots of Postcolonial Literature in Italy', *Forum for Modern Language Studies*, special issue on transnational African Literatures, ed. by Derek Duncan and Nelson Mlambo, 56 (2020), 66–77.

7   Ghermandi's *Regina di fiori e di perle* (Rome: Donzelli, 2007) is perhaps the most well-known text that uses the framework of literature to recount the Ethiopian memories of the Italian occupation. For a recent study of Scego's *Adua* (Florence: Giunti, 2015), see Lucy Rand, 'Transgenerational Shame in Postcolonial Italy: Igiaba Scego's *Adua*',

Scego necessarily forms part of a complex of texts and initiatives aimed at promoting a deeper awareness of the ongoing legacies of colonialism and how they can be contested.[8] Such a complex of interconnected works involves recent evocations of the reality of empire in Francesca Melandri's *Sangue giusto* and, more recently still, the Ethiopian–American writer Maaza Mengiste's *The Shadow King*.[9]

The importance of the work by the writers indicated above, the urgent topicality of the themes that they address and the intricacy with which they pursue ways of knowing are such that they are the subject of an expanding body of critical reflection that aims also to ensure that work of this kind is embedded in the curriculum at both school and university level.[10] It is increasingly difficult to imagine courses on Italian culture that do not address how legacies of colonialism are an essential part of what Italian studies as a disciplinary field aims to address. Part of the movement to ensure that prominence is given to the realities and legacies of Italian colonialism is to ensure that the differing positionalities that individuals and groups have occupied within the development of expansionist projects and their afterlife are studied in detail and placed within an integrated epistemological framework that allows one to see the truly intimidating

---

Journal of Postcolonial Writing, 56 (2020), 4–17. For an analysis of the way in which the Italian occupation has been represented in Ethiopian literature see Sara Marzagora, 'Nationalism: The Italian Occupation in Amharic Literature and Political Thought', in *The Horn of Africa and Italy: Colonial, Postcolonial and Transnational Cultural Encounters*, ed. by Simone Brioni and Shimelis Bonsa Gulema (Oxford and New York: Peter Lang, 2018), pp. 141–67.

8   On the material reminders of Italy's Fascist/colonial past and how their original intended significance can be contested by public awareness see Igiaba Scego, 'Cosa fare con le tracce scomode del nostro passato', *Internazionale*, 9 June 2020, <https://www.internazionale.it/opinione/igiaba-scego/2020/06/09/tracce-passato-colonialismo-razzismo-fascismo> [accessed 15 June 2020].

9   Francesca Melandri, *Sangue giusto* (Milan: Rizzoli, 2017) and Maaza Mengiste, *The Shadow King* (New York: W. W. Norton and Company, 2019). For a recent documentary on the uncovering of Italy's colonial past see *Pagine nascoste*, dir. Sabrina Varani, 2017. On *Sangue giusto* see Charles Burdett, 'Secrets and Lies: Francesca Melandri's *Sangue Giusto* (2017) and the Uncovered Memory of Italian East Africa', *Forum for Modern Language Studies*, 56 (2020), 49–65.

10   On the problematics of addressing the colonial past, see Brioni and Bonsa Gulema, eds, *The Horn of Africa and Italy*. On the importance of the wider discourse of postcoloniality, see Cristina Lombardi-Diop and Caterina Romeo, eds, *Postcolonial Italy: Challenging National Homogeneity* (New York: Palgrave Macmillan, 2012).

dimensions of what Mary Louise Pratt has famously described as the 'contact zone'.[11]

It is within this context that a further approach can be added to inquiry into an Italian presence in Africa, with all its ramifications and all its enduring complexities, and that is to look in detail at the publications that have been produced by associations that have acted as a focal point for the Italian inhabitants or former inhabitants of East Africa. Organizations of this kind are not numerous and what associations there are have been formed with quite different purposes in mind; some have set out with the intention of pursuing a distinct political agenda, while others have sought to steer clear of politics altogether.[12] The intention of this chapter is to concentrate on one such association, created around the journal *Mai Taclì*, while pointing to the wider cultural environment to which it alludes and of which it formed a part. The intention is to try to unlock some of the narratives that recur with greatest frequency and some of the most persistent tensions that have characterized the memory of the Italian presence in East Africa. By so doing, the chapter seeks to place this experience within the interrogation of the legacy of colonialism and in dialogue with the other forms of mobility that are examined in this volume.

Mai Taclì

Mai Taclì, meaning 'clear water' in Tigray, was first published as a four-page bi-monthly journal in December 1976 and continued to appear, with uninterrupted regularity, until the end of the twentieth century and through the whole of the first decade of this century.[13] The driving force behind the journal was its editor, Marcello Melani, who was assisted by an editorial team made up of, for the most part, a group of the former inhabitants of Asmara,

---

11 Mary Louise Pratt, *Imperial Eyes: Travel Writing and Transculturation* (Abingdon and New York: Routledge, 1992).
12 An example of an association with a strong political agenda is that which has coalesced around the journal *Il reduce d'Africa*. For a discussion of the differences between that journal and the group that has been drawn towards *Mai Taclì* as a means of recovering memories and shared experiences see Charles Burdett, 'Memories of Italian East Africa', *Journal of Romance Studies*, 1 (2001), 69–84.
13 The archive of *Mai Taclì* is now held at the Biblioteca Africana in Fusignano. I am grateful to Gian Carlo Stella from the Biblioteca Africana for permission to reprint photographs from issues of *Mai Taclì*.

the majority of whom had grown up in Eritrea and who, like Melani, had left the country in the 1960s.[14] Though the journal provided a focal point for reunions that occurred in various parts of Italy through the years, its primary purpose was to enable its readers to recover their memories and to share their experience of the past and it sought to accomplish this aim by adopting a variety of strategies.

To begin with, each edition of the journal was structured around the regular columns of its editorial team. These included the front-page commentary by the editor, 'Amici miei' [My friends], which reflected on the articles included in the edition. The editorial column was supported by the appearance of the observations – on disparate subjects connected with life in Eritrea and on the activities of its former Italian residents – of two of the most consistent contributors to the journal, Cesare Alfieri and Sergio Vigili.[15] From roughly the beginning of the 1990s *Mai Taclì* published a regular column by Marisa Baratti, which was structured around the evocation of specific sites in Eritrea and the personal memories that they conjured up (see below). The recurring pattern of the journal was given further substance by the contributions of figures such as Oscar Rampone, Nicky Di Paolo and Erminia Dell'Oro. With a background in journalism, Rampone was also the author of a novel on life in Eritrea, while the fiction writing of both Nicky Di Paolo and Erminia Dell'Oro on themes relating to the Italian presence in East Africa has attracted a good deal of critical attention.[16] The work of the regular contributors provided the readership with a stimulus to remember and a framework in which individual memories could be accommodated. The interaction of one piece of writing with another and the frequent differences of opinion on how to interpret the past necessarily added to the sense of a community of remembering. This sense of community was reinforced by the annual meetings of the subscribers and it was also reinforced by the journal's

---

14   The journal was published by a group of the former inhabitants of Asmara, the majority of whom were the children of bureaucrats and entrepreneurs who had settled in Eritrea in the late 1930s.
15   Cesare Alfieri published a column entitled 'Caravanserraglio', while that of Sergio Vigili was entitled 'Paillettes'. Other regular contributors included Rita Di Meglio and Gigliola Franzolini.
16   The title of Rampone's novel was *Avvenne in Eritrea* [It Happened in Eritrea] (Milan: Editrice Nuovi Autori, 1987). For more information on the critical reception of writers like Dell'Oro and Di Paolo, see Charles Burdett, 'Transnational Time: Reading Post-War Representations of the Italian Presence in East Africa', *Italian Studies*, 73.3 (2018), 274–88.

various initiatives to raise money to support institutions in Eritrea or to restore buildings in Asmara and in other towns in the country.

The invitation to remember resonated across the whole of what was once a sizable community of people living for the most part in Asmara and one finds within the journal, as a result, hundreds of individual acts of memory, written over decades.[17] It is generally the case that the writings are accompanied by the reproduction of photographs, drawn for the most part from the private albums of the journal's readers, and thus *Mai Taclì* represents an archive not only of written but also of visual material. In addition to the articles and photographs that appear in the journal itself, there are many works of creative writing that have been produced by regular contributors.[18] Thus, the journal was not only in itself an extensive archive of people's memories but also a point of reference within a larger network of textual production. Such is its significance as a repository of lived experiences that one might argue that it would be difficult to attempt to reconstruct a history of the Italian community in East Africa without referring to it.

What is certain is that if one is attempting to consider experiences that occur over time across a range of geographically distant sites – and thereby gain an enhanced perception of the shifting practices that collectively we refer to as Italian cultures – then a resource such as *Mai Taclì*, which offers a record of people's lives collected over decades, represents an important resource. Cultures are neither distinct nor separable and they are, above all, subject to change.[19] One of the most striking features of *Mai Taclì* is that it is so explicitly concerned with the alterations to people's sense of themselves and their environment that are wrought by the passage of time. Through the years in which the journal was published, one can see the ways in which the life stories of individuals are threaded together: how, in other words, memories of childhood or early adulthood in East Africa are constructed, how the circumstances of the present affect the perspective from which the

---

17   In 1978 the journal numbered over 1,000 subscribers.
18   The writing of Erminia Dell'Oro and Nicky Di Paolo has achieved a high level of recognition, but there are many other members of the Italian community in Eritrea who have published works of creative writing. To give just a few examples: Angelo Granara, *Cara Asmara, Eritrea* [Dear Asmara, Eritrea] (Rome: IPSE, 1993); Augusto Robbiati, *Il ponte (Oh Asmara, Asmara!)* [The Bridge (Oh Asmara, Asmara!)] (Monza: Bahà'i, 1994); Costantino Zangheri, *Era tutto provvisorio* [It Was all Provisional] (Milan: Italia Letteraria, 1987).
19   On this subject see Arjun Appadurai, *Modernity at Large: Cultural Dimensions of Globalization* (Minneapolis: University of Minnesota Press, 1996).

past is recalled, or how the experience of loss is negotiated. One can also see how people think about and record their perceptions of the changing physical appearance and working of the African environment that for many years they regarded as home. Lastly, by piecing together the descriptions and notations that are contained in so many writings over such a lengthy period of time or by exploring the meanings of such an extensive collection of photography one can develop an awareness of how the journal provides a record – constructed in however partial and subjective a form– of the unfolding of processes within the multicultural reality of Eritrea and Ethiopia.

In the words of the editor: 'Il carattere del giornale [...] è quello dei ricordi, dei racconti di vita vissuta, delle esperienze trascorse in Eritrea, della gioventù e anche, lo confesso, della nostalgia' [The character of the journal [...] is that of memories, of stories of lived life, of experiences in Eritrea, of youthfulness and, I confess, of nostalgia].[20] His observation usefully indicates both how Eritrea appears in the journal and how its apparition is located in time. The Eritrea, and to a much lesser extent the Ethiopia, that we read about in *Mai Taclì* is not constructed according to the principles of historical research but instead through the accumulation of individual memories. The journal, therefore, contains a written and visual record of all the sites that were most frequented by members of the Italian community: there is a wealth of pictures of the port city of Massawa; of the road that rises from the port to the plateau – 2,325 metres above sea level – where the capital is located; of the modernist buildings and avenues of the centre of Asmara; of the city's cathedral, Coptic church and central mosque; of the towns of Assab, Dekemhare and Keren. There are descriptions of the Italian schools in Asmara and of the working practices of the community.[21]

But the record is selective. The recollections are openly concerned with the self who remembers and they are intended for a community of readers familiar with the everyday life of the Italian community in East Africa. Thus, *Mai Taclì* does not give us an account of life in Eritrea that can make claims to be either objective or comprehensive. For all its complexity, it can clearly offer only a partial account by no means always aware of the positionality of the person who records the memory. It does, however, furnish us with the means to consider how people – with their powers

---

20 Marcello Melani, 'Amici miei', *Mai Taclì*, May–June 1997, p. 3. This and other translations from Italian are mine.

21 For a recent study of the history of Italian colonialism in Africa see Emanuele Ertola, *In terra d'Africa. Gli italiani che colonizzarono l'impero* (Rome-Bari: Laterza, 2017).

of imagination, their family connections, their professional and personal allegiances – are involved in a cultural configuration that is intimately connected with other collective social experiences and which, when placed in contiguous perspective with these experiences of displacement, can indicate features that are important to our understanding of the currents within the development of diasporic Italian cultures. If we isolate the body of work belonging to one or other of the contributors to *Mai Taclì*, then this point becomes clearer.

One of the most regular contributors to the journal was Marisa Baratti, who wrote for most issues from 1992 until her death in 2009. Her column of reminiscences, entitled 'Era una volta ...' [There was a time ...], does not follow a chronological sequence, rarely reflects explicitly on the meaning of memory, and does not offer a narrative of selfhood that is fully connected. Yet, if we look deeper into the way in which her articles are constructed, we can see that they do provide an imaginative way of framing personal identity. Each article in the series, 'Era una volta', evokes a place in a specific year of its existence and is accompanied by a photograph either of the place itself or of a group of people in close proximity to the location. The reader thus moves, say, from the port of Massawa in 1960 to Piazza Italia in Asmara in 1954, from the residential district Villaggio Paradiso in 1941 to Ghinda in 1962 or Kagnew Station a year earlier or Basciacùl a year later, from Viale Crispi in 1950 to Adi Quala in 1951 or to the Chiesa degli Eroi [The church of the heroes] in 1947. The effect of journeying from one place and one time to another is that the reader gains, incrementally, a sense of the spaces – in their changing appearances – that once constituted the external reality of the Italian community. However, the effect is more profound than that.

In evoking, simultaneously, a sense of self with a sense of place, Baratti is not presenting her life experiences as independent from the social context in which they occurred. Quite the reverse is true; she is emphasizing the inter-dependence of the record of her subjectivity and the rapidly changing historical circumstances in which both she and her family were involved. The impression of selfhood that her writings convey is, in common with most autobiography,[22] made up of the narration of the course of friendships, of imaginings, of moments from school or the beginning of professional life. But what makes her writing distinctive is the prominence that it accords to the

---

22 On this subject see Paul John Eakin, *How Our Lives Become Stories: Making Selves* (Ithaca, NY: Cornell University Press, 1999).

defining events within the life of the community as a whole. She remembers,[23] for example, participating in the rituals – such as the 'Natale di Roma' [The Roman Christmas] – organized by the Fascist authorities; she recalls the start of the war as well as the moment when British troops entered Asmara, passing through the residential area, Villaggio Paradiso, in which her family lived, on the road from Eritrea's second city, Keren;[24] she remembers the period in the camp at Sembel, waiting to be repatriated to Italy in July 1943, the night-time train journey on board a cattle truck to Massawa and the boarding of the two transportation ships, the *Giulio Cesare* and the *Duilio*; she recalls the return to Asmara after three years spent in Italy; the beginnings of renewed economic activity in the immediate post-war period, the presence of the American troops at Kagnew Station at the height of the Cold War and the forms of association that typified the lifestyle of Italians living in or around Asmara in the 1950s and 1960s.[25]

In all of these instances the reader gains a sense of the depth of Baratti's psychological and emotional responses to the events in which she, both as a child and as a young adult, finds herself involved: we learn of her fear for the wellbeing of her father at the camp in Sembel, her pride in helping her mother to make ends meet in the immediate aftermath of the war, her relationships with her sisters, the extent of her knowledge of Eritrean society, the origin of her interest in photography, even the nature of her speculations on mortality. But, above all, through the way in which she records her subjective understanding of the events and circumstances that characterized her life in Eritrea, we can see the coherence of the underlying beliefs of the Italian community, the sets of practices that defined its operation and the nature of its connections with mainland Italy. It is not surprising that her narration of confinement at the camp in Sembel or repatriation in the 'navi bianche' [white ships] echoes the defining features of the Italian community in Eritrea's memory of the Second World War.[26] One finds in her writing the same emphasis on the sense of bewilderment at the suddenness of Italian defeat, on the harshness of the behaviour of the British authorities in the wake of victory, and on the lack of

23 Marisa Baratti, '1937: 21 aprile, Amba Galliano', *Mai Taclì*, July–August 2003, p. 3.
24 Marisa Baratti, '1941: 1 aprile, Villaggio Paradiso', *Mai Taclì*, July–August 1996, p. 3.
25 For a detailed account of the modern history of Eritrea see Michela Wrong, *I Didn't Do It for You: How the World Used and Abused a Small African Nation* (London: Fourth Estate, 2005).
26 Marisa Baratti, '1943: 5 luglio, Sembel, sera', *Mai Taclì*, March–April 1996, p. 6. See also her article, '1943: Massaua, 6 luglio, mattina', *Mai Taclì*, November–December 2003, p. 3.

knowledge of what awaits her family on their return to Italy that one finds in many accounts in *Mai Taclì* on the experience of the war.

The experience of repatriation – relayed in the journal either through personal testimony or through historical recreations of the occurrence – was an exceptional event even within the circumstances of the war.[27] On three occasions, following the capitulation of Italian troops in East Africa, converted cruise ships (the *Duilio* and the *Giulio Cesare*, and the *Saturnia* and the *Vulcania*) were sent from Italy to the Eritrean port of Massawa to take large swathes of the Italian community in Eritrea back to Italy. The first of the three expeditions – each of which necessitated circumnavigating Africa – was made between March and June 1942, the second between September 1942 and January 1943 and the third between July and August 1943.[28]

The unprecedented and highly dramatic nature of the repatriation has earned its status as one of the key points in the memory of the former Italian community of Eritrea. The memory of the event was reinforced by the peculiarity of the historical moment in which each evacuation took place. As Gianfranco Spadoni wrote in an entry for the journal in 1996, drawing on his own experience, the Italy to which each group of internees returned was very different. While the first group returned to a country in which Fascism was still firmly in control, the second and third groups arrived in an Italy that had been devastated by the conflict. At the beginning of his article on the nature of the journey from Massawa to Taranto, Spadoni evoked the resonance of Baratti's writing on the subject:

> Nell'articolo '1943: 5 luglio, Sembel sera' [...] Marisa Baratti ha descritto in modo assolutamente perfetto la triste esperienza vissuta da donne, bambini, vecchi ed ammalati che dopo il campo di concentramento di Asmara e il carro bestiame finirono con l'imbarcarsi, nel torrido caldo di

---

[27] See Gianfranco Spadoni, 'Le navi bianche', *Mai Taclì*, September–October 1996, pp. 3–4. See also Maria Cescutti's diary of the experience of repatriation, 'Asmara, Addio!', *Mai Taclì*, September–October 2005, pp. 9–10. In her writing Cescutti gives her impressions on each stage of the journey. For another account of the journey see Franco Losacco, '1942–43 Viaggio di rimpatrio sul transatlantico Giulio Cesare', *Mai Taclì*, May–June 2003, pp. 12–13.

[28] For a detailed account of the navigation of the 'navi bianche' see Angelo Del Boca, *Gli Italiani in Africa Orientale*, vol. 3, 'La caduta dell'impero' (Milan: Mondadori, 1992), pp. 556–66. For reference in *Mai Taclì* to the sinking of the troop ship *Nova Scotia*, carrying Italian POWs from British occupied Eritrea, see Carlo Dominione, 'La tragedia del Nova Scotia', July–August 1982, pp. 4–5.

Massaua, sulla Duilio (io tra questi) e sulla Giulio Cesare. Ho rivissuto con te, cara Marisa, tutti quei momenti drammatici, anche se, l'eccitazione superava di gran lunga l'indignazione per il comportamento di un occupante arrogante e spesso prepotente.[29]

[In the article '1943: 5 July, Sembel evening' [...] Marisa Baratti has described in a way that is absolutely perfect the sad experience lived by women, children, old and sick people who after the concentration camp of Asmara and the cattle truck were embarked, in the torrid heat of Massawa, on the *Duilio* (myself among them) and on the *Giulio Cesare*. I have re-lived with you, dear Marisa, all those dramatic moments, even if [at the time] excitement overcame indignation for the behaviour of an arrogant and often overpowering occupier.]

Baratti's representations of the consequences of the Second World War are among the most striking examples of how personal memory serves to illuminate wider societal practices. But even in her record of life in the post-war period, we see the interplay between her subjectivity and collective organizational structures – or how, in other words, her narration of specific episodes, encounters or emotions reveals the tightly integrated network of associations, relations and repeated everyday work or leisure activities that constituted life in Africa for the Italian community. And we see this, perhaps most interestingly, in the photographs that accompany the prose of her articles. It is not simply that the photography provides a neutral visual record of events and circumstances from the past. It is rather that, in viewing the image, we assume the perspective of the photographer – entering his or her world, accepting the same conventions, drawing the same inferences, making the same distinctions between the sight-worthy and the invisible.

We see the same processes that we witness in the writings of Baratti at work in many of the reminiscences that are contained in *Mai Taclì*. Or rather, what we see in reading the journal as a whole is how a community is created through memory, how people's life stories are integrated within that community and how their sense of self is moulded by the experience of belonging. There is little doubt that the appeal of the journal for its original subscribers lay precisely in reading how the lives of a large range of people were in some way knitted together, how the community functioned over time and how it could be remembered

---

29 Spadoni, 'Le navi bianche', p. 3. See also Alberto Capitanio, 'Le navi bianche', *Mai Taclì*, January–February 1997, p. 12.

Asmara - Mercato dei generi alimentari.

Asmara - Mercato delle granaglie.

Fig. 4.1: Asmara, food market and corn seed market, *Mai Taclì*, May–June 1993.

years after its dissolution. The appeal of the journal also, no doubt, lay in the opportunity that it afforded its readers to re-experience the mode of perception and the organization of reality that were proper to the time. Every edition of *Mai Taclì*, for example, ended with a collection of photographs, 'Album', sent to the editor by the journal's readers. The collection allowed its viewers to imagine the reality of Asmara, say, or Keren or Dekemhare as they were once configured, with all their sights, sounds and familiar points of reference (Figure 4.1). The collection, to put this point differently, offered its viewers the chance of reinhabiting the mental and emotional universe of the time – of travelling with the imagination not just to a space but to an earlier stage within the intellectual and sentimental life of each individual.

Many of the writings of *Mai Taclì* – and many of the literary works produced by contributors to the journal – give expression to the affective dimension of memory in all its multiple manifestations. One finds, for example, reflections on how the memory of the spatial disposition of Asmara infiltrates the everyday consciousness of living in an Italian city.[30] One finds the narration of journeys to the graves of family members in the Italian cemeteries in Eritrea and Ethiopia as well as musings on how the living can attempt, imaginatively, to recover a sense of how the world appeared to the dead.[31] One finds the evocation of the interplay between the perception of the physical reality of Asmara with the remembered internal presence of the city.[32] One finds, in addition, longer explorations of the meaning of the feeling of nostalgia felt by so many of the former Italian inhabitants of Eritrea and which is defined, in some contexts, as 'il mal d'Africa' [longing for Africa].[33]

Yet, it is often the case that some of the shorter interventions are as effective in conveying the intensity of the emotional pull that memory exerts, the sense of partial estrangement from the present that it can induce and the desire to relive the sequence of the past that it engenders. In response to the narration, by Alessandro P., of a recent journey to Massawa,[34] Aldo Vannini sent a picture of himself and his wife to the editor, with a brief note:

> Nel leggere il resoconto di A.P. (ultima visita Asmara, Cheren, Massaua etc.) mi sono commosso, ricordando i bei tempi felici vissuti laggiù per oltre 10 anni con mia moglie purtroppo scomparsa 6 anni fa. [...] Ti mando una foto [...] dove con mia moglie siamo davanti alla nostra

---

30 Alce [pseudonym], 'Avanti tutta con il museo immaginario', *Mai Taclì*, January–February 1997, p. 3.
31 Stefano Anastasia, 'Un viaggio nella memoria', *Mai Taclì*, May–June 1996, p. 1.
32 Nina Castellani Spagnolini, 'A due passi dalla Croce del Sud ...', *Mai Taclì*, January–February 1997, p. 12.
33 See Gabriella Gasparini, 'Mal d'Africa: parliamone ancora', *Mai Taclì*, September–December 1982, p. 3 and Oscar Rampone, 'Ma è veramente misterioso il mal d'Africa?', *Mai Taclì*, January–February 1983, p. 3.
34 A. P., 'Massaua a marzo', *Mai Taclì*, November–December 1996, p. 4.

Cattedrale. Noi abitavamo a Ghezzabanda, eravamo felici. Avevo superato indenne la guerra, ho combattuto a Cheren col 106 Btg. Coloniale, ma qui devo lasciarti perché la commozione e i ricordi mi vincono.[35]

[Reading the article by A. P. (last visit to Asmara, Keren, Massawa etc.) I was moved, remembering the happy times spent there for more than 10 years with my wife who sadly passed away six years ago. [...] I am sending a picture [...] with my wife where we are in front of our cathedral. We lived in Gezabanda, we were happy. I had managed to get through the war uninjured, I fought at Keren with the 106 Colonial Brigade, but here I must leave you because emotion and memories overcome me.]

Transnational Memory

Each act of memory evokes an earlier self that was part, for whatever period of time, of the Italian community that was based around Asmara and each act of memory participates in the journal's recreation of the modes of social interaction that characterized the life of that community. However, though it may seem to evoke a moment that is frozen in time, every act of memory in reality represents a society in rapid and continual movement. Part of the interest of the journal lies, therefore, in how its record of individual experiences indicates societal or cultural shifts that were occurring during the years of a substantial Italian presence in the Horn of Africa and which may or *may not* have been evident to the individuals themselves. Or rather, the journal – if subjected to a certain type of reading – can heighten our awareness of the forces, whether ideological or material, that shaped – or were in the process of shaping – the society in which contributors to the journal spent a significant portion of their lives.

As I have suggested, one way in which we can consider *Mai Taclì* is as a photographic archive. Though it is true that most of the photographs that are reprinted in the journal are from the period running from the end of the Second World War through to the beginning of the 1970s, there are nevertheless quite a number of pictures that are from the era of Italian colonial rule and specifically from the 1920s and 1930s. The pictures do not set out to celebrate aspects of the regime, as is often the case in publications such as *Il*

---

35 Aldo Vannini, 'Andiamo, io ci vado a marzo', *Mai Taclì*, January–February 1997, p. 13.

reduce d'Africa. They do, however, serve to indicate that the period that was so fondly recalled by so many former residents in Eritrea was neither entirely disconnected from the years leading up to the war nor free from colonial connotations. By attempting to place the many photographs in chronological sequence, we can see how the family history of each contributor to the journal is caught up in the progress of the Italian colonial appropriation of East Africa. We can also see the succession of geopolitical events – the beginning of the Second World War, the establishment of the British administration, the withdrawal of Italian political influence – as they were experienced by those who lived through them. But, perhaps most interestingly, we can see how the urban landscapes that appear in the photographs do not appear simply as the background against which scenes of social significance are played out but as sites which themselves are in movement. One can see this most evidently in instances of the removal of the visible evidence of Italian presence in Eritrea. But one can see this also in pictures of Asmara; the city, with its wide boulevards and its impressive art deco buildings, was intended to be a symbol of modernity and the gateway to the expanding Italian empire. In the photographs we see the construction of the city and its changing visual aspect as it undergoes various stages of its history from site of expansionist ambition to capital of the newly independent Eritrea (Figures 4.2 and 4.3).

The photographs also exemplify that shifts in collective thought and imagination do not proceed in a sequential fashion. The long shadow that is cast by the visual imagery of the 1920s and 1930s is, on occasions, accompanied by the expression of views that are unwilling to accept the extent of the brutality that characterized, in particular, the latter stages of colonialism or the need for sustained inquiry into the origins and functioning of Italian rule over parts of East Africa. One finds, for example, a number of contributions that are prepared to contest the use of poisoned gas in the conquest of Ethiopia,[36] that are willing to insist on the role played by European powers in the tutelage of African countries,[37] or which express outrage at the interpretation of Italy's role in Africa that the volumes published by Angelo Del Boca in the 1980s and 1990s advanced.[38]

---

36 Paolo Beltremelli-Ceppi, 'La verità sull'uso dei gas', *Mai Taclì*, September–December 1986, p. 11.
37 Cesare Alfieri, 'Ma di chi è quest'Africa?', *Mai Taclì*, January–February 1987, p. 2. Reprinted from *La Gazzetta di Parma*, 17 January 1987.
38 Marcello Melani, 'Certe calunnie e ... certe verità', *Mai Taclì*, January–February 1998, p. 11, and 'Guai ai vinti!', *Mai Taclì*, March–April 2001, p. 5.

Fig. 4.2: View of Asmara, *Mai Taclì*, July–August 1997.

Fig. 4.3: View of Asmara, *Mai Taclì*, November–December 1997.

It is certainly true that a publication that appeared regularly over a number of decades enables us to see how, in their narration of past events, people reveal the degree to which they are prepared to appropriate and refer to the collective conceptual framework that surrounds them. It is also true that in the collection as it develops over the years we can trace, through the record of subjective experience, the arc of the Italian colonial and post-colonial experience: the establishment of Asmara as an important city in the 1930s and as a gateway to continued expansion, the consequences of entry into the Second World War, the gradual dissolution of the Italian influence in the region in the post-war years. The journal can also be seen as a site from which to view the temporalities in which Eritrea and Ethiopia are involved. But the question remains as to how far the experiences of the Italian community in East Africa were and are transnational – transnational, that is, in the sense of involving a radical alteration in the way in which personal identity is lived and remembered, in the way in which belonging to a determined culture is framed and, finally, in the way in which culture itself is conceptualized and remembered.[39]

At a certain level, the fragments of people's life stories that are recorded in *Mai Taclì* all exemplify a movement between and a coming together of traditions and modes of social interaction. This is true of the narrations that concern every sphere of life, whether the workplace, the domestic sphere, the institutional context or the spaces of leisure activity. As noted above, a city such as Asmara – recognized in 2017 as a UNESCO World Heritage Site – is a transnational phenomenon: built with African and Italian labour, its very existence testifies to the complex nature and temporality of contact between Italy and Eritrea.[40]

Yet, at another level, though there are many references to Eritreans and to features of Eritrean life, the contributions to *Mai Taclì* are written, almost exclusively, by Italians and the reality that is remembered is a reality in which the Italian community lived an existence that was in many ways isolated from the rest of the society in which it was situated. On the restoration of Haile Selassie to power, following the rapid collapse of colonial rule, Italian

---

39 On the production of forms of hybrid cultural identity that result from diverse experiences of the transnational see Steven Vertovec, *Transnationalism* (London and New York: Routledge, 2009), in particular pp. 4–13. For the material and conceptual complexity of the transnational when relating to memory see Chiara De Cesari and Ann Rigney, *Transnational Memory: Circulation, Articulation, Scales* (Berlin: De Gruyter, 2014).
40 For a recent study on this subject see Sean Anderson, *Modern Architecture and Its Representation in Colonial Eritrea: An Invisible Colony 1891–1941* (London: Routledge, 2017).

technological experience was considered an asset and permission to stay in the newly liberated country was granted to Italian citizens.[41] But the conditions of continued Italian presence in Eritrea and Ethiopia meant that there was something intrinsically precarious in its continuation and in the profundity of its connection with emerging post-war societies.

This precariousness is something that is reflected upon by a number of writings. In 1984 Fiorella Nuovo suggested that the post-war Italian presence in Eritrea was peculiar and that it needed to be the subject of further reflection.[42] For another contributor, who identified himself simply as R. B., the Italian community was defined by its very precariousness. He wrote that, for most inhabitants of the former colony, life in Eritrea was 'provisional':

> 'Provvisorio' perché il definitivo era l'Italia; si viveva in maniera 'transitoria', in attesa di tornare in Patria. Per tale motivo molti (me compreso) non si interessavano alla lingua, alla storia, ai costumi, agli usi, alla civiltà dell'Eritrea: attendevamo di tornare in Italia a riprendere la vita 'normale' dopo la parentesi eritrea che, credevo, sarebbe stata presto dimenticata. [...] Rimpiango di non essermi interessato, come avrei potuto e dovuto, all'Eritrea, di non aver studiato la lingua.[43]

> ['Temporary' because what was permanent was Italy; we lived in a way that was 'temporary', waiting to return to the homeland. For that reason, many of us (myself included) did not become interested in the language, the customs, the practices, the civilization of Eritrea: we were waiting to go back to Italy to begin again a 'normal' life after the Eritrean parenthesis which, I thought, would soon be forgotten. [...] I regret not devoting my interest, as I could and should have, to Eritrea, to studying the language.]

Though considerations such as the above indicate both how and why the nature of profound and sustained inter-cultural exchange was limited for so many of the former Italian residents of Eritrea, one can nevertheless seek – in the record of the experiences of a generation that *Mai Taclì* represents – instances of intense transcultural contact. Perhaps the most profound understanding of the lived reality of being part of different cultures – and

---

41   For a recent study on the legacy of Italian colonialism see Valeria Deplano and Alessandro Pes, eds, *Quel che resta dell'impero* (Milan: Mimesis, 2014).
42   Fiorella Nuovo, 'Leggero colonialismo', *Mai Taclì*, November–December 1984, p. 4.
43   R. B., 'Non era per nulla provvisorio', *Mai Taclì*, September–October 1997, p. 5.

sharing concepts and traditions from both – belongs to people of mixed ethnicity. Despite the introduction of the notorious race laws in the late 1930s, it is well known that a great many children of Italian and Eritrean or Ethiopian parents were born in the final years of the empire and grew up, for the most part in Eritrea, in the immediate post-war period.[44] Their experience of constructing personal identity both within and between different worlds and also, in many instances, of being exposed to varying kinds and degrees of racial prejudice offers the most complex example of a transnational life.

In the pages of *Mai Taclì* there is, unfortunately, no lengthy inquiry into the meaning of being of mixed ethnicity written by one or other of the prominent members of the community. This is not, however, to say that the cultural and social questions surrounding the life experiences of people of mixed ethnicity and the challenges caused by the legacy of racially motivated legislation are not addressed by the journal. There is, for example, the writing of Rita Di Meglio on the questions surrounding children of mixed ethnicity and the reprint of an article by the journalist Gustavo Selva on the introduction of racial segregation in the Italian empire and the need to develop a more general awareness of the consequences of the identifications made on the basis of conceptions of race.[45]

Interesting as the reflections of Di Meglio and Selva are, it is not uniquely in the pages of the journal that one should look for responses. Some of the most searching inquiries into the nature of the question are pursued through fiction. Nicky Di Paolo in his novel, *Hakim*, and, more centrally, Erminia Dell'Oro in *L'abbandono: Una storia eritrea* [The Abandonment: An Eritrean Story] rely upon the resources of plot, characterization and the imaginative involvement of the reader to take an exploration of the issues further.[46] *L'abbandono*, specifically, sets out to convey both the material consequences and the intimate psychological implications of an inter-ethnic relationship

---

44 For a detailed study of the implications of the introduction of legislation enforcing racial segregation see Barbara Sórgoni, *Parole e corpi: Antropologia, discorso giuridico e politiche sessuali interrazziali nella colonia Eritrea 1890–1941* (Naples: Liguori, 1998).

45 Rita Di Meglio, 'Alla faccia della tanto auspicata fratellanza', *Mai Taclì*, September–October 1999, p. 10 and 'Cosa hanno guadagnato gli italiani in Eritrea?', *Mai Taclì*, March–April 2002, p. 11. See also Gustavo Selva, 'C'è ancora l'Italia', *Mai Taclì*, September–December 1984, p. 14. The original article by Selva appeared in the *Gazzettino di Venezia*, 8 October 1984.

46 Erminia Dell'Oro, *L'abbandono: Una storia eritrea* (Turin: Einaudi, 1991), Nicky Di Paolo, *Hakim: Quasi quasi torno in Eritrea* (Milan: Wichtig Editore, 1994).

that is abandoned by the male protagonist. Both Di Paolo and Dell'Oro were among the most important contributors to *Mai Taclì* and both, through their fictional and non-fictional writing, have sought to place their memories and those of the Italo-Eritrean community in a multifaceted historical perspective. Within the wider world and within the academic community, a work such as *L'abbandono* has played a significant role in drawing attention to a question of intense social, cultural and historical importance.[47] But the novel has also been the object of a very interesting kind of reception in *Mai Taclì* itself, most notably in the review written by Oscar Rampone.[48]

Rampone was a writer and journalist as well as one of the most prominent figures in commenting – for the journal – on the reality, past and present, of the Italian experience in Africa. Thus, in reviewing *L'abbandono* he was not simply giving a personal opinion but writing from a position of considerable authority. Indeed, the most significant feature of his review was that he chose to interpret the question 'Come hai potuto?' [How could you?], posed with searing insistence by the female protagonist, Sellass, throughout the novel, as an interrogation not only of the work's male protagonist but of the history of the Italian community as a whole. The question is posed, to begin with, at the level of rational inquiry: the depiction of the conditions in which Sellass and her family live leads necessarily to an awareness of the wrongs perpetrated by colonialism and to the consequences of the racial laws introduced at the end of the 1930s. But, in Rampone's review, any answer to Sellass' question is not confined to an assessment of the consequences of past collective action: the strength of the literary encounter with the characters in Dell'Oro's novel evokes, in a merging of the fictional with the non-fictional, the memory of friendships, perceptions and situations. The novel acts as a means of access into the subjectivity of the reader:

> Capisco Erminia Dell'Oro, perché anch'io mi sono compenetrato nel dramma di tanti 'meticci'. Anch'io mi sono calato in essi e ho capito in che inferno senza fiamme vivono [...] Ho capito e sentito anche tutta la pena di quelli che, rassegnati, si abbandonano ad un'esistenza da paria. [...] Poema di ribellione iridiscente e disperata; e sopratttutto amore per

---

47 See Giuliana Benvenuti, 'Memoria e metissage nel romanzo italiano postcoloniale e della migrazione', in *Memoria storica e postcolonialismo: Il caso italiano*, ed. by Martine Bovo Romoeuf and Franco Manai (Brussels: Peter Lang, 2015), pp. 115–36.
48 Oscar Rampone, 'Sellass: Eritrea abbandonata', *Mai Taclì*, January–February 1992, p. 4.

queste creature che, grazie alla bravura della scrittrice, si moltiplicano in tanti Carlo, Sellass, Marianna e Gianfranco, che il colonialismo si è lasciati dietro senza voltarsi: colpa di cui solo la Dell'Oro e pochi altri sentono la gravità.

[I understand Erminia Dell'Oro, because I too have participated in the drama of so many 'meticci' [people of mixed ethnicity]. I also have identified with them and understood the hell without flames in which they live [...] I have understood and felt the pain of those who, resigned, accept the existence of an outcast. [...] An iridescent and despairing poem of rebellion; and above all of love for these people who, owing to the skill of the writer, become so many Carlo, Sellass, Marianna and Gianfranco, that colonialism left behind without turning round: a wrong the gravity of which only Dell'Oro and few others are able to feel.]

The emphasis not only in this section but in the review as a whole is on the meaning of understanding – whether it is achieved through empathy, identification or imagination – and its consequences for one's everyday relationship with one's self and with others. The effect of dwelling on the affective dimension of understanding is primarily to situate the reviewer in relation to the action of the story, to promote rapid changes in perspective and to destabilize any settled relationship with the past. In imagining himself – or rather the community to which he belongs – as in some sense the addressee of the question 'Come hai potuto?' [How could you?], Rampone refers to a collective sense of guilt that his review – and, of course, the novel – argues should inflect an Italian memory of the past. Such, however, is the sophistication of the reading to which the novel is exposed that Rampone, while conscious of the accusation that it carries, can also identify with the very question that is posed by Dell'Oro's character. Rampone's reading may be partial and it may not have appealed to other subscribers to *Mai Taclì*,[49] but it does alert us to the depth and complexity of the temporalities in which, whether consciously or not, the Italo-Eritrean community was and is involved.

---

49 See, for example, Melani's review, 'Perché non mi ha entusiasmato?', *Mai Taclì*, January–February 1992, p. 4.

Conclusion

Writing on the vestiges of empire, one of the foremost scholars of Italian colonialism, Angelo Del Boca, described *Mai Taclì* as a collection of 'episodi, sensazioni, emozioni, immagini, per ricostruire la storia di un mondo irrimediabilmente perduto e bramato, ma non rivendicato, non ricordato con astio o amarezza' [episodes, sensations, emotions and images aimed at reconstituting the history of a world that was irredeemably lost and longed for, but not demanded, not remembered with rancour or bitterness.][50] It may indeed have been the intention of *Mai Taclì* to avoid issues of immediate political concern, to concentrate on personal memory and to avoid the controversies surrounding the legacies of Italian colonial involvement in East Africa. Whatever the intentions of the journal were, however, it did not succeed in acting simply as a repository of people's memories. Irrespective of the intentions of their authors, the many hundreds of written memories that the journal contains inevitably offered explanations of the significance of the past, and one can see a number of distinctive interpretative strands emerge over the course of the existence of *Mai Taclì*.

There is, for example, a strand of historically focused writing that sought to place the experiences of the contributors to *Mai Taclì* within a historical context stretching back from the late nineteenth century. In this vein, between 2000 and 2001 Nicky Di Paolo published a series of lengthy articles that looked at the sharply distinguished periods that constituted the evolving story of the Italian presence in East Africa. In defending his reconstruction of historical events, Di Paolo wrote:

> Sono fiero di essere asmarino ed anticolonialista e non voglio fare processi alla storia ... In quanto alla mia scomoda 'storia', ripeto ancora una volta, è stato il frutto di una necessità interiore per cercare di capire tutto quello che nessuno mi aveva mai insegnato né cercato di spiegarmi sulla terra dove sono nato, dove è nato mio padre e dove sono vissuto felicemente tanti anni.[51]

> [I am proud to be a [former] resident of Asmara and an anti-colonialist and I do not wish to put history on trial ... Regarding my inconvenient

---

50 Angelo del Boca, 'L'Impero', in *I luoghi della memoria: Simboli e miti dell'Italia unita*, ed. by Mario Isnenghi (Rome-Bari: Laterza, 1996), p. 434.
51 Nicky di Paolo, 'L'Eritrea e gli asmarini', *Mai Taclì*, July–August 2001, p. 12.

[written] 'history', I repeat once more that it is the product of an interior necessity to try to understand what no one taught me or tried to explain to me about the land where I was born, where my father was born and where I lived happily for so many years.]

In contrast, one also finds within the journal (as noted earlier) an approach towards the past that was steadfastly opposed to acknowledging the findings of recent historiography and which sought to retain some of the tarnished narratives of the immediate post-war period. But the most common interpretation of the past that emerges – for the most part implicitly – from the recorded memories is, as I have attempted to suggest, as a period that was characterized by everything being in flux. In the narratives that unfold from one issue to another of the journal, the memories of the activities and impressions of youth are threaded through with a sense of the growing tension between Ethiopia and Eritrea, of acts of hostility towards the Italian community and of the precariousness of the community itself. The narration of experiences of disintegration and reconstitution characterize the majority of accounts of life in Africa shared by the former residents of Asmara. The past is interpreted as a site of instability, as a point or episode within shifting geopolitical forces that was destined to be lost. This interpretation, not necessarily consciously formulated, accounts in part for the strong affective dimension of many of the reminiscences of *Mai Taclì* and of the literary production of its contributors. It also accounts for one of the most intriguing features of the journal – the awareness expressed by many contributors that they experienced a reality whose cultural, political and ethnic complexity they apprehended but which they struggled fully to understand.

Part 2

Art, Objects and Artefacts

CHAPTER FIVE

'The Path that Leads Me Home': Eduardo Paolozzi and the Arts of Transnationalizing

Derek Duncan

Critical thinking is both a condition of and complement to art-making. (Doris Sommer)

Migratory aesthetics is an aesthetic of geographical mobility beyond the national state and its linguistic uniformity. (Mieke Bal)

The Artist as Transnational Subject

Sir Eduardo Paolozzi (1924–2005) was one of the most internationally successful British artists of the twentieth century. From his early collages to the massive public sculptures he produced late in his career, Paolozzi constantly experimented with material and form. His engagement with popular culture and techniques of mass production, as well as the aesthetics of the creative reassemblage of debris and waste, led him to explore an extraordinary range of artistic media. Critical and public interest in his work remains strong. A major retrospective exhibition was held jointly at the Whitechapel Gallery, London and the Berlinische Galerie, Berlin in 2017–18 and in 2018–19 the Scottish National Gallery of Modern Art in Edinburgh put on a combined Paolozzi/Andy Warhol exhibition under the title *I want to be a machine*. Warhol's famous quote pointed to their shared but very differently understood and expressed fascination with the mechanical world and the possibilities it offered for redefining art and the creative process, as well as the human subject. Visitors to the exhibition were also alerted to another link between the two artists: 'Both were sons of immigrant parents'. This statement on the first information panel immediately precedes a short summary of their common artistic interests, leaving the visitor to infer, perhaps, that their work bears some kind of biographical imprint. In drawing attention to Paolozzi's family origins, the exhibition operates in a well-established tradition. In the introduction to her substantial monograph on Paolozzi, Judith Collins notes that: 'He was an Italian-Scot, born of parents who were members of a large Italian community in Edinburgh', and compares the artist's industry with that of his father, who ran an ice-cream shop and confectioners in Leith.[1] Similarly, Daniel Herrmann, in the introduction to the book accompanying the Whitechapel Gallery exhibition, writes: 'As the oldest child of first-generation Italian immigrants to Edinburgh, he assisted his parents in their ice-cream shop. Surrounded by colourful arrangements of advertising, consumer goods and packaging in window displays, he grew up familiar with commercial design and consumer culture.'[2] Paolozzi himself wrote about growing up in a multilingual family environment and his early fascination with commercial and film culture, much of which was American.[3] He suggests that his family origins and bi-cultural upbringing somehow made a difference to his artistic practice and creative thinking. From this perspective, migration, both cultural and demographic, matters.

Paolozzi's status as a much-acclaimed British artist of Italian origin offers a suggestive template for the exploration of the complexities of language, legacy and cultural identity. His experience of speaking both standard and regionally inflected forms of English and Italian and moving across all four languages on a daily basis suggests a high level of linguistic competency, not solely in terms of fluency but, more particularly, in terms of the advanced skills of intercultural translation that linguistic flexibility fosters and requires. Such

---

1 Judith Collins, *Eduardo Paolozzi* (London: Lund Humphries, 2014), p. 6.
2 Daniel F. Herrmann, 'Eduardo Paolozzi: Pop Art Redefined', in *Eduardo Paolozzi*, ed. by Daniel F. Herrmann (London: Whitechapel Gallery, 2017), pp. 9–27 (p. 9).
3 Excerpts of Paolozzi's short autobiographical essays are most easily accessed in Robin Spencer, ed., *Eduardo Paolozzi: Writings and Interviews* (Oxford: Oxford University Press, 2000). This volume is an extraordinary compendium of Paolozzi's writing over his entire career. It works in counterpoint with Frank Whitford's 23-part interview with Paolozzi for the National Life Story Collection in which he recalls in detail his early life as well as his later career. The interviews are available at <https://sounds.bl.uk/Arts-literature-and-performance/Art/021M-C0466X0017XX-0100V0> [accessed 10 February 2020].

dexterity is poorly accommodated by the conflation of national language, territory and identity that has determined the monolingual boundaries of disciplinary thinking and practice in Modern Languages. This disciplinary monolingualism creates a sharp sense of dislocation when considered in terms of the multilingual spaces in which many people now live.

What follows is an account of a speculative transnational intervention in the field of language pedagogy. This intervention is not about language acquisition in the accepted sense, but instead works with the communication skills acquired through processes of language learning rather than the knowledge of a particular language. One of the challenges TML hoped to address was how to revise the modern languages classroom in order to give due emphasis to the movement of people and language, and its unexpected directions and outcomes.[4] We wanted to find ways of more closely approximating the cultural fluidity of contemporary social realities in which languages have migrated, not least with the aim of validating the critical intellectual and creative life skills that the users of two or more languages inevitably possess. Practices of translation and adaptation featured prominently as experimental frameworks in a series of intercultural research-led practice-based art projects conducted between 2014 and 2017 at two secondary schools in Edinburgh.[5] These projects, inspired by Paolozzi's multidimensional work, initiated not in Modern Languages but in Expressive Arts, where teachers more readily grasped the impulse to move between and across accepted boundaries. The feasibility of this intervention depended in large measure on the interdisciplinary ambitions of the Scottish education system's 'Curriculum for Excellence', a programme encompassing both primary and secondary education that explicitly attempts to foster exchange and connection across disciplines.[6] Its learner-centred approach and its emphasis on inquiry- and

---

4 TML, as indicated in the Introduction to this volume, is the acronym of 'Transnationalizing Modern Languages: Mobility, Identity and Translation in Modern Italian Cultures'. TML was a large research project funded by the UK's AHRC that ran between 2014 and 2016. Full details can be found on the project website <https://www.transnationalmodernlanguages.ac.uk> [accessed 10 February 2020].
5 I want to express my deepest thanks and gratitude to the teachers and pupils at Drummond and Castlebrae Community High Schools for the enthusiasm, hard work and creative imagination that they brought to this project. Their contribution was truly transformative.
6 Full details of the Curriculum for Excellence can be found at <https://education.gov.scot/education-scotland/> [accessed 10 February 2020]. The Curriculum is based around four fundamental capacities, whose aims include, for instance, the ability to

problem-based activities place subjectivity and locatedness at the heart of the educational experience, facilitating the kind of culturally sensitive, cross-disciplinary collaboration we wanted to explore.

The art projects started life as still fully to be defined elements of our AHRC research funding application, which placed us under the formal obligation to ensure that our research had 'impact' reaching out beyond academia into the wider world. Working with schools seemed like a feasible step to take on our 'Pathway to Impact', especially as the scheme under which we were funded was in part a response to the decline in formal modern language learning in schools across the UK. At the time of preparing our funding application, 'impact' was still a relatively new and, for some, controversial, dimension of research activity. In this still-evolving landscape I was aware that I hoped to engage partners and participants as active co-researchers – producers and not simply recipients of knowledge. Our introduction to the secondary school sector was facilitated by Norma Prentice, Head Teacher of Drummond Community High School, close to the centre of Edinburgh. Although, at the outset, our project seemed primarily language-based, Norma recognized its potential breadth, and we launched a pilot with Marcia Rose, the school's then teacher of Drama, who staged a translation/adaptation of Dario Fo's satirical play *Non si paga, non si paga*.[7]

Over the following three years Philippa Drummond, Head of Expressive Arts at Drummond, initiated and led a series of projects designed to explore questions of cultural translation and belonging through transnational artistic and critical practice. One year later, we began a similar collaboration at Castlebrae Community High School, another secondary school in Edinburgh, where we had been invited to work by Norma when she moved there on a temporary secondment that in the end became permanent.[8] Julie Philip, Head of Expressive Arts at Castlebrae, developed a series of parallel projects working in different artistic media.[9] Underpinned by the same

---

communicate in a variety of media, self-awareness, creativity and openness, and the appreciation of cultural diversity.

7   Readily available English versions of the play render the title in different ways suggestive of the creative space offered by translation as cultural practice: *Can't Pay? Won't Pay*, *They don't pay? We won't pay!* and *Low pay? Don't pay!*

8   Whereas Drummond Community High School is located in the centre of Edinburgh and has a mixed, multicultural intake, Castlebrae is on the city's outskirts in an area of multiple deprivation with a traditionally white and working-class student population.

9   The projects were curated under the title 'Art in Translation'. A video on the work with participant interviews can be found at <https://vimeo.com/158337501>.

research questions, the teachers' choice of different media through which to explore them offered evidence of the breadth of their possible applicability, but also of the need to find ways of expressing the questions that are relevant and inclusive with the respect to the interests and capacities of diverse constituencies. Reflecting on our research programme in light of the needs of our co-producers required a re-evaluation of how research could be disseminated. In the three years of our collaboration, project artwork was shown publicly at exhibitions in St Andrews, Edinburgh, and Cesena, as well as online.[10] It was also included in the two final TML exhibitions held in Rome and London, which constituted major research outputs.[11]

These art-based projects ran contemporaneously with the other strands of TML activity, so were neither secondary nor retrospective to the work of the academic research team. In essence, these projects were responding to the same research questions in a different critical medium. Although I had numerous conversations with Philippa and Julie about the overarching ideas that drove TML, it seemed essential for me to stand back and allow them to decide how to translate these ideas into the classroom setting. From the outset, I intuited that my own role was to stay in the background, barely an observer to a process that I had set in motion but did not have the necessary expertise to steer. My understanding of the role I was to play over the following years was very much inflected by Johannes Fabian's definition of how the ethnographer stands in relation to cultural performances they instigate to further their research: 'he or she is but a provider of occasions, a catalyst in the weakest sense, and a producer (in analogy to a theatrical

---

A shorter clip featuring the exhibition held at the Creative Exchange in Leith is at <https://www.youtube.com/watch?v=9QN5vOMW4yE&feature=youtu.be>. Further information on all the various projects and examples of the art work can be found on the Transnationalizing Modern Languages website. The site also contains information about art projects organized for adult learners at Drummond by Birgit Harris and interdisciplinary initiatives across art, social subjects and modern languages by Chris Hume and Tanya Smith at Castlebrae.

10 None of these exhibitions could have been staged without the commitment, support and creativity of Laura Pels Ferra and Kathleen Brown at the University of St Andrews.

11 Details and video clips of the two end-of-project exhibitions can be found on the TML website at <https://www.transnationalmodernlanguages.ac.uk/media-collection/exhibition-beyond-borders-transnational-italy/> [accessed 10 February 2020]. See also the three short essays on the process of staging the exhibitions by a member of the academic research team and the two curators: Derek Duncan, Giulia Grechi and Viviana Gravano, 'Beyond Borders: Transnational Italy', *Italian Studies* 74 (2019), 381–96.

producer) in the strongest'.[12] I saw myself at the weaker end of the scale, as a facilitator primarily providing the resource as well as the occasion for creative intervention. The art-work produced by these projects provided (among many other things) critical insight into how TML's academic research questions might be articulated in a different idiom. This knowledge offered particular insight into research as an ongoing and, indeed, time-consuming process, the value of which is not the singularity of a final output. The artwork also demonstrated the transformative role of creativity as a motor for research practice in its conceptualization, planning and realization.

Transnational Creative Practices

Pop Paolozzi! was the first of three projects led by Philippa involving pupils of different ages across the school. Starting with a general exploration of Paolozzi's work, the S1 pupils (aged 12–13) made site visits to the Scottish National Gallery of Modern Art, which houses a substantial Paolozzi collection, and to the shop that his parents ran at 10 Albert Street, quite close to the school. The fact that Paolozzi was a local as well as an internationally renowned artist added an important dimension of scale to this project and to the questions TML was investigating more broadly. The pupils also went to see *The Manuscript of Monte Cassino* (1991), his monumental three-piece commemorative sculpture situated outside the nearby St Mary's Metropolitan Cathedral, the traditional place of worship for Edinburgh's Italian community, which was attended by Paolozzi and his family in the 1930s.[13] The experiential, indeed tactile, dimension of the research led the students towards two

---

12   Johannes Fabian, *Power and Performance: ethnographic explorations through proverbial wisdom and theatre in Shaba, Zaire* (Madison, WI, and London: University of Wisconsin Press, 1990), p. 7.

13   The abbey of Monte Cassino, badly damaged in the Second World War, is close to Viticuso, the village in Lazio from where Paolozzi's family came. Latin text from the actual manuscript is inscribed on the ankle and foot. Paolozzi wrote that the text 'serves a double link between the Cathedral and the origins not only of my father and grandfather but to many Italians who came from these regions to make Scotland their home'. Quoted in Spencer, *Eduardo Paolozzi*, pp. 321–22. The sculpture also references Ludwig Wittgenstein, the Austrian philosopher, imprisoned at Cassino during the First World War, whose work, particularly on language, profoundly influenced Paolozzi. For a discussion of this link see Diego Mantoan and Luigi Persinotto, eds, *Paolozzi and Wittgenstein. The Artist and the Philosopher* (Basingstoke: Palgrave Macmillan, 2019).

different areas of his work: his use of vibrant colours, seen both in his early collages and in the ceramic work he designed for Tottenham Court Road Tube Station in London; and his interest in technology and mass production. Sweet packets recalling Paolozzi's childhood were used as the medium through which to investigate his use of colour, while the tubes and fittings used by plumbers provided the means through which to deepen an understanding of the artist's engagement with the mechanical world.[14] Pupils created their own prints, and the eight images felt to demonstrate most successfully the research done on Paolozzi's work were printed professionally at Edinburgh Printmakers Workshop and exhibited first at St Andrews University and then in Italy (Figure 5.1).

The exhibition was accompanied by a slideshow realized by Rachel Barnet and Thomas Munley, two second-year students of Italian at St Andrews who visited the school to talk to the pupils about their work and teach them some basic Italian. The slideshow begins and ends with the exhibition itself but mainly shows work in progress – sketches, paintings of sweets, circuit boards and piping, as well as photographs of the primary research material. The captions for the slideshow were in English and Italian. Some of them were hand-written, while others had been printed. Both contained what would conventionally been seen as errors of grammar and spelling. The retention of these linguistic imprecisions reinforced the premise that border-crossing cultural practices are always and necessarily in progress. Modifying them to adhere to the normative standard of either national language would misrepresent the site of their transnational provenance and utterance. This idea of cultural translation as work in progress informed all subsequent projects to underline the productively unfinished nature of any form of cultural exchange.

The second project was inspired by Paolozzi's interest in textiles. In the 1950s he taught textile design at the Central School in London. Later, he designed complex, brightly coloured tapestries, often as large-scale public commissions, some of which were woven at the Dovecot Studios in Edinburgh. Whereas *Pop Paolozzi!* was based in the local area, *Print Generation*, the second project, was more expansive, drawing self-consciously on the diversity of the pupils' cultural heritage to explore questions of transmission across both national and generational boundaries:

---

14   Paolozzi referred to such apparently insignificant objects as 'the sublime of everyday life'. Spencer, *Eduardo Paolozzi*, p. 88. The project was also part-funded by SNIPEF (Scottish and Northern Ireland Plumbing Employers' Federation), whose offices are close to the school.

Fig. 5.1: Artwork from *Pop Paolozzi!*

S3 students researched their own cultural heritage creating a dialogue between parents, grandparents and other family members. Their findings were then recorded in visual journals and took the form of patterns from various textile traditions and the design of family trees. Ten students were

'The Path that Leads Me Home' 135

Fig. 5.2: Slide from the *Pop Paolozzi!* presentation.

selected to participate in an artist-led workshop where the students learnt new techniques such as gelatin and intaglio printing. These delicately, layered prints reflect textile influences from countries such as Poland, Germany, England, Pakistan, Jamaica, Scotland, Australia and America and visually represent some of our research findings.[15]

Philippa emphasizes how research informed both the investigation into particular traditions of textile design and the production of new forms of artistic expression. By focusing their initial research on their families, the students were required to reflect on their own positionalities and identifications in relation to national traditions. This process of self-ethnography engaged the students in a conversation about lived quotidian transnational practice and dissolved any sense of tradition or belonging as self-evident. The opportunity to work with established artists invited into the project to communicate specific skills and techniques (Figure 5.3) led to the transformation of that sense of everyday inheritance. The students' very striking final prints are the creative research

15   Philippa Drummond, project brief.

Fig. 5.3: *Print Generation*: the printing process.

outputs of a process of formal and thematic investigation. The unprompted decision of each student to mix and combine rather than adhere to established national traditions and to blur formal boundaries in their artwork underscores the possibilities that research-led creative practice offers for the investigation of transnational cultural identity and mobility: '*I forgot it was meant to be related to our backgrounds.*'[16] Their prints are expressions of what Appadurai refers to as 'vernacular globalization'.[17]

The two projects briefly outlined were fundamental to how TML collectively was able to conceptualize Impact as an equal informing motor of research rather than as a derivative. Understanding creative practice as research activity in its own right fostered an appreciation of process as something more than simply an intermediate stage on the route to the finished outcome. New techniques suggested alternative pathways of investigation and again the durative nature of process as both a formal and expressive resource. Seeing the self as a critical limitation as well as a resource became an important lesson in

---

16   Quotes given in italics without attribution have been taken from anonymous feedback on the different projects.
17   Arjun Appadurai, *Modernity at Large: Cultural Dimensions of Globalization* (Minneapolis: University of Minnesota Press, 1996), p. 10.

methodology and practice as (self)enthography assumed a more pervasive role in our work. Skills and knowledge accrued through collaboration revealed the limitations of the single researcher as well as opening up opportunities for more expansive research mappings. The need for multiple voices and perspectives is affirmed by Katarzyna Marciniak and Bruce Bennett in their edited volume *Teaching Transnational Cinema*, where they point to the challenges to pedagogical competencies that working in a transnational context inevitably raises.[18] Films involving border crossing, whether aesthetic or geopolitical, rupture the confident imparting of knowledge premised on an area studies model of national exclusivity. Similarly, in the transnational or translingual classroom linguistic diversity may induce feelings of anxiety and disempowerment as teachers encounter languages that they don't know, or know less well than their students. Marciniak and Bennett reverse this apparent dilemma, insisting on the productive value of 'not-knowing' as a necessary moment of recognition in the development of transnational pedagogical practice. Indeed, attending to the experience of 'non-understanding' and learning to value and work with its generative impasses are fundamental skills in any process of language acquisition, and more broadly any apprenticeship in the humanities.

Finally, the question of how best to communicate research was raised by exhibiting publicly the art-work not simply as a mechanism of display but a shared, experiential, immersive medium and activity in which research was inhabited as an affective as well as intellectual mode of inquiry. Our perception of the value of investigating issues of transnational culture through the medium of artistic practice echoed the position of Mieke Bal on art and what she calls 'migratory aesthetics':

> The making of art is not an instance, an example to prove an academic point, nor an elevated form of cultural expression. Instead of these two things, which are equally problematic for a productive confrontation with the alleged otherness of migratory culture, it is a form of *facilitation* so that things can happen in a intercultural context that would not easily occur otherwise.[19]

---

18   Katarzyna Marciniak and Bruce Bennett, 'Introduction', in *Teaching Transnational Cinema: Politics and Pedagogy* (London and New York: Routledge, 2016), pp. 1–35 (esp. pp. 10–15).
19   Mieke Bal, 'Documenting What? Auto-Theory and Migratory Aesthetics', in *A Companion to Documentary Film*, ed. by Alexandra Juhasz and Alisa Lebow (Chichester and Malden, MA: Wiley Blackwell, 2015), pp. 124–44 (pp. 138–39).

I will now discuss briefly three further art projects that exemplify how Impact work properly constituted as 'forms of facilitation' can inform and enhance academic research agendas. All three draw on aspects of Paolozzi's work to stretch the disciplinary boundaries of transnational research and pedagogical practice. Yet perhaps their most potent effects were personal.

BOLT!

> THE PAST – pressing objects into a clay bed, pouring wax, making diagrams, charts of events, objects in bronze from the art founders ... THE PRESENT – wooden shapes cast in gun metal by engineers assembled like ships by BOLT & WELD. (Paolozzi)

One of Paolozzi's best-known pieces is Vulcan, an eight-metre-high sculpture in steel plate made for the Scottish National Gallery of Modern Art.[20] A maquette of the sculpture is held in St Andrews University's museum.[21] However, Paolozzi's exploration of the interface between the human and the mechanical world long predated his massive metallic statue of 1999. He had taught at the art school in Hamburg in the early 1960s, where he explored the city's shipyards and scrapyards, fascinated by the idea of prefabrication and by how ready-made pieces might be combined and used in new ways to create alternative objects and insights.[22]

In an interview with Édouard Roditi in 1960, Paolozzi talked about the pull of 'ordinary objects' and how he subjected them to multiple transformations to turn them into sculptural art:

> I work mainly with *objets trouvés*. Well I often feel if one of us chances to find a particularly nice and spooky-looking piece of junk like an old discarded boiler, he can scarcely avoid using it as a trunk or body of a figure, if only because its shape suggests a body to anyone who sets out to do this kind of assembly-work. Then one only needs to weld something

---

20 For an image of the sculpture and a brief description see <https://www.national-galleries.org/art-and-artists/54424/vulcan> [accessed 10 February 2020].
21 For an image of the maquette see <https://www.st-andrews.ac.uk/adlib/Details/collect/2845> [accessed 10 February 2020].
22 Jon Wood, 'The Silver Sixties: Paolozzi's Sculpture Abroad', in *Eduardo Paolozzi*, ed. by Herrmann, pp. 150–61 (p. 155).

smaller onto the top to suggest a head, and four limb-like bits and pieces onto the sides and bottom to suggest arms and legs, and there you have the whole figure, which has come to life like a traditional Golem or robot ... .[23]

Paolozzi's monumental sculptural work and his aesthetic of the repurposed object provided a springboard for a project based at Castlebrae. *BOLT!* was a figure approximately eight feet tall constructed out of recycled materials, a creative quotation of Vulcan (Figure 5.4). The trunk was made out of two water containers and the limbs of discarded plastic parts and copper wire. Once complete, the sculpture was painted a luminescent industrial black.

The piece was the work of the Young Achievers, a group of eight or so boys with a range of educational challenges taught outside the regular curriculum in a planned programme of experiential and outside learning. The programme was directed by James Donald, Future Improvement Co-ordinator at the school, who had lived in Italy and retained a particular interest in Italian language and culture. Most of the boys had low literacy levels in English and were unlikely to engage productively with conventional modes of language teaching. In keeping with the group emphasis on experiential learning, James devised a programme of study in which the boys gained hands-on, practical contact with Italian culture. They cooked Italian food, made an outdoor pizza oven out of concrete and took photographs in the style of Oscar Marzaroli, the Italian-born Scottish photographer best known for his black and white images of working-class Glaswegian children in the 1960s. One of the classroom walls became the 'Muro' on which they recorded their work and the vocabulary they learned.

BOLT! was, however, their most significant initiative. Constructed over a number of weeks, it was first shown at a TML workshop held in Castlebrae School, and then as part of a larger exhibition at the Byre Theatre in St Andrews. A number of the artists travelled to St Andrews to see the exhibit and, for many, this trip was the first time they had been out of Edinburgh. Some also presented the work to participants at the Castlebrae workshop, explaining their role and the process of its construction. The participants were mostly academics from UK universities as well as from Italy and their unusual presence in the environment of Castlebrae significantly altered the meaning of the school as a cultural space. The presenters often

---

23 Spencer, *Eduardo Paolozzi*, p. 88.

Fig. 5.4: Making *BOLT!*

had to modify their pronunciation and lexical choices to compensate for the inability of participants to understand what they heard as heavily accented English. For the artists, the experience was transformative in significant ways, as they saw that what they had been doing could be perceived as a significant cultural intervention. The opportunity to talk publicly about this work also led to shifts in self-perception: *'Lots of people are interested in what I do.'*

By reworking the idiom of its expression (polished steel to painted debris), its location (temple of modernist high culture to council estate) and the set of cultural responses it engenders, *BOLT!* translates Paolozzi's Vulcan in myriad ways. Arguably, the work involved transforming discarded and waste material into art, yet *BOLT!* can also be read in terms of the Young Achievers' own process of transformative self-translation as they moved into the public sphere through the space of Italian culture. In this sense, *BOLT!* is more than the painted figure made out of debris, but is rather the cumulative set of mostly intangible, yet nevertheless transformative, effects brought about through improvised, transnationalizing practices of communication and relationality.

Castlebrae in the World

> The transnational is not bound by the binary of the local and the global and can occur in national, local or global spaces across different and multiple spatialities. (Lionnet and Shih)

Castlebrae in the World was the umbrella name given to the series of projects led by Julie Philip at Castlebrae that aimed to create spaces of global connectivity for pupils whose local area was marked by social deprivation and cultural isolation. Around the time these projects started, one of Paolozzi's most famous and certainly most seen public projects was the focus of significant media attention. The brightly coloured mosaics that he had designed for Tottenham Court Road tube station in London were threatened by renovation works, but after a public campaign it was decided to preserve as much of the mosaic installation as possible.[24] Paolozzi had said that he wanted the mosaics to represent, on a metaphoric level, the vibrant multicultural life above ground, a response that again has been seen as symptomatic of Paolozzi's Italian heritage.[25] Julie recognized in the tiles and in their story a way of

---

24 Gary Drostle, who was involved in restoring the mosaics, gives an informative and insightful account of the process: <https://www.drostle.com/recreating-paolozzis-great-mosaics-for-tottenham-court-road/> [accessed 10 February 2020].

25 Richard Cork, 'Art and the London Underground: From Marinetti to Paolozzi', in *Eduardo Paolozzi Underground*, ed. by Richard Cork (London: Weidenfeld and Nicolson, 1986), pp. 28–42 (p. 40).

capturing pupils' interest in the global afterlife of a local artist. Julie felt that the vibrancy of Paolozzi's palette, the mosaics' strong narrative and the tactile dimension of the medium itself would appeal to pupils with uneven levels of literacy and technical accomplishment. The pupils produced a range of striking ceramic tiles reminiscent of Paolozzi's large-scale panels. However, the project assumed a more significant, transnational dimension when it was extended to a group of adult learners attending English language classes at the school. The students came from a wide range of countries, including China, Spain, Poland, Hungary and the Sudan, and English was their own *lingua franca*. At this point, the project became transnational on an experiential level and the art room at Castlebrae the site of a series of unplanned cultural encounters. In the initial stages of the shared project, the school pupils, who were slightly more experienced in working with clay, led skill exchange sessions with the adult learners. These sessions were the first time that members of either group had come into direct contact. School pupils learned not only to explain ceramic techniques but also how to communicate with people with varying levels of proficiency in English. As the relationship developed, the adult learners began to teach the pupils more about their own cultures and languages.

> *I have worked with two groups of ESOL [English for Speakers of Other Languages] students. It was a really different and unique experience as we don't usually have the opportunity to work with adults in any other subject at school. I enjoyed teaching them some clay techniques, my teacher said I was good at explaining things, especially to people who did not come from Scotland. I learned some new facts about their countries.*

Collectively, the groups produced larger-scale tiles that graphically brought different cultures and traditions into proximity: 'People in Sudan and throughout Arabic countries, shake hands when they greet, like in Scotland.'

Like *Bolt!*, but in very different ways, the transformative value of the project lay in the relationships that it allowed to happen and the transnational connections that it forged. While the pupils were exposed to a multiplicity of languages and cultures through the project, they did not engage in language learning as such, yet nevertheless developed and practised skills of translation and inter-cultural mediation that modern languages as a discipline fosters.[26]

---

26   Michael Warton's highly influential HEFCE 'Review of Modern Foreign Languages provision in higher education in England (2009)' <https://discovery.ucl.ac.uk/id/eprint/329251/2/hereview-worton.pdf> [accessed 10 February 2020] refers to a

An emphasis on participation at a local level allows the transnational to be apprehended as an integral feature of everyday experience: *'We are studying English and living in Scotland so we want to settle here and that's what the tile is about.'*

As mentioned, the overarching aim of the *Castlebrae in the World* initiative was to encourage pupils experiencing often quite a high degree of social isolation to see themselves as globally connected. The success of the ceramics project was to domesticate that connectivity by revealing it to be an existing albeit previously unattended-to aspect of what was already close to hand. In addition to the personal validation that this might have given the pupils, the exhibitions also contributed to the award of an SQA National 5 qualification in Creative Industries.[27] Thirty-six pupils have gained this award, part of the SQA's 'Skills for Work' programme, one of the stated aims of which is to 'help young people develop their self-confidence'.[28] The success of these art projects is difficult to calibrate, but does not reside solely in an evaluation of the quality of the art-work. The development of self-confidence in transnational communication requires different tools of assessment. One way of thinking of this in relation to the work of the project is in terms of Doris Sommer's contention: 'Success in art and everything else depends on coproduction.'[29] Coproduction elevated the making of ceramic tiles in imitation of Paolozzi's Tottenham Court Road mosaics into a transformative instance of transnational education.

> The images are the panda from China and the flower too, and the snow leopard and jasmine are from Pakistan, as well as the traditional food, the samosas and the dumplings. And we have the buildings, the Badshahi Majid, the largest mosque in Lahore, and the flags. And over here the Scottish flag

potential '"lost generation" of linguists and inter-cultural thinkers' in light of the by-now well-attested decline in the availability and take-up of languages in UK education. I would suggest that the projects outlined in this essay indicate how higher-order 'inter-cultural thinking' may be developed in other curriculum areas as a means of supporting language learning and recognizing linguistic knowledge and skills acquired outside the curriculum by, for example, often fluent and flexible home speakers.

27 Details of the award can be accessed at <https://www.sqa.org.uk/sqa/69525.html> [accessed 10 February 2020].
28 Details of this programme can be accessed at <https://www.sqa.org.uk/sqa/79148.9433.html> [accessed 10 February 2020].
29 Doris Sommer, *The Work of Art in the World: Civic Agency and Public Humanities* (Durham, NC, and London: Duke University Press, 2014), p. 8.

and the local castle to here, Craigmillar Castle, and a bag of chips, and a fox. We'd like to do more of this in the future. Its been fun working with the clay, and working together.

The development of a shared artistic mode of expression between pupils and adult learners, native and non-native speakers of English, realized through the work in clay is an instance of what Mezzadra and Neilson refer to as an 'improvised patois', a strategy of successful communication between those without a shared language. It is, they contend, '[t]he discourse of foreigner to foreigner, which creates a language that is common precisely because it is forever in translation and rooted in material practices of co-operation, organization, and struggle.'[30] While Julie 'facilitated' (to reprise Fabian's term) the work, the lived, vernacular experience of intercultural exchange conducted in English across languages and through the medium of art reinvents the meaning of locality, just as it revises understandings of the imprint of biography or ethnicity on artistic practice.

Leonardo

The idea of innovation is linked to the idea of translation. (Paolozzi)

The idea or, rather, practice of translation was central to *Leonardo*, undoubtedly the most technically complex of all the projects undertaken. Devised by Philippa Drummond, it used the notebooks of Leonardo da Vinci as a starting point to explore the interest that he and Paolozzi shared in scientific innovation and interactions between technology and the human body.[31] As a student at art school in Edinburgh, Paolozzi had honed his drawing technique by tracing Leonardo's sketches, and the Italian artist and polymath was a recurrent figure in his work.[32] More pertinently, in 1986 he created the

---

30 Sandro Mezzadra and Brett Neilson, *Border as Method, or, the Multiplication of Labor* (Durham, NC: Duke University Press, 2013), p. 275.
31 A quotation from Leonardo's *Notebooks* is inscribed on Paolozzi's sculpture *Head of Invention* at Butler's Wharf in London. The piece is a homage to James Watt, the Scottish inventor.
32 Collins recalls that a cloth reproduction of Da Vinci's *Last Supper* purchased from Indian travelling salesmen had been the only work of art in Paolozzi's family home (p. 18). Elly Thomas notes Paolozzi's stated preference for a carpet with an image of the Mona Lisa over the painting itself attributing this preference to his 'fascination with the processes by

large-scale sculpture *For Leonardo,* which sits outside the Alte Pinakotek in Munich, named in semi-ironic homage to the Renaissance polymath. Inspired by sci-fi artist Davis Meltzer's illustration of human cancer cell activity visible only through a microscope, Paolozzi's cast iron piece translates Meltzer's already translated stylization into an accessible piece of public art.

Leonardo was delivered as an 'Interdisciplinary Learning Project' (IDL) followed by a group of pupils in their final year of study, mostly specializing in science subjects. This elective art class required them to translate their established interests into a different disciplinary idiom. Whereas *Pop Paolozzi!* and *Print Generation* had been elaborated conceptually in relation to specific places, *Leonardo* worked with ideas of mobility, mediation and processes of transformation at a more abstract level. The dense lesson plan reproduced below sets out the ways in which multiple processes and practices of intermedial translation were explored over the ten weeks of *Leonardo*'s duration.[33] Beginning with an historical investigation into Leonardo's *Notebooks,* the students then undertook a series of intense formal experiments involving different techniques and technologies of representation. The students drew, photographed and documented their research in handmade books and on iPads, exploring scale as well as perspective. They identified key terms relating to their specific projects, which were then translated into Italian with the help of Jacopo Colombini, a PhD student at St Andrews and member of the TML team. These words were then subjected to an additional transformation through the use of mirror writing, a technique adopted by Leonardo himself as a means of making his own notes less legible to other people. The high point of the ten weeks was a visit to Edinburgh Printmakers, where students were introduced to photo-lithography colour printing under the guidance of studio director Alastair Clark.[34] The students had already prepared sketches of their work on acetate (Figure 5.5).

> Photo-lithography is based on the premise that oil and water do not mix. Students exposed their acetates onto light-sensitive aluminium photo plates. The positive marks (their line drawings) repelled water. A wet

---

which images shift through translation': *Play and the Artist's Creative Process: The Work of Philip Guston and Eduardo Paolozzi* (New York: Routledge, 2019), p. 65.

33   I am very grateful to Philippa Drummond for giving permission to reproduce her course outline. It gives an excellent insight into the quality and quantity of work demanded of the pupils in the course of the project.

34   Alastair explains and demonstrates this technique in an illuminating video: <https://www.youtube.com/watch?v=8Cf-e_a2gxY> [accessed 10 February 2020].

Fig. 5.5: Leonardo: the printing process.

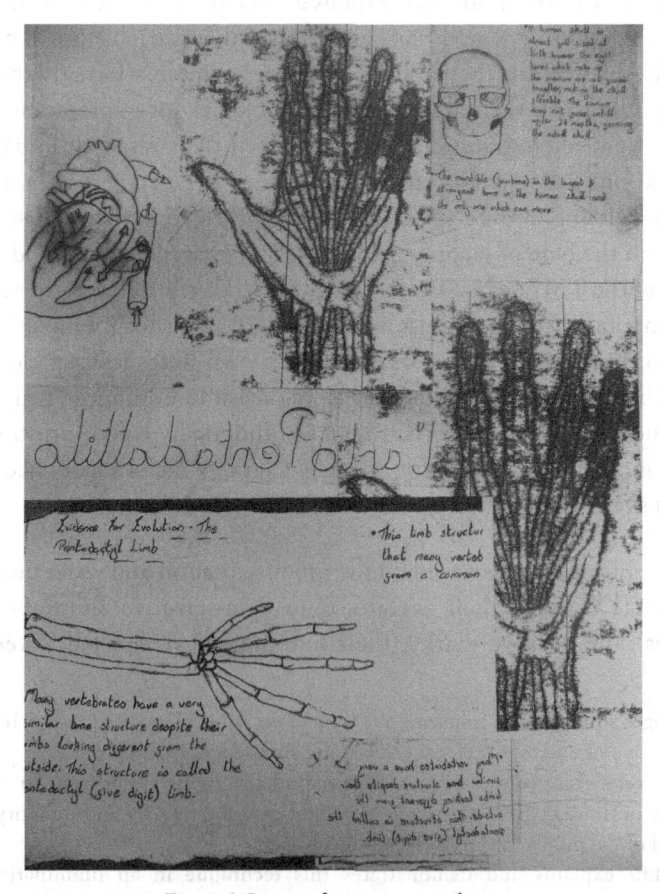

Fig. 5.6: Leonardo: science and art.

sponge is then wiped over the plate, and the water sits only in the negative areas. When the oil-based ink is later applied it does not lie in these negative spaces (or gaps), only in the drawn lines. The prints successfully captured the sensitivity of their drawings and text, which were later printed using a litho press in coloured layers onto paper.[35]

Leonardo notebooks: observation and invention

Week 1 Introduction to TML project
PPT Introduction to Leonardo's notebooks
Leonardo Alphabet Activity

Students select a discipline to work within, e.g. Geology, Astronomy, Botany, Architecture, Engineering etc.

Week 2 Observational drawings of selected objects
White pencil on black paper. Different angles and viewpoints
Week 3 Observational studies based on selected objects
Brown pen on white paper
Create a handmade sketchbook for the museum trip
Week 4 Visit to National Museums of Scotland

Using iPads, photograph objects from the collection that relate to selected themes. Five-minute observational sketches of the objects photographed.

Week 5 Visit of Jacopo Colombini from the Italian department at St Andrews

Pupils work collaboratively with students to select key vocabulary to translate into Italian. Mirror writing activity. Mono-printing key words on a variety of scales.

Week 6 Developing design ideas for inventions based on observational studies

Students matched with a mentor/teacher from another subject. Dialogue on key features/characteristics of the objects, plant, animals etc. they have drawn.

---

35   Philippa Drummond, private communication, 19 February 2020.

> Week 7   Creating small 3D models of their inventions or doing 2D sketches
>
> Week 8   Photographing models and composing acetates of their work. Layering of observational drawings, mirror writing and models.
>
> Ten students were selected to go to Edinburgh Printmakers workshop for a whole day of printing.

The constant shifting across media and technical processes as a means of investigating both the formal properties of the material world and technologies for their reproduction/representation mirrors the creativity inherent in all forms of translation. The immiscibility of oil and water through which the prints are realized in a series of transformative stages is highly suggestive of the productive work of difference manifest in practices of intercultural translation. In the final section of the project, the pupils began to think about their inventions in terms of biomimicry, moving beyond a transcultural aesthetic to effect what might be called a real-world intervention (Figure 5.6). This move affirms Paolozzi's sense of the contingent dynamics of translation and innovation. Biomimicry is a modality of trans-thinking emphasizing connection rather than division. The Biomimicry Institute itself claims, for instance, that 'Biomimicry offers an empathetic, interconnected understanding of how life works and ultimately where we fit in',[36] a definition resonating with the more inclusive yet difficult understandings of the transnational encounter, returning the technological to the human body.

By Way of Conclusions

> Minor transnational subjects are invariably invested in their respective geopolitical spaces often waiting to be recognized as 'citizens' to receive the attendant privileges of full citizenship. (Lionnet and Shih)

Feedback on all the art projects emphasized how enjoyable they had been (Figure 5.7). Artists enjoyed, among many other things, the tactile sensations of working with clay, the visits to Edinburgh Printmakers and seeing their work on

---

36   <https://biomimicry.org/what-is-biomimicry/> [accessed 3 September 2020].

'The Path that Leads Me Home' 149

Fig. 5.7: Enjoyment.

display in the exhibitions. While such pleasure is not to be sniffed at, and indeed should stand, in some form, at the core of any creative project and process, attention to what Sommer calls the 'ripple effects' of collective art practice may sharpen the sense of where the pleasure actually lies and what the stakes of pleasure might actually be.[37] This pleasure exceeds the parochial cheeriness with which community multicultural initiatives are sometimes received.

These 'ripple effects' are palpable in this arresting reflection by one of the artists at Castlebrae (Figure 5.8): *'In my tile I wanted to make it look like I am part of the landscape looking out over Arthur's Seat, Salisbury Crags and down the path to my home in Craigmiller [...] My favorite tile is the one with my eye and the path that leads me home.'* To create an artwork in the hope of seeing

---

37 Sommer, *Work of Art in the World*, p. 7.

Fig. 5.8: 'The path that leads me home'.

oneself as 'part of the landscape' implies an almost exorbitant investment in what art might achieve. It equally invites speculation on both the degree of cultural dispossession that makes such an investment sought after in the first place and on the optimism of the search for the 'path' that might lead home. Carolyn Steedman writes about the 'landscape' in similarly disconcerting terms as a figure of aspiration in the child's critical imagination. It is the core metaphor in her interpretative reconstruction of her working-class mother's life at the margins of social acceptability, and her own entanglement with it: 'Where is the place that you move into the landscape and can see yourself?'[38]

38   Carolyn Steedman, *Landscape for a Good Woman: A Story of Two Lives* (London: Virago, 1986), p. 142.

The point of moving into the landscape is to move into 'historical time, one of the places where vision establishes the child's understanding of herself as part of the world'.[39] As noted earlier, the hope that pupils and adult learners might become 'part of the world' lay behind *Castlebrae in the World* as a project of cultural intervention. For me, this hope echoes that expressed by Eve Sedgwick in her essay on the possible achievements of intense cultural engagement:

> Hope, often a fracturing, even a traumatic thing to experience, is among the energies by which the reparatively positioned reader tries to organize the fragments and part-objects she encounters or creates. Because the reader has room to realize that the future may be different from the present, it is also possible for her to entertain such profoundly painful, profoundly relieving, ethically crucial possibilities that the past, in turn, could have happened differently from the way it actually did.[40]

Few artists can have worked more consistently with 'fragments and part-objects' than Paolozzi, who was enduringly unsure of his own place in the landscape. Writing in 2000, some years before Paolozzi's death, Spencer suggests that this ambivalence lay behind his initial identification with Wittgenstein and 'his own feeling of living in an alien world': 'For all the honours he has been awarded, Paolozzi still feels Italian, and an outsider. For him acts of genius, whether of philosophy, technology, or art, have added poignancy when performed by individuals on the margins of a society, or by people who are its victims ... .'[41] This sense of ambivalence or alienation complicates the path from ethnicity to artistic production referred to at the beginning of this essay. In his interview with Roditi, Paolozzi makes the point that his sculptures are not made of the *objets trouvés* themselves, but of casts in the form of the original pieces. The *objets trouvés* 'survive in [his] sculptures only as ghosts of forms that still haunt the bronze'.[42] This haunting perhaps offers a way of thinking about how Paolozzi figures the shadow of life's imprint on art, and also art's capacity to represent haunting as a modality of living.

39 Steedman, *Landscape*, p. 143.
40 Eve Kosofsky Sedgwick, *Touching Feeling: Affect, Pedagogy, Performativity* (Durham, NC, and London: Duke University Press, 2003), p. 146.
41 Spencer, 'Introduction,' in *Eduardo Paolozzi*, pp. 1–43 (pp. 3–4).
42 Spencer, *Eduardo Paolozzi*, p. 90.

In his memoirs, Paolozzi recalled a childhood lived across cultures. Born and brought up in Edinburgh, he was sent by his father to attend summer camps in Italy run by the Fascist government, an experience he remembered with great fondness. In 1940, after Italy entered the Second World War, Paolozzi and other male members of his family were arrested and imprisoned. While he was released after three months, his father, uncle and grandfather all died aboard the *Arandora Star*, a requisitioned liner carrying 'enemy aliens', mostly Italian and German nationals, resident in the UK to Canada.[43] Torpedoed by a German submarine, the ship sank with the loss of 865 lives. For Paolozzi, Herrmann reflects, '[t]he events were formative'.[44] The fatal consequences of compromised citizenship weighed heavily on Scotland's historic Italian community.[45] Paolozzi's deformed, brutalized figurative sculptures of the 1950s have been seen as expressive of the violence of the Second World War. Hal Foster asks a perhaps provocative question that goes straight to the heart of the mimetic impulse informing some readings of his work: 'Could it be that Paolozzi brutalised his figures in order to register not only the violence of this historical process but also to recoup that very violence as a belated form of protection against it?'[46] Might the same question be asked about *Bolt!* and the reparative energies its makers put into and extracted from its creation?

A further haunted deformation, symptomatic of his compromised citizenship, could be heard in Paolozzi's voice or accent, which Raymond Mason, his fellow sculptor, felt was at odds with where he was from: 'He [Paolozzi] said he was Italian and that he had been brought up in Leith, but he expressed himself in a chipped English much nearer Mayfair.'[47] Similarly,

43 For more details on the sinking of the *Arandora Star* and the memorial in St Peter's Italian Church, London, see the chapter by Jennifer Burns in this volume.
44 Herrmann, 'Eduardo Paolozzi: Pop Art Redefined,' p. 10.
45 A memorial to the Scots–Italians lost on the *Arandora Star* was inaugurated in St Andrews Cathedral in Glasgow only in 2011, after a long campaign. See <http://www.italiancloister.org.uk/> [accessed 10 February 2020]. Other, albeit smaller, memorials can be now found across the UK and in Italy. For an account of the sinking see Terri Colpi, *The Italian Factor: The Italian Community in Great Britain* (Edinburgh and London: Mainstream Publishing 1991), pp. 115–29. Colpi also lists the names of the Italian men lost at sea, including those of Paolozzi's father, Alfonso, and his maternal grandfather and great uncle, Pietro and Emilio Rossi.
46 Hal Foster, 'Ikons of Survival', in *Eduardo Paolozzi*, ed. by Herrmann, pp. 30–41 (35).
47 Quoted in Collins, *Eduardo Paolozzi*, p. 21.

in an episode of Radio 4's *Great Lives* dedicated to Paolozzi, Matthew Parris, Antonio Carluccio and Christopher Frayling debate inconclusively the artist's hybrid, yet undoubtedly noteworthy, pronunciation.[48] Speculatively, the unlocatability of Paolozzi's accented voice is the 'found object' of a transnational subject articulating the embodied ambivalence of an acclaimed artist whose life was played out in the shadow of the uncertain entitlements of full national citizenship. The ESOL students at Castlebrae were, of course, working towards qualifications attesting to their proficiency in English in order to apply successfully for permanent residence or naturalization: *'The students' confidence increased markedly as the weeks went by both in terms of working with the clay and talking about it. It has been very good for their spoken English.'* Their marked voices, like those of Paolozzi, and indeed of the school pupils, are, for those closer to the centre, audible signs of marginality. These varying linguistic investments in cultural belonging illuminate Rey Chow's suggestion that 'language is where the often perilous crossings of epistemic thresholds leave their material traces.'[49]

Over the course of these experiments in transnational pedagogy, Paolozzi's work has been an invaluable resource and source of infinitely varied inspiration. Simon Martin's assessment of the mosaics in Tottenham Court Road as forming 'one vast collage that sums up Paolozzi's non-hierarchical approach to culture in the widest sense of the word'[50] anticipates a way of conceptualizing inter-cultural education respondent to the possibilities of local connectivity. The collaborations that his work fostered have been creative and instructive, and shed light on and expressed deep tensions in feelings of belonging, place, mobility and citizenship. They have been about cultures of translation and about the adaptive skills required through transnational practices of communication. They echo Sommer's claims that 'full citizenship requires high-order literacy'[51] and that 'citizenship' is about 'participation rather than legal status'.[52] The 'ripple effects' of such work are, however, perhaps best encapsulated by

---

48 *Great Lives: Eduardo Paolozzi*. Radio 4. First broadcast 23 August 2011. Available at <https://www.bbc.co.uk/sounds/play/b013f976> [accessed 10 February 2020].
49 Rey Chow, 'On Captivation: A Remainder from the "Distinction between Art and Non-Art" written with Julian Rohrhuber', in *Entanglements, Or Transmedial Thinking about Capture* (Durham, NC: Duke University Press, 2012), pp. 31–58 (p. 33).
50 Simon Martin, *Eduardo Paolozzi: Collaging Cultures* (Chichester: Pallant House, 2013), p. 100.
51 Sommer, *Work of Art in the World*, p. 6.
52 Sommer, *Work of Art in the World*, p. 112.

Sedgwick's summative assessment of not unrelated cultural work: 'What we can best learn from such practices are, perhaps the many ways selves and communities succeed in extracting sustenance from the objects of a culture – even of a culture whose avowed desire has often been not to sustain them.'[53]

53 Sedgwick, *Touching Feeling*, pp. 150–51.

CHAPTER SIX

Moving Objects: Memory and Material Culture

Margaret Hills de Zárate

Objects and People

The relationship between people and objects in contemporary material culture studies is described by one of the area's most prolific authors in the UK, Daniel Miller, as an 'integrative' field, drawing across disciplines to examine a 'core relationship between objects and people'.[1] Such an approach challenges 'the historical disciplinary division between the social and natural sciences, where materials have been designated as the methodological and empirical domains of the natural sciences and culture and social relations as the domains of the social sciences'.[2] Instead, culture and society are understood by some authors as being created and reproduced by the ways in which people make, design and interact with objects. This view proposes that things make people as much as people make things.[3] In seeing the material properties of things as central to the meanings an object might have, the main proponents of this view of material culture studies are critical of the idea that objects are merely symbols that represent aspects of a pre-existing culture or identity.[4] The key area of

---

1 Daniel Miller, 'Things Ain't What They Used to Be', *Royal Anthropological Institute News*, 59 (1983), 5–7 (p. 7).
2 Sophie Woodward, 'Object Interviews, Material Imaginings and "Unsettling" Methods: Interdisciplinary Approaches to Understanding Materials and Material Culture', *Qualitative Research*, 16 (2016), 359–74.
3 See Daniel Miller, *Stuff* (Cambridge: Polity, 2009), p. 22.
4 See Alfred Gell, *Art and Agency: An Anthropological Theory* (Oxford: Clarendon 1998); Daniel Miller, *Material Culture and Mass Consumption* (Oxford: Basil Blackwell,

contestation in the literature on material culture thus rests on the question of agency and the ways in which objects can produce particular effects and allow, orientate and permit certain behaviours or cultural practices.[5]

Agency and Objectification

The question of agency is developed by Miller through the concept of objectification.[6] This notion is central to the many studies that seek to explore the intertwined, and often dialectic, relationships between people and things: that is to say, how things, once created, work themselves to reproduce or transform the social contexts in which they are encountered and move;[7] or, as Miller puts it, 'social worlds are as much constituted by materiality as the other way around.'[8]

Objectification is a concept that provides a certain way of understanding the relationship between subjects and objects. It 'attempts to overcome the dualism in modern empiricist thought in which subjects and objects are regarded as utterly different and opposed entities, respectively human and non-human, living and inert, active and passive'.[9] As noted by Tilley, 'Through making, using, exchanging, consuming, interacting and living with things people make themselves in the process ... without the things – material culture – we could neither be ourselves nor know ourselves. Material culture is thus conceived as being inseparable from culture and human society.'[10] The concept of objectification can already be located in the

1987); Miller, *Stuff*; Christopher Tilley, *Metaphor and Material Culture* (Oxford: Blackwell, 1999).
5   See Woodward, 'Object Interviews, Material Imaginings and "Unsettling" Methods'; also Sophie Woodward, 'Material Culture', *Oxford Bibliographies* (2013), available at <https://www.oxfordbibliographies.com/view/document/obo-9780199766567/> [accessed 29 February 2020].
6   See Miller, *Material Culture and Mass Consumption*; and, by the same author, 'Why Some Things Matter', in *Material Culture: Why Some Things Matter*, ed. by Daniel Miller (Chicago, IL: University of Chicago Press, 1998), pp. 3–25.
7   Tilley, *Metaphor and Material Culture*, p. 76.
8   Miller, 'Why Some Things Matter', p. 3.
9   Christopher Tilley, 'Objectification', in *Handbook of Material Culture*, ed. by Christopher Tilley, Webb Keane, Susanne Küchler, Mike Rowlands and Patricia Spyer (London: Sage, 2006), pp. 60–73 (p. 61).
10   Tilley, 'Objectification', p. 61.

work of Cooley and his discussion of the 'looking glass self'.[11] Hicks notes that 'the varieties of material culture studies that developed in the 1980s built upon the emergence of "material culture" as an object of enquiry in twentieth-century archaeology and anthropology, which in turn developed from museum-based studies of "technology" and so called "primitive art" during the late nineteenth century.'[12] Material culture has been central to anthropology since its inception and, as Hoskins points out,

> anthropologists since Mauss (1924; 1954) and Malinowski (1922) have asserted that the lines between persons and things are culturally variable, and not drawn in the same way in all societies. In certain contexts, persons can seem to take on the attributes of things and things can seem to act almost as persons.[13]

In short, an historical overview of 'objectification' points to studies of traditional exchange systems and to research that details how objects can be given a gender, name, history and ritual function while, at the same time, some people have their very humanity depreciated, so as to approach the status of objects.[14] When a person internalizes the perspective of the other, of an external observer, self-objectification occurs. Taking such a third-person perspective of the self is not unusual; on the contrary, all people can and do think about the self as an object at various times.[15] As

11   Charles Horton Cooley, *Human Nature and the Social Order* [1902] (New York: Charles Scribner's Sons, 1922), pp. 152–53.
12   Dan Hicks, 'The Material-Cultural Turn: Event and Effect', in *The Oxford Handbook of Material Culture Studies*, ed. by Dan Hicks and Mary C. Beaudry (Oxford: Oxford University Press, 2010), pp. 25–98 (p. 26).
13   Janet Hoskins, 'Agency, Biography and Objects', in *The Oxford Handbook of Material Culture*, ed. by Hicks and Beaudry, pp. 74–84 (p. 75); see also Woodward, 'Material Culture'; and Hannah Arendt, *The Origins of Totalitarianism* (London: Penguin Modern Classics, 1968).
14   On these topics see Arendt; Hoskins; Igor Kopytoff, 'Slavery', *Annual Review of Anthropology*, 11 (1982), 207–30; Igor Kopytoff and Suzanne Miers, 'African "Slavery" as an Institution of Marginality. Introduction', in *Slavery in Africa: Historical and Anthropological Perspectives*, ed. by S. Miers and I. Kopytoff (Madison: University of Wisconsin Press, 1977), pp. 1–81; Martha C. Nussbaum, 'Objectification', *Philosophy & Public Affairs*, 24 (1995), 279–83.
15   Cooley; see also Diane M. Quinn, Stephenie R. Chaudoir and Rachel W. Kallen, 'Self-Objectification and Performance: A Review and Integration', in *Self-Objectification in Women: Causes, Consequences, and Counteractions*, ed. by Rachel. M. Calegero, Stacey

Strathern suggests: 'People objectify or present themselves to themselves in innumerable ways but must always do so through assuming a specific form. It is also the case that persons are objects of the regard of others, through performances of all kinds.'[16]

Event as Object

Strathern also maintains that 'the idea of a concrete, incidental event holds much the same place in the anthropological worldview as does the idea of a concrete, incidental artefact.'[17] In her view, 'a certain perception of event is implied in the way that Western anthropologists have often understood the work of historians, which mirrors the way they have also understood museologists and those interested in material culture.'[18] This leads her to suggest that we should extend our concept of artefact or object to performance and to events.

This perspective has been helpful in thinking about the numerous group events I participated in throughout the course of the research I carried out as part of the Transnationalizing Modern Languages (TML) project,[19] which involved liaising with the multitude of Italian societies and associations in Buenos Aires. Through these contacts I was able to hold a series of 'object workshops' and individual interviews. As an ethnographer can adapt and draw upon a mix of methods appropriate to a situation, so research and data collection take the form of diverse experiences. An open as opposed to closely structured format was preferred for both workshops and interviews, as it is only as the conversation progresses that the next question emerges in the 'co-production of ethnographic knowledge, created and represented in the only way it can be, within an interactive Self/Other dialogue'.[20]

Tantleff-Dunn and J. Kevin Thompson (Washington, DC: American Psychological Association, 2011), pp. 119–38.

16   Marilyn Strathern, 'Artifacts of History: Events and the Interpretation of Images', in *Culture and History in the Pacific*, ed. by Jukka Siikala (Helsinki: Transactions of the Finnish Anthropological Society, 1990), pp. 154–78 (p. 158).

17   Strathern, p. 159.

18   Strathern, p. 174.

19   For a description of the research project 'Transnationalizing Modern Languages', see the Introduction to this volume.

20   Barbara Tedlock, 'From Participant Observation to the Observation of Participation: The Emergence of Narrative Ethnography', *Journal of Anthropological Research*, 47 (1991), 69–94 (p. 82).

Pre-existing published scholarship on the Italian societies in Buenos Aires provides us with the historical background to the settings in which my research for TML took place, situating it within the context of Argentine nation building. The oldest of these Italian societies was founded by artisans and businessmen of the Risorgimento in the 1850s. Many of those who established the first mutual benefit society for workers – 'Unione e Benevolenza' [Union and Benevolence], founded in 1858 – were political exiles from the First Italian War of Independence (1848–1849) and were decidedly Republican.[21] Political and religious aspects were formally excluded from the activities and deliberations of the organization, with the exception of 'demostraciones de sentimientos patrioticos' [demonstrations of patriotic sentiment].[22] Despite this resolution, however, the turmoil in Italy at that moment made it impossible to eliminate all political questions from the activities of the society. The tension between monarchists and republicans intensified until finally, in 1861, when Italy was declared a unified nation-state, the association fragmented. The republicans stayed in 'Unione e Benevolenza', while the monarchists created a new society, the 'Società Nazionale Italiana' [Italian National Association].[23] During the 1870s, building on the precedents established by these two societies, new associations were created and new trends in the organizational life of the Italian community became evident. According to Baily, the most important was that of 'campanilismo' [parochialism or provincialism] and regionalism, which led to the creation, in 1876, of the first society based on local Italian origin, with members claiming shared roots in a specific Italian village or region. In 1879 the first society based on local neighbourhood belonging in Argentina was also established, in a district of Buenos Aires. By 1910 the overall number of associations had risen to about 4,000 and while some, such as 'Unione Meridionale' [Southern Union] and 'Primo Circolo Napolitano' [First Neapolitan Circle], continued to be formed by the growing number of immigrants from southern Italy, others were neighbourhood associations created in the peripheral and/or traditionally Italian areas of the city.[24] They included the mutual aid associations ('Società di Soccorso Mutuo'), which

---

21   Donna Gabaccia, *Italy's Many Diasporas: Elites, Exiles and Workers of the World* (Abingdon: Routledge, 2003), p. 121.
22   Samuel L. Baily and Andrea Scarli, 'Las sociedades de ayuda mutua y el desarrollo de una comunidad italiana en Buenos Aires, 1858–1918', *Desarrollo Económico*, 21 (1982), 485–514 (p. 489). This and other translations are mine.
23   Baily and Scarli, p. 489.
24   Baily and Scarli, p. 490.

were born during the era of the great emigration, in the late nineteenth and early twentieth centuries, to help migrants overcome difficulties in their new home country and provided pensions, medical payments and other benefits for their members. By paying a small monthly membership fee, members could be helped for some time in the case of illness, unemployment, disability or loss of work.

Munck observes that at the turn of the century the mutual aid societies were unique in the sense that they were almost all founded by immigrant workers and thus represented both 'an association of immigrants for immigrants and an association of workers'.[25] However, Schneider, referencing a detailed study undertaken by Scarzanella (1981), shows how at the same time an urban industrial elite of Italian origin had developed in Buenos Aires. This elite 'maintained strong links of patronage with the local Italian working class, its workforce and consumers, through the control of numerous mutual aid associations and Italian finance and banking'.[26] Gandolfo, Devoto and Bernasconi,[27] among others, also point to the disproportionate, largely middle-class leadership and predominantly working-class membership of the societies. An analysis by Gandolfo of the socio-economic profiles of the presidents of 87 mutual aid societies in office between 1878 and 1920 shows that the majority were professionals (37%), followed by small industrialists (14%), rich merchants (12%) and grand industrialists (10%).

The arrival of a massive wave of migrants in need of help between 1880 and 1914 created problems for the mutual aid societies and other ethnic associations in terms of the resources required to incorporate these new members into their communities. At the same time, concerns also arose among the Argentine elites regarding the assimilation of the migrants. This development, coupled with the rise of a labour movement dominated by Italian workers, presented a challenge to the hegemony of both Italian and Argentinian

---

25 Ronaldo Munck, 'Mutual benefit societies in Argentina: Workers, nationality and Trade Unionism', *Journal of Latin American Studies*, 30 (1998), 573–90 (p. 577).
26 Arnd Schneider, *Futures Lost: Nostalgia and Identity among Italian Immigrants in Argentina* (Oxford: Peter Lang, 2000), p. 69.
27 Romolo Gandolfo, 'Las sociedades italianas de socorros mutuos de Buenos Aires: Cuestiones de etnicidad y de clase dentro de una comunidad de inmigrantes 1880-1920', in *Asociacionismo, trabajo e identidad etnica: Los italianos en América Latina en una perspectiva comparada*, ed. by Fernando J. Devoto and Eduardo J. Miguez (Buenos Aires: CEMLA-CSER-IEHS, 1992), pp. 311– 32; see also Fernando J. Devoto, *Historia de los italianos en la Argentina* (Buenos Aires: Editorial Biblos, 2006) and Alicia Bernasconi, 'Las asociaciones italianas en Argentina entre pasado y presente', *AdVersuS*, XV (2018), 40–55.

elites.[28] The original aim of the Argentinian political elites was to 'promote the immigration of "white" Anglo-Saxon immigrants from Northern Europe, or at least Basques and migrants from Piedmont, both of whom were associated with hard work and respect for authority'.[29] It is important to point out that the concept of 'race' as used in this context by nineteenth-century intellectuals was cultural and historical, rather than biological:[30] distinctions between migrants were made not because of inherited or genetic qualities but because they belonged to different cultural, linguistic and religious traditions.[31] However, these views were later confounded by the spurious but influential writings of Cesare Lombroso (1871/1892) and others, who proposed a hierarchy of races with white northern Europeans, including Northern Italians, at the top, followed by 'less white' southern Europeans, including southern Italians, thus 'linking them to a notion of racial inferiority'.[32]

In Argentina, the original ideological framework for immigration had been laid out by Domingo Faustino Sarmiento, one of the founding fathers of the liberal republic, who saw European immigration as the cornerstone upon which the new Argentina would be built.[33] In this model, as noted by Tanja Bastia and Matthias vom Hau, the 'intrinsic connection between the "racial identity" of these migrants, their supposed habits and biological dispositions, and capacity for progress' would transform Argentina into a modern and 'civilized' country. However, as the same authors point out, 'the immigrants who arrived in Argentina were not those envisioned. The majority originated from Southern European countries, in particular Italy and Spain, and were not considered fully "white" by Argentinian elites.'[34] Ironically, it was Sarmiento – a major proponent of immigration – who came to see the Italian mutual

28   Samuel L. Baily, *Immigrants in the Lands of Promise: Italians in Buenos Aires and New York City, 1870–1914* (New York: Cornell University Press, 1999), pp. 191–92.
29   Fernando J. Devoto, *Historia de la Inmigración en la Argentina* (Buenos Aires: Editorial Sudamericana, 2003), p. 239.
30   Tulio Halperin Donghi, '"¿Para qué la inmigración?" Ideología y política inmigratoria y aceleración del proceso modernizador: El caso Argentino 1810–1914', *Jahrbuch Für Geschichte Von Staat, Wirtschaft und Gesellschaft Lateinamerikas*, 13 (1976), 438–39.
31   Jeanne DeLaney, 'National Identity, Nationhood and Immigration in Argentina: 1810–1930', *Stanford Electronic Humanities Review*, 5 (1997), 116–19.
32   Peter D'Agostino, 'Craniums, Criminals, and the "Cursed Race": Italian Anthropology in American Racial Thought, 1861–1924', *Comparative Studies in Society and History*, 44 (2002), 319–43 (p. 320).
33   Schneider, p. 73.
34   Tanja Bastia and Matthias vom Hau, 'Migration, Race and Nationhood in Argentina', *Journal of Ethnic and Migration Studies*, 40 (2014), 475–92 (pp. 478–79).

aid societies, schools and press as obstacles to assimilation. He denounced the Italian government for extending citizenship to children born of Italian parents in Argentina and publicly denounced proposals to further the growth of Italian schools.[35] Shortly before his death in 1888, he would proclaim that Buenos Aires was 'a city without citizens … growing and expanding, we shall build, if we have not already built, a Tower of Babel in America'.[36]

By the 1900s, the benefits and shortcomings of mass migration had become the focus of public controversy and support for the idea of European migration as pivotal to the construction of a modern and 'civilized' nation had given way to debates concerning the transformation of a heterogeneous society into a 'homogeneous nation'. The focus of the political class had by then shifted on to how to 'nationalize' the migrant population, while the concerns about the political and legal integration of migrants that had previously preoccupied Sarmiento, his colleagues and their contemporaries were replaced by concerns about the cultural integration of migrants and about how to make Argentines.[37]

The meticulous research undertaken by Bastia and vom Hau reveals how these dominant discourses about migration shifted from 'portraying migrants as a crucial element of development towards depicting them as an economic and social problem, a shift which needs to be understood within the context of Argentinian nation-making and the institutionalized notion of Argentina as a white nation of European descendants'.[38] While the dominant perception in the nineteenth century was that the arrival of immigrants from northern Europe would secure the 'whitening' of Argentina, by the early twentieth century eugenic thinking had become part of a 'package of "progressive" ideas for social improvement and modernization'[39] and official discourses portrayed the whiteness of Argentina as an already established fact.[40]

It is this latter period that is the setting of Laura Pariani's 2007 novel *Dio non ama i bambini* [God does not love children], in which, by employing a strategy of re-ethnicization, she complicates the dominant narrative of an

---

35   Baily, p. 78.
36   Jose Luis Romero, *A History of Argentine Political Thought* (Stanford, CA: Stanford University Press, 1963), p. 177.
37   Baily, p. 192; Bastia and vom Hau, p. 481.
38   Bastia and vom Hau, p. 487.
39   David Smith, 'Key Concepts and Theories About Race', in *Race and Criminal Justice*, ed. by Hindpal Singh Bhui (London: Sage, 2008), pp. 9–30 (p. 12).
40   Galen Joseph, 'Taking race seriously: Whiteness in Argentina's national and transnational imaginary', *Identities: Global Studies in Culture and Power*, 7 (2000), 333–71 (p. 335).

easy and rapid Italian assimilation into Argentine culture in Buenos Aires at the turn of the twentieth century, highlighting ethnic difference and thus reminding readers that Italians were initially considered inferior to and less civilized than northern Europeans.[41] In Quijada's view, 'The Argentine imaginary tends to disavow the ethnic mosaic underpinning it. For many decades Argentina has seen itself [...] as a people of European culture and homogenously "white" in phenotypical terms' and has preferred to 'ignore the indigenous, black, and other non-white or non-European influences on Argentine history thus consolidating a collective perception of a nation allegedly uniform in cultural, ethnic and racial terms'.[42]

The importance of the Italian societies, in this context, as a social space aiming to secure survival in a country lacking any structure providing social protection, cannot be underestimated. However, another of the societies' important functions was to enable new migrants, through the network of face-to-face relationships, to establish connections and friendships, which helped to secure their initial insertion in local communities. The question of whether Italian ethnic associations have actually favoured or hindered integration is addressed by Favero, who suggests that 'their main role has been ... to preserve the integrity and health of the social actor, saving him from anonymity and marginality';[43] and, as Bernasconi observes, that assistance to members went far beyond material relief:

> in all the statutes (which were strictly observed) obligations of accompaniment to sick 'socios' were established and stipulated the obligation to attend the wake in case of death and to accompany the funeral procession with the standard banners of the society. Many Italian associations also built pantheons in local cemeteries to ensure a worthy burial for their 'socios'.[44]

41   Francesca Minonne, 'Re-Ethnicizing Italians and Argentines: Laura Pariani's *Dio non ama i bambini*', *The Italianist*, 37 (2017), 86–99 (p. 87).
42   Monica Quijada, 'Introduccion', in *Homogeneidad y nación. Con un estudio de caso: Argentina, siglos xix y xx*, ed. by Mónica Quijada, Carmen Bernand and Arnd Schneider (Madrid: Consejo Superior de Investigaciones Científicas, Centro de Humanidades, Instituto de Historia, 2000), pp. 7–14 (pp. 9–10).
43   Luigi V. Favero, 'Mechanisms of Adaptation and Integration of Italian Immigrants in Argentina: From Social Spaces to the Interpretative Paradigms of Ethnic Identity', *Centre for Migration Studies Special Issues*, 'Special Issue: The Columbus People: Perspectives in Italian Immigration to the Americas and Australia', 11 (1994), 113–24 (p. 120).
44   Bernasconi, p. 42.

Such events and enactments can be defined as forms of identity performance that concern phenomena involving social, not personal, identity. Identity performance pertains specifically to social identities, deliberately performed with the intention of manifesting one's relation to a group identity. Through such performances, people may seek to consolidate particular understandings of their groups through identity enactment.[45] Klein, Spears and Reicher propose that identity consolidation can operate on social identity at two different levels. Individuals may act to secure their social identity as members of a particular group (identity consolidation) while, on the other hand, members of a group may act together to secure the recognition of their shared social identity (identity mobilization). Identity performance can be used to consolidate identities in relation to in-group audiences, but can also be used to mobilize in-group members into supporting specific political projects. Of particular relevance in relation to Argentine nation building is their view that 'one of the major ways in which identity performance relates to collective mobilization is through the definition of social identity and it is precisely because social identity shapes collective action that those who are interested in shaping society will be interested in defining identities.'[46]

As Judith Butler points out, 'performance emerges from shared social worlds ... and relies upon, and reproduces, a set of social relations, practices, and institutions that turn out to be part of the very performance itself.' Moreover, 'performance brings with it the chance to re-create community through various preparatory collaborations among objects, others, and technologies.' These collaborations, that make the performance possible, are described by Butler as 'a choreography of objects, networks, and processes that cross the human and the nonhuman'. She asks whether 'the human and object worlds that together make a performance possible' are also 'what make up the performance'.[47] Butler further asks:

---

45   Samuel Pehrson, Clifford Stevenson, Orla. T. Muldoon and Stephen Reicher, 'Is everyone Irish on St Patrick's Day? Divergent expectations and experiences of collective self-objectification at a multicultural parade', *British Journal of Social Psychology*, 53 (2014), 249–64 (p. 250).
46   Oliver Klein, Russell Spears and Stephen Reicher, 'Social Identity Performance: Extending the Strategic Side of SIDE', *Personality and Social Psychology Review*, 11 (2007), 28–45 (p. 35).
47   Judith Butler, 'Performativity', in *In Terms of Performance*, <http://intermsofperformance.site/keywords/performativity/judith-butler> [accessed 11 April 2019].

Fig. 6.1: Italian dances, Feria de Las Colectividades, Morón, Buenos Aires Province, April 2015. Author's own image.

Are such worlds carried and conveyed, made or unmade, in the performances that we do and are the ones we see and hear or register in some other way, those that lay claim to our responsiveness and, by acting on us, tacitly restructure how we sense the world at all?[48]

48 Butler.

Fig. 6.2: Dancers, Feria de Las Colectividades, Morón, April 2015. Author's own image.

The 'Feria de Colectividades' [Community Fair] takes place in Morón, a small city to the west of Greater Buenos Aires, where local communities from the surrounding provinces of Catamarca, La Pampa, Tucumán, Santiago del Estero and Salta come together to enjoy typical local food and regional produce, traditional dances and music. It is an annual event supported by the local municipality and the 'Sociedad Italiana de Morón' [Italian Society of Morón], originally the 'Società Italiana di Mutuo Soccorso in Morón' [The Italian Society of Mutual Assistance in Morón], created in 1867 by the large number of Italians who migrated to this city following the arrival of the railroad in 1859.[49] In the photos reproduced as Figures 6.1 and 6.2, the young women are wearing costumes typically associated with the tarantella dance, popular in the south of Italy. Somebody made these sleeveless black bodices, laced with colourful ribbons, and the blouse, which is always white. The silk or cotton skirts are full, coming to just below the knee and worn with petticoats. The traditional tarantella dancing skirts are red, green, blue

49 Graciela Luisa Sáez, Carlos María Birocco and Mariela Canali, eds, *Morón, de los orígenes al bicentenario* (Morón: Municipalidad de Morón, 2010).

and black. Black is chosen here for all dancers in the troupe. The small apron is sheer, to allow the colour of the skirt to show through; stockings are white and shoes black. The choreographed, synchronized flag waving seems to be more contemporary, perhaps a recent addition, given that the 'Tricolore' [tricolour] in its current form has been in use only since 19 June 1946 and was only formally adopted in Italy on 7 January 1948. In the arts, this might be thought of as eclecticism: the merging, blending or assimilation of several originally discrete traditions. I have not yet been able to find any other examples of Italian folk dances involving flags apart from performances by the 'sbandieratori' or flag-wavers, the twirlers and throwers who perform at a range of celebrations in Italy. There the thrower, who is usually male, uses both hands to move the flag in a sitting, lying or kneeling posture.

It was at this event that I made the initial contact with key members of the 'Sociedad Italiana de Morón', and it was in Morón that the first Object Workshop was held on 22 April 2015. The event was attended by nine participants.

Moving Objects

The theme of 'moving objects' emerged, inductively, from participants' accounts of objects or things that have moved from one place to another and serves to emphasize the shifting meanings attached to these objects through space and time. Things move with people and people move with things. Objects are bought and sold, stolen, gifted and traded by way of social relations, leading the French sociologist Marcel Mauss to comment that 'the circulation of goods follows that of men ... all in all, it is one and the same.'[50] Following Mauss, a number of scholars have sought to understand the role of objects by likening them to people, an approach adopted by Kopytoff, who proposes that we ask the same range and kinds of cultural question that we ask about people, to arrive at biographies of things.[51] Kopytoff also suggests that such a biographical approach be culturally informed, for things, just as people, are culturally constructed and cultural biographies of things 'make

---

50 Marcel Mauss, *The Gift: The Form and Reason for Exchange in Archaic Societies* [1925] (Abingdon: Routledge, 2001), p. 59.
51 Igor Kopytoff. 'The Cultural Biography of Things: Commoditization as Process', in *The Social Life of Things: Commodities in Cultural Perspective*, ed. by Arjun Appadurai (Cambridge: Cambridge University Press, 1986), pp. 64–91 (p. 66).

salient what might otherwise remain obscure' about the culture in which things take part[52] – all the more so when they are in motion:

> In doing the biography of a thing, one would ask questions similar to those one asks about people: What, sociologically, are the biographical possibilities inherent in its 'status' and in the period and culture, and how are these possibilities realized? Where does the thing come from and who made it? What has been its career so far, and what do people consider to be an ideal career for such things? What are the recognized 'ages' or periods in the thing's 'life,' and what are the cultural markers for them? How does the thing's use change with its age, and what happens to it when it reaches the end of its usefulness?[53]

Kopytoff's essay 'The Cultural Biography of Things' was included in Arjun Appadurai's influential edited collection *The Social Life of Things: Commodities in Cultural Perspective* (1986), which opens with the proposition that things can be said to have 'social lives' and goes on to draw attention to the ways in which objects are continually moved about and recontextualized, in a process of commodification and decommodification. Commodities are defined as 'things' that 'at a certain phase in their careers and in a particular *context*, meet the requirements of commodity' and a commodity can be any 'thing' intended for exchange.[54] However, defining commodities as things exchanged 'means looking at the commodity potential of all things rather than searching fruitlessly for the magic distinction between commodities and other sorts of things'.[55]

In his essay, Kopytoff also emphasizes the possibility of commodities or objects gaining social meanings in spheres other than those determined by exchange, focusing specifically on the process of singularization. Drawing upon Durkheim, who suggests that societies need to set apart a certain portion of their environment, as sacred,[56] Kopytoff proposes that the drive to commodification is countered in the form of culture, whereby 'excessive commodification is anti-cultural – as indeed so many have perceived it or sensed it to be – and

---

52 Kopytoff, 'The Cultural Biography of Things', p. 86.
53 Kopytoff, 'The Cultural Biography of Things', pp. 66–67.
54 Arjun Appadurai, 'Introduction: Commodities and the Politics of Value', in *The Social Life of Things*, pp. 3–63 (pp. 3–9).
55 Appadurai, 'Introduction', p. 13.
56 Émile Durkheim, *The Elementary Forms of Religious Life*, trans. by Joseph Ward Swain (London: George Allen & Unwin, 1915; original French edn 1912), Book 1, Chapter 1, Part 3, pp. 60–65.

singularization is one means to this end'.[57] Culture ensures that some things remain singular and resists the commodification of others, but it may also singularize or resingularize what has been previously commodified.

Singularization

As one might expect, singularization happens differently in different societies. Singularization can be extended to things that are normally commodities: these are singularized by being pulled out of their usual commodity sphere. In complex societies, singularization usually occurs through a personal or private process, when a person singularizes a commodity or a significant object, such as an heirloom, and declines to exchange it. However, objects may be simultaneously perceived as commodities and singularizations, when two different value systems are at work: that of the marketplace and that of the 'closed sphere of personally singularized things': 'What to me is an heirloom is, of course, a commodity to the jeweller, and the fact that I am not divorced from the jeweller's culture is apparent in my willingness to price my priceless heirloom.'[58]

Kopytoff goes on to point out that the individual is often caught between the cultural structure of commoditization and their own personal efforts to bring a value order to the universe of things, recognizing that there is a longing for singularization in complex societies. This insight is borne out by research that examines how consumers decommodify, singularize and personalize objects so that they become irreplaceable, priceless or inalienable.[59] The personal sphere of exchange is independent of the marketplace and based on values that come from aesthetic, moral or religion concerns. When a 'thing' simultaneously participates 'in cognitively distinct yet intermeshed exchange spheres, one is constantly confronted with seeming paradoxes of value'.[60] This paradox is perpetuated as a thing goes in and out of commoditization and

57 Kopytoff, 'The Cultural Biography of Things', pp. 73–74.
58 Kopytoff, 'The Cultural Biography of Things', p. 80.
59 Russell W. Belk, 'Possessions and the Extended Self', *Journal of Consumer Research*, 15 (1988), 139–68; Carolyn F. Curasi, Linda L. Price and Eric J. Arnould, 'How Individuals' Cherished Possessions Become Families' Inalienable Wealth', *Journal of Consumer Research*, 3 (2004), 609–22; Kent Grayson and David Shulman, 'Indexicality and the Verification Function of Irreplaceable Possessions: A Semiotic Analysis', *Journal of Consumer Research*, 27 (2000), 17–30.
60 Kopytoff, 'The Cultural Biography of Things', p. 82.

singularization, is attributed a marketplace value or none, and a blurring of the lines takes place between the human and the non-human, the material and the immaterial.

The Object Workshop Group as Event

The specific objective of the workshops I organized in Argentina as part of the TML project was the exploration of transgenerational Italian identity through objects. Participants were invited to bring any object that represented their relationship, in a real or symbolic way, to their Italian heritage. The orientation of the workshop, although thematic, was essentially non-directive. In this context, the cultural object is understood as any material or immaterial object likely to function as a producer, attractor or container of meaning:

> The cultural object, whether symbolic or material, is rooted in society and in history, functions to subjectivize and socialize both the individual and the group. As a malleable object which is intermediary, containing and mediating ... the cultural object plays an essential role in constructing the relation to self, others, and group.[61]

Working in groups with objects is particularly fruitful as the themes that emerge in response to individual accounts trigger participants' responses to each other but also to the object itself. These responses include non-verbal cues – that is, what people do non-verbally in a sequence of offering, accepting, holding, looking at and passing objects from hand to hand.

Recent research points to an overly predetermined account of resonance in the existing literature, which, rather than seeing resonance as an emergent process, treats the experience of resonance as a bounded moment or only as a connection to the past or present, as opposed to a forward-moving agent.[62] My understanding of resonance in the 'Object Workshops' is largely congruent with the position put forward by McDonnell, Bail and Tavory, who do not treat

---

61 Emmanuel Diet, 'The Cultural Object and Its Mediating Functions', *Connections*, 1 (2010), 39–59 (p. 39).
62 Terence E. McDonnell, Christopher A. Bail and Iddo Tavory, 'A Theory of Resonance', *Sociological Theory*, 35 (2017), 1–14; Christopher A. Bail, 'Cultural Carrying Capacity: Organ Donation Advocacy, Discursive Framing, and Social Media Engagement', *Social Science & Medicine*, 165 (2016), 280–88.

cultural objects as either 'resonant' or 'not resonant' and do not assume that some cultural objects inherently or inevitably resonate with certain cultural themes or conclude that resonance is a product of familiarity or alignment. The authors argue, instead, that while resonance may emerge through a process of alignment not all 'congruent' objects lead to resonance. On the contrary, a cultural object may begin as incongruent only to 'resonate' given the right situation. This applies, in particular, in the case of interactions within groups as well as in cases where actors face situations that they have never encountered, or that do not fit neatly into any of the available cultural schema within their worldview. This is a view grounded in relations among objects, people and situations. It is anchored in people's experience of resonance and emphasizes 'novelty' as essential to that experience, on the basis that resonance is most likely and strongest when the 'solution' offered by the object is neither too familiar nor too resistant to interpretation or extension.[63] As noted by Diet:

> The cultural object, whether symbolic or material, rooted in society and in history, functions to subjectivize and socialize both the individual and the group. As a malleable object which is intermediary, containing, mediating and transforming ... the cultural object plays an essential role in constructing the relation to self, others, and group.[64]

The Object Workshop (a novel experience for participants) provided the 'right situation' for this kind of experience and, while the materials brought by participants shared some apparent commonalities, participant narratives were both personal and unique, allowing for different perspectives to be shared and resulting in the emergence of resonance as well as of themes that were then explored through discussion. In the first workshop, in Morón, the interpretation of Italian transgenerational identity by one participant of Japanese origin was future-orientated, for instance, through her daughter's marriage to an Italian and their (as yet unborn) children, who would share this identity.

In Buenos Aires an impeccably dressed older Calabrian man came to the group held at the 'Ente Friulano Assistenza Sociale Culturale Emigranti' [Friulian Emigrants' Social Cultural Assistance Centre]. He wondered if, as a Calabrian, he would be allowed to participate and, later, as he signed the consent to participate (retrospectively at the end of the session), he

---

63   McDonnell et al., 'A Theory of Resonance', p. 2.
64   Diet, p. 39.

apologized for his handwriting, explaining that he had received very little schooling because he had had to work. Like many of his generation, he had come to Argentina in the 1950s, when levels of illiteracy were still high in southern Italy. According to UNESCO documentation from 1952 (based on data from a national survey dating from 1931), the rates were estimated at 40 per cent illiteracy in Sicily, 46 per cent in Lucania and 48 per cent in Calabria.[65] This was a problem that, during the Fascist regime, was largely passed over in silence and appeared to have been forgotten, yet academics such as Carlo Levi explicitly remarked upon it:

> Anyone can see the relationship between illiteracy and poverty. A map illustrative of its distribution would show that it goes hand in hand with barren land, bad sanitary conditions, malaria, and the lack of industries, communications and public works. Miserably poor families must put their children to work early. They send the boys to watch over herds of goats grazing on the desolate clay, and put the girls to cooking, cleaning, watching over the babies, weaving baskets and carrying jars of water from the distant well. The school is, in most cases, far away; there is not enough money to buy books and notebooks, and frequent illness keeps the children at home.[66]

'La Sociedad Obrera Italiana de Ensenada' [The Italian Workers' Society of Ensenada], originally 'Società Operaie di Mutuo Soccorso' [Society of Workers' Mutual Aid], is located in the port of Ensenada in Buenos Aires Province, specifically on the Ensenada de Barragán, a small bay on the Río de la Plata, some 40 kilometres south-east of Buenos Aires. The 'socios' [members] – many from Basilicata, Calabria and Naples – had come to Ensenada in the aftermath of the Second World War. They arrived either with their families, as children, or alone, as young men, to work in the port or the petroleum industry established in here in 1925.

On the day of the workshop nobody had brought a concrete object but, instead, participants shared stories or songs from Naples. One of those who sang actually came from Naples. He spoke of his working life, of working all day in one job, before going on to work an evening shift elsewhere. These songs were his objects. A man who, as a child, had left Basilicata with his

---

65 Carlo Levi, 'Southern Italy Fights the Battle of Illiteracy', *UNESCO Courier*, 5 (1952), 3–5 (p. 3).
66 Levi, p. 3.

Moving Objects 173

Fig. 6.3: Object Workshop, Morón, Buenos Aires Province, May 2015.
Author's own image.

mother and baby brother for Genoa, where they got on the boat to Argentina, spoke of the journey they had made to join his father and older brothers. He had never seen snow before arriving in Genoa and had no shoes, only woven sandals. The family had no money for lodgings. A woman let them stay in her house and, during the night, the baby soiled the bed sheet. His abiding memory was of the terrible cold and of his mother sobbing, as she washed that sheet in freezing water, in the dark.

In Morón, apart from a young male dancer, the group was entirely composed of women. Many brought domestic objects, but also documents, photographs, and a dress made and worn by a participant's grandmother. A retrospective viewing of the photographs of these objects *in situ* (Figure 6.3) does not capture the animated discussion revolving around them, but rather recalls a fragment of a still life – a genre which, essentially, depicts anything that does not move or is dead: a celebration of material pleasures or a warning of the ephemerality of those pleasures and the brevity of human life. These objects have been detached from an original scene, which is invariably described by participants and involves other people in one way or another.

Here they are arranged as a temporary assemblage, to be photographed as a referent to the group discussion, ostensibly for the purposes of documentation, but with the implied message of 'that has been'.[67]

However, the recordings, transcripts of interviews, notes of observations and reflections taken at the time tell another, a different, story, in which these objects are brought to life. Nobody in this group had ever been to Italy, but several participants dreamed of going. The little Sicilian horse and cart ornament was not something brought back from a holiday, it was a found object that was carefully restored by the dancer, whose grandparents came from Sicily, a place which he hopes to visit through one of the trips organized by the association. The photographs included in Figure 6.3 are of the ancestors of the Japanese participant, but there are other images, just outside the photographic frame: a Jewish mother who escaped Nazi Germany, a dress that belonged to a Galician grandmother, the mementos of a gypsy guitarist who migrated to Argentina in 1948 after fighting in Africa and Albania. Later, in an interview with his daughter in law and his granddaughter, I was to learn of his youth in Mola di Bari, Puglia, where he played guitar in a Tango orchestra; of his experience in Libya and what he thought of Mussolini; of his life in Argentina; and of his passion for the theatre and for the traditional Italian Nativity scenes known as 'presepi', which he built every year, each one different from that of the previous year, but all mostly constructed of found objects, until 1997. He died preparing his last 'presepe', just before Christmas, that year.

Personal reflections are based upon a willingness to engage fully with the topic of inquiry and one's own internal processes throughout the research process.[68] This engagement, which is not limited to the researcher but extends to all those who collaborate with them, can be framed as heuristic inquiry, a methodology that Henare suggests is a more open approach to analysis and which allows 'things', as and when they arise, to offer theoretical possibilities.[69]

---

67 Roland Barthes, *Camera Lucida: Reflections on Photography* (New York: Hill and Wang, 1981), pp. 76–77.
68 Linda Finlay, 'Negotiating the Swamp: The Opportunity and Challenge of Reflexivity in Research Practice', *Qualitative Research*, 2 (2002), 209–30.
69 Amira Henare, Martin Holbraad and Sari Wastell, eds, *Thinking Through Things: Theorising Artefacts Ethnographically* (Abingdon: Routledge, 2007), p. 3.

Time

Marilyn Strathern points to a connection between the study of objects and the study of time. She favours a non-linear historical appreciation of things, which suggests that 'objects simultaneously allow a past and a future in a present, whatever that may be, in light of cultural and contextual differences'.[70] The research undertaken by Savolainen and Kuusisto-Arponen, on the other hand, focuses on the narrated memories of former child evacuees and how these are formed in the interplay of the social, the spatial and the material.[71] Nora's 'sites of memory' are understood by these authors as 'meaning-carrying linkages between tangible reference points and memory' and they point out that 'memories and narratives of the past require points of reference, sites of memory of a sort, which can be particular named places, but also objects or documents, dates or crystallized and often-repeated stories, or even mindscapes.'[72] They conclude that the significance of these tangible reference points, these sites of memory, is dependent on their presence in both the past *and* the present.

Dr F. was the first member of his family to return to the town of Pergine Valsugana, Trentino, since his grandparents' departure with their remaining children (several had died) for Argentina in 1913. He recalls witnessing his grandparents kneeling by their bed in prayer in the house where they lived with his parents when he was a small child. Many years later, when visiting the church that his grandparents had attended in Pergine, he realized that, 40 years after leaving Italy, they had continued exactly the same practice in Argentina:

> Having entered that church, I started crying … a memory I have of my grandmother. I used to play with a small globe with a little Statue of a Virgin inside … when I turned it over, snow fell. When I started to investigate the family papers, I found a paper postcard from Montagnaga di Pine, a small town, in which there is a very miraculous Virgin, about ten kilometres from Pergine. I still have not been there, but I have to go, but I have come to the conclusion that my grandparents were from that town where there are many families with the same name. My grandparents

---

70 Strathern, p. 158.
71 Ulla Savolainen and Anna-Kaisa Kuusisto-Arponen, 'The Interplay of Memory and Matter: Narratives of Former Finnish Karelian Child Evacuees', *Oral History*, 44 (2016), 59–68.
72 Savolainen and Kuusisto-Arponen, p. 60.

lived there and then went down to the city that was a little bigger ... that is Pergine ... they had children who were born in Montagnaga and others who were born in Pergine. They made a pilgrimage on foot from Trento to the church at Montagnaga where there was the Virgin, and it was this Virgin that I played with, when I was four or five years old.[73]

Dr F. was visibly moved when recounting this event. We had looked at many documents together, but it was the memory of playing with the little statue of the Virgin Mary in the globe that seemed to have provided the most tangible reference point. This supports the assertion that 'narrated memories, both written and oral, are formed in this interplay between embodied recollections with the inter-action of matter, such as sources and mementoes, and the immaterial, such as affects and emotions.'[74] In turn, this suggests that 'the investigation of the discursive-material nature of memories is a key to deeper understanding of the affectual dynamics of remembering, telling and writing.'[75]

In thinking about what it has meant to be Italian in Buenos Aires over the historical period referred to here, Quijada's framework, which distinguishes three phases in the process of the construction of discourses of national homogeneity in Latin America, has proved particularly helpful. The first phase is that of the new elites and the formation of a civic nation composed of free and virtuous citizens. This model collapsed in the second half of the nineteenth century and was replaced by that of a 'civilized nation'. The category of 'civilization' was, however, limited to 'the urban and the European' and was influenced by ideas about a 'biologically' determined racial hierarchy that involved the demarcation of the lines of national inclusion and exclusion. The final phase commenced at the beginning of the twentieth century, with the discourse of the integrated nation and the creation of a unified national community based on cultural and racial mixing.[76] While, as Minonne notes, today being of Italian descent is regarded as a positive trait and has no bearing on an individual being able to claim an Argentine identity,[77] whether Quijada's final phase has been achieved is still debated and debatable. Both Joseph and Bastia and vom Hau query this, with reference to the 1980s and 1990s, when 'anti-immigration attitudes fed on ideas about national homogeneity and racial

73 Transcript of recording from interview with Dr F., 29 April 2015. My translation.
74 Savolainen and Kuusisto-Arponen, p. 59.
75 Savolainen and Kuusisto-Arponen, p. 60.
76 Quijada.
77 Minonne.

purity' and 'Problems such as poverty, bad housing or the persistence of shanty towns were portrayed as caused or aggravated by non-white immigration from Bolivia, Paraguay and Peru.'[78]

At the beginning of this century, the Consulate General of Italy in Buenos Aires made a partial survey of the associations in Buenos Aires, Morón and Lomas de Zamora. This revealed that 30 societies founded before the First World War were still active. In total, the Consulate's list includes 253 Italian associations within its constituency, of which a quarter (63) were founded after 1990.[79] Their purposes are very different from those of the oldest societies: only four have as their object mutual assistance, 36 are regional, while 15 have cultural purposes. There are also seven new federations of a regional nature, as opposed to those associated with the Italian government, a phenomenon that Bernasconi suggests is related to the current (and sometimes recently revived) relations of migrants and their descendants with Italy.[80] On the other hand, the creation of 'paesano' [village] associations with devotional purposes, involving the celebration of the patron saints, experienced its greatest intensity in the 1960s and 1970s, probably because of the influence (and in some cases, concurrence) of at least two factors: certain that they would not return, migrants sought to meet to celebrate their saints in Argentina; at the same time, in a period marked by military dictatorships (1966–73 and 1976–83), an institution with religious purposes had far less difficulty in establishing itself legally. Argentina's economic collapse in 2001–02 saw an estimated 300,000 people leave the country, among them many young Italians. However, according to the Argentinian National Directorate of Migration, 10,450 Italians initiated residency procedures between 2004 and 2013; 83 per cent of these applications were registered between 2008 and 2013, which, as Minonne notes, is just the latest development in 'a network of global migratory flows that is constantly in flux'.[81] The persistence of memory ensures that enduring attachments for people, places and objects are all entangled in this network, which stretches across generations and oceans. As Tilley notes, in this never-ending panorama of presence and absence 'an absence of something may be as crucial as its presence.'[82]

78 Bastia and vom Hau, pp. 487–88; see also Joseph.
79 Consolato Generale d'Italia a Buenos Aires, *Le Associazioni Italiane della circoscrizione consolare* (Buenos Aires: Consolato Generale d'Italia, 2003).
80 Bernasconi.
81 Minonne, p. 96.
82 Christopher Tilley, 'Ethnography and Material Culture', in *Handbook of Material Culture*, pp. 258–72 (p. 260).

CHAPTER SEVEN

Visualizing Spatialization at a Crossroads between Translation and Mobility: Italian Australian Artist Jon Cattapan's Cityscapes

Eliana Maestri

Introduction: The Arts Scene in Multicultural Australia

Home to the Victorian College of the Arts and the Royal Melbourne Institute of Technology, Melbourne has trained generations of professional artists, especially since the implementation of Australian multiculturalism, initiated in 1973 by the then immigration minister Al Grassby, a member of the Whitlam Labor government.[1] The confluence between increasing interest in the arts, as ideal media for the multiplicity of voices in multi-ethnic Australia, and the impact of the Whitlam government's measures, inaugurating cultural liberalization, laid the groundwork for successful initiatives in the arts.[2] As

---

1 Katherine Smits, 'Justifying Multiculturalism: Social Justice, Diversity and National Identity in Australia and New Zealand', *Australian Journal of Political Science*, 46 (2011), 87–103.
2 Ien Ang and Greg Noble, 'Making Multiculture: Australia and the Ambivalent Politics of Diversity', in *Making Culture: Commercialisation, Transnationalism, and the State of 'Nationing' in Contemporary Australia*, ed. by David Rowe, Graeme Turner and Emma Waterton (London and New York: Routledge, 2018), pp. 140–53; Sandra Forbes, 'Government and the Arts in Australia', *World Literature Today*, 67, Contemporary Australian Literature (1993), 494–98; Chris McAuliffe, *Jon Cattapan: Possible Histories* (Melbourne: Miegunyah, 2008), p. 24; Julian Meyrick, *Australian Theatre after the*

Jennifer Craik also maintains, from 1968 Australia saw a '*rapid expansion* of arts and cultural organisations' and from 1975 a 'dynamic reform of cultural administration'.[3] Australians, including those from working-class, less affluent or disadvantaged communities,[4] were encouraged to enjoy the arts scene and, possibly, carve out a professional career in the arts and humanities. Young artists, born to migrant parents but raised in Australia during the transition from the 'White Australia' policy to one of multiculturalism, were persuaded that they could 'engage confidently with global culture'.[5] Not only were they accorded unprecedented governmental support, they were also stimulated to explore the Australian art world as well as situate its artistic sensitivity within a wide-ranging web of transnational connections. As Jon Cattapan, a product of that time and the focus of this chapter, states: 'The sense of coming out of a European orbit became important' and motivated him to leave Australia temporarily.[6] Artists, curators and art historians felt the need to travel to Europe and connect with their cultural and artistic roots.

In the seventies and eighties, young artists of Italian descent found themselves amid cultural spaces and human energies, which pushed them even further to surf the globe and connect with their roots. Together with other young Italian Australians, these artists experienced what Cattapan called 'a generational shift, [...] com[ing] out of their migrant background and [...] find[ing] themselves being part of a new culture but attending to the old culture a little bit'.[7] Despite the fact that, in the majority of cases, Italian families did not approve of their children's careers in the creative arts sector – as they wanted them to become 'respectable' doctors or engineers[8] – they implicitly increased their desire to leave for Europe and connect with 'that cultural lineage' located within their country of origin.[9] Because of their

---

New Wave: Policy, Subsidy and the Alternative Artist (Leiden: Brill Rodopi, 2017), pp. 1–5; Geoffrey Milne, *Theatre Australia (Un)limited: Australian Theatre Since the 1950s* (Amsterdam and New York: Rodopi, 2004), p. 217; Eugene van Erven, *Community Theatre: Global Perspectives* (London and New York: Routledge, 2001), p. 209.
3   Jennifer Craik, *Re-Visioning Arts and Cultural Policy: Current Impasses and Future Directions* (Canberra: ANU E, 2007), p. 7, italics in original.
4   Ang and Noble, pp. 141–42.
5   McAuliffe, *Cattapan*, p. 24.
6   Jon Cattapan, Unpublished interview with Eliana Maestri (2014).
7   Cattapan, Interview with Maestri.
8   Laura Hougaz, *Entrepreneurs in Family Business Dynasties: Stories of Italian-Australian Family Businesses Over 100 Years* (Cham: Springer, 2015), pp. v, 170.
9   Cattapan, Interview with Maestri.

relentless attachment to their Italian heritage, first-generation Italians, settled in Australia before and/or after the Second World War, resisted assimilation and indirectly paved the way for Australian multiculturalism,[10] while arousing the curiosity of their offspring for Italy and the world beyond Australia. This curiosity complicates and enriches our understanding of the Italian diaspora to Australia and across the world. Therefore, it needs to be studied in a systematic and comprehensive way. This chapter intends to address this need and encourage future research on how second-generation Italians in Australia have been affected by migration and how they have articulated this legacy and 'layer into [their] thinking',[11] with particular attention to the visual arts. A number of academic volumes and research projects have been devoted to the investigation of Italy *out of* Italy, namely a country constructed and reconstructed in oral and written discursive narratives of migration across times and spaces. A zone that remains unexplored is the visual and, in particular, how visual artists of Italian descent reflect on the malleability of Italian identity and culture through the production of artistic expressions displaying the main components of a transcultural and translingual nation in motion: mobility, language and space.[12]

How do Australian artists of Italian descent display their journeys across continents and imaginary lands? How do their travels to European and non-European destinations help them translate and visualize the transcultural discourses of their parents' country of origin, situated within a web of global connections? How do they interpret their hybrid identity, translate their multilayered life narratives into visual artworks and contribute to the problematization of Italian culture constantly redesigned by mobility, movement and migration? As 'roots are forms of narration [...] providing

---

10   Stephen Castles, 'Italians in Australia: Building a Multicultural Society on the Pacific Rim', *Diaspora: A Journal of Transnational Studies*, 1 (1991), 45–66 (p. 64); Stephen Castles, 'Italians in Australia: The Impact of a Recent Migration on the Culture and Society of a Postcolonial Nation', in *The Columbus People: Perspectives in Italian Immigration to the Americas and Australia*, ed. by Lydio F. Tomasi, Piero Gastaldo and Thomas Row (New York: Fondazione Giovanni Agnelli, Centre for Migration Studies, 1994), pp. 342–67 (pp. 361–62).
11   Cattapan, Interview with Maestri.
12   An example is provided by Fred Gardaphé, 'In the Name of the Father and the Son: Italian Migrations in the Art of Joseph and William Papaleo', in *Harbors, Flows, and Migrations: The USA in/and the World*, ed. by Vincenzo Bavaro, Gianna Fusco, Serena Fusco and Donatella Izzo (Newcastle upon Tyne: Cambridge Scholars Publishing, 2017), pp. 487–509.

routes through the world',[13] how do they engage with cultural and linguistic constructs across borders while straddling manifold worlds? As they are also speakers of languages that are rooted to a place that is a translated space, how does their competence in the Italian language contribute to their visual translation and mediation of perceptions of Italy and other cultures? Being part of an inspiring multicultural makeup in Australia and the receivers of practices of migration and conservation of Italian traditions, these artists display thought-provoking translations of the Italian diaspora in a global context. Intrigued by Italian culture and un/familiar Italian spaces, the second and subsequent generations have performed the complex role of transnational and transcultural mediators.[14] As Michael Cronin and Sherry Simon confirm: 'Mediators are involved in [...] a range of activities which exceeds mere translation – they are multilingual authors, self-translators, often active in a variety of intercultural and inter-artistic networks, often migrants, with hybrid identities, who develop transfer activities in several geo-cultural spaces'.[15] Whereas the Italian Australian artists' transnational interests have led them to navigate worlds across continental borders and trace, as Rita Wilson argues, 'the dialectic between the local and the global',[16] their transcultural position has helped them negotiate meaning specifically between Italian generations, spaces and languages.

A Space–Language Approach to Cattapan's Artwork

Owing to spatial constraints, I will seek to answer the questions outlined above by discussing one second-generation Italian in Australia: Jon Cattapan, eminent Melbourne-based visual artist and current director of the Victorian College of the Arts. Born to Italian parents in the fifties and raised at the dawn of multicultural Australia, Cattapan's development as a person and as an artist has capitalized on cultures, ethnicities, artistic practices and generations: 'My

13   Iain Chambers quoted in Rita Wilson, 'Cultural Mediation through Translingual Narrative', *Target*, 23 (2011), 235–50 (p. 235).
14   Eliana Maestri, 'Quale Europa? In Italia o in Australia? Percezioni e visioni europee degli italiani australiani di seconda e terza generazione', in *Cultura e costruzione del culturale: Fabbriche dei pensieri in Italia nel Novecento e verso il terzo millennio*, ed. by Ilona Fried (Budapest: Ponte Alapítvány, 2014), pp. 263–98.
15   Michael Cronin and Sherry Simon, 'Introduction: The City as a Translation Zone', *Translation Studies*, 7 (2014), 119–32 (p. 123).
16   Wilson, p. 236.

father used to say if you are a migrant you're always gonna sit with your bum on two chairs, you know? And it is an interesting way of thinking about it, you are always between two places a little bit'.[17] His living in-between and within multiple places and cultural affiliations makes his work highly autobiographical, mobile, hybridized and, almost by default, 'translational'. The translational 'describes the complex process of cultural signification produced under the impact of [...] displacements, migrations, relocations and diasporas and the unprecedented development of transnational electronic communications and media systems'.[18] Practised by an inhabitant of multiple cultures and languages, translation represents this artist's *modus operandi*, providing him with methods, frames and processes of signification and negotiation as well as spatial figuration and linguistic representation. In light of the fact that translation appears as an integral component of his socio-cultural relations and artistic practices, how is this practice conceptualized in his visual artwork? This chapter will focus on the way Cattapan translates the interplay between spatial mobility, language practices and Italian identity into artistic spaces and how these spaces raise awareness of translation as a fundamental approach to the visualization of diasporic experiences.

I will avail myself of language-based theories of space and thick translation, which, although they do not seem to share common ground, prove to be useful in casting light on how Cattapan, as a visual artist with a migrant background and long-standing ties to multiple places, addresses questions of space and language. In other words, they will be useful in understanding how spaces and languages are conceptualized, visualized and translated into a layered and thick zone. In particular, I will draw on cultural theorist Henri Lefebvre's studies of space and cities,[19] which inaugurated the spatial turn in the humanities in the seventies and are still key in understanding how language and space affect one another in today's society.[20] Despite the

17 Cattapan, Interview with Maestri.
18 Wilson, p. 236.
19 Henri Lefebvre, *The Production of Space*, trans. by Donald Nicholson-Smith, English 1st edn 1991 (Oxford: Basil Blackwell, French 1st edn 1974); Henri Lefebvre, *Writings on Cities*, trans. by Eleonore Kofman and Elizabeth Lebas (Oxford: Blackwell, 1996).
20 Harvey Molotch, 'The Space of Lefebvre', *Theory and Society*, 22 (1993), 887–95; Ceri Watkins, 'Representations of Space, Spatial Practices and Spaces of Representation: An Application of Lefebvre's Spatial Triad', *Culture and Organization*, 11 (2005), 209–20; Stuart Elden, 'There Is a Politics of Space because Space Is Political: Henri Lefebvre and the Production of Space', *Radical Philosophy Review*, 10 (2007), 101–16;

subsequent elaboration of Lefebvre's theories, especially in the fields of urban planning, geography and philosophy, Christina Higgins maintains that we still need to pay attention to his theories of space, in particular when migration is the focal point.[21] Lefebvre's conceptualizations of space as an interactive and multidimensional entity can contribute to the study of 'how spaces – including nation-states, but also spaces of language instruction and language use – are produced through the intersection of human activity, including the imagining of spaces as belonging to particular ethnicities, religions, genders, and languages'.[22] By accommodating the imagination of multiple spaces, the visual arts (including language-based ones) lend themselves to the study of spatialization and its translation into optical experiences. Lefebvre advocates the use of translation as a strategy to uncover the ideological layers involved in the construction and creation of space, but he does not suggest any practical application of it. Therefore, I will attempt to compensate for this theoretical gap by turning to language-based theories of thick translation, which acknowledge and encourage the production of layered, or thick, texts in translation, namely translations dense with explanations about the textual strata of the original. Finally, a number of prominent translation studies scholars have looked at how acts of translation shape urban spaces and are affected by them.[23] None of them, however, invokes Lefebvre's theories of space or integrates them with recent translation theories. By benefiting from the confluence of theories of spatiality and translation, I therefore aim to enrich this promising field of research and pave the way for new and exciting methodological approaches to the study of the visualization of space, and in particular urban and migrant spaces.

Jani Vuolteenaho et al., 'Language, Space, Power: Reflections on Linguistic and Spatial Turns in Urban Research', in *Language, Space and Power: Urban Entanglements*, ed. by Jani Vuolteenaho, Lieven Ameel, Andrew Newby and Maggie Scott, Studies across Disciplines in the Humanities and Social Sciences, 13 (Helsinki: Helsinki Collegium for Advanced Studies, 2012), pp. 1–27.

21 Christina Higgins, 'Space, Place, and Language', in *The Routledge Handbook of Migration and Language*, ed. by Suresh Canagarajah (London and New York: Routledge, 2017), pp. 102–16.

22 Higgins, p. 102.

23 Tong King Lee, *Translating the Multilingual City: Cross-lingual Practices and Language Ideology* (Bern: Peter Lang, 2013); Sherry Simon, *Cities in Translation: Intersections of Language and Memory* (London and New York: Routledge, 2012); Sherry Simon, *Speaking Memory: How Translation Shapes City Life* (Montreal, Kingston, London and Chicago: McGill-Queen's University, 2016); Cronin and Simon, pp. 119–32.

Migrants and the City

If we look at Cattapan's artistic output to date, we can identify, almost immediately, a shared ground: the city and its architecture. Cronin and Simon point to migrants' attraction to the city as 'a space of productive diversity'[24] and desire, as Lefebvre would also say. In his study on the impact of migration and globalization on urbanization, Lefebvre maintains that the city represents a magnet with forces that pull on a number of citizens, including migrants.[25] While advocating diversity and centrality, these citizens claim the right to use and occupy the city and make it into their own space. Despite being theorized in the sixties, Lefebvre's reflections on migrants' right to the city as a critical and productive site are still pertinent. For example, to demonstrate the relevance and applicability of Lefebvre's theories to today's society, Higgins maintains that racist slogans against Middle Eastern migrants bounced back and forth within Sydney's city centre in 2005, alienating recently arrived migrants, 'policing space and contesting different groups' rights to space'.[26] Despite the power of racist attitudes in resisting new ideas about urban transformations to accommodate newcomers, migrants' contributions to the anatomy and morphology of the city prove to be inevitable and unavoidable. Cronin and Simon claim that 'mediators [among whom are migrants] are the true *architects* of common repertoires and frames of reference, e.g. a model of an urban, national or international culture'.[27] In addition, as 'a society is a space and an *architecture* of concepts',[28] migrants contribute not only to the physical construction of cities and nations but also to the conceptual creation of them.

Clear references to iconic urban landscapes, notoriously inhabited by multi-ethnic populations, have been part of Cattapan's practice throughout his long-standing professional career. His imaginary architectures, urban mappings and cityscapes (relating to cities such as Melbourne, Rome, New York, Venice and Singapore) display uneasiness and restlessness. Fragmented and reassembled according to visual and acoustic principles, his cities reveal anxieties and the artist's sensitivity to their configuration. In the interview I conducted with him in 2014, Cattapan discusses 'the cityscape phase' as a significant turning point in his career. This moment, inaugurating the beginning

---

24 Cronin and Simon, p. 119.
25 Lefebvre, *Writings on Cities*, p. 34.
26 Higgins, p. 109.
27 Cronin and Simon, p. 123, my italics.
28 Lefebvre, *The Production of Space*, p. 139, my italics.

of his growing attention to the city as a complex phenomenon, can be traced back to his seven-month visit in 1985 to Castelfranco Veneto, a moment often recollected and documented in publications, interviews (including mine) and the statements he has made about his Melbourne exhibitions and cultural events worldwide. In Cattapan's work, urban landscapes and cityscapes are composite and layered territories so that 'people can claim their own'.[29] 'Layering', which 'has very much to do with the idea of the city',[30] is a fabrication method, figurative device and semantic notion. It conceptualizes the artist's work and reveals transcultural and transnational approaches to the visual, similar to the techniques activated by cultural and linguistic translation as mediation.

Movement and Travel between Places: Cattapan's Italy

Mobility and movement between urban places and spaces, spaces conflated into multifarious, transnational cities, represent Cattapan's signature trait. In order to illustrate this, I discuss Cattapan's artistic practices before and after his New York residency. He states:

> This [that sense of layering] came out after a period of living in New York. [...] I had this idea, very simple idea, that the expressive stuff which was underneath my work [...] had become completely abstracted, and had a vague landscape sense, and then over the top of that I could drop [...] this architectural, this cityscape which looked a little bit like pixilation.[31]

Cattapan's 'cityscape phase', started, as stated above, during the artist's visit to his Italian place of origin and was refined during his travels, study tours and arts residencies in various parts of the world, including New York (1989–91), Canberra (1992), Venice (2007 and 2014) and Rome (2014).[32] Just before embarking for New York, Cattapan completed his *Documentary: Melbourne as Rome*,[33] which represents an attempt to reflect on his everlasting bond with

---

29　Cattapan, Interview with Maestri.
30　Cattapan, Interview with Maestri.
31　Cattapan, Interview with Maestri.
32　Jon Cattapan, 'Jon Cattapan Biography', *Jon Cattapan*, <http://www.joncattapan.com.au> [accessed 4 December 2019].
33　Jon Cattapan, *Documentary: Melbourne as Rome*, 1989, oil on linen, 210 × 183 cm, private collection, from McAuliffe, *Cattapan*, p. 94.

Italian culture and the composite nature of urban morphology.[34] Unlike the paintings produced after his New York period, based on layering techniques and digital juxtapositions of images of transnational architectural elements onto international urban landscapes (a technique refined, as we shall see, later in his life), this work is 'only' a metaphorical superimposition of two cities: Melbourne and Rome – namely, not just Melbourne in isolation but a surreal evocation of Rome.[35] Here, the allegorical and figurative charges are particularly meaningful, because they attribute spatial and translational traits to this piece of work. As Lefebvre claims, metaphors belong to the realm of space, because they reveal both '*fascination* [...] with a natural space that has been lost and/or rediscovered' and 'displacement, and hence also transposition and transfer'.[36] The entire painting is indeed layered with acts of displacement and transfer (from Melbourne to Rome and back), which are also fundamental attributes of the translation process. Loredana Polezzi reminds us that 'the connection between translation and mobility is often traced back to the etymological roots, the Latin word *translatio* indicating the movement or transfer of objects and people across space'.[37]

Cattapan visited Rome on various occasions, and the realization of *Documentary: Melbourne as Rome* was inspired by his passion for metropolitan centres and cinema.[38] In this work, neither Melbourne nor Rome has distinct or specific traits, but the fluidity of colour, the intensity of the blue and the multiplicity of shadows and spotlights create spatial points of contact between the background and the foreground, the general and the particular, as well as the Australian city and the Italian capital. This anaphoric reminiscence becomes a visual and kinaesthetic way to be in two places simultaneously, evoking transnational movement and mobility – the quintessential elements of migration – and shortening the distance between desired lands. As art historian Chris McAuliffe also claims, 'contrary to its title, *Documentary: Melbourne as Rome*, 1989, sets aside location and fact. It is not an image of Melbourne but a registration of the artist's longing for another place: the kind of city seen in *Roma* (1972), Fellini's

---

34   McAuliffe, *Cattapan*, p. 99.
35   McAuliffe, *Cattapan*, p. 90.
36   Lefebvre, *The Production of Space*, p. 140, italics in original.
37   Loredana Polezzi, 'Mobility', in *The Routledge Encyclopedia of Translation Studies*, ed. by Mona Baker and Gabriela Saldanha, 2nd edn 2009 (London and New York: Routledge, 1998), pp. 172–78 (p. 172).
38   Chris McAuliffe, *The Drowned World: Jon Cattapan, Works and Collaborations* (Melbourne: Ian Potter Museum of Art, University of Melbourne, 2006), p. 13.

genre-busting combination of memoir, documentary and allegory'.[39] The figurative evocation of Rome translates the artist's longing for a space to belong and projects his imagination into a transnational locus, conjuring another diasporic experience in his life. In Cronin and Simon's words, one could maintain that *Documentary: Melbourne as Rome* also 'reveal[s] the passages created among communities',[40] framing diasporic routes and language encounters with the other.

Rome is not the only Italian attraction for Cattapan. At the beginning of my interview he states that visiting the Veneto region and studying major Renaissance artists (such as Giorgione) elicited in him a 'pronounced response to Italian art'[41] and encouraged him to use the city of Melbourne as the ideal setting of his work, with, however, clear Italian reminiscences. These reminiscences bring back to life not only Rome but also Venice:

> And it is with me to this day that the idea of Melbourne, which is my city, is somehow deeply ingrained in the work I make, comes out of that moment and takes me all the way back to Venice, which if I had the opportunity to live between Melbourne and Venice that is probably what I would do.[42]

Venetian tropes – in particular, fluidity, 'masking' (another way of creating layers) and the 'ultramarine blue'[43] – appear to be incorporated into depictions of Cattapan's Melbourne (see, for instance, *The Melbourne Panels*).[44] And this complex layering of brushstrokes and tropes (further studied during his 2014 printmaking residency, Bulgari Art Award, at the Scuola Internazionale di Grafica, Venice)[45] adds an extra dimension to the artist's translational practice, paying tribute to his origins and fictional sources. McAuliffe skilfully identifies Italian writer Italo Calvino's influence on Cattapan's work: 'Calvino again showed the way when his narrator, Marco Polo, declared: "Every time I describe a city I am saying something about Venice ... To distinguish the

39 McAuliffe, *Cattapan*, p. 90.
40 Cronin and Simon, p. 119.
41 Cattapan, Interview with Maestri.
42 Cattapan, Interview with Maestri.
43 Cattapan, Interview with Maestri.
44 Jon Cattapan, *The Melbourne Panels*, 2003, oil on linen, three panels 185 × 168 cm each, from Cattapan, 'Works', *Jon Cattapan*, <http://www.joncattapan.com.au> [accessed 4 December 2019].
45 Cattapan, 'Jon Cattapan Biography'; Cattapan, Interview with Maestri.

other cities' qualities, I must speak first of a city that remains implicit. For me it is Venice'".[46] Cattapan's spatial practice underpins his creative work, while also pointing up his desire to move fluidly between global and local realities as well as fictionalized and construed locations.

The Linguistic Construction of Space and Cattapan's Spatial Inscriptions

Movement and travel across boundaries and cultures – including the Italian one – characterize other pieces of work produced by Cattapan in the following decades, namely after *Documentary: Melbourne as Rome*. The movement is produced by the evocation of multiple cities at once. Cattapan corroborates this idea:

> It is not one city. It is a cut-and-paste job. There is a little bit of Sydney, a bit of New York, a bit of London, a bit of Singapore. It creates this kind of composite city, if you like. That was a way of talking about the city as a global phenomenon at a conceptual level.[47]

In particular, his *Under New York* (1990) installation, assembled in New York, and *The City Submerged* (1991–), an ongoing cycle of works, which he started during his residency at the Australia Council's Greene Street Studio, New York, and which he further evolved back in Australia,[48] are emblematic of this kinaesthetic mood. In New York, Cattapan refined the layering technique devised previously and also his understanding of space. Here, Calvino's *Invisible Cities* represented a source of inspiration and 'poetic frame' for the artist.[49] The novel provided the artist with the tools to reflect not only on the multifarious urban configurations evolving into infinite and intertextual layers of subsequent and contiguous cities but also on the constructed nature of the metropolitan space. McAuliffe's book-length study of Cattapan's aesthetics does not mention this element, which is supplanted by observations on the vagueness and evanescence of the displayed cities. According to McAuliffe's analysis, almost all the work completed in the 1990s and after 2000 displays

---

46   McAuliffe, *Cattapan*, p. 109.
47   Cattapan, Interview with Maestri.
48   Jon Cattapan, Email to Eliana Maestri (22 October 2018).
49   McAuliffe, *Cattapan*, p. 106.

cities that are less and less localized and identifiable.[50] They challenge viewers' visual and sensory perceptions, especially as various transcultural urban landscapes are blended together. However, I believe that an in-depth linguistic-orientated analysis of the artificiality of these cities, in light of Lefebvre's theories of space, will help us unveil other intrinsic connections between the artist's migrant background, his visual constructions and his transnational/ translational vision of the world.

Lefebvre worked on the production and construction of space and 'the dialectical relationship which exists within the triad of the perceived, the conceived, and the lived'.[51] In particular, he emphasizes the linguistic fabrication of space and the interrelation between social practices and the textualization of space by using language-inflected terminology and metaphors. Spaces are marked by signs produced and used by individuals within and around specific spaces.[52] Spaces are, therefore, not simple containers of signs. They are appropriated, manipulated, inscribed and designed by them: 'Conceptions of space tend [...] towards a system of verbal (and therefore intellectually worked out) signs'.[53] Signs can be verbal as well as non-verbal, including languages created by communities within specific linguistic landscapes. In other words, language, one of the greatest human productions, partakes in the social practices shaping human relations actualized in space and fashioning perceptions and consumptions of space, which is revealed to be real and factual as well as artificial and simulated.

Space, invested with spatial inscriptions and other language practices and discourses on space, is, consequentially, a huge, complex and multilayered text governed by ideologies and 'susceptible of coding and decoding'.[54] In his chapter 'Walking in the City', for example, de Certeau, deeply affected by the study of the language–space interplay, describes the view of the whole of New York City from the top of the World Trade Center as an intricate fabric of words and letters: 'The tallest letters in the world compose a gigantic rhetoric of excess in both expenditure and production'.[55] Looking at the language–space interface entails not only the acquisition of spatial reading skills but

50 McAuliffe, *Cattapan*, p. 138; McAuliffe, *The Drowned World*, p. 5.
51 Lefebvre, *The Production of Space*, p. 39.
52 Lefebvre, *The Production of Space*, pp. 140–41.
53 Lefebvre, *The Production of Space*, p. 39.
54 Lefebvre, *The Production of Space*, p. 141.
55 Michel de Certeau, *The Practice of Everyday Life*, trans. by Steven F. Rendall (Berkeley and Los Angeles, CA, and London: University of California, 1984), p. 91.

Fig. 7.1: *Untitled*, 1990 (From *Travel Suite* 1990–2015). Gouache and watercolor on paper, Collection National Gallery of Victoria; image courtesy the artist.

also the identification of 'spatial *textures* which are informed by effective knowledge and ideology'.[56] In this light, cities and urban environments, with a high concentration of dwellers, are actually 'city-texts' or textual cities spreading across vast linguistic landscapes.[57]

Cattapan's iconic cities (especially the ones visualized after his New York residency) are all textually produced landscapes traversed and inscribed by dots. His *Untitled* (1990) piece of work, belonging to the *Under New York* installation (presented in 1990 at the Nathalie Karg Gallery, New York) and also *Travel Suite*, a more recent collection (1990–2015) illustrating 'the beautiful ability of drawing to act like a visual travel diary',[58] is emblematic. This painting, like others in the above collections, strikes us as being full of dots, in different numbers, shapes or forms. Whereas in McAuliffe's reading of Cattapan's artwork these dots *are* data, namely synecdoches standing for the whole and being metonymically part of entire systems of data,[59] in my

56 Lefebvre, *The Production of Space*, p. 42, italics in original.
57 Jani Vuolteenaho et al., p. 10.
58 Cattapan, Email to Maestri.
59 Cattapan quoted in McAuliffe, *Cattapan*, p. 149.

analysis they are signs and symbols *translating* data, namely information, numbers, files, facts, figures, digits and statistics produced and processed by information systems and digital technologies. Therefore, whereas for McAuliffe, 'a dab of paint is a pixel, which in turns calls to mind the vast realm of information technology'[60] and also 'pixilated streams of data' or 'dense webs of data flows',[61] for me a dab of paint is a signifier, and – as I shall discuss further below – a form of language, including the verbal one. In other words, looking at these dots as symbols and translations helps us consider in depth the translational, semiotic and constructed nature of these signs, codifying meanings and messages and, especially, the interaction between semiotic systems, languages and spaces.

In addition, the 'dots' that Cattapan talks about, both in the interviews included in McAuliffe's 2008 monograph and in my 2014 interview, mark a shift in the artist's visual rhetoric over time. Works produced in New York and Canberra, for instance, are dominated by streams of lights whose dots reflect the haziness typical of luminescent particles emanated from office windows by such electronic devices as computers, laptops, screens, mobile phones and other forms of digital communication and data transmission.[62] In the artist's latest works, the dots sometimes lose the electric brightness typical of light bulbs, computer screens or dashboards and acquire circularity, which emblematizes such icon-driven technologies as Androids, iOS home screens or, even, control panels from decades ago. Occasionally, these dots turn into unsophisticated symbols and simple signs, which, according to primitive iconicity, resemble rounded bodies and circle-shaped referents and signifiers (see, for example, the *Atonal Group* (Cannaregio) series produced during the 2014 Venice Printmaking residency, or other works on the city, such as *Days of the Festival*).[63] Borrowing Mondrian's words, Gunther Kress and Theo van Leeuwen explain the simplicity that our scientific world tends to attribute to elementary geometrical characters such as 'circles': 'Circles [...] have been regarded as pure, quasi-scientific "atoms" of the visible world, a "pure manifestation of the elements". [...] And they have been thought to have the power to

60   McAuliffe, *Cattapan*, p. 149.
61   McAuliffe, *Cattapan*, pp. 123, 177.
62   McAuliffe, *Cattapan*, pp. 110, 123.
63   An example is Jon Cattapan, *Atonal Group* (Cannaregio 7), 2014, mixed media on paper, 130 × 130 cm, from Cattapan, 'Works', *Jon Cattapan*, <http://www.joncattapan.com.au> [accessed 4 December 2019]; Jon Cattapan, *Days of the Festivals*, 2007, oil on linen, 168 × 195 cm, from Cattapan, 'Works', *Jon Cattapan*, <http://www.joncattapan.com.au> [accessed 4 December 2019].

Fig. 7.2: *The Bookbuilder*, 1992. Oil on linen, Collection Artbank Australia;
image courtesy the artist.

directly affect our nervous system'.[64] Not accidentally, Cattapan also defines his dots or circles as 'pulses'[65] – namely, heartbeats, throbs, rhythms, vibrations and palpitations inducing human contact and visually translating basic forms of signification, writing and communication. Kress and van Leeuwen elucidate: 'Circles and curved forms generally are the elements we associate with an organic and natural order, with the world of organic nature [...]. Angularity we associate with the inorganic, crystalline world, or with the world of technology, which is a world we have made ourselves'.[66] In light of this, Cattapan's dotting technique is a strategy to visualize not only technologically transmitted data but also natural or primeval forms of communication, which attempt to mirror the unsophisticated simplicity of verbal interaction devoid of scientific, specialized or technical devices mediating and complicating interaction.

64 Gunther Kress and Theo van Leeuwen, *Reading Images: The Grammar of Visual Design*, 2nd edn 2006 (London and New York: Routledge, 1996), p. 53.
65 Cattapan, Interview with Maestri.
66 Kress and van Leeuwen, p. 55.

The confluence of various types of visual sign, icon and code, including the linguistic one, is diachronically exemplified by *The Bookbuilder* (1992). In my reading of McAuliffe's analysis, *The Bookbuilder* represents a significant turning point, marking the start of Cattapan's 'datascape phase'.[67] Referring to this piece of work, Cattapan confirmed that 'as soon as I saw it, I thought, "I know what to do now – it fed me for a very, very long time"'.[68] In *The Bookbuilder*, the information and communication systems invading the global city are represented by both heaps of books, namely the foundation, structure and scaffolding of 'a medieval building', and 'myriad lights, pinpricks of information, each light seeming to tell a story'.[69] The painting is accompanied by two vignettes complementing the work and visualizing the fact that in the past buildings were made 'from books instead of bricks. Each book is like a dot',[70] and, therefore, of written and verbal signs. Nowadays, however, other forms of communication, including electronic and digital transmission of data, further complicate the shaping of urban spaces. Dots and circles, scattered across the canvas and marking harmoniously innumerable points of contact between two superimposed cities, Melbourne and New York,[71] merge skilful forms of communication, verbal and digital, developed chronologically across centuries. These languages translate and convert information into meaningful symbols, electronically managed, filed and distributed across/around these two major urban centres. In light of this, these linguistic codes and symbols represent visual layers or, better, 'narrative layers',[72] which do not simply coat pre-existing fragmented layers of the artist's textual cities. These codes are 'deeply embedded'[73] into the painted space: they are part and parcel of the city-texts and, as a consequence, of the articulation of their urban morphology, syntagmatic relations and social–spatial practices: 'They [the works] also tell stories of local environment'.[74]

67   McAuliffe, *Cattapan*, pp. 136–46.
68   Paul Dalgarno, 'Jon Cattapan: A Portrait of the Artist as a New Director', *ART150: Celebrating 150 years of art*, <https://art150unimelb.edu.ac> [accessed 18 November 2018].
69   Cattapan in McAuliffe, *Cattapan*, p. 146.
70   Cattapan in McAuliffe, *Cattapan*, p. 146.
71   Cattapan in McAuliffe, *Cattapan*, p. 146.
72   Cattapan, Interview with Maestri.
73   Cattapan, Interview with Maestri.
74   Christine Dauber, 'An Interview with Jon Cattapan', *M/C: A Journal of Media and Culture*, 5 (2004), <http://journal.media-culture.org.au/0207/cattapaninterview.php> [accessed 18 November 2018].

In explaining the textual layers located in Sydney, Alastair Pennycook and Emi Otsuji illustrate the same nexus between space, action and languages that can be found in Cattapan's work: 'Layers are not about the mere overlapping of texts on flat surfaces; rather, they need to be seen in terms of sedimented activities and practices that are still in motion'.[75]

Actions overwrite the city with textual messages, and the city responds by emitting messages. As Lefebvre maintains:

> The city was and remains *object*, but not in the way of particular, pliable and instrumental object: such as a pencil or a sheet of paper. Its objectivity, or "objectality", might rather be closer to that of the *language* which individuals and groups receive before modifying it, or [...] to that of a cultural reality, such as the *written book*. [...] On this book, with this writing, are projected mental and social forms and structures. [...] The city *writes* and *assigns*, that is, it signifies, orders, stipulates. What? That is to be discovered by reflection.[76]

Languages are cities and cities are languages that construct houses, buildings, bridges and skyscrapers and, in doing so, they orientate and disorientate the citizen or the traveller whose itineraries spread among meanders of letters, words, texts and text messages and whose goal is to discover what the city has to offer and communicate.

Cattapan as a Multimodal and Multilingual Migrant Artist

I conclude that Cattapan's visualization of metropolitan sites is a way to draw fictitious, translational trajectories between imaginary and real cities and express his desire to be in multiple spaces and places at the same time. Cattapan's paintings are also a way to embark upon imaginary journeys out of Australia and back to European, American or Asian cities, without abandoning or ignoring – as discussed above – his Italian origins but unveiling and empowering them. Finally, his paintings are playful attempts to reflect on the confluence of signs and languages that surround and write our lives. Second-generation migrants are renowned for their tentative competences

---

75   Alastair Pennycook and Emi Otsuji, *Metrolingualism: Language in the City* (London: Routledge, 2015), p. 139.
76   Lefebvre, *Writings on Cities*, p. 102, italics in original.

in the second language,[77] sensitivity to other cultures, and desire to bring them to life in computer-mediated spaces – for example, WhatsApp and text messages with Italian relatives and friends based in the country of origin.[78] Languages are seen by Cattapan as a 'grid'[79] that prevents the viewer from seeing things and entering his depicted spaces. These grids, visualized in his work (for example, in *Exhibition Group Study*),[80] could be interpreted as distant and unreceptive, especially when they translate languages that are not mastered completely or practised daily. But my 2014 interview with Cattapan also reveals that he sees languages as a way to feel at home in a country[81] as well as social practices at work in urban settings and, simultaneously, at one with them: 'All [the dots are] [...] deeply embedded there'.[82] These practices cannot be disengaged from the internet, which dominates our era and influences our language–space behaviour.[83]

Melbourne-based writer and curator Kyle Weise analysed the professional use of computer-assisted techniques in Cattapan's artistic production but he overlooked the artist's migrant background, translational activities and interaction with the computer-modulated languages in/of the city. In his review of Cattapan's digital methods of data visualization, Weise sees Cattapan's pixel-style dots as 'networks and relationships that entangle us' or as 'networks of communication and media that dominate our landscape'.[84] Emphasis is placed more on the 'ephemerality and intangibility of the digital realm'[85] than on the linguistic fabrication of the city. Data and cities are seen as two separate entities (the latter suffering the consequences of the former) rather than a confluence of forces and social practices (including verbal

---

77 Antonia Rubino, *Trilingual Talk in Sicilian-Australian Migrant Families: Playing out Identities Through Language Alternation* (Basingstoke and New York: Palgrave Macmillan, 2014).
78 Antonia Rubino, 'Italian in Australia: Past and New Trends', in *Innovation in Italian Teaching* (Brisbane: Griffith University, 2002), pp. 1–15 (p. 9).
79 Cattapan, Interview with Maestri.
80 Jon Cattapan, *Exhibition Group Study*, 2012, archival inkjet print with acrylic and pencil markings, ED 5, each unique 60 × 80 cm (image size), from Cattapan, 'Works', *Jon Cattapan*, <http://www.joncattapan.com.au> [accessed 4 December 2019].
81 This is exemplified by the joy of discovering that 'Catapan' is also the name of a Venetian alley (Cattapan, Interview with Maestri).
82 Cattapan, Interview with Maestri.
83 Cattapan, Interview with Maestri.
84 Kyle Weise, 'Jon Cattapan: Data-scapes', *Eyeline: Contemporary Visual Arts*, 78/79 (2015), 42–49 (p. 42).
85 Weise, p. 43.

communication) generated by and generating specific spaces. Furthermore, there is no mention of the implied viewers – multilingual, multi-ethnic and multi-skilled – populating global and cosmopolitan urban centres. Cattapan's artwork, made in the heart of cosmopolitan cities with their mobile population of migrants and travellers, invites the viewer to unpack the layers that the city has acquired over time: its resemblance to other cities, its acoustic cacophony, the changing face of its signposted buildings and its textual and spatial co-creation at the hands of multilingual speakers and users of different electronic and digital devices.

Like Weise, McAuliffe neglects the interplay between multimodality and migration in Cattapan's artwork. He recognizes the artist's attempt to depict the mobility and fluidity of metropolitan sites, concepts that Cattapan draws from postmodern and poststructuralist philosophers, including Zygmunt Bauman, Jean-François Lyotard, Fredric Jameson, Gilles Deleuze and Félix Guattari.[86] Furthermore, McAuliffe repeatedly stresses the artist's intention to represent the flow of data, 'information, people and capital',[87] and the ensuing mobile qualities that the global city acquires. According to him, modern cities attract the artist because of their nomadic and mobile traits (defining the condition of urban postmodernism), not because of their migratory history or background – an aspect that is not discussed by this art historian.[88] The adjective 'migrant', along with its problematic and politically loaded connotations grounded in reality, is never employed by McAuliffe. It is supplanted instead by such cosmopolitan, trendy and, at times, abstract terms as 'mobile', 'fluid' or 'bohemian', terms that convey, as he claims, a postmodern sense of elusiveness, evasiveness, uncertainty, instability and slippage.[89] As a consequence, in his view, the postmodern society depicted by Cattapan is 'a "post-industrial society", a "consumer society, media society, information society, electronic society"',[90] but not a migratory society. Migration is, however, celebrated by the inclusivity that marks the artist's collection *Travel Suite*. While bringing together artworks from various residencies and travels (New York, India, Korea, etc.), *Travel Suite* 'lets the individual works migrate' and hails 'travel sensations, especially colour'.[91]

86   McAuliffe, *Cattapan*, pp. 100, 138, 141, 149.
87   McAuliffe, *Cattapan*, p. 149.
88   Only Karen Burns mentions this briefly in a conversation with Cattapan, transcribed and included in McAuliffe, *The Drowned World*, p. 13.
89   McAuliffe, *Cattapan*, pp. 100, 141.
90   Jameson quoted in McAuliffe, *Cattapan*, p. 141.
91   Cattapan, Email to Maestri.

In addition, McAuliffe claims that Cattapan's art is a way to portray the 'mutation [of the city] in the digital age',[92] its apocalyptic fate or its evanescent and transient nature, aspects also explained by the artist in various online interviews and talks. However, despite the fact that he briefly mentions Cattapan's migrant background,[93] McAuliffe does not reflect at any length on how the artist's position, as a member of a multimodal and polylingual community, shapes his artistic practice, aesthetics and world vision. Cattapan's migrant roots are not discussed alongside the multimodal or semiological nature of his artwork.[94] Moreover, McAuliffe never refers to Cattapan as Italian Australian or second-generation Italian, but simply as Australian, shadowing his ability to inhabit multiple spaces and linguistically varied communities, including the Italian one. This aspect in fact emerged to a considerable degree during my 2014 interview, which confirms the importance that Cattapan ascribes to his upbringing 'out of a migrant background' and within 'the large Veneto community in Melbourne'. Knowing that 'there is a network of people coming out of the same culture [...] [and providing] another cultural layer into your thinking' appears to be fundamental in Cattapan's reflections on his identity formation and artistic development.[95] These layers are not easy to disentangle or articulate, because, as Cattapan maintains, they are subconscious and in-built: 'It is an intuitive thing. You let it wash over you and it is there'.[96] These layers are therefore part of the artist's identity as a second-generation Italian and a lens through which he sees Melbourne, the world and human relations, relations mediated by languages and codified signs.

Cattapan's Acts of Translation

As Lefebvre observes: 'If I compare the city to a book, to a writing (a semiological system), I do not have the right to forget the aspect of mediation. I can separate it neither from what it contains nor from what

---

92 McAuliffe, *Cattapan*, p. 113.
93 McAuliffe, *Cattapan*, pp. 21, 171.
94 Only *Carrying*, a piece about refugees in Australia, is discussed in the light of Cattapan's migratory background, but not in relation to his digital art practice (Jon Cattapan, *Carrying*, 2002, oil on linen, 195 × 240 cm, from McAuliffe, *Cattapan*, pp. 170–71).
95 Cattapan, Interview with Maestri.
96 Cattapan, Interview with Maestri.

contains it, by isolating it as a complete system'.[97] Being mindful of mediation means that we must not forget that the painting is a medium or that second-generation Italian Australians are transcultural mediators. However, it also means that the city-book is a construction and modulation. In light of this, we should investigate how acts of mediation, transmission, alteration and, therefore, translation of semantic practices, fashioning the urban space and fabricating the urban text, are performed. In order to do so, Lefebvre suggests a number of 'intellectual operations and reflective approaches', including 'translation'.[98] Translation is a method to 'decipher' urban reality, replicate its fabrication mechanisms and analyse inscriptions and projections of relations and processes onto the city-book. According to Lefebvre, translation can unearth what is not immediately visible, palpable, transparent, evident or noticeable on the semiological surface of the city.[99] The city writes and is overwritten by a multiplicity of acts and city-languages, complicating its landscape and architecture: 'Both natural and urban spaces are, if anything, "over-inscribed": everything therein resembles a rough draft, jumbled and self-contradictory'.[100] Confusion climaxes multiple times – for example, when 'the specific code of the urban is an incomprehensible modulation, a version, a translation without the original or origins'.[101] Translation represents the key to understanding the opacity of reality and its layers. As Lefebvre explains: 'The whole is not immediately present in this written text, the city. There are other levels of reality which do not become *transparent* by definition'.[102] These levels or layers are the outcomes of transcriptions performed by the hand of ideological and social–spatial practices of interaction.

So, how can translation help us unearth what is not immediate or obvious? What kind of translation practices does Cattapan apply to his work? What kind of acts of translation does his work display? Cattapan's paintings are all produced under the sign of translation and this is obvious through his ability to depict not only flows of people and capital but also digital transmissions of data bytes and movements of information, which are translational by definition (see, for example, *Study After Endless* (Melbourne), 2014).

---

97   Lefebvre, *Writings on Cities*, p. 102.
98   Lefebvre, *Writings on Cities*, p. 102.
99   Lefebvre, *Writings on Cities*, pp. 102–03, 107–08.
100 Lefebvre, *The Production of Space*, p. 142.
101 Lefebvre, *Writings on Cities*, p. 108.
102 Lefebvre, *Writings on Cities*, p. 102, italics in original.

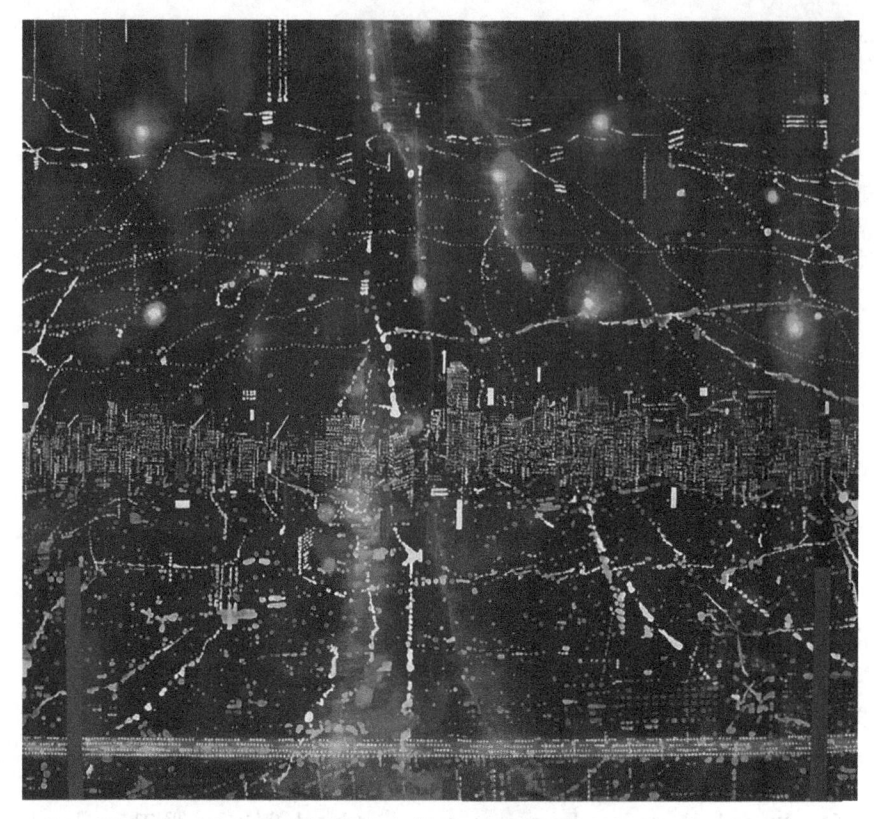

Fig. 7.3: *Study after Endless* (Melbourne), 2014. Digital print and gouache on paper; image courtesy the artist and STATION.

As Michael Cronin confirms:

> The variability of outputs of these machines [laptops] is made possible, in part, by the universal convertibility of binary code, the ability of words, images, sounds to be converted to the universal language of code. In this sense, the radical changes that have been wrought in all areas of life as a result of the advent of information technology are to be placed under the sign of convertibility or *translation*.[103]

---

103   Michael Cronin, *Translation in the Digital Age* (London and New York: Routledge, 2013), p. 3, my italics.

During 2004 and 2006 interviews with Christine Dauber and Julie Copeland, respectively, Cattapan articulates his strategies of data visualization by illustrating his computerized devices, software (e.g. Adobe Photoshop) and 'translation' approaches.[104] On both occasions, Cattapan explains that the latest paintings of his 'datascape' phase (starting with his 1992 work in Canberra) have been produced by actualizing processes of translation, namely renditions of 'visual image[s] back into painting'.[105] In order to do so, cityscapes are scanned and superimposed digitally and then 'marked' or 'translated' manually by the painter:

> The beautiful thing about it is that you start off with something which is captured ... literally the information is captured digitally, but in *translation* it becomes very much about a unique kind of mark making. So although I may be trying to replicate at times the look of the pixel or of a digital screen ... when you're actually right in front of the work ... you become aware of the fact that there's texture, that there's clumsiness, that there are particular kinds of marks that are in my ... painterly handwriting.[106]

The painter's manual marks aim to replicate the pixel-style dots and, therefore, all the signs, codes and languages that populate the cityscape at hand. In light of this, translation should be seen not just as remediation, a conversion of visual images into digital ones as highlighted, for instance, by Weise.[107] It should be seen as 'thick' translation – namely, a 'productive' strategy that aims to translate a text by thickening its fabric with personal input and subjective interpretations:[108] 'The hand-made mark becomes highly subjective as an interpretive tool, and therefore much as I might try to simply replicate the collage, what results is a painterly colouration and discrete mark-making process of overlays that speaks about painting itself'.[109]

Processes of thick translation, initially theorized by Kwame Anthony Appiah and then refined by Theo Hermans, Michaela Wolf, Martha Cheung

---

104   2004 interview with Dauber in McAuliffe, *Cattapan*, p. 138; 2006 interview with Copeland in McAuliffe, *Cattapan*, p. 195.
105   Cattapan quoted in McAuliffe, *Cattapan*, p. 195.
106   Cattapan quoted in McAuliffe, *Cattapan*, p. 195, my italics.
107   Weise, p. 44.
108   Kwame Anthony Appiah, 'Thick Translation', *Callaloo*, On 'Post-colonial Discourse': A Special Issue, 16 (1993), 808–19 (p. 817).
109   Cattapan quoted in McAuliffe, *Cattapan*, p. 138.

and Catherine Boyle,[110] have been hailed for their ability to do justice to the multilayered complexity of texts in translation. These scholars consider interlinguistic translation, understood as transfer from language A to language B, one-dimensional and limiting. As texts are multilayered and polyphonic objects intrinsically embedded in their cultural and linguistic setting,[111] translation processes ought to contemplate experimental and multidimensional ways to render their thickness, texture and fabric. As a possible solution to the subjective interpretation and rendition of the textual complexity in translation, annotations and glosses,[112] paratextual prefaces and footnotes,[113] explications and digressions[114] should be visibly added to the translated text. If, on the one hand, this 'extra-textual apparatus distances the reader from the narrative', on the other hand it enhances the translational nature of the text and raises awareness of the subjective agency of the translator.[115] Cattapan's marks and dots enrich his texts–objects–translations of multiple cities or cities in motion by incorporating inscriptions and writings that, while highlighting the constructed nature of the painting (as Cattapan says), gloss up the painting, annotating the mechanisms that participate in the transformation of the global city: the polygonal conjunction of artificial urban-inflected sign systems.

Why is it important to understand Cattapan's approach, which here I define as thick translation? What insight can this appreciation offer into the work of this artist, as a second-generation Italian Australian? And, finally, what ideologies and power does his work uncover and denounce? Cattapan's urban narrative phase coincides with his attempt to explore the dangers and the anxieties amplified by globalization. The artist reminds us that globalization

---

110 Theo Hermans, 'Cross-Cultural Translation Studies as Thick Translation', *Bulletin of the School of Oriental and African Studies*, University of London, 66 (2003), 380–89; Michaela Wolf, 'Feminist Thick Translation: A Challenge to the Formation of Feminist Cultural Identity?' *Tradução e Comunicação*, 12 (2003), 115–31; Martha P. Y. Cheung, 'On Thick Translation as a Mode of Cultural Representation', in *Across Boundaries: International Perspectives on Translation Studies*, ed. by Dorothy Kenny and Kyongjoo Ryou (Newcastle upon Tyne: Cambridge Scholars Publishing, 2007), pp. 22–36; Catherine Boyle, 'On Mining Performance: Marginality, Memory and Cultural Translation in the Extreme', in *Differences on Stage*, ed. by Alessandra De Martino, Paolo Puppa and Paola Toninato (Newcastle upon Tyne: Cambridge Scholars Publishing, 2013), pp. 207–23.
111 Appiah, p. 817.
112 Appiah, p. 817.
113 Wolf, p. 121.
114 Hermans, p. 387.
115 Wolf, pp. 121, 125.

and the circulation of money, objects and people that it generates increase endless replication mechanisms across the world.[116] The solipsistic repetition, reproduction and exportation of elements, features and characters across borders (also facilitated by mobility and technology) lead to standardization practices, uniformity and, consequently, as the artist claims, fear of sameness and identity crisis.[117] These fears and crises are projected onto Cattapan's implied viewers, identified with travellers, travellers looking at cityscapes and topographical similarities from an airplane window[118] and, according to my interpretation of the artist's work, with second-generation migrants. In the words of Cronin, 'travellers go to far-off places, tell their readers that the "exotic" is an illusion, that everywhere has now become much the same and the writers themselves are the last witnesses of differences which are about to disappear forever'.[119] Second-generation migrants share the same worries and uncertainties as the ones felt by global travellers, but they personalize and internalize them further. Current second-generation migrants in Australia, for example, fear sameness *in situ*: they dread losing their ethnic traits and being absorbed into an undistinguishable and anonymous blotch.[120] Being the children of first-generation migrants to pre-multicultural Australia, they have experienced the brutalities and racism of the 'White Australia' policy and have struggled to comply with assimilation requirements devoid of any form of respect for cultural heritages other than the White British one. 'If you were Italian, you were the other', Cattapan confirms.[121]

Therefore, Cattapan's layered cities, produced through digital superimpositions of scanned images of urban landscapes, translate cities into cities into cities ad infinitum and highlight their ethnic strata and semiotic complexity. To borrow Simon's words, his cities are 'a crossroad of codes [...] where there is a heightened awareness of the plurality of meaning systems, of the testing of the limits of expression, where dissonance is understood as a productive force'.[122] The different dotting pattern that characterizes every image of Cattapan's cities marks the original contribution of the artist as

---

116 McAuliffe, *Cattapan*, p. 123.
117 McAuliffe, *Cattapan*, pp. 106, 123; Cattapan, Interview with Maestri.
118 McAuliffe, *Cattapan*, p. 141.
119 Michael Cronin, 'Speech Acts: Language, Mobility, and Place', in *Travel and Ethics: Theory and Practice*, ed. by Corinne Fowler, Charles Forsdick and Ludmilla Kostova (London and New York: Routledge, 2014), pp. 16–30 (p. 21).
120 Maestri, pp. 288–89, 292.
121 Cattapan, Interview with Maestri.
122 Simon, *Speaking Memory*, p. 6.

second-generation migrant to the depicted landscape and, at the same time, their uniqueness and linguistic specificity, unlike what McAuliffe advocates.[123] Despite being dystopian (and, consequently, intrinsically diasporic), they are not 'any' city, displaying the same traits and features as any global city in the world. The layers and strata, contributing to their unique con/fusion and setup, visualize their resistance to ideological processes of assimilation, domestication and blending, implemented by the 'White Australia' policy before the seventies and encouraged by standardizing processes of globalization after that. According to Cronin, globalization has activated two global translation mechanisms: translational assimilation and translational accommodation.[124] While the former forces migrants to adjust to their new language environment by translating themselves into their cultural surrounding, the latter allows them to benefit from translation services and techniques so as to resist language loss and keep cultures and traditions alive. Italian migrants in Australia have fought to preserve their cultural legacies and this tenacious attachment to their roots, passed onto their children, has paved the way for Australian multiculturalism. Migrants' unique contribution to the Australian urban and linguistic landscape is celebrated by Cattapan's work, and this is clear especially when we consider the manual addition of pixel-style dots and marks to his work. These 'thick' marks, translating verbal, visual, electronic and acoustic systems, are an attempt to grasp the urban-inflected signs and languages spoken by generations of migrants and, as a consequence, an effort to acknowledge their distinctive contribution to the physiognomy of the polylingual and polysemic city. By translating the global city in a thick manner, Cattapan celebrates his subjective imprint on the city life as a child 'raised out of a migrant background'[125] and the migrants' attempt to enrich and complicate the multifaceted, multilingual and multicultural identity of their city. Like words or dots, his pieces of visual artwork represent prominent modes of signification and provide 'narrative layers'[126] whose signified and idea, in Lefebvre's words, 'correspond to a specific use of [...] space, and hence to a spatial practice that they express and constitute'.[127]

---

123   McAuliffe, *Cattapan*, p. 138.
124   Cronin quoted in Kaisa Koskinen, 'Linguistic Landscape as a Translational Space: The Case of Hervanta, Tampere', in *Language, Space and Power*, ed. by Vuolteenaho et al., pp. 73–92 (p. 90).
125   Cattapan, Interview with Maestri.
126   Cattapan, Interview with Maestri.
127   Lefebvre, *The Production of Space*, p. 16.

Conclusion

Cattapan's migrant position, between heritages and cultures, encourages him to reflect on the meaning of migration, mobility, movement, verbal and non-verbal languages and sign systems. The latter complicate the cityscape, but they also unveil a relentless attempt to celebrate the diversities and differences sculpting urban layouts and linguistic landscapes. Despite their complexity and multilayered nature, these landscapes conserve the exceptionality and inimitability of the global city. Not only are the assonances or dissonances between the languages brought into the picture (literally speaking), but the interface between computer-assisted spaces and physical spaces is also displayed and challenged. The aim is not to represent the dominance of technology over space or the ensuing sense of powerlessness it creates. Nor is it to show the viewers' inability to engage intelligibly with technology or the untranslatability of digitization processes, discussed, for example, by Weise.[128] The aim is to represent multiple forms of diaspora across spaces and places, including the richness of virtual ones. Mediating diaspora as a second-generation migrant does not entail translating an in-between place *per se*, which, in Maria Tymoczko's and, before her, Anthony Pym's views,[129] is a fantasy. It entails inhabiting multiple places – just like Cattapan's migrant father, metaphorically sitting on two chairs – and translating multiple spaces at the same time: 'One must conceptualize the translator not as operating *between* languages, but as operating [...] in a system inclusive of both'.[130] Cattapan's cities are not exclusively Italian or Australian. They are a mixture of various nationalities, which, despite their hybridity or contradictions, pay tribute to the artist's ethnic roots and origins.

Finally, Cattapan's translated cities encourage his viewers (migrants and travellers) to reflect on the agency and power that they exercise and to become social agents in charge of the constant transformation, adjustment and accommodation of the city. Cities are not just 'inferno' or 'sites for migration, displacement and bi-cultural otherness' inhabited by migrants as

---

128 Weise, pp. 42–49.
129 Anthony Pym, 'Alternatives to Borders in Translation Theory', *Athanor*, Lo stesso altro, 12 (2001), 172–82.
130 Maria Tymoczko, 'Ideology and the Position of the Translator: In What Sense Is the Translator "in between"?' in *Apropos of Ideology: Translation Studies on Ideology, Ideologies in Translation Studies*, ed. by María Calzada Pérez (Manchester: St Jerome, 2003), pp. 181–201 (p. 196), italics in original.

the 'dispossessed'.[131] And migrants are not just others or passive individuals, lost in translation and overwhelmed by 'global media and technology [...] effacing indigenous local cultures'.[132] Migrants, endowed with multilingual and technical competences, are the backbones of urban environment, its scaffolding and foundations. Empowered by Cattapan's paintings, viewers are constantly invited to reflect critically on their contribution to the urban morphology of the place they inhabit and on the interaction with the space that hosts them. Cattapan's 'thick' translated cities reveal a clear attempt to acknowledge the migrants' writing of the city, namely 'what is inscribed and prescribed on its walls, in the layout of places and their linkages', and the migrants' sensitivity to 'the *language* of the city', namely 'particularities specific to each city which are expressed in discourses, gestures, clothing, in the words and use of words by the inhabitants'.[133] Cattapan's migrant background informs his work and urges him to pay respect to the multicultural, multilingual and multisemiotic diversity of the migrants' city.

Acknowledgements

I would like to express my gratitude to Prof. Rita Wilson for her generous support and guidance as co-investigator of my 2014 MEEUC Research Fellowship, Monash University, Melbourne. Thanks to this project, I met Jon Cattapan and started an ongoing conversation with him. His insights have helped me to appreciate not only his genius but also the exciting potential of intersections between translation and the visual arts.

---

131 John Conomos, 'Jon Cattapan', *Eyeline: Contemporary Visual Arts*, 27 (1995), <https://www.eyelinepublishing.com/eyeline-27/review/jon-cattapan> [accessed 24 September 2020].
132 Conomos.
133 Lefebvre, *Writings on Cities*, p. 115.

CHAPTER EIGHT

An Exhibition about Italian Identities: *Beyond Borders*

Viviana Gravano and Giulia Grechi*

Premises

The BEYOND BORDERS: *Transnational Italy/OLTRE I CONFINI: Italia Transnazionale* exhibition was the result of a close collaboration between the 'Transnationalizing Modern Languages' (TML) research team and *Routes Agency. Cura of Contemporary Art,* a contemporary art curatorial collective founded by art historian Viviana Gravano and visual anthropologist Giulia Grechi. Assuming the form of a usable 'object', the exhibition sought to represent not only the research material, but also – crucially – the innovative methodology proposed by the TML team. The exhibition also incorporated the work of the TML's artist in residence, the photographer Mario Badagliacca.[1] What follows aims to explain the theoretical framework informing the organization of the exhibition from a curatorial perspective, and presents the process of sharing and negotiation in which we, as curators, and the TML researchers were engaged. The exhibition travelled between different locations: first Rome (British School, 2016), then London (Italian

---

* The sections 'Premises', 'Showing Stories' and 'Interactivity' are by Viviana Gravano; 'A house of fiction', 'Experiencing Experience' and 'It Is Forbidden Not to Touch' are by Giulia Grechi. English translation by Georgia Wall.
1 'Italy Is Out' was a project by Mario Badagliacca, artist in residence for TML: a series of 14 colour photographs consisting of portraits of people and the personal objects that tell the story of their family and their connections with modern Italian cultures. The intention was to collect life stories involving Italian communities and individuals who belong to different generations.

Cultural Institute, 2016), New York (Calandra Institute, 2017), Melbourne (Italian Museum, 2017), Addis Ababa (Italian Cultural Institute, 2017) and finally Tunis (Italian Cultural Institute, 2018).

It is, first of all, necessary to consider the core principles of the project to understand the rationale behind the type of exhibition that was ultimately proposed: a traditional 'display' risked short-circuiting the very research methodology it aimed to represent. At the heart of TML's reflections on the study of modern languages and cultures was the idea that language and culture are not expressions of a monolithic national reality linked to one territory and exported in that form to other parts of the world. Rather, Italian culture is considered to exemplify the diasporic nature of most modern languages and cultures. It was not, therefore, a case of identifying the essential characteristics of a given culture, but of capturing the constant transformation it undergoes 'at home' and in the various communities that in some way derive from it.

We could say that the exhibition began with a reflection on the concept of 'the invention of tradition',[2] an attempt to create an environment in which different interpretations of 'italianità' could be seen for what they are: narratives created by these communities in close relationship with their surrounding environment, which diversify according to personal, lived experience. Paraphrasing the title of an important exhibition in Turin marking the 150th anniversary of Italian unification in 2011, what we needed was not an exhibition of Italy, but an exhibition about Italians.[3]

Another core principle of the TML project was the idea of polyphonic narratives: a *collection* of stories that rejected encyclopaedic-style definitions and descriptions, offering instead a chorus of (at times, dissonant) voices that would eliminate any risk of recounting THE history of Italian culture. The TML researchers were working on public and private memories in different parts of the world, on the historical formation of different Italian communities, on new forms of Italian communities abroad and on the significant contemporary cultural diversity within Italy prompted by contemporary migration to the peninsula. It was immediately clear to us that the exhibition had to capture this rich and complex collection of material gathered in what we

---

2 Eric Hobsbawm and Terence Ranger, *The Invention of Tradition* (Cambridge: Cambridge University Press, 1983); *L'invenzione della tradizione* (Turin: Einaudi, 1987).
3 Studio Azzurro, *Fare gli italiani. 1861–2011. Una mostra per i 150 anni della storia d'Italia* (Milan: Silvana Editoriale, 2011).

might term, following Paolo Bertella Farnetti, a practice of *Public History*, or 'history from below'.[4]

Beyond Borders had to be a fluid space, where emotional, private and even intimate stories could meet and encounter official, institutional and historical narratives, offering a hybrid perspective that refrained from judgement and presented the user with various opportunities for identification with or, indeed, rejection of the perspectives offered. A significant example that we feel it is important to cite: how to approach the history and more recent fate of Italian communities in former colonies? Our critical positioning regarding colonialism, as curators who focus on the postcolonial, did not prevent us from allowing space in the exhibition for the story of the years of Italian colonialism and of Italians in those former colonies today. The juxtaposition of images in the 'school room', for example, and the selection of audio narratives does not present a judgement or offer a hierarchy of importance of these conflicting memories. Instead, it places the viewer within a circuit that allows them to assume their own position, to develop a subjective sense of identification or rejection. The exhibition was intended not to provide answers but to generate questions, offering up the material on 'display' for continual reinterpretation or translation.[5]

The final essential premise was the conscious methodological heterogeneity of the research approaches of the various members of the TML team. The different types of material collected, the diverse range of people involved in the project and the use of multiple research languages were conceptual prerequisites, rather than consequences, of a perspective that sought to avoid at all costs a taxonomic, catalogue-style classification. The biographies of the researchers

---

4   This reference is to the particular Italian interpretation of the term 'public history' as elaborated by historian Paolo Bertella Farnetti and the Associazione Italiana Public History, who are developing an Italian approach to public history. Paolo Bertella Farnetti, Lorenzo Bertucelli and Alfonso Botti, *Public history. Discussioni e pratiche* (Milan: Mimesis, 2017).

5   'Now, the subject is he who collects images. The subject is therefore a reader. I myself, in my book, have simply engaged in an "act of reading" one of the *Mnemosyne* panels created by Warburg, who in turn engaged in an "act of reading" certain objects (the clay and bronze divination tools used by sages in antiquity to interpret omens in animal livers) which in turn are objects of "reading" (of man's destiny)'. Georges Didi-Huberman and Isabella Mattazzi, 'L'immagine inquieta: una conversazione con Georges Didi-Huberman', *Doppiozero*, 22 May 2012 <http://www.doppiozero.com/materiali/interviste/l%E2%80%99immagine-inquieta-una-conversazione-con-georges-didi-huberman> [accessed 20 February 2020].

themselves, conceived in turn as a possible research object of the project, were a key factor in the decision to create a particular type of final exhibition.

It was apparent from the very first conversations we had with the researchers that each object was composed of three narrative layers, and that this intrinsic feature had to be made visible in the exhibition. At the first level was the object itself, be it text, photo, video, etc., which presented its own history; a second level of narration came from the story, the experiences impressed on the object by the person who had given it to the researcher; the third interpretative level, crucial for us, was the emotional engagement of the researcher, the relationship between the object and its 'donor' with their research and personal biography. To this we need to add, or rather 'mix in', a fourth level: the perception of these three levels we held as curators together with the creative team who worked with us to produce the exhibition.

Each of these passages highlights the importance of the term 'translation', a word at the heart of TML and one that became the fundamental principle guiding the curatorial decisions for *Beyond Borders*. Each '(s)oggetto', each subject–object, engaged in the translation of a continually redefinable meaning. Each 'object' exhibited, each installation, brings with it the donor's translation of its history, the translation offered by the researcher to whom it was 'donated' and the translation proposed by ourselves as curators, by our transformation of those objects and stories into a public image, in turn translated by the technological language employed in the exhibition.[6]

Showing Stories

From the onset, there was a tension between the aims of *Beyond Borders* and its very nature as an exhibition. Creating an exhibition, which, as such, had to address a certain academic notion of 'documentation', raised the key question of how we could reflect on the mechanism of the practice of 'exhibiting'; how we could critically engage with a historically hierarchical vision where space 'teaches' and visitors 'learn'. Temporary exhibitions, like museums, rest on an ordering, normative vision, both in terms of the conceptual organization of the objects they present and in the material display of the space they construct.

The very structure of an exhibition must provide a direction of travel; the visitor should feel carried by the flow of a river that urges her/him to navigate

---

6   Andrea Balzola and Paolo Rosa, *L'arte fuori da sé. Un manifesto per l'età post-tecnologica* (Milan: Feltrinelli, 2011).

a clear path. This prevailing idea of 'exhibition', born in the museums of the nineteenth century, continues in large part to dominate museum spaces, which consider the user as a(n) (s)*oggetto* who must be educated. The primary objective of the exhibition space is to affirm the authority of its own vision. If its peremptory and assertive structure can be questioned by anyone who enters, it will cease to exist in ontological terms. Each visitor entering an exhibition knows that she is looking for a little experience of 'truth' that, room by room, will be displayed and demonstrated for her/him.[7]

In 1969 curator Harald Szeeman created an exhibition entitled *When Attitudes Become Form* at the Kunsthalle in Bern.[8] The title itself invades the exhibition space with a subtle virulence. On show are not forms, but attitudes; the processes and operating modes that transmute into forms. The potential visitor already knows that they will not find pre-sculpted forms, pre-written truths, pre-modelled aesthetic bodies; they will be able to participate in their creation, in their process/ing. The open-plan exhibition saw works and objects 'placed' haphazardly in the spaces of the Kunsthalle, often at risk of being trampled by visitors, and without any clear explanation, so that one unidentifiable work merged with the next.

Szeemann's installation was the product of an intense collaboration with the participating artists, in terms of not only the location of the objects/works in the space but also the construction of an open path that leaves room for the bodily improvisation of the spectator. The lack of a designated path simultaneously puts the visitor at ease and embarrasses them, obliging them to assume the responsibility for their decisions, putting them in a state of anxiety and fear on account of the disruptive, even violent agent of change they may become in doing so.[9]

---

7 To understand the profound difference between the notion of exhibition understood as static, didactic place and a conceptualization of the exhibition as a territory of shared experience with the visitor, it is useful to refer to Michel De Certeau's distinction between 'place' and 'space' in *L'invention du quotidien*. 'Place', like the written word, refers to a clearly defined, largely stable and identifiable site; 'space' is like the word when it is spoken, a territory marked by the trajectories that cross it and continually translate and redefine it. Michel De Certeau, *L'invention du quotidien* (Paris: Union générale d'éditions, 1980), p. 175.
8 Harald Szeemann, *When Attitudes Become Form. Live in Your Head. Works – Concepts – Processes – Situations – Information* (Berne: Stampfli + Cie Ltd, 1969).
9 'Works, concepts, processes, situations, information (we consciously avoided the expressions 'object' and 'experiment') are the 'forms' through which these artistic expressions are expressed. They are forms derived not from pre-formed pictorial

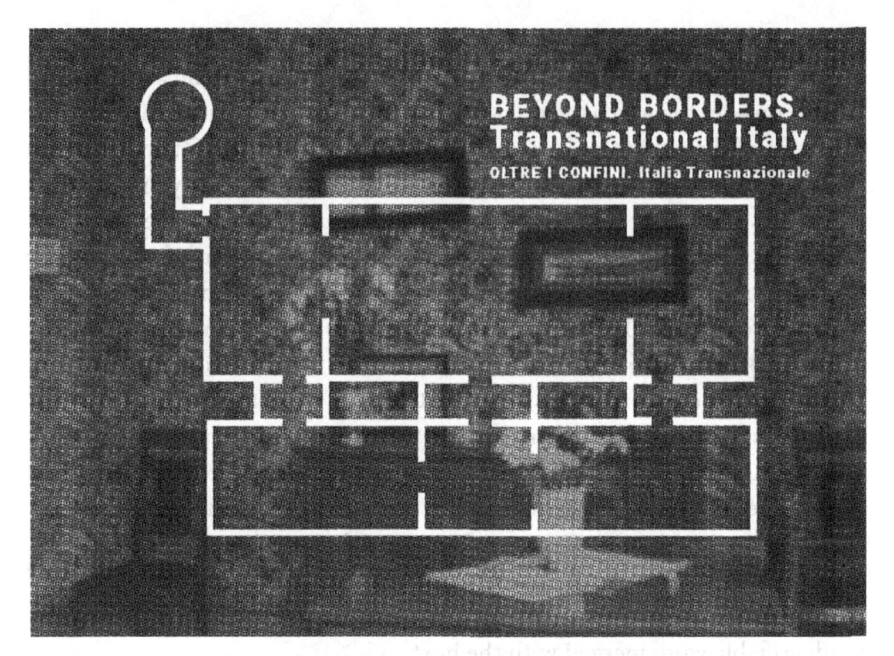

Fig. 8.1: Plan of the exhibition *Beyond Borders: Transnational Italy*, British School at Rome, 2016. Poster design by Carolina Farina.

This condition of insecurity, the possibility as users of managing oneself within a space, are two of the principles guiding the construction of *Beyond Borders*. The exhibition's first venue, The British School at Rome – practically speaking, an ideal venue for the exhibition, although our use of the space had profound ideological connotations – allowed us to simulate a house: an entrance from the street, a hallway, a corridor, a living room with a corner for homework, a kitchen, two bedrooms (adult and child) and a reference library (Figure 8.1). Each room, as we discuss subsequently, has traces that help identify it, but the space remains an open territory, without walls, in which the visitor can move freely, retrace their steps, walk quickly or slowly, listen, see, touch.

opinions, but from the experience of the design process itself. This dictates both the choice of material and the form of work as the extension of gesture. This gesture can be private, intimate, or public and expansive. But the process itself always remains vital; it is handwriting and style simultaneously. Thus, the meaning of this design lies in the fact that an entire generation of designers has undertaken to give form to the nature of design and designers in term of a natural process.' Szeeman, *When Attitudes Become Form*, p. 3.

Visitors had to experience a feeling of freedom such that they could choose to stay for three hours or twenty minutes, to walk or sit and stay a while, even to sit in an armchair and read. The exhibition invites you to traverse it with 'spatialising actions', a condition that almost any exhibition could and should promote. In reality, however, the imposition of a distance between the body of the user and 'objects' on display, the cadenced and regular space, impose a sense of time that, even allowing for all possible variation, remains within the canonical paradigm of the museum as a place of education.

The exhibition had first of all to disrupt the perception of the 'documents' on show to enable a more intimate and personal engagement, according to an internal, rather than external, time. We can think of *Beyond Borders* as a 'social apparatus', a *dispositif*, following Gilles Deleuze's definition:

> In the first instance it is a tangle, a multilinear ensemble. It is composed of lines, each having a different nature. And the lines in the apparatus do not outline or surround systems which are each homogenous in their own right, object, subject, language, and so on, but follow directions, trace balances which are always off balance, now drawing together and then distancing themselves from one another. Each line is broken and subject to *changes in direction*, bifurcating and forked, and subject to *drifting*. Visible objects, affirmations which can be formulated, forces exercised and subjections in position are like vectors and tensors.[10]

Interactivity

Beyond Borders was informed by the 'museum as narration' model of the exhibition, as defined by the artist collective Studio Azzurro:

> Oggi quando pensiamo a un 'museo', ci appare quindi l'idea di un laboratorio, un organismo vitale che sa dialogare con le persone parlando la lingua della nostra epoca e che sa trasformarsi interattivamente nel confronto e nella partecipazione, così come sa proporre una 'visione' in continua evoluzione senza però cedere a soluzioni di intrattenimento immediato.

---

10   Gilles Deleuze, 'What is a *dispositif*?', in *Michel Foucault: Philosopher*, ed. and trans. by Timothy J. Armstrong (London and New York: Routledge, 1992), pp. 159–68.

Today when we think of a 'museum', what we have in our minds is a workshop, a vital organism which can dialogue with people by speaking the language of our time and which can be interactively transformed by comparison and participation, just as it can offer a continually evolving 'vision' without resorting to facile entertainment.[11]

Two aspects of Studio Azzurro's definition concern us here: the notion of museum/exhibition as a workshop in which the spectator actively participates, and the idea of a shifting vision in which interactivity is not just an illusory game but a way of addressing the visitor's perceptions.

Beyond Borders had to be an innovative academic output, sharing these research findings with audiences who would not normally have access to them. At the same time, it needed to reflect the complex meanings of the materials collected by the TML team without turning into the sort of superficial 'show' becoming increasingly common in many museums. The question was: how could one reflect appropriately the weight of the exhibition's content and, at the same time, attract a wider audience? The solution came via the significant participatory approach that broadened the curatorial staff of the exhibition. We invited architects Laura Negrini and Carmelo Baglivo from the Baglivo-Negrini studio in Rome to work with us alongside video maker Simone Memé and software developer Giulio Pernice, both experts in building interactive exhibition systems.

Collaboration with Simone Memé and Giulio Pernice was fundamental to the construction of the narrative element that represented the structural particularity of *Beyond Borders*. We needed to find a way for the four levels of 'translation' or of 'interpretation' explained previously to become legible narratives, accessible on a visual and multisensory level. The expressive potential of each 'object' on display, beyond its obvious history, was carefully analysed. Each document appeared to us as a potential activator of diverse sensory, emotional and affective experiences. We had to place the viewer *inside*, and not just in front of, the myriad of stories told and tellable; offer them total freedom of movement. The intention was that the knowledge and emotions of the researchers, curators, donors and future visitors be commingled, situating us all in an open exchange that, from a perceptive point of view, would be wilfully uncontrollable. We chose, therefore, to use the form of interactive technology that is largely invisible, and which could

---

11   Studio Azzurro, *Studio azzurro. Musei di narrazione* (Milan: Silvana Editore, 2011), p. 6. This and other quotations from Italian are translated by Georgia Wall.

An Exhibition about Italian Identities: Beyond Borders

Fig. 8.2: The Passageway with photographs by Mario Badagliacca, 'Italy Is Out',
Beyond Borders: Transnational Italy, British School at Rome, 2016.
Photo by Carolina Farina.

be activated through analogue, everyday objects or actions such as sitting on a chair at a dining table or perching on a school bench and looking at a blackboard that is actually a projection.

Interactivity in itself is not about some generic concept of participation; it is about insisting on giving back to the spectator the pleasure of making a choice, and a request for responsibility. Time was another essential question: each spectator had to be able to decide whether and how to stop using the different parts of the exhibition, in this way choosing their own interaction time. There were no hints that a specific feature could be 'exhausted', which would imply that we had set a beginning and an end of the experience – instead, everyone had the opportunity to create their own time. The possible spatial and temporal variations offered to users were not only an act of 'generosity' towards those visiting the exhibition but became an essential tool for further research related to the perceptions of spectators faced with a particular object/document.

In *L'arte fuori da sé*, Andrea Balzola and Paolo Rosa discuss a new type of interactivity that they define as 'participatory':

La prospettiva di questa interattività artistica è rovesciata: il pubblico è protagonista dell'interazione invece di subirne le procedure con cui si suggerisce la possibilità del passaggio dalla semplice produzione di dati finalizzati all'uso commerciale e di controllo alla produzione di segni significativi sul piano emotivo, autoformativo e comunitario.

The perspective of this artistic interactivity is reversed: the public is the protagonist of the interaction rather than object of its procedures, which suggests the possibility of a transition from simple data production aimed at commercial and monitoring uses, to the production of significant signs on an emotional, self-development and community level.[12]

This is an interactivity that positions the viewer as an actor, not merely a recipient. This decision brings us back to our opening reflections on the possibility of constructing *Beyond Borders* not as a place of 'learning' but as a space of 'self-development' – for all those who worked to produce it or visited it.

A House of Fiction[13]

> I am the one
> who always goes away.
> Because I must –
> With my home intact
> But always changing
> So the windows don't match
> The doors anymore – the colours
> Clash in the garden –
> And the ocean lives in the bedroom.
> I am the one
> Who always goes

---

12   Balzola and Rosa, p. 94.
13   I refer here to Homi Bhabha's analysis of 'domestic' stories in novels recounting postcolonial experience: 'to live in the unhomely world, to find its ambivalences and ambiguities enacted in the *house of fiction*, or its sundering and splitting performed in the work of art.' Homi Bhabha, *The Location of Culture* (New York: Routledge, 1994), p. 18 (my emphasis).

> Away with my home
> Which can only stay inside
> in my blood – my home which
> does not fit
> with any geography.
> (Sujata Bhatt)

In an exhibition space constructed not as a place of passive absorption of knowledge elaborated elsewhere, but of active, interactive and multisensory engagement, we proposed an experimental narrative path: an exhibition not of objects but of stories. Here, the visitor can choose to identify with or reject the narratives that may trigger personal or historical memories and generate a complex sense of affect; they can see even the most familiar objects from a different point of view, question that 'infra-ordinary'[14] space that opens up between the folds of everyday life, of habit, where we construct, contest and perform our cultural identity, often without realizing.[15]

We inhabit our culture – and our 'mother tongue' – like a home.[16] With doors and windows closed to the outside world we can defend an 'endogamic' identity from contamination with other cultural trajectories or open up to the outside to welcome difference, making the house a porous space, a contact zone, rendering our own domesticity intimately connected to that wider world. It is, after all, in the home that we learn as children – almost by osmosis – the roles, rituals, meanings and techniques that our culture offers us as normative models and instruments of social integration. It is through the domestic space that we acquire, in various ways, the cultural skills that will make us feel 'adequate'; the 'body techniques' of sleeping, eating, walking that Marcel Mauss identifies as supposedly natural and yet are in fact where we are most thoroughly cultural beings,[17] in that the culture to which we belong indicates a map of meaning that helps us feel 'natural' within that environment. In Italian, as indeed in English, there is a very strong etymological link between the idea of 'inhabiting' and 'habit'. Both words derive from the Latin *habitus*: where we

---

14 George Perec, *L'infra-ordinaire* (Paris: Éditions du Seuil, 1989).
15 Images and a short film of the exhibition are available online: <http://www.routesagency.com/portfolio/beyondborders/>.
16 We presented the following reflections also in 'Exhibiting Transnational Identities and Belongings. Italian Culture beyond Borders', *Italian Studies*, 74 (2019), 386–91.
17 Marcel Mauss, 'Le tecniche del corpo', in *Teoria generale della magia e altri saggi* (Torino: Einaudi, 1991; first edn 1936).

live is where we are creatures of habit; where a space, certain relationships or a way of being in the world is habitual.

This process of 'cultural incorporation' becomes particularly complex for subjects whose life experience is inherently transcultural, who identify simultaneously with two or more cultures – as Sujata Bhatt evokes in the poem above. The feeling of never being at home, or always feeling at home, regardless of where that might be; this experience of being 'unhomed', which is not to say 'homeless',[18] today corresponds to the trajectories of many people's identifications of belonging. They may be far from home in many ways; perhaps they have moved to a different place from where they were born, or would like to, or they have *not* moved, but have watched their family space and city radically change; perhaps they find themselves living between different cultures and languages, where a sense of belonging becomes even more complex and multifaceted, or perhaps they experience the shock of recognizing 'the-world-in-the-home, the-home-in-the-world'.[19] Homi Bhabha describes this feeling of 'unhomeliness' as a disturbance that comes from becoming unable to distinguish 'the world' and 'the home', the public and the private, in their traditional positions.[20]

This complex interrelation between private and public, story and history, cultural norms and the creative or contradictory ways they are translated into subjective experience was the departure point for the metaphor around which *Beyond Borders* was constructed, linking the exhibition to an understanding of domesticity and of living as practices of continuous reinvention of the self and personal cultural identity. We asked, can an exhibition be a home? Is it possible to feel at home at an exhibition? Can an exhibition make us understand something of our experience of inhabiting not only a home, but also ourselves, our cultural identity, our memories, our community? Through the various installations, we created an environment that visitors would find familiar, an emotional space, an *atmosphere*[21] that would be immediately identifiable as a house,[22] a house of fiction.

18   'To be unhomed is not to be homeless, nor can the "unhomely" be easily accommodated in that familiar division of social life into private and public spheres.' Homi Bhabha, 'The World and the Home', *Social Text*, 31/32 (1992), 14–53 (p. 141).
19   Bhabha, 'The World and the Home', p. 141.
20   'The intimate recesses of the domestic space become sites of history's most intricate invasions. In that displacement the border between home and world becomes confused; and, uncannily, the private and the public become part of each other, forcing upon us a vision that is as divided as it is disorienting'. Bhabha, 'The World and the Home', p. 141.
21   Tonino Griffero, *Atmosferologia. Estetica degli spazi emozionali* (Rome: Laterza, 2010).
22   Of course, we based our 'house' on the Italian cultural stereotype of a home, conscious

An Exhibition about Italian Identities: Beyond Borders 219

Fig. 8.3: The Living Room, *Beyond Borders: Transnational Italy*,
British School at Rome, 2016. Photo by Carolina Farina.

Fig. 8.4: The Bedroom, *Beyond Borders: Transnational Italy*,
British School at Rome, 2016. Photo by Carolina Farina.

Within each installation, a simple, familiar object evokes the space of the 'room' (a kitchen cabinet, bedside tables, an armchair). Once the atmosphere of the home was clear and immediately recognizable, we worked (paradoxically) on *removing* key objects to complete the picture. For example, six 'real' chairs were placed around a table that was physically absent, instead projected as an image (Figure 8.3); between the two 'real' bedside tables, the bed was also a projection (Figure 8.4). Spontaneous, 'natural' gestures activated the installations, so sitting down at the set table triggered video content to appear on the empty plates. The purpose of the missing object was twofold: on the one hand, it creates an imbalance, defying expectations; on the other, it makes space for the visitor's imagination – while the material objects make the environment easy to recognize, the physical absence of one key element and its substitution with a visual image transforms it into one of many possible tables, inspiring the visitor to complete the picture, projecting onto that image *their* table, or *their* bed. The space, in this way, becomes habitable: the visitor can fill it with their memories and experiences, similar or diverse. The missing material object is as important as those present, encouraging the visitor to articulate a personal interpretation and facilitating their identification, triggering a playful yet profound reflexivity.

Experiencing Experience

The hypertextual structure of the narration and the multitude of documentary fragments make it possible to evoke the story in a non-linear version that is not seen from a single viewpoint. The presentation of the events through the

---

of its particularity and without any intention to generalize it as a universal concept of living. On final project visits to Addis Ababa and Tunis this was one of the first questions raised in meetings with university students: the fact that the exhibition represented a model of a house that did not correspond to a way of living in many other cultures or in poorer sections of the population in other parts of the world. These observations were extremely interesting for us. When we initially designed *Beyond Borders*, Rome, London and New York were the only planned locations. Further sites, specifically Addis Ababa and Tunis, emerged later, and the issue of the pertinence of the chosen domestic environment to cultural traditions distinct from our own is crucial in these cases. A workshop with students from La Manouba University in Tunis was aimed precisely at questioning and problematizing the organization of the exhibition and research and led to the creation of a new installation which was added to the exhibition in February 2018.

Fig. 8.5: The School, *Beyond Borders: Transnational Italy*, British School at Rome, 2016. Photo by Carolina Farina.

collating of original documents or oral narrations creates an accumulation of fragments that surpasses an organic, unitary explanation.[23]

We explained above that *Beyond Borders* worked with at least three intertwined interpretative levels: the fieldwork process, where the material in question was first presented; the researchers' own reading of the materials they had collected; the representation of those same materials in the exhibition itself. Fieldwork is based on the act of listening, with the researcher – be they an anthropologist, sociologist or historian – listening to the subject recount their culture in their own terms. The researcher bases their own narration on this account, in this way adding another degree of interpretation, 'an interpretation of an interpretation',[24] following the first interpretation offered by the subject who belongs to the culture in question. This implies that the work of the researcher is essentially an imaginative act that seeks to 're-present' a person's culture or history through the terms in which they were narrated.

---

23   Fabio Cirifino, Elisa Giardina Papa and Paolo Rosa, *Studio Azzurro. Musei di narrazione. Esperienze interattive e affreschi multimediali* (Rome: Silvana Editoriale, 2011), p. 14.
24   Clifford Geertz, *The Interpretation of Cultures* (London: Macat, 1988).

What the researcher effectively produces is a 'fiction' – not in the sense of something false or unreal, but in the original meaning of the Latin word *fictio*: something formed or fashioned.

In this sense, the researcher's story is a point of view, born in and of a provisional field of reciprocity. This raises a further point: 'the line between mode of representation and substantive content is as undrawable in cultural analysis as it is in painting; and that fact in turn seems to threaten the objective status of [...] knowledge by suggesting that its source is not social reality but scholarly artifice.'[25] This threat should not be seen as a danger, says Geertz, because the strength of our explanations lies not in a mass of raw, uninterpreted data but rather in the possibility of understanding and recounting the forms through which a subject lives and communicates personal experience on a symbolic level; that is, 'against the power of the scientific imagination to bring us into touch with the lives of strangers'.[26]

In *Beyond Borders*, therefore, there are three levels of experience connected to three levels of interpretation: firstly that of the subjects who recounted their experience, then that of the researchers who construct their narrative based on this account, and finally the curators' reading of the two previous levels, which leads to a further level of *fictio*, of imagination: the house as a device in which all the various levels of the story can be articulated. There is in fact another, essential, level that closes the circle: the fourth level of interpretation is the experience of the visitor. In *Antropologia dell'esperienza*, Victor Turner states that 'experience is a journey, a test (of oneself, of one's assumptions about others), a ritual landscape, self-exposure' ['l'esperienza è un viaggio, una messa alla prova (di sé, delle proprie supposizioni sugli altri), un paesaggio rituale, un esporsi'].[27] An *exposure*; *setting out*, to meet other stories, similar or foreign to one's own.

It Is Forbidden Not to Touch[28]

> Whose house is this? Whose night keeps out the light in here?
> Say who owns this house? It is not mine. I had another sweeter
> [...].

---

25 Geertz, p. 25.
26 Geertz, p. 25.
27 Victor Turner, *Antropologia dell'esperienza* (Bologna: Il Mulino, 1984), p. 112.
28 Cirifino et al., p. 31.

> The House is strange. Its shadows lie.
> Say, tell me, why does its lock fit my key?
> (Toni Morrison, *Home*, 2012)

Beyond Borders was an exhibition of stories inspired by Studio Azzurro's 'museums as narration': exhibition spaces conceived of as 'learning ecosystems', immersive environments where the objects present do not have intrinsic value but trigger a story. Rather than acting as a container for institutional memories, artefacts or masterpieces, this exhibition space is a site of collective reworking of memory and identity recounted in a non-linear way, signalling fractures rather than continuities, the lapses – what doesn't fit, what is on the tip of your tongue. A space in which there is not a narrative to be read, but to be *practised*, a space where the visitor is urged to play an active role by projections calling upon, and amplifying, our cognitive and sensory potential. Such a 'narrative habitat' is also a space that can 'restore sense to the senses', where gesture, affect, and emotion are 'interpretative agents'[29] that help the visitor to identify with the memories of others, penetrating History through stories.

The embodied and collective dimension simultaneously underlines the significance and the beauty of the visitor's act, because they are not only an active part of the museum narrative but also the performativity and the 'aesthetics' of the exhibition space, recalling in this sense the poetic, ethical and political value in this term's etymology, 'the disposition to sense acutely'.[30]

This kind of 'performing museology' opens up a metalinguistic and reflective space, revealing the museum as a site where embodied social practices – specifically, where playfulness – can be a tool for the visitor to acquire awareness of their own role as an 'interpretative agent',[31] who finds in the exhibition traces of their own possible experience or living memory.

Dubbed 'anthropoetic' by Paola Rosa, this mixture of poetic and anthropological elements within an installation becomes itself *an affective art working*: a site that can hold the emotional strength of memorialization strategies, that can activate visitors' bodies and their sensorial nature and go beyond the urge to simply 'show', working instead with the embodied dimensions of the senses, constructing in this way a porous and profoundly political space.

---

29   Balzola and Rosa.
30   Paul Gilroy, David Howes and Douglas Kahn, eds, 'Introducing Sensory Studies', *The Senses and Society* 1 (2006), 5–8.
31   Helen Rees Leahy, *Museum Bodies: The Politics and Practices of Visiting and Viewing* (Farnham: Ashgate, 2012).

> The affective museum works with poetics to assist visitors to look through that which was hidden and rendered opaque in traditional linear displays [...]. Poetics here demands physical, emotional and intellectual labour, from design, content and programming, and from visitors. It importantly moves us to reflect on the ethics of colonial encounters, the stories we tell about self and others, and to relate this to our lived experiences today and in the global future.[32]

Immersing the visual in its sensory embeddedness can stimulate a form of sensorial and affective reappropriation of the space and stories shown. The subjects, represented with their voices and their stories, the researchers, the entire working group and the visitors combine to create a sort of 'interstitial intimacy' that questions the distinction between the public and the private, the past and the present, the intimate and the social; the 'binary divisions through which such spheres of social experience are often spatially opposed. These spheres of life are linked through an "in-between" temporality that takes the measure of dwelling at home, while producing an image of the world of history'.[33]

---

32 Viv Golding, 'Museums, Poetics and Affect', *Feminist Review* 104 (2013), 80–99.
33 Bhabha, *The Location of Culture*, p. 13.

Part 3

Mobilities of Memory

CHAPTER NINE

Pitigliano, Maryland? Travelling Memories and Moments of Truth

Barbara Spadaro

Pitigliano is a beautiful, ancient town in southern Tuscany, also known as 'La piccola Gerusalemme' (Little Jerusalem). Built on a tuff rock that overlooks vineyards, olive groves and thermal springs, Pitigliano sits within a network of Etruscan paths, Roman roads and medieval fortresses between Siena, Perugia and Rome. In the sixteenth century, when restrictive measures for the Jews in Venice and the Papal States inaugurated the age of the urban *ghetti* in Europe,[1] numerous Jews found a new home in Pitigliano and for a couple of centuries their commercial networks linked the Italian states to the global trade of the port city of Livorno. While exchanging colonial goods from the Sahara to Europe via Tripoli, these networks also provided the vehicle for Sephardic culture to move across the whole of Europe and beyond.[2] In the nineteenth century the Jews of Pitigliano accounted for 12 per cent of the entire population of 3,000, which was a high percentage of Jewish population for a single Italian town at the time (within the Jewish population in Italy of approximately 50,000): this gave rise to the nickname of Little Jerusalem.[3] Yet

---

1 Angelo Biondi and Carlo Fè, *Gli ebrei a Pitigliano. La Piccola Gerusalemme* (Grotte di Castro: Tipografia Ceccarelli, 2009); Anna Foa, *The Jews of Europe after the Black Death* (Berkeley: University of California Press, 2000), translated from the Italian by Andrea Grover.
2 Francesca Trivellato, *The Familiarity of Strangers: The Sephardic Diaspora, Livorno, and Cross-cultural Trade in the Early Modern Period* (New Haven, CT: Yale University Press, 2009); Sarah Abrevaya Stein, *Plumes: Ostrich Feathers, Jews, and a Lost World of Global Commerce* (New Haven, CT: Yale University Press, 2008).
3 Biondi and Fè, p. 8.

soon Jewish emancipation (the process that would recognize Jews as entitled to social equality and citizen rights in nineteenth-century Europe) and Italy's unification would open new paths to the Jews as citizens of a secular state driven towards industrial modernity and expansionist projects.[4] Thus many *ebrei pitiglianesi* (Jews of Pitigliano) embraced the urban life of the big cities[5] to participate in the transnational making of the new nation, whether from Italy or abroad. In 1876 Giannetto Paggi – a Jew from Pitigliano, a teacher and an ardent Italian patriot – set off from Livorno at the invitation of a lady of a family from the Jewish trading elite of Tripoli, Carolina Nunes-Vais. At the time of European imperialism in the Mediterranean, the North African elites wanted to provide their children with a European-style education, and Paggi accepted to become a tutor in Libya.[6] With the Italian occupation of Tripoli in 1912 and the establishment of colonial rule, Giannetto Paggi became *the* celebrated pioneer of Italian 'civilization' in Tripoli, until the Fascist anti-Semitic laws hit his children – who had themselves become teachers in his Tripoli school – casting a dark and long shadow on the Jews of Italy and Libya. Giannetto Paggi's grandchildren 'returned' to Italy in 1967 – when they were actually expelled as colonialists and Jews from an increasingly nationalist Libya – and came to live in Rome.

In 2015 I visited Pitigliano with a great-grandchild of Giannetto Paggi, with the intention of exploring this thread of family history within the interconnected histories of Italy and Libya. Pitigliano seems to have forgotten Libya and Italy's colonial adventures; and, despite all the interest and energies recently invested in the preservation of the Jewish heritage of the town (a subject to which we will return), the story of Giannetto Paggi had also been overlooked until the arrival of another visitor, the founder of the Jewish Institute of Pitigliano (JIPI).

The story of Giannetto Paggi allows us to explore the mobility of Italian culture and memory. On one level – which we could call factual – this story

---

4 Carlotta Ferrara degli Uberti, *Making Italian Jews: Family, Gender, Religion and the Nation 1861–1914* (London: Palgrave McMillan, 2017).
5 Roberto G. Salvadori, *La comunità ebraica di Pitigliano dal XVI al XX secolo* (Florence: Giuntina, 1991), p. 127.
6 Renzo De Felice, *Ebrei in un paese arabo. Gli ebrei nella Libia contemporanea tra colonialismo, nazionalismo arabo e sionismo (1835–1970)* (Bologna: il Mulino, 1978), pp. 79–80; Roberto Nunes-Vais, *Reminiscenze Tripoline* (Florence: Uaddan, 1982). For a recent overview of the studies on educational ideologies and practices in the Italian colonies see Matteo Pretelli, 'Education in the Italian Colonies during the Interwar Period', *Modern Italy*, 16 (2011), 275–93.

sheds light on the linguistic and cultural exchanges that have been shaping the history of Italian imperialism since the nineteenth century whilst informing the concepts of Italianness inside and outside Italy. This story, in other words, illuminates the transnational dimension of Italian history and culture. It also illuminates a series of tensions and fractures – the occupation of Tripoli, the Italian anti-Semitic laws, the expulsion of Italians from independent Libya – that pushed and pulled individual and collective trajectories between the centre and the margins of Italianness. The memories of Giannetto Paggi and his descendants have been inscribed in narratives of colonialism and migration, reclaimed from *débris*, fragments and objects, and translated into other languages and media. This process illuminates histories of affinity and identification with the past that enable us to understand how memory 'travels'[7] by negotiating the linear and homogenizing narratives of History (for example, the History of Italy, of Italians, or of Italian Jews).

This chapter explores the memories of Giannetto Paggi and Pitigliano by establishing a dialogue with people who tell their stories: members of the Paggi family who were 'repatriated' to Italy, and the founder of the Jewish Institute of Pitigliano in Maryland. I will return shortly to the intricate geographies of these memories, but first I will outline the theoretical and methodological itinerary of this chapter. By engaging with my interviewees and their private archives, my aim has been to develop a type of cultural history of memory that, inspired by Luisa Passerini's approach, 'does not aim only at recovering accumulated subjectivity, but through its methodology [...] produces new forms of understanding of oneself as a subject of history [...] a type of cultural history that does not only study the past, but also produces cultural content in the present'.[8] I consider the intersubjective process between interviewer and interviewees as the cultural content in question: a transformative knowledge exchange that leads participants to a fresh understanding of themselves as subjects of memory and history, and to new forms of history writing (i.e. this essay). To put it in Passerini's own words, this means developing a method for 'the analysis of texts – written, oral, visual – interpreted within a disciplinary horizon which includes history and anthropology' and which acknowledges how what used to be regarded as objective (for example, scholarship and the writing of History) is now understood as intersubjective. Passerini

---

7   Astrid Erll, 'Travelling Memory', *Parallax*, 17 (2011), 4–18.
8   Ioanna Laliotou, 'On Luisa Passerini: Subjectivity, Europe, Affective Historiography', *Women's History Review*, 25 (2016), 408–26.

draws from 'Kracauer's idea of the historian as a rhabdomancer, who uses her subjectivity as a tool for connecting to the past [...] creating new connections between the past and the present'.[9] My practice of history writing as an intersubjective, transformative process that foregrounds the self-reflexivity of the historian is also indebted to Francesco Ricatti's concept of 'emotion of truth' in the interview exchange. This 'is not to be addressed as an epistemological tool to obtain objective factuality, but rather as a gnoseological issue about the emotional relationship between past and present, and its impact on individual lives and social experiences'.[10] This gnoseological issue foregrounds the intersubjectivity embedded in any form of storytelling, including history writing. By disrupting the historical narratives in my academic background – as well as the theories and disciplinary tools that I intended to employ – the 'moments of truth' of my fieldwork opened up new dialogues with my interviewees that highlight the performative and intersubjective nature of memory in culture. Hence, more than on the retrieval of factual information, the chapter focuses on the processes of identification of my interviewees with the stories of Giannetto Paggi and Pitigliano, which shed light on the negotiation of narratives of Italianness and Jewishness. By engaging with the 'moments of truth' in the fieldwork, my aim has been to acknowledge my interviewees as subjects rather than objects of historical research, and to encompass in this study their emotional and cultural investment in the stories being told – in other words, the forces that make these memories 'travel'. By teasing out these movements as complex webs of interconnection – both imaginative and intersubjective – the chapter endorses Naomi Leite's ethnography of affinity as a research perspective on individual and collective processes of identification.[11] And, by engaging with language and translation within these productive, intersubjective processes, the chapter adopts the translational lens developed in the TML research framework.[12]

9 Ara H. Merjian, 'Gender, Historiography, and the Interpretation of Fascism: An Interview with Luisa Passerini', *Qui Parle: Literature, Philosophy, Visual Arts, History*, 13 (2001), 157–63.
10 Francesco Ricatti, 'The Emotion of Truth and the Racial Uncanny: Aborigens and Sicilians in Australia', *Cultural Studies Review*, 125 (2013), 125–49, p. 128.
11 Naomi Leite, *Unorthodox Kin: Portuguese Marranos and the Global Search for Belonging* (Berkeley: University of California Press, 2017), p. 8.
12 Charles Burdett, Nick Havely and Loredana Polezzi, 'The Transnational/Translational in Italian Studies', *Italian Studies*, 75 (2020), 223–36.

Pitigliano, Maryland?

Judith Roumani is co-author of the article 'From Pitigliano to Tripoli, via Livorno: the Pedagogical Odyssey of Giannetto Paggi',[13] and the founder of the Jewish Institute of Pitigliano (JIPI), a non-profit organization established in the 2000s to engage with the Jewish heritage of the Tuscan hill town from the perspective of both Italy and the US. The article, written in English, was published in *Sephardic Horizons*, the multilingual online journal that Roumani has been editing for ten years, while writing and publishing numerous contributions on the history and culture of the Jews of Libya. Within a life-long history of individual and collaborative research projects on Sephardi literature, history and culture, Judith Roumani also acted as translator (into English) of the first comprehensive Italian study on the history of the Jews of Libya – Renzo De Felice's *Ebrei in un paese arabo*.[14] I contacted her to ask for an interview about these activities for my study on the memory of the Jews from Libya. Her first reply was that she was wondering whether she would be of much help, because she had no Jewish or Libyan origins, but had been married to a Libyan Jew from Benghazi (Jacques Roumani) for 46 years. Rather than diminishing it, this only reinforced my interest in her profile as a carrier and translator of these memories. Her position also allowed us to explore unexpected topics in our interview – notably the complex web of her cultural, emotional and linguistic engagement with Pitigliano and the story of Giannetto Paggi seen among other Sephardic stories. The disruption also allowed us to establish a connection through our common languages: after the initial email exchange in Italian, we agreed to switch to English – her preferred language and the language of my academic publications – and most of all to enjoy the translanguaging.

Our Skype interview between Rome and Miami started from the question of languages: those spoken by the Roumanis, a family of Jewish

---

13 Ariel Paggi and Judith Roumani, 'From Pitigliano to Tripoli, via Livorno: The Pedagogical Odyssey of Giannetto Paggi', *Sephardic Horizons*, 2 (2012) <https://www.sephardichorizons.org/Volume2/Issue4/paggi.html> [accessed 13 March 2020].

14 Renzo De Felice, *Ebrei in un paese arabo*; English trans. by Judith Roumani, *Jews in an Arab Land: Libya, 1835–1970* (Austin: University of Texas Press, 1985). Renzo De Felice was a preeminent historian of the twentieth century and was commissioned by Raffaello Fellah and other Jews from Libya to write this monumental study precisely in order to inscribe their history into the history of Italy.

traders who in 1960 moved from Benghazi to the US, where she married Jacques. This was a family of Libyan Jewish traders that – like many others in their circles – had a fluid relationship with European concepts of citizenship and language: they would give their children French names and an Italian education, and 'took the ferry to go to Italy for vacation: to Rome, Castelli Romani, Siracusa …'.[15] These were the most recurrent places in the memories of the family, who spoke mostly Italian and the Judeo-Arabic from Benghazi; the latter, as Judith emphasizes, was spoken mainly by Jacques' father: 'the mother preferred Italian and the children had been in America for about eight years by the time I met them. They did speak English, it was the preferred language, but they would also mix languages together, depending who they were speaking to. And then there was, of course, Hebrew.'[16]

Judith met Jacques Roumani at the British Library in London: he was a doctoral student from Princeton researching the history of colonial Libya in the Public Records Office and she was a language student at King's College with a strong interest in Ladino, Judeo-Spanish and Sephardi history and culture. Jacques was the first real life Sephardi that she met, and this encounter became an incentive to pursue Sephardi studies and later to convert to Judaism. Today she considers herself an orthodox Jew with Jewish American children and grandchildren, within a wider Sephardi world; but, as she puts it, laughing: 'I come from the middle-class, from the middle of the Midlands I tell people, a town called Northampton.'[17] When Judith arrived in the US in 1968 to enroll on her doctorate and pursue Sephardic studies, by 'sitting with Jacques and his family at many Shabbat meals and other meals, listening …'[18] she also started picking up Italian. She became fascinated by the translanguaging of the Roumanis, and embraced it:

> The family would mix three, four languages in one sentence, it was so interesting … Sometimes I would think I was learning a word in Italian but it turned out it was Arabic instead! There was no concept that the language should be pure – I am sure you notice this a lot with Libyan Jews, it's more a utilitarian approach to language than a perfectionist.[19]

15 Interview with Judith Roumani, 23 December 2019, in English.
16 Interview with Judith Roumani.
17 Interview with Judith Roumani.
18 Interview with Judith Roumani.
19 Interview with Judith Roumani.

Because of the unpleasant memory of the ways in which languages had been taught to her in England, Judith never took Italian classes, preferring to rely on her Spanish and Latin to engage with the translanguaging of her in-laws:

> I grew up monolingual until eleven and studied French and Spanish in school in the traditional way, with books of grammar and vocabulary and so on. I think the way we were taught was very difficult and made me feel inhibited about speaking French or Spanish because I was always in the back of my mind referring to the dictionary or the grammar book in my head to see if I was getting things right.[20]

She eventually became fluent in Italian largely in order to be closer to Jacques' parents, who she had noticed were becoming increasingly isolated in the US, where they had arrived with adult children and where they knew nobody like themselves. Like their contemporaries, Jews from Libya displaced in Europe and Israel,[21] this couple from Benghazi who went to Italian schools and idealized Italy couldn't identify totally with the small Sephardi community in their US context – made up of Jews from the Middle East, Iraq and Egypt – nor with the Italian American community, even though the rite of family gatherings was 'a visit to the Little Italy to have a pizza, an *espresso*, or buy a little coffee *macchinetta* ... and they were happy to buy a few pieces, food ...'.[22] Over the years, Italian for Judith and Jacques remained a language of intimacy – one to use in adult conversation when in the presence of their American children, and a language for working, travelling and connecting with the rest of the world.

Pitigliano came into the life of the Roumanis purely by chance. Judith had read about the Little Jerusalem in Edda Servi Machlin's *The Classic Cuisine of the Italian Jews*,[23] a successful memory cookbook that introduced the US to Italian Jewish food and culture through recipes and memories of the life of her family in Pitigliano between the 1920s and 1940s. Published in 1981, the cookbook became a catalyst for developing US notions of Italian Jewish

---

20 Interview with Judith Roumani.
21 Piera Rossetto, 'Mémoires de diaspora, diaspora de mémoires: juifs de Libye entre Israël et l'Italie, de 1948 à nos jours', PhD dissertation, EHESS-University of Venice Ca' Foscari (Paris and Venice, 2015); Barbara Spadaro, 'Remembering the "Italian" Jewish Homes of Libya: Gender and Transcultural Memory (1967–2013)', *The Journal of North African Studies*, 23 (2018), 811–33.
22 Interview with Judith Roumani. Italics indicate Italian.
23 Edda Servi Machlin, *The Classic Cuisine of Italian Jews. Traditional Recipes and Menus and a Memoir of a Vanished Way of Life* (New York: Everest House Publishers, 1981).

culture, prompting the career of Edda Servi Machlin as a food writer within 'the burgeoning middle-class American "foodie" culture of the Eighties, with its hedonistic interest in food scholarship and the recovery of "authentic" international cuisines and modes of preparation'.[24] Judith was fascinated by the nicely written descriptions 'that brings the place to life'[25] and by the old photographs in the volume – particularly one of women and men making *matzah* for Passover by the communal oven – which lingered in her imagination for many years. However, it was only in 1999, when a couple of Italian friends invited the Roumanis to Pitigliano, that she visited the town.

That was a time of burgeoning Jewish heritage tourism: former sites of Jewish life in Europe attracted visitors whose experiences were immortalized in widely translated books, such as Rivka and Ben Zion Dorfman's *Synagogues without Jews* and Jonathan Safran Foer's novel *Everything Is Illuminated*.[26] In Pitigliano, after decades of secularization, migration, anti-Semitic laws and abandonment, the local Jewish buildings, now in ruins, were identified as a resource to distinguish the place from all the other beautiful hill towns in Tuscany, attract tourism and develop a new economy. At that point, only three people were registered members of the local Jewish community: less than the quorum (*minyan*) of ten adult male Jews required for communal worship by the prevalent Jewish Orthodoxy in Italy, but enough to participate in the new civic commitment towards the Jewish heritage of the town. *La piccola Gerusalemme* (Little Jerusalem) was established as a civic association of Jewish and non-Jewish residents of Pitigliano;[27] Elena Servi, a local Holocaust survivor, was appointed as president, and the restoration of the synagogue began. During their first visit Judith and Jacques were invited to a prayer in the reopened synagogue with members of the local association and conceived the idea that Pitigliano needed a living Jewish community:

---

24 Laurence Roth, 'Toward a Kashrut Nation in American Jewish Cookbooks, 1990–2000', *Shofar*, 28 (2010), 65–91 (p. 69); Neil Getzlinger, 'Edda Servi Machlin, 93, Champion of Italian Jewish Cuisine, Dies', *The New York Times*, 1 September 2019 <https://www.nytimes.com/2019/09/01/obituaries/edda-servi-machlin-dead.html> [accessed 15 March 2020].

25 Interview with Judith Roumani.

26 Rivka Dorfman and Ben Zion Dorfman, *Synagogues without Jews and the Communities that Built and Used them* (Philadelphia, PA: Jewish Publication Society, 2000); Jonathan Safran Foer, *Everything Is Illuminated* (Boston, MA: Houghton Mifflin Harcourt, 2002).

27 La piccola Gerusalemme <http://www.lapiccolagerusalemme.it/Pages/associazione.asp>; Facebook page <https://www.facebook.com/pg/lapiccola.gerusalemme/posts/?ref=page_internal> [accessed 13 March 2020].

You know, I read so many books about what happened to Jewish communities without Jews, there is a book called *Synagogues without Jews* with really heartrending photographs of synagogues especially in Eastern Europe, and a book by Ruth Ellen Gruber, an expert on Jewish heritage on how communities and municipalities deal with the remnants of Jewish communities [...] our idea was different: we wanted to bring Jews back to Pitigliano, so we started an organization called the Jewish Institute of Pitigliano, and we tried different things.[28]

To disseminate information about the history of Jews in Pitigliano, encourage people to visit and promote publications about the Jewish culture of Pitigliano, Tuscany, Italy, and Sephardic Jews in general,[29] the Jewish Institute of Pitigliano began to organize a summer school, public lectures, art and book exhibitions in Pitigliano and in Maryland. They offered classes in Italian Jewish cuisine that would build on the popularity of Jewish Italian food in the US and encourage the local production of *kosher* food. They endorsed the campaign of the sister association *La piccola Gerusalemme* to sell local *kosher* wine to fund the restoration of the Jewish cemetery, and invited friends for a Passover trip. Most of their efforts to encourage the return of Jewish life to Pitigliano were not successful – the summer school and the Passover programme, for example, never actually happened, although the exhibit of Jewish arts was successful in helping the local museum. After a few intense years of initiatives in Italy and in the US, Judith decided to concentrate on her research and publications – the online journal *Sephardic Horizons* and a couple of book projects – rather than on package trips that would require the resources and skills of a corporate travel agent.[30] However, those years of local, transnational and online activities enhanced the profile of Pitigliano as a destination for Jewish heritage tourism within emerging circuits in Italy and the reclaiming of local Sephardic histories.[31] Furthermore, through the

---

28   Interview with Judith Roumani. Ruth Ellen Gruber is the author of *Virtually Jewish: Reinventing Jewish Culture in Europe* (Berkeley and London: University of California Press, 2002).
29   <https://jipitaly.org/index.php/about/> [accessed 13 March 2020].
30   The online journal *Sephardic Horizons* can be found at: <https://www.sephardichorizons.org/> [accessed 13 March 2020]; the first manuscript has been published as Jacques Roumani, David Meghnagi and Judith Roumani, eds, *Jewish Libya: Memory and Identity in Text & Image* (Syracuse, NY: Syracuse University Press, 2018); Judith Roumani is currently at work on a monograph.
31   See the continuous stream of articles in the international press featuring Pitigliano

website of the JIPI, Judith still connects with people who share her interest in Italian Jewish culture and who acknowledge her expertise and connection to Pitigliano as well as to the global Sephardi community:

> Many people write to me, from many places in England and the US, because the website is in English: it's amazing. They ask where to stay, how to visit the synagogue, how to have a *bar mitzvah* in Pitigliano ... I would refer them to *La piccola Gerusalemme*, that runs the museum – they have tours, a little shop and the wine of Pitigliano.[32]

Through the website Judith feels 'in touch with people all over the world, in several languages: I correspond with people in Italian, Spanish, Ladino, and I think there is a lot of interest in the journal, *Sephardic Horizons*. I try to bridge my two interests, Sephardi culture and Pitigliano'.[33] From an ethnographic perspective[34] it is worth stressing that digital communication is only one dimension within a web of interconnections made of annual visits to Pitigliano, personal relations and research projects that materialize Judith's lasting, transnational emotional ties with the place. The journal, the online contacts with potential visitors and our interview are further examples of the multidimensionality of this web of interconnections. By investing in multiple forms of connectivity, by learning and translating languages, by producing and sharing information and educational materials and by teaming up with people around common interests, Judith has articulated her feelings of affinity with Italian, Jewish and Sephardi culture. As a result of this impulse, the JIPI has developed a variety of ways to represent, connect, consume and identify with the past of the Jews of Pitigliano while engaging with local and transnational narratives of Jewishness – whether *Pitiglianesi*, Sephardi, Libyan or American. This is a productive process of translation which, as Loredana Polezzi has put it, 'bounces off in different directions, producing new interpretations, inspiring new creations, and never hitting the

---

and other former sites of Jewish life in Italy as destinations for heritage tourism, for example: Vered Guttmann, 'A Passover exodus to Italy's Little Jerusalem', *Haaretz*, 28 March 2012 <https://www.haaretz.com/1.5209234> [accessed 13 March 2020]; Elisabetta Povoledo, '500 Years after Expulsion, Sicily's Jews Reclaim a Lost History', *The New York Times*, 24 April 2017 <https://nyti.ms/2pWkBrf> [accessed 8 October 2020].
32 Interview with Judith Roumani.
33 Interview with Judith Roumani.
34 Leite, pp. 27–28.

same spot – even when it travels back to what we may think of as its point of origin'.[35] In other words, this is a transformative and transcultural process that makes memories travel.

The website of the JIPI features articles and photographs by Judith and other volunteers. While being the main author of the online content, over the years she has relied on help from friends and now on a professional webmaster. The photo galleries on the website[36] invite the virtual visitor to engage with the Jewish heritage of Pitigliano; one album, for example, is dedicated to the *Doors, archways and gateways to Jewish Pitigliano: entrances to the Past or to the Future?*, a title that explicitly links the viewer to the past and the future of the local Jewish heritage. This narrative is further developed in the album *Jewish life in Pitigliano*, which showcases sites of religious, domestic and everyday life of the Jewish community over time, as featured in old photos as well as in the promotional material (a citymap, a menu, cards, leaflets and so on) of the contemporary tourist facilities. These materials evoke sensorial aspects of the Jewish life of Pitigliano that are now commodified for tourist experiences – for example, the ritual baths now incorporated in a local Hotel Spa, and the bakery that produces traditional Jewish pastries and certified kosher food. Similarly, the old community oven is featured as a main hub, specular to the synagogue, of Jewish life over the centuries – which further enhances the narrative of Edda Servi Machlin's memories and the value of the pastries and bread for the experience of the local Jewish heritage.[37]

The photo album also testifies to the place of Pitigliano within the transnational memory of the Holocaust and the collaborative practices that secure its transmission. The plaque placed by the association *La piccola Gerusalemme* in 2001 in memory of the local Jews killed in concentration camps is paired with photographs of the local survivors in the act of disseminating their stories: Elena Servi is photographed with an interviewer and Ariel Paggi, a local great-grandnephew of Giannetto, is seen in the act of

---

35 Loredana Polezzi, 'Translation', in *Translating Cultures: a Glossary*, ed. by Charles Forsdick and Leila Kamali (in press).
36 These are linked to the JIPI Flickr account <https://www.flickr.com/photos/jipitaly/albums> [accessed 15 March 2020]. There are no comments appended to the Flickr albums.
37 See Vered Guttmann's writing for examples of the emphasis on ideas of Jewish 'authenticity', particularly the interview with Elena Servi on how to make the perfect homemade matza: Vered Guttmann, 'How to Make Perfect Homemade Matza in Just 18 Minutes', *Haaretz*, 3 April 2012 <https://www.haaretz.com/1.5211014> [accessed 15 March 2020].

showing the plaque to Judith, the visitor. Only two more images of local Jews are featured in the album: the nineteenth-century portrait of Giuseppe Consiglio, a local philanthropist and founder of a school for poor Jewish children, and a contemporary photo of a couple standing among an olive grove who welcome with a smile the virtual visitor. These pictures inscribe the spatial and sensorial elements of Jewish life into a narrative of belonging that mobilizes what Naomi Leite has termed the 'cultural logics of kinship' within individual and collective processes of identification occurring across time and across vast distances.[38]

To complete the photo gallery, a reproduction of the logo of Salomone Belforte – a 200-year-old publishing house whose books were distributed from Livorno across the Mediterranean and the Middle East – testifies to the prestige of the local Jewish tradition in the Sephardi world. During our interview, Judith returns a few times to this point, and also to the wider research interests that inform her narrative in her article on Giannetto Paggi. The title of the article sets out an itinerary 'from Pitigliano to Tripoli via Livorno'[39] – or, as she puts it in the interview, 'from the *Collegio Rabbinico* (rabbinic college) of Livorno, which was a great centre of education for Jews at the time'[40] to Libya. The article stemmed from the encounter of the Roumanis with a descendant of Giannetto, Ariel Paggi, a member of the family branch that stayed in Tuscany; they exchanged their knowledge on the colonial and Italian side of Giannetto's story, sharing fascinating documents from institutional and private archives and co-writing the article featured, in English, in *Sephardic Horizons*.[41] The article traces the history of Pitigliano since the Middle Ages, highlighting the contribution of the Jews to the cultural, economic and political life of Tuscany, Italy, Europe and the US and listing those who achieved distinction in Jewish and secular fields.[42] Giannetto Paggi is presented as the first Jew from Pitigliano to become a

---

38 Leite, p. 5.
39 Paggi and Roumani.
40 Interview with Judith Roumani, Italian in italics.
41 Interview with Judith Roumani. The article is in English. A short version in Italian of the article can be found in the Jewish magazine *Hazman Veharaion. Il tempo e l'idea*, 21 January 2012 (2013), 23 <http://www.mevakshederekh.info/Portals/0/Il_tempo_e_idea/IL_TEMPO_E_L_IDEA_XXI_1_12.pdf> [accessed 15 March 2020].
42 The last name in this list is Edda Servi Machlin, described as 'a resident of New York and author of several cookbooks, responsible for bringing Italian Jewish cuisine (based on the Jewish cuisine of Pitigliano) to the knowledge of Americans'. Paggi and Roumani, n. 8.

public employee, and a series of biographical details illuminate the micro and macro level of his commitment to the dissemination of Italian language and culture in Libya: for example, his children and grandchildren married into local Jewish families, and their Italian names (Vittorio Emanuele, Jole, Garibaldi, Arnaldo) testify to feelings of attachment and identification on the part of local elites to prominent figures of the history of Italy. The article also lists the public relevance of Giannetto's initiatives, as he opened a series of Italian-language schools, was president of the local section of the Dante Alighieri Society and received a number of honours before his death in 1916. He was further honoured with a state funeral and a plaque, both featured in Judith and Ariel's article.[43]

Giannetto's life in Libya is considered in the light of the Jewish experience during the first decades of the Italian state, when participation in highly charged emotional processes of nation-building (the Risorgimento, colonial expansion in Africa, the First World War) intertwined with the reconfiguration of narratives of Jewishness and anti-Semitism. The article highlights how he would negotiate his Jewish and Italian background with the local Jewish community in Libya, since only a small group of families were open to his ideas of modern and secular education. Furthermore, his school arrived in Tripoli in a context in which many other institutions – Ottoman, Jewish, Muslim and missionary (both Christian and Jewish, i.e. the *Alliance Israelite Universelle*) – promoted different and competing ideas of education. Being inspired by universalist values and open to all, Giannetto Paggi's school provoked many clashes and required him to 'to tread carefully [...] with Italian Jewry, Libyan Jewry, Italian foreign and colonial policy, as well as Libyan Muslims'.[44] Hence, he welcomed the takeover of his school by the Italian government in 1882, and the subsequent reform that strengthened the Scuole Italiane all'Estero (Italian schools abroad) through the Ministry of Foreign Affairs. The alignment to Italy's expansionist agenda is explicit in the official report to the Ministry of Education quoted in the article, in which Paggi claimed that: 'Due to the patriotism and the self-sacrificing spirit of the teaching staff, [the school] was a bastion of social education, a school for patriotism, an effective instrument for the propagation of our language, and an efficient means of peaceful penetration.'[45] The article concludes that, for

---

43 Paggi and Roumani, fig. 6. The honorific titles mentioned are *Cavaliere d'Italia* (Knight of Italy) and *Medaglia d'oro della città di Tripoli* (Gold medal from the City of Tripoli).
44 Paggi and Roumani.
45 Paggi and Roumani.

Paggi, the promotion of Italian education (and implicitly of Italian ways of life, including modern health and hygiene and Western attitudes) was the best way to succeed 'in his goal of opening Libyan Jewry to a new, modern way of seeing the world.'[46] As Judith puts it in the interview: 'You have to admit nowadays, it is a colonialist enterprise that he was serving; but Jews were very proud to be Italians, to represent the interest of Italy, even those who were born in Libya and had somehow acquired Italian citizenship at the time.'[47] By coalescing these Italian, Western and modern ways of seeing the world, the success story of the integration of the Jews of Pitigliano into Italian modernity pairs with Giannetto Paggi's success story in colonial Libya, echoing a recurrent pattern in Jewish narratives and with it the complexity of Jewish memories and histories of European imperialism.[48] One way to explore this complexity is to ask what it would mean to be Italian for Jews such as the Paggis when the anti-Semitic laws expelled them from Giannetto's school and from Italian citizenship; or, later, when they became *'rimpatriati'* ('repatriates') from Tripoli to Italy. Focusing as it does on Giannetto's life, Judith and Ariel's article doesn't say; instead, I explored these questions with the Paggis in Rome.

Pitigliano: Rome

My interviewee, Paola Giuili, begins by picking up an elaborate ornament from a display of silver objects:

> This lady was the daughter of the famous Giannetto Paggi: Clelia. There was also another of his daughters teaching in the school, Ida, but you'll never find her in the records, she gave sewing classes for pleasure; whereas Clelia used to teach the pupils to read, to write, and all kinds of nice things ... When the racial laws arrived, she too, like everybody, lost her job, and for four years she stayed at home. See [pointing to the dates 1904–1948 stamped on the silver] she started teaching in 1904, when

---

46 Paggi and Roumani.
47 Interview with Judith Roumani.
48 Lisa Moses Leff, *The Sacred Bonds of Solidarity: The Rise of Jewish Internationalism in 19th Century France* (Stanford, CA: Stanford University Press 2006); Abigail Green, 'The British Empire and the Jews: An Imperialism of Human Rights?', *Past and Present*, 199 (2008), 175–205; Joshua Schreier, *Arabs of the Jewish Faith: The Civilizing Mission in Colonial Algeria* (New Brunswick, NJ: Rutger University Press, 2010).

Fig. 9.1: Fonte della Sapienza. Author's own photograph.

grandad Paggi was still alive [...] and she worked until 1948 – clearly they didn't put minus four on here.[49]

The ornament in question – a silver sculpture representing *la fonte della sapienza*, the source of knowledge (Figure 9.1) – was a present given to Clelia for her retirement, along with a silver box on which is engraved: 'Gli insegnanti della Scuola Roma alla Sig.na Paggi Clelia, Tripoli 1948' (To Miss Paggi Clelia from the teachers of Roma School, Tripoli 1948). 'These remained at my mom's, and obviously once we returned here – once we

---

49 'Questa signora era la figlia del famoso Giannetto Paggi, Clelia – e Ida, ce n'era un'altra. Tutte e due insegnavano alla scuola, ma Ida non la troverai mai scritta, insegnava a ricamare, lo faceva per piacere. Clelia invece era proprio nell'organico della scuola, insegnava alle elementari, a leggere, a scrivere, tutte queste belle cose qua. Quando ci sono state le leggi razziali anche lei, come tutti, per quattro anni è stata a casa. Ha cominciato a insegnare nel 1904 quando il nonno Paggi era ancora vivo, perché lui è morto nel '16 [...] fino al '48 – non hanno chiaramente messo meno quattr'anni.' Interview with Paola Giuili, Rome, April 2015, in Italian, my translation. This excerpt of the interview featured in the TML exhibition *Beyond Borders: Transnational Italy/Oltre i confini: Italia transnazionale*, Rome, London, New York, Melbourne, Addis Ababa and Tunis, 2016–18. See the essay by Viviana Gravano and Giulia Grechi in this volume.

arrived! – she would keep them.'⁵⁰ Ida and Clelia lived with their relatives, the idea of women living on their own being inconceivable to a family from Tripoli's Italian elite; they were still living together under the racial laws while struggling to survive with no jobs and in social isolation. When Clelia died her objects passed to her niece, along with other memories of the Paggis, such as albums of photographs, records and newspapers cuttings. My interviewee, Paola, a great-grandniece of Giannetto Paggi, arrived – rather than 'returned', as she specifies – in Rome in 1967, fleeing the political turmoil that targeted Jews all over the Arab world in the wake of the Six-Day War. In Libya this anticipated the expulsion of all Italians by order of Gaddafi's revolutionary regime in 1970. The expulsion was a trauma for families such as the Paggis, who had lived in Libya for generations at that point, and even more so for the old Sephardi and local Jewish families – such as Paola's paternal family – who could trace their roots in Libya back for centuries, or possibly millennia.⁵¹ Like many others in their circle, the Paggis took shelter in Rome and tried to regain their belongings with the help of friends and intermediaries.

By looking at photographs and records, Paola and I find other pieces of the story of Giannetto Paggi, which testify to the narratives cultivated within the family and to the trajectories of members marginal to the success story of Giannetto – like aunt Ida, whose energetic personality is still vivid in Paola's memory in spite of the scarcity of material records. As we engage with the objects, more tensions and fractures emerge: for example, the tensions between the memory of struggle and isolation suffered by the family under the racial laws, and the celebratory dates that erase those times stamped on the silver sculpture discussed above (which, nevertheless, is still treasured by new generations).

By interviewing a few members of the family, I have engaged with very different processes of identification with these memories, and my questions, remarks and interpretations acted as part of the external reality with which my interviewees negotiate their internal self.⁵² As previously mentioned, I was

50 'Questo era ovvio che rimanesse da mamma, era ovvio che una volta tornati qua – venuti qua! – li avrebbe tenuti.' Interview with Paola Giuili, Rome, April 2015.
51 Harvey E. Goldberg, *Jewish Life in Muslim Libya: Rivals and Relatives* (Chicago, IL, and London: University of Chicago Press, 1990); De Felice, *Jews in an Arab Land*.
52 Between 2012 and 2015 I interviewed seven members of the family from three different generations, one of their partners and a close friend from Tripoli. The interviews were conducted as individual and group sessions, in their homes and in public places in Rome. See also Piera Rossetto and Barbara Spadaro, 'Across Europe and

interested in the intersubjective nature of the fieldwork and in the disruptive 'moments of truth'[53] that mark stories as potentially dissident within the narratives of Italianness and Jewishness present in my academic background. One of these moments occurred when Paola took a bunch of photographs from an old plastic bag marked with the logo of Schostal. Schostal is a Jewish clothing shop immortalized in the canonical novel of Italian Jewish literature, Natalia Ginzburg's *Lessico famigliare*, which, having informed my scholarly background, shaped my early idea of a Jewish Italian family. When I saw the bag this all seemed validated, to the point that I asked Paola whether the use of a Schostal bag was intentional, assuming her familiarity with the shop and the novel. Yet she denied both, and became interested in my sudden enthusiasm for a plastic bag: she questioned me about the shop, the novel and how they relate to the history of Italian Jews, being a student of Jewish history herself. By disrupting my canon of Italian Jewishness, this episode helped me to move from research that validates existing narratives to a knowledge exchange that, through the disruption and negotiation of those narratives, illuminates the constant mobility of memory.

The Schostal bag stood out for me among the many bags and boxes full of photographs, records and memories of the Paggis. The newspaper cuttings of Giannetto Paggi's state funeral, the numerous honours awarded to him and to Clelia (such as the *Medaglia d'Oro della Guerra di Libia*, Gold Medal for the Libyan War, signed by Mussolini, and the congratulations from Pitigliano for the 25th anniversary of Giannetto's teaching), along with the photographs of official events and ceremonies from the colonial era (nationalist celebrations in Trento and Trieste, fundraising events of the Italian Red Cross), materialize a series of emotional ties to the Italian motherland and testify to the deep monarchist sentiments of the main curator of this family's collection: Nella, Paola's mother. Paola described for me her complex relationship with her mother's memory of the colonial period and of the Fascist anti-Semitic laws: in her opinion, Nella suffered so intensively the social isolation of that time that for the rest of her life she wanted only to forget it, denying the responsibilities of Mussolini and the monarchy:

> My mother was a Fascist like everybody at the time, but a Fascist of monarchic sentiment: the last monarchist of Italy, I used to say to her

---

the Mediterranean Sea. Exploring Jewish Memories from Libya', *Annali di Ca' Foscari*, 50 (2014), 37–52.
53 Ricatti, p. 127.

– how is it possible, with these fine examples of the Savoia family? – but she saw it all through rose-tinted spectacles. [...] What she suffered with the most was not the loss of her job but the change in people's attitude, the fact that people would no longer greet her in the street. Being a Paggi, she was used to being invited to the most exclusive parties, being photographed as the girl who presented the flowers to the Governor in public ceremonies ... she went from being a protagonist of what she considered a golden age, to being ... nothing [...] She was furious with people whom she considered inferior who all of a sudden treated her as inferior ... I understand her trauma, but that is precisely why I was so angry when she defended the Duce! After all she suffered because of him![54]

It was only after decades of confrontation that Paola persuaded her mother to write a statement and apply for the status of *vittima di persecuzione razziale* (victim of racial persecution). In that statement, Nella defines herself as a *cittadina italiana di fede ebraica* (Italian citizen of Jewish faith), proud of her grandfather Giannetto, who arrived in Tripoli from Pitigliano in 1876 'to fight the tremendous illiteracy and pave the way for the colonizers' – as she puts it, echoing the 1916 plaque reproduced in a number of images and cuttings of the family collection.[55] The statement takes pride in the *italianità* (Italianness) of the whole Paggi family and in their confidence in Fascism and the fatherland. It defines the racial laws as a betrayal – an absurdity that caught them unprepared and incredulous of being made guilty of their Jewishness, provoking pain and discomfort in those who faced this

54 'Mia madre era fascista come tutti all'epoca ... di fede monarchica, l'ultima monarchica rimasta in Italia dicevo io, come si fa con questi esempi di Savoia ... ! Ma vedeva tutto sempre da un'angolatura dorata. [...] La cosa che le pesava di più non era aver perso il lavoro ma il cambiamento dell'atteggiamento della gente. Il fatto che la gente non la salutasse più. Lei come facente parte della famiglia del fondatore della scuola era sempre invitata ai ricevimenti dell'ambasciata, non è più stata chiamata. Lei era la bambina che portava i fiori al governatore che arrivava ... lei da protagonista di un'epoca che lei reputava meravigliosa, è diventata ... niente. Ce l'aveva soprattutto con le persone inferiori che a un certo punto si mettono a trattare lei come inferiore ... io la capisco per questo trauma di passare dalle stelle alle stalle ma proprio per questo comunque mi arrabbiavo con lei per come continuava a difendere in duce, proprio per come ne aveva sofferto!' Interview with Paola Giuili, Rome, 21 April 2013, in Italian, my translation.
55 Nella Giuili Paggi's statement, private record. The plaque in honour of Giannetto Paggi was placed on the facade of the school in Tripoli at his death in 1916. The text, in the rhetoric of the time, stresses his contribution in paving the way for Italians arriving in the footsteps of Rome to accomplish the destiny of the Italian fatherland.

turnaround by friends and acquaintances, and an instinctive distrust in their children, raised and fed in that discomfort. As we read these lines, Paola and I discuss the attitude of other Paggis of her mother's generation who, like Nella, after the fracture of the anti-Semitic laws couldn't reconcile their Jewishness and their Italianness and preferred not to speak about those years 'so as not to embarrass Italy'.[56] This resonates with the findings of scholarship on the early Jewish narratives within the Italian commemoration of the Holocaust, whose emphasis on stories of survival has long obfuscated the facing of the trauma of anti-Semitism in Italy.[57] While sharing these insights, Paola moves to tell me about the pivotal moments that changed her relationship with the main narratives of the family's past and propelled the development of her personal perspective.

The first 'moment of truth' for Paola occurred at the British Library, where she came across a copy of Primo Levi's *Se questo è un uomo* (*If This Is a Man*)[58] and for the first time read about the Holocaust:

> It was gripping. I sat there reading for three days because I had no idea, although I was already past my twenties ... my parents had never mentioned it, at school history finished at the First World War, I knew that Mussolini was the leader of Fascism, that the Jews had troubles from the Germans, I'd heard about Anna Frank, but that was it.[59]

This pushed her to ask questions about the Holocaust to older people that she would meet in Italy and later to further engage with these stories as a volunteer in a civic association of victims of political and racial persecutions. This expanded her knowledge and encouraged her questioning of the

---

56 'Per non mettere in imbarazzo l'Italia'. Interview with the Paggis and Nunes Vais, Rome, 12 March 2013.
57 Ruth Nattermann, 'Italian Commemoration of the Shoah. A Survivor-Oriented Narrative and Its Impact on Politics and Practices of Remembrance', in *A European Memory? Contested Histories and Politics of Remembrance*, ed. by Bo Stråth and Małgorzata Pakier (Oxford: Berghahn Books, 2012), pp. 204–16.
58 Primo Levi, *Se questo è un uomo* (Turin: F. De Silva, 1947); first translated into English by Stuart Woolf: *If This Is a Man* (London: The Orion Press, 1959).
59 '... e io sono rimasta lì per tre giorni incollata a leggere perché io non sapevo niente, ma avevo già più di 20 anni. I miei non mi avevano detto niente, a scuola finivi con la Prima Guerra Mondiale, sapevo che Mussolini era stato capo del fascismo. Sapevo che gli ebrei avevano avuto dei problemi dai tedeschi, sapevo del diario di Anna Frank, tutto qui.' Interview with Paola Giuili, Rome, 21 April 2013.

Fig. 9.2: Paola in the classroom of aunt Clelia, Tripoli 1947. Courtesy of Paola Giuili.

narratives in which the family's past had been presented to her, notably those around Italianness and Fascism: 'By volunteering for the antifascist organization, by reading these stories, I have discovered a new world, becoming more and more adamant, more and more anti-Italian-Fascist.'[60] By engaging with the stories of victims of Fascist and racial persecution in Europe she begun to trace parallels and connections that filled the gaps that had resulted from the silence in her family and helped her to understand her mother's emotional relationship with the past: 'My mother was full of anger ... I see what happened as an infinite tragedy: here [in Italy] the Jews were deported to concentration camps, there [in Libya] they were stripped of their dignity [...] and all this informed behaviours and mentalities in the times to follow.'[61]

60 'Io ho lavorato per l'Associazione dei perseguitati politici italiani antifascisti ... io leggendo queste storie ho scoperto un mondo nuovo e da lì mi sono sempre più irrigidita, sono diventata sempre più anti-italiana-fascista'. Interview with Paola Giuili, Rome, 21 April 2013.
61 'Mia madre era piena di rabbia ... io vedo questa cosa come una tragedia infinita: qui li hanno portati nei campi di concentramento, lì gli hanno tolto la dignità [...] ma poi anni dopo era rimasta questa mentalità'. Interview with Paola Giuili, Rome, 21 April 2013.

As an example of the long-term effect of the antisemitic laws and of her ongoing negotiations with the past, Paola shows me an old photograph taken in the classroom of aunt Clelia, where she is sitting on an improvised bench among children visibly older than her (Figure 9.2). At the time of the photo she was four years old and still attending playschool in a Catholic institution where one day one of the nuns ordered that Jews in the classroom raise their hand. 'I saw five or six children raising their hands, I didn't understand what she meant. Then she said: "Now Catholic children, raise your hands". About twenty children raised theirs and so I just raised mine.'[62] Speaking of the episode at home, her mother told her that they were Jews, and there was no need to follow others because everyone is different. This soothed Paola's lingering discomfort, until the next day when the same nun called her a liar in front of the class and sent her for punishment: 'You can't imagine what happened inside me, the shock ... I thought my mom had betrayed me, I refused to go back to school and my parents ended up putting me in my aunt's class, you see? [pointing to herself in the photograph again]'.[63] To explain to me the slow and ongoing processing of her memories of anti-Semitism, Paola adds: 'I understood all this only much later, but these are very important things. This [episode] happened in 1947, and I know only what happened after the war, but I can imagine what happened beforehand. These things all leave a mark on you.'[64] As these memories emerge, Paola must negotiate conflicting feelings towards her sense of Italianness and her sense of Jewishness.

> Giuili and Paggi, two different stories indeed. My [paternal] grandfather was from Benghazi, and here I return to the fact that Arabs and Jews were friends. After 1967 it was the Arabs who helped us, so I get really angry when people emphasize the conflicts with the Arabs. Today nobody

---

62   'Vedo che alzano la mano 5 o 6, io non sapevo cosa volesse dire. Alzi la mano chi è cattolico, una ventina la alzano e la alzo anche io.' Interview with Paola Giuili, Rome, 21 April 2013.
63   'Non ti puoi immaginare quello che è successo dentro di me, ho pensato che mia mamma mi avesse tradito, ho avuto uno shock notevole, non volevo piu andare a scuola, tanto che hai visto [si riferisce alla foto], l'anno dopo non sono più andata dalle suore ma nella classe dove insegnava mia zia'. Interview with Paola Giuili, Rome, 21 April 2013.
64   'Ma io tutto questo l'ho capito solo dopo. Queste cose sono molto importanti. Questo è successo nel 1947, io conosco solo quello che è successo dopo la guerra, ma mi immagino quello che è successo prima. Queste cose lasciano tutte dei segni.' Interview with Paola Giuili, Rome, 21 April 2013.

Fig. 9.3: Miriam and Elia Giuili (1920s).
Photograph by Gaetano Nascia, Benghazi. Courtesy of Paola Giuili.

remembers what the Fascists did, and I can't accept it. [...] Now everybody is [going on about] 'damn Arabs' nobody speaks of the damn Fascists.⁶⁵

Paola was born in Tripoli to the niece of Giannetto Paggi, who married into a family of Jewish traders from Benghazi. 'They Italianized the name in *Giuili* from the Arabic Juili', she says, taking out a beautiful portrait of her Benghazi grandparents (Figure 9.3). The photograph of the couple is similar to others that I had been shown by other interviewees, and that, along with the transliteration of family names, bear signs of the transculturality of turn-of-the-twentieth-century North African Jewish families. Taken in a professional studio and framed to be displayed, these portraits mark the emerging of new forms of self-representation, featuring the confidence of new generations embracing the future. The lady sits, dressed in a long skirt made of local fabric, worn with a white shirt and a headband – an outfit that all my interviewees would identify as traditionally Jewish. The man stands on her left sporting a mustache and dressed in a dark suit. They pose against a studio background made of pieces of European furniture. Most importantly, they are sitting in the studio of Gaetano Nascia, *the* Italian photographer of Benghazi, who did portraits for many other families from those same circles who were embracing this new form of self-representation.⁶⁶ Along with this portrait, Paola brings out other photos of her Benghazi ancestors dressed in European suits: she is visibly touched by their transcultural elegance and, in particular, by an uncle wearing spectacles, which to her conveys a special intellectual grace.

Paola grew up in the 1950s and 1960s, decades of financial prosperity and underlying political tension in which colonial representations of Italian and indigenous Jews still informed Libyan society: 'My grandfather would play chess with Idris before he became king and I was privileged whilst other Libyan Jews were dismissed by Italians, they were considered as inferior.

---

65 'Giuili e Paggi, davvero due storie diverse, mio nonno era di Bengasi. E qui ritorno al fatto che arabi ed ebrei erano amici. Io l'ho già detto, dopo il '67 a noi chi ci ha aiutato sono stati gli arabi. Perciò io mi arrabbio veramente moltissimo quando mettono in evidenza le controversie con gli arabi. Adesso nessuno si ricorda di quello che hanno fatto i fascisti, e io questo non lo posso accettare. Adesso tutti [a dire] "maledetti arabi" e nessuno parla di quanto sono stati maledetti i fascisti.' Interview with Paola Giuili, Rome, 21 April 2013.
66 Francesco Prestopino, *Una città e il suo fotografo. La Bengasi coloniale (1912–1941)* (Rome: La Vita felice, 1999); Ameglio Fargion, *Frammenti di ricordi e di memoria* (Rome: Edizioni Nuova Cultura, 2005).

Sometimes even by us ...'.[67] This represents another thread of her reflections on the colonial past of the family, namely the distance between the Jews of the cosmopolitan elites, such as the Paggis and the Juilis, and those of the *hara* (the Jewish quarter in the walled city). These Jews, who made up the majority of the 30,000-strong Jewish population of Libya in the 1920s, resisted Giannetto Paggi's call for secularization under the Italian flag and were confined to the status of indigenous people by the Fascists, deported to concentration camps, and later marginalized by the urban middle classes in independent Libya.[68] Most of them fled the country for Israel in 1948, but in the 1950s and 1960s the Jewish quarters of Tripoli and Benghazi were still populated by many of them, and still resonated with Judeo-Arabic dialects.[69] Over the years, Paola has been reflecting on the stereotypes and dismissive attitudes of their circles towards the Arabs and the Jews of the *hara* with a like-minded friend who had a trajectory across social and cultural contexts in Libya and Europe similar to hers. Paola invited this friend, identified simply as G., to join the interview and share our conversation: within her collaborative attitude towards my research – which went from putting me in contact with friends and relatives all over Europe to engaging in individual and group interviews – this invitation represented an example of Paola's investment in our knowledge exchange as part of her wider and multi-directional processing of these memories. G. showed interest in my research questions on the

---

67 'Mio padre con Idris ci giocava a scacchi prima che diventasse re, io sono anche stata privilegiata, ma gli altri, gli ebrei libici erano schifati dagli italiani, perché erano percepiti come inferiori, a volte anche da noi stessi.' Interview with Paola Giuili, Rome, 21 April 2013.

68 Harvey E. Goldberg, 'The Jewish Community of Tripoli in Relation to Italian Jewry and Italians in Tripoli', in *Les relations intercommunautaires Juives en Méditerranée occidentale – XIIIe–XXe Siècles. Actes du colloque international de l'Institut d'Histoire des Pays d'Outre-Mer (Gis Mediterranée Aix-En-Provence) et du Centre de Recherches sur les Juifs d'Afrique du Nord (Institut Ben-Zvi, Université de Jerusalem)*, ed. by Jean Louis Miège (Paris: Editions du CNRS, 1984), pp. 79–84; De Felice, *Ebrei in un paese arabo*; Liliana Picciotto, 'Gli ebrei in Libia sotto la dominazione italiana', in *Ebraismo e rapporti con le culture del Mediterraneo nei secoli XVIII–XX*, ed. by Martino Contu, Nicola Melis and Giovannino Pinna (Florence: La Giuntina 2003), pp. 79–106; Eric Salerno, *Uccideteli tutti. Libia 1943: Gli ebrei nel campo di concentramento fascista di Giado: Una storia italiana* (Milan: Il saggiatore, 2008).

69 Harvey E. Goldberg, 'The Notion of "Libyan Jewry" and Its Cultural and Historical Complexity', in *La bienvenue et l'adieu. Migrants Juifs et Musulmans au Maghreb, XV–XX siècle*, ed. by Frédéric Abécassis and Karima Dirèche (Casablanca: Centre Jacques-Berque, 2012), pp. 121–34.

long-term effects of the different regimes of citizenship for indigenous and metropolitan Jews enforced by the Italian empire. She and Paola related my questions about their snobbish attitudes towards people from the *hara* to the widespread classism and the narrow-mindedness of the world of their youth. As an exemplar of the feelings to which they have been returning over the years, they speak about languages and about their emerging discomfort about never learning Arabic or any of the Judeo-Arabic dialects of Libya, despite being born in Tripoli and studying Classical Arabic at school for years. They explain that social and family conventions – in their families, as in others of their circles[70] – did not help their lack of motivation: 'My mother was so against it, to the point that she was happy when we had a mute maid, so we couldn't pick the language up from her. She wanted us to live the world of the Giovani Italiane [Young Italians, the Fascist girls organization], she was proud of her black and white uniform.'[71] As we analysed further examples of Italian representations of Arabs and indigenous Jews and how they fed into the haughty attitude of their generation, G. remarked on how the entanglement with this complex chapter of their lives has also fed their friendship over the years, and, despite the conflicting sentiments, remains open to new relations and understanding: 'We were so young, we didn't understand it at the time, our world was so small; later we were ashamed. And now we are trying to understand, together.'[72]

Pitigliano, Italy

In 2015 Paola Giuili and I visited Pitigliano. We drove from Rome and spent the day wandering around the passages and archways of the medieval town, visiting the synagogue and the community oven in the Jewish museum, tasting the local food and the traditional Jewish pastries, which we also purchased for friends in Rome. We spoke to people at the museum and

---

70 Spadaro.
71 'Ma mia madre non voleva, era felice quando abbiamo avuto la donna di servizio muta, così non imparavamo l'arabo. Lei ha cercato di farci vivere il mondo delle Giovani Italiane, era molto fiera del suo vestitino bianco e nero'. Interview with Paola Giuili, Rome, 21 April 2013.
72 'Ma eravamo delle ragazzine, queste cose da ragazza non le capisci, vivevamo in un mondo così chiuso ... dopo ci siamo vergognate e adesso stiamo arrivando a capire, insieme'; G. (second interviewee). Interview with Paola Giuili and others, Rome, 21 April 2013, in Italian, my translation.

in the shops, eventually mentioning Giannetto Paggi and Tripoli; and we were directed to Elena Servi and to the website of the Jewish Institute of Pitigliano for more information. This was the fieldwork trip of two friends united by a common interest, driven by similar questions and by the desire to experience a place that holds so much mythology and significance for both of us. Paola ended up sensing 'a Jewish essence of the place', as she termed it. I realized – and confirmed by interviewing Judith – that the trajectories linking Pitigliano and Tripoli that I was so confident of retrieving at the beginning of my journey were neither linear nor obvious to my interviewees. Yet, by engaging with the 'moments of truth' in this fieldwork, I was able to explore my interviewees' webs of imaginative and emotional interconnections with the stories of Giannetto Paggi and Pitigliano, and by extension with narratives of Italianness and Jewishness. These webs are intersubjective and testify to the continuous negotiations with narratives of the past; they are multidimensional, encompassing a variety of practices; and they are also translational, as they produce new narratives and representations, new processes of identification and a new understanding of ourselves as subjects of history and culture.

CHAPTER TEN

Misplaced Plants: Migrant Gardens and Transculturation

Ilaria Vanni

Introduction: Gardens, Contact Zones, Misplacements

> We have a lot of Italian gardeners here in Haberfield. And there are a couple of controversies. One Italian gardener is really upset because he enters the Haberfield Association's garden competition every year and never wins, because his style of gardening is not Federation. So, we were talking as the gardening committee about having a separate section in the competition, an Italian gardening category. (Angelina, 2018)

The story of the Italian gardener who enters a garden competition every year and who never wins was told to me and my co-researcher by Angelina, herself an accomplished gardener and daughter of Italian migrants from Treviso, in an oral history interview on the home gardens of Sydney Inner West. I chose to start with this story because it prompted me to think of gardening in relation to transculturation and place-making. How Italian migrants make place has been the continuing theme of my ongoing cultural research with Italians and Italian Australians in Sydney, exploring modes of belonging in relation to material culture. I wanted to understand some of the ways in which the dynamics resulting from the encounters of different actors and cultural formations in a multicultural city such as Sydney are enacted in everyday practices.[1] Gardening is one such practice.

---

1 Amanda Wise, 'Sensuous Multiculturalism: Emotional Landscapes of Inter-Ethnic Living in Australian Suburbia', *Journal of Ethnic and Migration Studies*, 36 (2010), pp. 917–37.

Fig. 10.1: Front garden, some traces of the original Federation design and a copy of Michelangelo's David, Ilaria Vanni, 2017.

In the context of this chapter I define gardening as social, cultural, material and environmental practices shaped by and shaping the relations between people and plants, and I propose an understanding of migrant gardens in terms of transculturation. Francesco Ricatti, writing about Italian migration histories in Australia, notes how transculturation can help to shift the discourse of migration to Australia, which 'still privileges a narrative of gradual evolution: from the complete rejection of migrants by Australian society, to a push towards assimilation first, integration later, and finally multiculturalism'.[2] On the contrary, adopting a transcultural approach means to attend to reciprocal influences, exchanges and encounters. In this chapter I think of transculturation following its Latin American beginnings, as a set of concomitant and entangled processes, as Paul Allatson shows in his genealogy of the concept.[3] Two cultural theorists are especially relevant

---

2   Francesco Ricatti, *Italians in Australia. History, Memory, Identity* (Cham: Palgrave Macmillan, 2018).
3   Paul Allatson, *Key Terms in Latino/a Cultural and Literary Studies* (Maiden, MA, and Oxford: Blackwell Publishing, 2007), pp. 229–32.

for their attention to place and transculturation: Mary Louise Pratt and Silvia Spitta.[4]

Pratt, in *Imperial Eyes: Writing and Transculturation*, used transculturation to stress the reciprocity of exchanges between colonial centres and peripheries and to query the way in which the peripheries influenced the metropolis, including 'the latter's obsessive need to present and re-present its peripheries and its others continually to itself'.[5] Pratt also offers another useful, and influential, concept: the contact zone – 'social spaces where disparate cultures meet, clash, and grapple with each other' and 'the space of colonial encounters, the space in which peoples geographically and historically separated come into contact with each other and establish ongoing relations, usually involving conditions of coercion, radical inequality, and intractable conflict'.[6] I borrow, move and scale down this concept to describe the entanglement and co-presence of trajectories and people previously separated by geographical and historical factors in Inner West Sydney suburban gardens. The gardens in this chapter are micro contact-zones where knowledge and practices are remixed and translated in a new environment: they materialize the movement and encounters of people, animals, objects and plants. Unlike contact zones, gardens in these multicultural suburbs are not sites of violent inequality and coercion, but are often a theatre of contentions where, along the edges and fences, relationships and negotiations are played out.

Thinking about gardening entails also paying attention to the materiality, design, plant life and animal life of gardens. Spitta's *Misplaced Objects* (2009) offers inspiration for the title of this paper and a frame to reflect on material culture and transculturation. To explain the idea of misplacement, Spitta tells the story of entanglements between objects that belong or not to certain places. Her first example is Moctezuma's headdress, which appeared in Europe around 1500 as a metonym of an unknown culture. Spitta, referencing Foucault (1973), asks what such an object did to the European 'order of things', the epistemological structure that ordered the known world. To answer this question, she explores the idea of misplacement. In the process of travelling from one place to another, misplaced objects disrupt the established order of things and force

---

4 Mary Louise Pratt, *Imperial Eyes. Travel Writing and Transculturation* (London and New York: Routledge, 1992); Silvia Spitta, *Misplaced Objects: Migrating Collections and Recollections in Europe and the Americas* (Austin: University of Texas Press, 2009).
5 Pratt, p. 6.
6 Pratt, pp. 4 and 6.

a 'profound reshuffle of the known'.[7] For Spitta objects are able to generate epistemological, cultural and geographical shifts as they migrate from one place to another. [8] As things move into new contexts, they appear 'incongruous' and make everyday spaces different, or they rearrange 'the order of things'.[9]

Transnational and translocal mobilities, such as the ones of Italian migrant gardens, also entail misplacements. Activities, things, memories, plants and language are not simply uprooted and lost, they are reshuffled and reconfigured out of their usual location and into a new arrival environment. Migration can be experienced as *spaesamento* (loss of one's bearings, unhomeliness, bewilderment, feeling out of place), which demands a reorientation of relations among objects, language, practices and memories.[10] But this reconfiguration also changes the arrival environment, and reorganizes its 'order of things'.[11] Misplacement in this sense does not mean being in the wrong place or out of place. Instead, this concept captures the double action of being changed by the process of translation that is ingrained in transnational and translocal mobilities, and of altering the receiving cultures.

The plants I encounter in this research are also misplaced. They are plants in motion: they move and resettle, and, in this process, they contribute to change places, practices and, in the case of some invasive species, entire ecosystems. The concept of 'misplacement', therefore, also entails changing and making new places. In the case of Italian and Italian Australian gardens in Australia misplaced plants, instead of being plants out of place, are key actors in place-making.

My argument, therefore, is that Italian Australian gardens are contact zones that make present transcultural processes in various ways: as rifts and remixes of established cultural and environmental landscapes, as translations of other places in a new environment, and as material and sensory entanglements between humans and plants, and sometimes animals. This sense of gardening as remix, translation and entanglements of cultural, social and environmental practices contributes to a more nuanced understanding of transculturation by focusing on gardening as an everyday practice and by

7   Spitta, p. 5.
8   Spitta, p. 4.
9   Spitta, p. 4.
10 Ilaria Vanni, 'Oggetti Spaesati, Unhomely Belongings: Objects, Migrations, and Cultural Apocalypses', *Cultural Studies Review*, 19 (2013), 174–95 and Francesco Ricatti, *Embodying Migrants: Italians in Postwar Australia* (Bern: Peter Lang Publishing, 2011).
11 Spitta, p. 4.

Fig. 10.2: Planty transculturation in a front garden: flowers inspired by cottage garden design, a native fern tree, olive and mango trees, Ilaria Vanni, 2017.

directing attention to its material and sensory dimension. This particular focus also highlights how transculturation is not a matter that depends exclusively on humans: plants play a role in place-making in transnational Italies.

Misplaced Gardens

As I write this chapter, I glance at my tiny urban garden of mixed ornamental and edible plants. There is a new addition. It is mustard greens (*Brassica juncea*). I grew these plants from seeds collected from a street seed library in Tasmania. *Brassica juncea* is not a common vegetable in Italian gardens, but it reminds me of a spontaneous brassica I used in wild green salads when I lived in Tuscany, la *senape bianca*. I was also interested in the loving care of the gardener that collected the seeds and donated them to a seed library in a recycled envelope with a handwritten label; in the promise of flavours I haven't tasted in years; in the passing of stewardship from the unknown gardener to me; and in the journeys of mustard greens. These trajectories, the relations they generate between localities, affects and people, and the material and sensory dimension they create are key to an understanding of transnational place-making as embedded in everyday emotional lives.

Gardens loom large in these migrant geographies and are the subject of several studies and documentation projects.[12] *My Backyard, Your Backyard* (2012), for instance, a documentary conceived and produced by the Italian Social Welfare Organisation of Wollongong (a richly multicultural city in south-east Australia) is an example of the pivotal role of gardens in the lives and emotional geographies of first-generation Italian migrants. Adopting a transmedia storytelling approach across different platforms, including documentary film and social media, *My Backyard, Your Backyard* tells the story of seven gardeners presenting various points of view, such as the garden as memoir; the garden as the site of material–cultural traditions, such as tomato-sauce making; the garden as a place enabling social relations; and the garden as a site of enjoyment, wellbeing and love.[13]

This interest is mirrored in the vast, multidisciplinary academic literature on gardening, too vast to be discussed in this chapter. Instead, I build on the growing portion of scholarship that focuses specifically on domestic gardens.[14] Researchers have examined plant–human relations in suburban gardens through the lenses of material practices,[15] environmental conservation,[16] sustainability,[17] emotions[18] and sites of entanglements between the wild and the familiar.[19]

---

12 Madeleine Regan, 'Veneti Market Gardeners 1927: From the Veneto to Frogmore and Findon Roads 1920s to 1970s', 2006 <https://venetimarketgardeners1927.net/> [accessed 2 September 2020]; Anna Du Chesne, '"It's in the Blood!" Belief, Knowledge, and Practice in Italian Migrant Gardens of the Northern Rivers Region', Southern Cross University, 2016; Ilaria Vanni Accarigi, 'Terra Sogna Terra, The Italian Garden Project, and My Backyard, Your Backyard', *Italian American Review*, 6 (2016), 142–46.
13 Vanni, 'Terra Sogna Terra'.
14 Lisa Law, 'The Tropical Backyard: Performing Environmental Difference', *Geographical Research*, 2019, 1–13; Ilaria Vanni Accarigi and Alexandra Crosby, 'Remapping Heritage and the Garden Suburb: Haberfield's Civic Ecologies', *Australian Geographer*, 50 (2019), 1–20.
15 Emma Power, 'Human–Nature Relations in Suburban Gardens', *Australian Geographer*, 36 (2005), 39–53.
16 Lesley Head, Pat Muir and Eva Hampel, 'Australian Backyard Gardens and the Journey of Migration', *Geographical Review*, 94 (2004), 326–47.
17 Sumita Ghosh and Lesley Head, 'Retrofitting the Suburban Garden: Morphologies and Some Elements of Sustainability Potential of Two Australian Residential Suburbs Compared', *Australian Geographer*, 40 (2009), 319–46.
18 Mark Bhatti, Andrew Church, Amanda Claremont and Paul Stenner, '"I Love Being in the Garden": Enchanting Encounters in Everyday Life', *Social & Cultural Geography*, 10 (2009), 61–76.
19 Franklin Ginn, *Domestic Wild: Memory, Nature and Gardening in Suburbia* (London, New York: Routledge, 2016).

Gardens have also been considered as important sites in understanding diasporic geographies in terms of continuities and changes in intangible cultural heritage.[20] Gardens are where the complexities of engagement with place come into being in multiple variations that depend on ethnicity as well as generation.[21] The relation between gardens and migration has also been explored in terms of maintenance of cultural relationships and as site of nostalgia but also as a way to develop a sense of ownership and control over the environment.[22] Migrant gardens inject diversity in the landscape of Australian suburbia, through creative and material labour that shapes spaces of connection to the country of origin as well as to Australia and other cultures, changing with class as well as with ethnicity.[23] More recently, gardening practices have been recognized as a form of everyday multiculturalism through which complex negotiations involving senses, sensibilities and emotions between migrants and non-migrants take place.[24] Gardens here are intended as assemblages engaging with the environment and with cultural difference. Shan and Walter, for instance, relate gardens to 'ways through which human and nonhuman beings come together to foster everyday multiculturalism, which we define not only as coexistence but also the production of hybrid knowing and knowledge across cultural differences'.[25] In relation to cultural diversity, van Holstein and Head point also to the 'pluralism of environmental relationships' brought by migrant communities.[26] Domestic garden literature reveals a further aspect, the

20   Helen Armstrong, 'Migrants' Domestic Gardens: A People Plant Expression of the Experience of Migration', in *Proceedings of International Conference, Towards a New Millennium in People–Plant Relationships*, ed. by Tarran & Wood Burchett (Sydney: University of Technology Sydney, 1998), pp. 28–35.
21   Lesley Head, Pat Muir and Eva Hampel, 'Australian Backyard Gardens and the Journey of Migration', *Geographical Review*, 94 (2004), 326–47.
22   Sonia Graham and John Connell, 'Nurturing Relationships: The Gardens of Greek and Vietnamese Migrants in Marrickville, Sydney', *Australian Geographer*, 37 (2006), 375–93.
23   George Morgan, Cristina Rocha and Scott Poynting, 'Grafting Cultures: Longing and Belonging in Immigrants' Gardens and Backyards in Fairfield', *Journal of Intercultural Studies*, 26 (2005), 93–105.
24   Hongxia Shan and Pierre Walter, 'Growing Everyday Multiculturalism: Practice-Based Learning of Chinese Immigrants Through Community Gardens in Canada', *Adult Education Quarterly*, 65 (2015), 19–34.
25   Shan and Walter, p. 21.
26   Ellen van Holstein and Lesley Head, 'Shifting Settler–Colonial Discourses of Environmentalism: Representations of Indigeneity and Migration in Australian

sensory work that happens in gardens: plant choices and garden design and care are affected by, for instance, sensory experience and perception.[27] Drawing on this body of research, to foreground sensory, environmental and material practices and emotional geographies the fieldwork for this paper was designed as a combination of sensory ethnography and oral histories.

These methodologies can be defined as a set of practices based on qualitative methods that take into consideration sensory categories, experiences and perceptions to investigate how knowledge and meaning are produced through embodiment in everyday life.[28] Participatory observation, ethnographic interviews and visual research such as video and photography are some of the associated methods employed.[29] Paying attention to the sensory dimension is also relevant in studies of multicultural situations to explore how cultural practices shape and are shaped by engagements and regimes of the senses.[30] A focus on senses other than sight to analyse culturally diverse urban spaces as 'sensescapes'[31] has led to a growing body of studies in a variety of disciplines including education,[32] linguistics[33] and sociology.[34]

If we consider sensory preferences from a transcultural point of view, we can see how, for instance, growing a certain type of chicory from seeds from

Conservation', *Geoforum*, 94 (2018), 41; see also Lesley Head, Natascha Klocker and Ikerne Aguirre-Bielschowsky, 'Environmental Values, Knowledge and Behaviour: Contributions of an Emergent Literature on the Role of Ethnicity and Migration', *Progress in Human Geography*, 43 (2019), 397–415.
27   Chris Tilley, 'The Sensory Dimensions of Gardening', *Senses and Society*, 1 (2006), 311–30.
28   Sarah Pink, *Situating Everyday Life: Practices and Places* (London: Sage, 2012).
29   Sarah Pink, 'Sensory Digital Photography: Re-Thinking "Moving" and the Image', *Visual Studies*, 26 (2011), 4–13.
30   Wise, 'Sensuous Multiculturalism'.
31   Emiliano Battistini and Marco Mondino, 'For a Semiotic Multisensorial Analysis of Urban Space. The Case of Ballarò and Vucciria Markets in Palermo Introduction: From Landscape to Urban Sensescape', *Punctum*, 3 (2017), 12–26.
32   Stephanie Springgay, '"The Chinatown Foray" as Sensational Pedagogy', *Curriculum Inquiry*, 41 (2011), 636–56.
33   Alastair Pennycook and Emi Otsuji, 'Making Scents of the Landscape', *Linguistic Landscape*, 1 (2015), 191–212.
34   Kelvin E. Y. Low, 'The Sensuous City: Sensory Methodologies in Urban Ethnographic Research', *Ethnography*, 16 (2015), 295–312 and Elaine Swan and Rick Flowers, 'Lasting Impressions: Ethnic Food Tour Guides and Body Work in Southwestern Sydney', *Gender, Work & Organization*, 25 (2018), 24–41.

Fig. 10.3: Bananas and olive trees, Ilaria Vanni, 2018.

Italy, as one of the gardeners we met does, is a way to extend to Australia a taste for bitter greens. Similarly, bananas, begonias and ferns reference the childhood landscape of tropical North Queensland, where one of the gardeners we met grew up, and where the lushness of the native environment inspired her life-long love of gardens. In brief, the way a garden looks and feels, and if it looks and feels 'right', is determined by culturally bound sensory preferences. These preferences, though, are not fixed, but are, rather, a process of reconfiguration and regrounding.

Reconfigurations: Storied Gardens

Alessandro Portelli has described oral history as the 'work of relationships' between past and present, memory and narrative, interviewer and interviewee, and orality and written or recorded narratives.[35] Unlike other forms of interview, oral histories are characterized by storytelling and by

---

35 Alessandro Portelli, 'What Makes Oral History Different', in *Oral History, Oral Culture, and Italian Americans*, ed. by Luisa Del Giudice (New York: Palgrave Macmillan, 2009), pp. 21–30.

moments of realization, awareness, and, ideally, education and empowerment during the narrative process [...]. Oral histories allow for the collaborative generation of knowledge between the researcher and the research participant. This reciprocal process presents unique opportunities, continual ethical evaluation (heightened in the electronic age), and a particular set of interpretive challenges.[36]

Most importantly, Portelli notes, oral histories allow the study of a process, which is important if we foreground transculturation as a set of processes. During our interviews the relational character of knowledge making described by Portelli came to the surface in the form of conversational tangents and wanderings through gardens. Plants often diverted the narrative with their presence, played cameo roles in vignettes and brought memories into focus, prompted the remembrance of other places and social relations in the space of the garden and led to sudden realizations on gardening as a process. We learned, for instance, about experiments gone wrong (a hot house is too hot in the Australian summer and seedlings die, tomatoes are planted but the soil is sandy and too dry and requires continuous watering) and tinkering gone well (native violets that reclaim the space of a Japanese garden among the pebbles, compost that sprouts trees). The garden as a whole, and particular plants, generated storytelling around broader historical contexts, such as Italian migration to Australia and the history of a particular suburb. This plant-based storytelling also illuminated some of the social processes embedded in the gardens, whether sharing practices with friends and families or developing social connections around cuttings and the common interest in gardens, or disagreements with neighbours.

Two oral histories, one from Gina, a first-generation Italian gardener from Pescara, in central Italy, and one from Angelina, a second-generation gardener from North Queensland, offer a counterpoint to the more common representation of Italian Australian gardens in terms of kitchen gardens producing an abundance of Italian vegetables.[37] Instead, these two stories

---

36 Alessandro Portelli, 'Oral History. A Collaborative Method of (Auto)Biography Interview', in *The Practice of Qualitative Research*, ed. by Sharlene Nagy Hesse-Biber and Patricia L. Leavy (London, Thousand Oaks, CA: Sage, 2005), pp. 149–94.

37   Oral histories: Gina, 20 July 2017; Alexandra Crosby, Angie Gallinaro and Ilaria Vanni Accarigi, 'Trees, Urban Gardening and the Importance of Birds: A Conversation with Angie Gallinaro – Mapping Edges', *Mapping Edges*, 2018 <http:/www.mappingedges.org/project/angie-gallinaro/> [accessed 2 September 2020]. Alexandra Crosby, Vincent Crow and Ilaria Vanni Accarigi, 'The Garden Suburb: A Conversation with Vincent

illustrate well the diversity of Italian Australian gardens and the processes of translation, reshuffling and entanglement that, as discussed above, are at the core of transculturation. These two gardens, with their co-presence of misplaced plants coming not only from diverse eco-regions but also from diverse cultural histories, can be read as botanic contact zones.

We start in Marrickville, a large, mixed, low- and high-density residential and light industrial suburb that is home to several waves of migration, most notably Greek and later Vietnamese. In recent years Marrickville has also become home to a younger demographic and is earmarked as one of the creative hubs of Sydney. Many of the houses in the low-density areas have established gardens. The multicultural history of the suburb, with the support of local wildlife that helps to spread seeds and pollinate, is materialized in these gardens, with abundant cross-overs of plants from different eco and geographical regions. During one of our research walks, for instance, my co-researcher drew my attention to a backyard where a mango, a papaya and an olive tree stand side by side. This kind of botanical remix of the tropical and the Mediterranean is common in Sydney's Inner West. In the backyard we could also see broad beans, peas, a fig tree, salad leaves, broccoli, herbs – including parsley – growing everywhere, fennel and tomatoes, and decided to talk with the gardener.

Gina migrated to Australia from Pescara in the 1960s. Her family lived in a *masseria* (a farmhouse with land), where the family grew all their vegetables. They did so helped by farm animals, such as cows, chickens and sheep, that produced abundant manure and were fed on food scraps. When she relocated to Sydney Gina started a garden in her backyard. This quite literal regrounding entailed a series of adaptations and translations, which construct place by remixing memories and experiences of agricultural practices and knowledge in Italy with the requirements of the new environment. This remixing becomes clear in the way Gina uses her current garden as a mnemonic device to bring back memories of the *terra* near Pescara. Her narrative connects together plants, animals and gardening techniques from Italy with her Australian urban backyard. Switching smoothly across the two temporal dimensions of the past back in Italy, spoken in the present tense, and the Sydney Inner West present, Gina highlights a series of translations and reconfigurations, both at a material and linguistic level. 'My mother used to have a piece of land near the river, you could put beans there, *fava*, spinach, and you never

---

Crow – Mapping Edges', *Mapping Edges*, 2018 <http://www.mappingedges.org/project/vincent-crow-garden-suburb/> [accessed 2 September 2020].

Fig. 10.4: A backyard in Marrickville remixes tropical and Mediterranean plants, Ilaria Vanni, 2017.

have to water because when you dig the soil there is water underneath, and everything grows.' The river plays a central part in Gina's understanding of soil composition, as she explains that the sediments produced abundant black, fertile soil and bore water, ensuring that the soil did not dry up; in addition, 'we have a lot of manure because everybody, every house, have farm animals'. By contrast, her Sydney backyard is built on silty sand: it dries up quickly and needs to be fertilized with manure. Manure needs to be bought, because Gina cannot keep animals in the city. Her brother, with whom she arrived in Australia, lives in the hills outside Adelaide, and 'has chickens everywhere', so that he can grow a variety of plants, including olive trees to make oil. 'He believes in chickens', she explains, because they eat food scraps, so that nothing goes to waste. In the city, although chickens are allowed, Gina was threatened with a fine because her rooster used to wake up the neighbourhood at dawn. So, her chickens had to go, and now food scraps are buried in the backyard.

This is how the papaya we saw from the street happened to be in Gina's garden: it just grew from seeds. Gina is particularly proud of her papaya, an exotic tree in Italy: pawpaw, she corrects us, not papaya (both papaya and pawpaw are from the same tree *Carica papaya*, a native of Mexico and widespread in south-east Asia and now Australia. In Australia the yellow fruit is called pawpaw, while the red-fleshed fruit is called papaya). The mango, papaya and mandarin are good trees for Sydney's climate, and couldn't be grown in the *masseria*, where winters are much harsher. Also, they are not so easily attacked by fruit flies. Queensland fruit flies (*Bactrocera tryoni*) play an important role in her narration: fruit flies, she explains, showing us the ubiquitous plastic bottles with honey traps dangling from fruit trees, deposit their eggs in fruit such as tomatoes, cucumbers and peaches. These particular fruit flies, she continues, appeared because one of their neighbours from Lebanon has a pomegranate tree, and let the fruit spoil on the ground. Gina's family had nectarines, peaches, pears and apples in Italy, but 'peaches are very bad with fruit flies'. That is why peach trees are often replaced by thicker-skinned mangos. Other fruit trees, such as *nespoli* (*Eriobotrya japonica*) grow in Gina's garden like they did in her family's *orto*, but she explains that 'in Italy the *nespole* taste different, because different soil produces different fruits, and because the city is polluted. Everything tastes different, everyone complains: the spaghetti don't taste nice, the meats don't taste nice, the water tastes different because there is no calcium.'

The second garden is in Haberfield, which, as described at the beginning of this chapter, is a historic suburb in Sydney Inner West. The significance of Haberfield as the 'Garden Suburb' is the result of a campaign by a group of committed residents who from 1974 lobbied for the recognition of Haberfield as an urban conservation area.[38] The architectonical style is called Federation because it was in fashion when the six Australian colonies became the Commonwealth of Australia in 1901. Stylistically it is a remix of Queen Anne, Arts and Crafts and Californian Bungalow (this later style emerged around 1913/14 and continued into the late 1920s, and reflects a growing US influence on urban design in places such as Australia and New Zealand), with decorative elements inspired by Australian flora and fauna. The wide tree-lined street and the federation houses surrounded by gardens were decisive factors in the recognition of the heritage value of the area. Haberfield is also famous as one of the suburbs where Italian migrants settled in large numbers and introduced a different way of gardening based on productive *orti*. Angelina, the gardener of this story, identifies herself and her gardening style as Italian Australian,

---

38 Crosby et al., 'The Garden Suburb', and Vanni Accarigi and Crosby, 'Remapping Heritage and the Garden Suburb'.

to stress the difference between her garden and both that of first-generation Italians and the British-inspired cottage and Federation gardens in the area. As such, her garden is an interesting counterpoint to the way Italian gardens are often imagined as kitchen gardens.

Angelina's story starts in Far North Queensland, where her parents migrated from Treviso. After nine years as a cane cutter her father bought a tobacco farm. This meant that Angelina's parents did not have much time to dedicate to tending an *orto*, although her mother had a vegetable patch. Her love for gardening did not start, as did Gina's, in her family farm, but in the lush Australian bush: 'the most important thing is that I grew up in the country and I have a major appreciation of nature. You will see the influence of being from Queensland: at the back I've got a rainforest, a wet forest. Alongside there is also a dry forest, because I grew up in Mareeba. Then I have the orchard, my passionfruit and my bananas, which reflect where I grew up.' In Haberfield this love of nature means experimenting in the garden, learning from and being guided by native plants growing in the area, and making a significant contribution to the environment by maintaining trees that are part of a green corridor where native birds live. Gardening, in this sense, is an act of environmental stewardship that recognizes that gardens are part of wider urban ecologies.

Moving to Haberfield in the late 1980s meant translating and remixing the love of nature and native plants with Federation heritage, but also with the vegetable garden and orchard left by the previous owners of her house. Having a career meant that Angelina needed a garden that required only minimum care, and an interest in vegetables started only after retirement. This interest was sparked by her involvement as a volunteer in an edible schoolyard programme that teaches primary school children to grow vegetables, compost and eat garden-to-table, and not according to family traditions. Growing vegetables in this story acquires different meanings, shifting from a symbol of necessity to a lifestyle choice. This particular regrounding highlights cultural differences, and it is played along the north–south divide that at times persists in the self-representation of Italian Australians. Cultural difference is materialized in the choice of plants and finds its iconic image in the prickly pear (*Opuntia ficus-indica*):

> There were Sicilians who lived here before me and they had their typical prickly pears. And their fig trees. They had citrus trees. The citrus trees, I've relocated along the fence, what I call my orchard. I got rid of all the prickly pears because I'm from Northern Italy so prickly pears is not something that I particularly like. Unfortunately, I got rid of all

Fig. 10.5: Garden whimsy in Haberfield, Ilaria Vanni, 2018.

the fig trees and I'm really very disappointed about that because I now appreciate fig trees, but that's where I put the native forest.[39]

Cultural differences are further articulated, and explained as a difference in taste and in the understanding of gardening as a practice: on one hand gardens are about producing food, on the other about the appreciation of nature. 'There are cultural differences in our suburb … Italians like tidy gardens, they like everything to be productive, and they don't like leaf litter. They like everything clean. I want to feed the birds and trees create a lot of shade which keeps the house cool.'

Migrant gardens as contact zones, therefore, are made through remixes and reshufflings of cultural and social practices and of plants and environments that were previously separated by geographies and histories. Gardens are also sites of intense reconfigurations and readjustments, creating new environments that are made through the material and sensory entanglements of humans, plants and animals.

39   Crosby et al., 'Trees'.

Regrounding: Gardens as Translators and Mediators

I think of my garden as a series of rooms. (Angelina Gallinaro, 2018)

In the stories of Italian Australian gardeners, gardens are described as fundamental components of homes, not simply in a real estate sense of land ownership (although of course there is also that), but as symbolic and material sites that make settling and the sense of 'feeling at home' possible. Gardening is important in the context of transnational mobilities because it generates place through a continuum of practices and sensory worlds. It is, quite literally, the materialization of 'uprooting and regrounding', as Ahmed, Castañeda, Fortier and Sheller defined the relationship between home and migration.[40] In their book, home is not understood as a static point of origin or of destination. Rather, both home and mobility are part of the same dynamic and are in relation to each other through material, symbolic and affective connections. The authors call the constellation of practices that generates these connections 'uprooting and regrounding'.[41]

Gardens are a fundamental part of this process exactly because they require a continuous cycle of uprooting and regrounding, through which place is made. This place-making shapes and is shaped by everyday life with its accumulation of actions, knowledge, experiences and memories. For instance, choosing specific plants, using certain tools to cultivate the garden, designing a container garden of herbs or the support for tomatoes, or planting in a determined order provide a continuity of practices and memories. Continuity in this context is not intended as repetition of the same, but rather as the ongoing translation of a practice, gardening, into different circumstances and environments. Like other processes of translation, this continuity is not seamless, as it involves misplacement and readjustment.

Peach trees are a good example of a misplaced plant in Sydney and of the reshuffling described by Spitta.[42] Many gardeners we met had tried to grow peach trees, but they all came to the same conclusion: that peach trees suffer in the subtropical climate of coastal south-east Australia, and that they are easily attacked by fruit flies, which spoil the fruit. Peach trees are, literally,

---

40   Sara Ahmed, Claudia Castañeda, Anne-Marie Fortier and Mimi Sheller, *Uprootings/Regroundings. Questions of Home and Migration* (Oxford, New York: Berg Publishers, 2003).
41   Ahmed et al., p. 2.
42   Spitta, p. 21.

Fig. 10.6: Mango and olive trees, Ilaria Vanni, 2017.

misplaced in Sydney. The loss of peaches, though, entailed the introduction of a new fruit tree in Italian gardens. Mango trees, native to South Asia, and producing fruit with a thicker skin, are now planted in the place of peaches side by side with olive trees, in gardens and verges in Sydney suburbs (as in the garden described earlier). This creative response (planting a tropical tree) to a gardening problem not known in Italy (fruit flies) entails a translation of flavours: the sweet summer stone fruit from peach becomes mango.

The adjustments described above are reflected also at a linguistic level. Gina, for instance, would use words from her Italian linguistic repertoire when she needed to indicate specific configurations of land, animals, people and plants that have no equivalent in Australia. Words such as *la terra, la masseria, l'orto*, while they can be translated as land, farmhouse and vegetable garden, fail to capture the specific relations between house and land, the distance between the productive zone and the house, and the presence of farm animals. The documentary *My Father's Backyard* provides examples of translanguaging: *fensa* (the garden fence), *blocco* (block), *yarda* (backyard). These words are created by adding a vowel at the end of an English word and appear in several conversations with other Italian Australian gardeners. These words are not simply semiotic innovations. Rather, they capture material transformations because they indicate new physical elements, and the practices they engender, which exist in the contact zone of Italian Australian gardens but did not exist in Italy. Italian village houses and farmhouses generally did not have a wooden fence delimiting a block of land. They do not have a yard, or backyard either. As Gina recounted during our interview, vegetables were grown in *orti*, and *orti* were either in a productive zone, often including animals such as chickens, at some distance from houses, or, in the case of people living in villages, in smaller allotments in the surrounding areas. Migrating to Australia, many Italians had to translate these place-making practices and hide the production of vegetables at the back of the house, maintaining the front for ornamental plants, because: 'If you grew vegetables in your front garden as well as the back, you were considered a real Wog.'[43] As the narrator in *My Father's Backyard* remarks: 'The Italian backyard in Australia is very Australian.'[44]

As it is clear from the examples above, when thinking of translation processes I refer to a specific understanding of the term that captures tinkering, substitutions and readjustments. John Law illustrates this dynamic in his description of metaphors to describe the transitions between different types of 'order rubbing against each other'. Law explains: 'translation also implies betrayal: *traduction, trahison*. So, translation is both about making equivalent, and about shifting. It is about moving terms around, about linking and changing them.'[45]

Similarly, the gardens and plants in this chapter act as translators, shifting the terms of uprooting and regrounding, moving between different orders, locations, sensory worlds and histories. Seeding, propagating, growing, taking care of plants, sometimes of small animals such as chickens, rabbits and birds, attending to visiting wildlife, simply 'being' in the garden, thinking about the design of specific areas, experimenting, cutting flowers, exchanging cuttings with other gardeners, learning about native plants, harvesting, cooking, eating, recycling scraps are some everyday practices through which place is made. In addition to being a regrounding practice, gardening also involves the speculative ability to imagine what a site will look like and plan it in collaboration with plants. Plants actively contribute to place-making:

43 Armstrong, 'Migrants' Domestic Gardens'.
44 Sandra Pires, *My Backyard, Your Backyard* (Australia: ITSOWEL/Why Documentaries, 2012).
45 John Law, 'Actor Network Theory and Material Semiotics', in *The New Blackwell Companion to Social Theory*, ed. by Bryan S. Turner (Chichester: Wiley-Blackwell, 2009), p. 144.

gardeners talk, for instance, about trees generating welcoming, shady sites, of gardening as following what plants want to do – for instance, transplanting seedlings popping up in the compost heap, or letting native plants grow freely. The result of the interplay between past experience, imagination, design and plant life generates particular aesthetics: places made of smells, flavours, sights, sounds, moods and textures.

Plants also mediate social relations through, for instance, sharing, as recounted by the narrator in one of the seven short films in the documentary *My Backyard, Your Backyard* titled *My Father's Backyard*: 'A big part of gardening is giving, and we always had enough veggies to share with everyone.' In this sense, plants can be seen as assembling artefacts, conduits that mediate across geographies, environments and histories and create new meanings and relations at the intersection of people and social practices.[46] Garden fences are also assembling artefacts: in another short film in *My Backyard, Your Backyard* two neighbours, Frank and Fred, are separately interviewed about each other's gardens. The following is an excerpt from the conversation and illustrates well what I call 'fence relations', indicating the complex relationships generated by the encounter of cultural diversity along garden fences:

> Fred: 'They buy a pig and make salami, this can go on for two or three days ... boiling the pig or whatever, the fire going, the smoke coming across our washing.'
> Frank: 'Here no one calls anyone. All my neighbours are on my side. I give him pizza and this and that and he says thank you.'
> Fred: 'I had a small garden myself, but after watching Frank in action, the expanse of his garden, I thought I can't compete with this man and I might as well join him and find whatever information I can get out of him to make my garden better.'
> Frank (giggling): 'He has done a bit here, a bit there, he has three sections ... He doesn't want anything from the garden ... the fico d'india (prickly pear – classified an invasive in Australia) he doesn't want, figs, olives, he doesn't want.'
> Fred: 'The only thing Frank doesn't have is rhubarb. Frank says non piace non piace (I don't like it) so I keep it for my family.'[47]

---

46   Alastair Pennycook and Emi Otsuji, 'Fish, Phone Cards and Semiotic Assemblages in Two Bangladeshi Shops in Sydney and Tokyo', *Social Semiotics*, 27 (2017), 434–50.
47   Pires, *My Backyard, Your Backyard*.

Fig. 10.7: A fence, prickly pear, gorse, and olive tree, Ilaria Vanni, 2018.

Sometimes fence relations are conflictual, and become fence feuds, as Angelina put it:

> There are cultural differences in our suburb. I've been here 30 years. My family is from northern Italy by the way, and I am a divorcee. For instance, my neighbours are Sicilian, married. My trees were already here when they bought their house, right, I think it was probably 10 years later. They invited me in for coffee, and then the next day they asked me to cut all my trees down and get rid of my dogs. That was the beginning of the end so to speak. The beginning of our feud.[48]

Fence relations are interesting because they show how the entanglement between gardeners and plants generates different and often incommensurable senses of place: productive kitchen gardens and ornamental ones, gardens designed for vegetable consumption and gardens designed as environmental stewardship, lush and barren gardens, and so on. When considering specifically Italian migrant gardens, these choices also have class and generational

48   Crosby et al., 'Trees'.

connotations: first-generation migrants had to cultivate *orti*, because many of the vegetables in their diet were not available in Australian greengrocers, and because having an *orto* was a way to eat well and be resilient. Second-generations garden as a choice and lifestyle, because, as is explained in the short documentary *My Father's Backyard*, 'parents wanted a better life for kids, and that meant not having to produce one's own veggies.'[49]

Conclusion

This chapter has explored what gardens may mean in the context of transnational Italies. It began with the definition of transculturation as a set of processes and focused on transculturation in relation to place-making. It did so following Mary Louise Pratt's concept of contact zones as spaces of encounters between people and things previously separated by historical and geographical factors, and Silvia Spitta's notion of misplacement as the uprooting and reshuffling of cultural configurations. It brought this literature together with recent writing on migrant gardening as cultural and social practices. This strategy allowed me to explore gardens as contact zones at the intersection of transculturation, place-making and plant–human entanglements.

What has emerged from this study is that migrant gardens are not sites where sensory worlds from other places, in this case Italy, are recreated. They are instead sites of complex entanglements and of cultural, social and environmental mediation. The understanding of gardens draws attention to the material and sensory dimension of transculturation and to the way in which transcultural practices occur and make place. For instance, a liking for prickly pears is linked to being from southern Italy, soil is described in terms of how it feels to touch – rich and wet, or sandy and dry; papayas, banana and mango trees are adopted for their flavour; growing 'Italian' fruit and vegetables means growing a sensory landscape, even when 'everything tastes different'. It is important to stress that the kind of place that is made through gardening is at the same time deeply localized and produced by the entanglements among Australian geology and nature, Italian horticultural knowledge, people, cultivated plants and plants that decide to grow spontaneously, soil, small animals, wildlife, personal memories, ideas from contemporary gardening trends, the wider history of migration, and social

---

49 Pires, *My Backyard, Your Backyard*.

relations in a multicultural suburb. The attention to material and sensory entanglements is important in order to expand the notion of transculturation beyond discursive practices, which, while significant, tend to pass over the relevance of embodied experiences of transculturation in everyday lives.

Acknowledgements

This chapter was researched and written on Gadigal and Wangal land: I acknowledge the traditional custodians of this land, and pay my respects to elders, past, present and future. This project was supported with a local history grant by the Inner West Council of NSW. I am deeply grateful to all the gardeners I spoke with in the course of this research for their enthusiasm in sharing their garden and garden stories with me. The research for this project was conducted with Dr Alexandra Crosby, as part of our collaborative work as Mapping Edges Research Studio. I wish to thank Alexandra for sharing, commenting and generally taking care of good thinking. I also wish to thank Associate Professor Paul Allatson, Dr Emi Otsuji, Dr Lucia Sorbera and Dr Alice Loda for taking time to read and comment on the draft of this chapter.

CHAPTER ELEVEN

The Chinese Community in Italy, the Italian Community in China: Economic Exchanges and Cultural Difference

Chiara Giuliani

The graphic novel *Chinamen. Un secolo di cinesi a Milano* [Chinamen. A century of Chinese people in Milan],[1] tells the story of the Chinese community in Milan through images, short captions and archival documents. According to this book, one of the first Chinese men to arrive to Milan was Wu Qiankui:

> Wu Qiankui era un commerciante cinese [...] e commerciava statuine in pietra e tè. [...] Era già stato a Brescia nel 1904 dove [...] aveva conosciuto Cesare Curiel, un commerciante meneghino [...]. I due si incontrarono nuovamente alla Grande Esposizione. Tra commercianti s'intendevano bene. Oltre all'amicizia condividevano una parte degli affari.[2]

> [Wu Qiankui was a Chinese merchant [...] who traded stone figurines and tea. [...] He had already been in Brescia in 1904 where [...] he had met Cesare Curiel, a Milanese businessman [...] The two men met again at the Great Exhibition. Among businessmen they understood each other well. Beyond friendship, they had some businesses in common.]

---

1 Matteo Demonte and Ciaj Rocchi, *Chinamen. Un secolo di cinesi a Milano* (Levada di Ponte di Piave (TV): Becco Giallo, 2017). All translations of original Italian texts are my own except for Nesi's book, for which I will use the published translated text.
2 Demonte and Rocchi. No page numbers in the first part of the volume. Indicatively pp. 3–4.

That was 1906, and Milan was hosting the *Esposizione Internazionale* [World Expo]. The presence of a Chinese representative at the Expo was considered an honour and an event in itself, to the point that Wu was welcomed by a number of personalities of the time. Beyond the curiosity linked to the exotic flair that the Chinese contingent brought, the local authorities as well as the citizens of Milan were interested in trading with them and in familiarizing themselves with the Chinese culture, so different from their own. Roughly a century after that Expo, in 2015, Milan hosted another Universal Exhibition, in which China was not just one among many countries but rather one of the protagonists. In addition to its national pavilion, the Vanke Pavilion and the China Corporate United Pavilion in the official Expo area, China was also the only country to have an annex in the city centre, called the City Pavilion, to further celebrate the relationship between the two countries.[3] The Expo, a key moment in Sino-Italian diplomatic and commercial dynamics, was preceded by a tour in China during which the Italian organizers promoted the event by creating direct links with the Expo held in Shanghai in 2010. At that event Italy set up a 3,600-square-metre pavilion reproducing a typical Italian city and displaying *Made in Italy* products.[4] These examples are indicative of two elements that characterize the relations between Italy and China so far: historic connections and the economic nature of those connections.

From the 1920s a Chinese community started to take shape in Italy, and in 2018 there were 309,110 Chinese people officially registered in the country.[5] However, attitudes towards the People's Republic of China have

---

3 For more information see Gatti Stefano, ed., *Expo Milano 2015, Official Report* (Milan: Expo 2015 Spa, 2018) <http://www.expo2015.org/wp-content/uploads/2019/10/OFFICIAL%20REPORT%20EXPO%20MILANO%202015-PDF-ENG.pdf> [accessed 21 November 2019]; for the City Pavilion see 'China City Pavilion', *Vudafieri Saverino Partners*, 2016 <https://www.vudafierisaverino.it/projects/architecture/china-city-pavilion> [accessed 21 November 2019]. For an analysis of the Expo 2015 see Viviana Gravano, *Expo show. Milano 2015. Una scommessa interculturale persa* (Milan: Mimesis, 2016).

4 'Il Padiglione Italia – "La città dell'uomo"', *Italia Expo Shanghai 2010* <http://www.expo2010italia.gov.it/ita/padiglione-Italia%20-citta-uomo.html> [accessed 30 July 2017].

5 Laura Giacomello et al., eds, *La comunità cinese in Italia. Rapporto annuale sulla presenza dei migranti* (Rome: Ministero del lavoro e delle politiche sociali: 2018), p. 5. For more information on Sino-Italian relations in the twentieth century see Laura De Giorgi and Guido Samarani, *Lontane, vicine. Le relazioni fra Cina e Italia nel Novecento* (Rome: Carocci, 2011).

been rather ambiguous, especially since China's entry into the World Trade Organization in 2001. On the one hand, the Italian government and key figures in the world of finance have underlined the necessity of establishing a strong and lasting economic dialogue with China. On the other hand, the presence of a sizeable Chinese community and their businesses (be they factories, shops or restaurants) in Italy has been perceived as a problematic and dangerous element for the Italian economy and society, a perception that has contributed to the understanding of China as an economic threat.[6]

This chapter analyses the representations of the economic exchanges between Italy and China as articulated in a series of fictional and non-fictional texts about the Chinese community in Italy and the Italian community in China.[7] I argue that these representations, by focusing on cultural differences, are working towards the distancing of two countries and two peoples that the global economic order has brought into a new proximity. To this end, I will consider Edoardo Nesi's *Storia della mia gente* [Story of my people] and Hu Lanbo's *Petali d'orchidea* [Orchid's petals].[8] I will include three texts written by Italian expats in China, namely TomcatUSA's collection of blogposts *Te la do io la Cina* [I'll give you China], Antonella Moretti's novel *Prezzemolo & cilantro. Storie di donne italiane in Cina* [Parsley and cilantro. Stories of Italian women in China] and MartinoExpress's autobiographical account *Lǎowài, un pratese in Cina. Diario di un expat da Chinatown all'estremo oriente* [*Lǎowài*, a Pratese man in China. Diary of an expat from Chinatown to the far East].[9]

On 11 December 2001 China officially became the 143rd member of the World Trade Organization, an event that Italians perceived as the

---

6 See, for instance, Gaoheng Zhang, *Migration and the Media: Debating Chinese Migration to Italy, 1992–2012* (Toronto: Toronto University Press, 2019). See also Maurizio Marinelli and Giovanni Andornino, eds, *Italy's Encounters with Modern China: Imperial Dreams, Strategic Ambitions* (New York: Palgrave Macmillan, 2013).
7 The Chinese community in Italy is a very heterogeneous group. It includes people who arrived in the 1920s and 1930s, Sino-Italians and migrants who arrived in the last few decades. For the purpose of this essay I will focus on the latter group, as it is the one considered in the novels selected.
8 Edoardo Nesi, *Storia della mia gente* (Milan: Bompiani, 2010); Edoardo Nesi, *Story of My People*, trans. by Antony Shugaar (New York: Other Press, LLC, 2013). Lanbo Hu, *Petali di orchidea* (Siena: Barbera, 2012).
9 MartinoExpress, *Lǎowài, un pratese in Cina. Diario di un expat da Chinatown all'Estremo Oriente* (Florence: goWare, 2017); Antonella Moretti, *Prezzemolo & cilantro: Storie di donne italiane in Cina* (Liepzig: Amazon Distribution CreateSpace, 2016); TomcatUSA, *Te la do io la Cina* (Milan: Mursia, 2008).

official confirmation of what they already suspected: China is a powerful economic competitor.[10] The case of Prato is paradigmatic to understand such a perception. As Antonella Ceccagno points out, 'Prato is the place in Italy where fears, widespread at a national level, of being destroyed by China are compounded by fears that Chinese migrants in Prato are taking over the district.'[11] In addition to the already-established historic community, since the mid-1980s the majority of Chinese migrants have settled in those areas where manufacturing was the predominant activity.[12] Prato was the ideal environment, as it used to host one of the major industrial districts in Italy for garments and the production of textiles, and at the end of the last century it was experiencing a period of stagnation.[13] Gradually, the growing number of Chinese migrants arriving in Prato started to be perceived as a frightening invasion. The spreading of Chinese factories and the worsening situation of Italian-owned manufactures were (and are) seen as consequential events.[14] And yet, they are not. According to Paolo Martinello, former president of the BEUC (the European Consumer Organisation), the abolition of the 'Accordo Multifibre' [Multi Fibre Arrangement] in 1994, a treaty that, since the 1970s, obstructed imports from growing economies (including China) and facilitated those originating from other countries, was an unsettling event for Italian and European manufactures. Despite the ten-year notice before the actual ending of the agreement, not all Italian enterprises prepared properly for this and industrial districts such as Prato were heavily hit by this change.[15] The resulting crisis coincided with the rising success of Chinese-owned factories in Prato, a development that was soon interpreted as the main cause of Prato's decline.

10   'WTO | NEWS – WTO Ministerial Conference Approves China's Accession – Press 252', *WTO* <https://www.wto.org/english/news_e/pres01_e/pr252_e.htm> [accessed 28 August 2017].
11   Antonella Ceccagno, 'The Hidden Crisis: The Prato Industrial District and the Once Thriving Chinese Garment Industry', *Revue Européenne Des Migrations Internationales*, 28 (2012), 43–65 (p. 59).
12   Antonella Ceccagno, 'The Mobile Emplacement: Chinese Migrants in Italian Industrial Districts', *Journal of Ethnic and Migration Studies*, 41 (2015), 1111–30 (p. 1113).
13   Stefano Adamo, 'The Crisis of the Prato Industrial District in the Works of Edoardo Nesi: A Blend of Nostalgia and Self-Complacency', *Modern Italy*, 21 (2016), 245–59 (pp. 246–47).
14   Adamo, p. 247; Ceccagno, 'The Hidden Crisis', p. 59.
15   Paolo Martinello, '"Made in Italy" tra vecchi e nuovi protezionismi', *Consumatori, diritti e mercato*, 5 (2007), 64–78 (pp. 64–65).

Instead of recognizing the lack of organization, as suggested by Martinello, Edoardo Nesi, author of the semi-autobiographical novel *Story of My People*, places the blame for the crisis on Chinese migrants. Nesi depicts the downturn of his hometown and identifies Chinese workers and businessmen as the ultimate culprits. His book, winner of the Premio Strega in 2011, is marked by rhetorical nostalgia for a prosperous industrial past, which is complemented by discriminatory and stereotypical depictions of the Chinese community. As Silvia Ross points out:

> Questa strategia permette a Nesi di offrire una specie di consolazione ai suoi lettori italiani che si trovano in condizioni disagiate o che affrontano la disoccupazione, ma contemporaneamente offre loro – può darsi involontariamente? – un Altro al quale affibbiarne le colpe (almeno in parte), un Altro che è, guarda caso, cinese.[16]
>
> [This strategy allows Nesi to offer some solace to his Italian readers who find themselves in impoverished conditions or that are unemployed, while providing them – unwittingly perhaps? – with an Other to blame (at least partially), an Other who, guess what, is Chinese.]

And if, on the one hand, the Italians are depicted as the victims of a ruthless economic system, on the other Nesi hints that, by breaking the law and by relying on unfair competition, Chinese migrants have bought the Pratese stronghold of *Made in Italy*, turning China and its economic power into the perfect scapegoat. As explained by both Ross and Adamo, Nesi blames the Chinese and globalization, but also Italian politicians and economists who have not only allowed Chinese entrepreneurs to take possession of the Italian marketplace but have also tricked Italian businessmen into investing in China. Since China's entry into the WTO, the attention of the Italian media has been directed towards this country and the economic opportunities it offered, encouraging Italian entrepreneurs to establish new and more solid collaborations with China. Within a few years, a number of agencies were created with the purpose of facilitating these economic exchanges. For instance, the *Fondazione Italia Cina* was established in 2003 by the economist and businessman Cesare Romiti to improve the image and practices of Italy's presence in China and to support Italian

---

16   Silvia Ross, 'Globalizzazione e alterità. I cinesi di Edoardo Nesi', *Narrativa nuova serie*, 35/36 (2014), 143–55 (p. 145).

businesses.[17] Similarly, the association *Only Italia* was created from an idea of former President of the Chamber of Deputies Irene Pivetti in order to export *Made in Italy* products worldwide, but with a stronger focus towards China.[18]

Pivetti's vision is questioned by Nesi, who strongly criticizes such enthusiastic views. Throughout the novel, the author laments that Italian economists were wrong and that globalization turned out to be a one-way process in which Chinese parties profitably invest in Italy but Italians are not able to do the same in China, at least not those who own small and medium enterprises, which, in Italy, represent the majority.[19] He states:

> Evidently another thing the economists didn't know was that when you get to China with your lovely assortment of samples, on the very first day, it becomes obvious that you don't have snowball's chance in hell, because the Chinese don't need you or your products – and when it comes to that, the Chinese immediately went into business with the Neapolitans, as Roberto Saviano tells us in such great detail, in his book *Gomorrah* – and they don't need you or your products, which they have long since copied and are currently selling everywhere around the world, including in China, for pennies on the dollar.[20]

The connection Nesi makes between Chinese people and Neapolitans draws on very common stereotypes, which he legitimizes by referring to Saviano's work *Gomorrah* and his reputation as a respected journalist.[21] Nesi's opinion on China is not an exception. Giorgio Prodi, in analysing the German Marshall Fund's *Transatlantic Trends* report, states:

> The 2012 edition of this study shows a relative majority of polled Italian citizens seeing China as more of an economic threat than an opportunity

---

17 'Presentazione', *Fondazione Italia Cina* <http://www.italychina.org/it/la-fondazione/chi-siamo/presentazione-fondazione/> [accessed 13 June 2017]. The Fondazione Italia Cina, especially in more recent years, is also very keen in developing cultural and scientific collaborations between the two countries.
18 'Chi siamo', *Only Italia* <https://www.only-italia.it/chi-siamo/> [accessed 13 July 2017].
19 Giorgio Prodi, 'Economic Relations between Italy and China', in *Italy's Encounters with Modern China*, ed. by Marinelli and Andornino, pp. 171–99 (p. 171).
20 Nesi, *Story of My People*, pp. 135–36.
21 Roberto Saviano, *Gomorra* (Milan: Mondadori, 2006).

[...] 56 percent of Italians believe that their country and China have such different values that cooperating on international problems is impossible. Italy has rarely perceived China as a strategic partner for its business, political, and diplomatic interests.[22]

According to the report, the majority of Italians believe that the heart of the problem lies in the fact that China and Italy do not share the same 'values'. This issue emerges regularly in Sino-Italian discourse, where the differences between the two countries and the two cultures are constantly highlighted. Prodi continues his analysis by identifying more practical motifs behind Italian companies' limited success in China. In his opinion, Italy has never considered China as an equal partner not only in terms of business but also from an institutional point of view, a factor that has undoubtedly undermined Italy's financial efforts in China, along with 'a severe lack of coordination between the myriad institutional and private actors [that] has adversely affected their capacity to make an impact'.[23] The reluctance to recognize China as an equal partner, shown in the lack of interest in creating more solid cultural and institutional exchanges,[24] was also confirmed by a study on how a disregard for Chinese culture and customs has influenced the performance of Italian firms in China. According to Rubens Pauluzzo, who analysed the role played by cultural determinants in the success of Italian enterprises in the PRC:

> Italian companies' strategies in the Chinese marketplace are often characterised by a lack of attention towards cross cultural management themes. Due to their scarce knowledge of local cultural backgrounds and to their small scale, that often does not allow them to afford cultural training costs, Italian companies do not adequately evaluate and implement cross cultural policies and practices.[25]

This became clear in November 2018 when Italian fashion brand Dolce & Gabbana posted a racist campaign to advertise *The Great Show*, a high-profile

22   Prodi, p. 172.
23   Prodi, p. 193.
24   See, for instance, Paolo Borzatta, 'La strategia dell'Italia in Cina', *Agichina* <http://www.agichina24.it/blog-paolo-borzatta/notizie/la-strategia-dellrsquoitalia-in-cina> [accessed 13 July 2017].
25   Rubens Pauluzzo, 'How Cultural Determinants May Affect HRM: The Case of Italian Companies in China', *Research and Practice in Human Resource Management*, 18 (2010), 78–95.

fashion show to be held at Shanghai's Expo Center on 21 November. Dolce & Gabbana had to cancel the show after being publicly accused of racism. The three short promotional videos that preceded the show were released on all social networks, including the Chinese social media platform Sina Weibo, and featured a female Chinese model dressed in a red D&G garment trying to eat traditional Italian dishes (pizza, spaghetti and a Sicilian cannolo) with chopsticks, while a male voice-over directs and mocks her attempts with sexual stereotypical allusions. In addition to this, a screenshot of an Instagram conversation in which Gabbana insulted China and the Chinese people was leaked. The company tried unsuccessfully to explain this by affirming that the account was hacked, but they were forced not only to release a video of official apologies to China and its people but also to cancel the show, while models and celebrities publicly announced their withdrawal from the event and their dissociation from the brand. This had enormous consequences for the success of the Italian company in China, as boycott actions were launched on social media and supported by many Chinese retailers and department stores refusing to sell D&G items.[26]

In addition to compromising the advance of Italian firms in China, this inability to recognize the importance of understanding and adapting to China's culture and customs oddly mirrors one of the accusations levelled against the Chinese community in Italy, namely that of being 'closed' and unwilling to embrace Italian culture.[27] The results of Pauluzzo's study mentioned above also challenge the tendency of Italian enterprises to blame Chinese people's lack of fair play in order to provide a different reason for their failures. Throughout the book, Nesi suggests how China's success is mainly

---

26 For more information on the D&G debate see Fabian Jintae Froese et al., 'Challenges for Foreign Companies in China: Implications for Research and Practice', *Asian Business & Management*, 18 (2019), 249–62 (p. 251); Stephy Chung and Oscar Holland, 'Dolce & Gabbana Cancels China Show amid "Racist" Ad Controversy', *CNN*, 2018 <https://www.cnn.com/style/article/dolce-gabbana-shanghai-controversy/index.html> [accessed 12 November 2019]; Benjamin Haas, 'Chinese Retail Sites Drop Dolce & Gabbana amid Racist Ad Backlash', *The Guardian*, 23 November 2018 <https://www.theguardian.com/world/2018/nov/23/dolce-gabbana-vanishes-from-chinese-retail-sites-amid-racist-ad-backlash> [accessed 12 November 2019]; '"Racist" D&G Ad: Chinese Model Says Campaign Almost Ruined Career', *BBC News*, 23 January 2019 <https://www.bbc.com/news/world-asia-china-46968750> [accessed 12 November 2019].
27 Roberta Raffaetà, Loretta Baldassar and Anita Harris, 'Chinese Immigrant Youth Identities and Belonging in Prato, Italy: Exploring the Intersections between Migration and Youth Studies', *Identities*, 23 (2016), 422–37 (p. 423).

linked to counterfeiting, unfair competition and labour exploitation. In the chapter entitled 'Immediately', Nesi, invited by the police, takes part in a raid on a Chinese-owned warehouse. In addition to using vocabulary normally associated with animals throughout the narration to describe both the place and its inhabitants,[28] the author affirms: 'And yet, how are we supposed to live side by side with such widespread and glaring criminal behavior, practiced by thousands of people, all members of a single ethnic group, who show total disregard for our system of law – that is, when they are even aware of it?'[29] Nesi is frustrated here by the state of the warehouse, which used to belong to an Italian businessman who, forced by the economic crisis, sold it to a Chinese entrepreneur: what was once a cog in the Pratese economic system is now managed by Chinese migrants who work and – more problematically – live there.[30] Nesi's generalization of all Chinese as a 'single ethnic group' that disregards Italian laws is reinforced by the description of the warehouse as the setting of inhuman dynamics of labour exploitation.

Yet if, on the one hand, the difficult work conditions and the low salaries of the Chinese migrants in Italy are denounced as disrespectful of human rights, on the other, these are among the appealing aspects that push Italian firms to open new factories in China. For instance, the protagonist of Hu Lanbo's semi-fictional novel *Petali d'orchidea* decides to start a joint venture with a partner in China, taking advantage of the low cost of production: 'Ragionai che in Italia un paio di scarpe costava circa trentamila lire di manodopera, mentre in Cina la manodopera era molto più a buon prezzo.' [I realized that in Italy the cost of labour would be 30 thousand liras for a pair of shoes, while in China the labour would have been much cheaper].[31] According to Gaoheng Zhang, in this book Hu 'consciously addresses the flattened and stereotypical representations of the average Chinese immigrant in Italy in *Cinacittà* and other similar depictions',[32] among which we can certainly include Nesi's. Equally relevant is the description provided

28 For more details on Nesi's language see Ross, p. 149.
29 Nesi, *Story of My People*, p. 115.
30 Ceccagno pointed out how this housing arrangement is also a way to speed up Chinese employers' and employees' routes to success. Antonella Ceccagno, 'Compressing Personal Time: Ethnicity and Gender within a Chinese Niche in Italy', *Journal of Ethnic and Migration Studies*, 33 (2007), 635–54 (p. 647).
31 Hu, p. 166. On gender and industry see Mark Chu, 'Industry and Gender in Recent Representations of Sino-Italian Relations', *Modern Italy*, 24 (2019), 383–99.
32 Gaoheng Zhang, 'Contemporary Italian Novels on Chinese Immigration to Italy', *California Italian Studies*, 4 (2013), 1–38 (p. 25).

by the same character of her very first experience as a businesswoman, when attempting to produce shoes in Italy and to export them to China. At the moment of collecting the merchandise from the Italian contractor she realizes that the quality is much lower than she had expected, a complication that could jeopardize both her chances of selling the products and the deposit she has already paid to the factory:

> Quando il cliente ricevette il primo lotto di merce mi telefonò alle tre di notte, imbestialito perché la pelle di tutte le scarpe non aveva un colore omogeneo. [...] Era questa la tanto decantata qualità dei prodotti italiani? [...] Andai a cercare il proprietario e gli chiesi spiegazioni. La sua risposta fu: 'È una caratteristica della vera pelle'. 'Allora come mai voi italiani non indossate scarpe di colori diversi?' gli dissi.[33]

> [When the customer received the first batch of goods, he phoned me at 3am enraged because the leather in all shoes did not have a homogeneous colour. [...] Was that the highly celebrated quality of Italian products? [...] I went looking for the manager and asked for explanations. His answer was: 'It is a feature of real leather'. 'Then why don't you, Italians, wear shoes of different colors?' I asked.]

The behaviour of the Italian contractor, who is trying to sell low-quality products to his Chinese customer, reiterates Italy's unwillingness to recognize China as an equal partner. Moreover, it confirms Zhang's statement about the author's attempt to provide a counter narrative to a public discourse in which low quality and unreliability are part of the common description of Chinese enterprises and *Made in China* products when compared with the highly praised *Made in Italy*.

Even if Italian small and medium enterprises generally struggle to find their place in China, some did manage to successfully take advantage of this new economic opportunity. According to the *Rapporto Annuale-Cina 2019* [Annual Report-China 2019], compiled by the Centro Studi per l'Impresa, Fondazione Italia Cina, at the end of 2018 there were almost 2,000 Italian enterprises in China and Hong Kong, including joint ventures and wholly foreign-owned enterprises, with exports to the value of 13.2 billion euros.[34]

33   Hu, pp. 163–64.
34   Fondazione Italia Cina, 'Rapporto annuale Cina 2019', *Ministero degli Esteri*, <https://www.esteri.it/mae/resource/doc/2019/07/highlights.pdf> [accessed 12 November 2019];

Additionally, as reported by the *Rapporto Fondazione Migrantes* [Fondazione Migrantes's Report] in 2019, up to 9,320 Italians lived in China.[35] This figure, provided by the AIRE (the official registry of Italian nationals living abroad), includes only those Italians who have officially moved their residency to China; therefore, the real number might actually be higher. In 2014 the *Fondazione Migrantes* released a report analysing contemporary Italian migration to China with the evocative title *Sulle orme di Marco Polo. Italiani in Cina* [In Marco Polo's footsteps. Italians in China] as part of the project AMICO – Analisi della Migrazione degli Italiani in Cina Oggi [Analysis of Italian Migration in China Today].[36] This volume offers an account of the Italians in China, including useful statistical information on their jobs, their backgrounds and their expectations. As well as praising Italian know-how, especially in terms of *Made in Italy*, food, work ethic and other elements (among which football skills are included), the report presents a derogatory view of China. The volume includes a collection of interviews with Italian expats, who emphasize their success in spite of all the challenges they are faced with. A suitable example of these attitudes is represented by the section on Daniela Nuzzaci, brand manager for Ferrero in Shanghai:

> La sua è stata una terapia d'urto, che ha destabilizzato il suo staff, a cui a chiesto competenze creative, pareri sui prodotti e commenti critici: tutto quello a cui i cinesi non sono abitutati. Anche questo significa caricare di valore aggiunto il *know-how* italiano. [...] 'La lontananza di vedute tra me e i miei colleghi cinesi è incolmabile – dice Daniela – perché non danno valore alle cose: sperperano i soldi in cose inutili, si comportano con superficialità pensando che tutto gli sia dovuto.' Ma nonostante ciò Daniela continua a battere il pugno sul tavolo e a pretendere un avvicinamento culturale almeno nel lavoro che forse non arriverà mai.[37]

> [Hers was a shock therapy that destabilized her staff. She demanded creative competences, opinions and feedback on products: something

---

'Info Mercati Esteri, Homepage Cina', *Ministero degli Esteri* <http://www.infomercatiesteri.it/paese.php?id_paesi=122#slider-1> [accessed 12 November 2019].
35 Fondazione Migrantes, *Rapporto italiani nel mondo 2019* (Assisi (PG): Tau, 2019), p. 509.
36 Giovanna Di Vincenzo, Fabio Marcelli and M. Francesca Staiano, eds, *Sulle orme di Marco Polo. Italiani in Cina* (Todi (PG): Tau Editrice, 2014).
37 Di Vincenzo et al., p. 86.

Chinese people are not used to. This too is a way of increasing the value of the Italian know-how. [...] 'The gap between my views and those of my colleagues is immense – says Daniela – because they don't value anything: they waste money on useless things, they behave superficially thinking that they have a god-given right to everything.' Nevertheless, Daniela keeps beating her fist on the table and requires a cultural rapprochement that, at least at work, may never arrive.]

The reference to the 'lontanza di vedute' [gap between views] refers back to the different values indicated by the *Transatlantic Trend* report as one of the determining factors in the complicated Sino-Italian exchanges. The addition of the adjective 'incolmabile' [immense] to describe the ways in which Chinese people differ from Italians and the impossibility of 'un avvicinamento culturale' [cultural rapprochement] are elements that work to reaffirm the cultural distance between the two countries – a cultural distance that can be comprehended as cultural difference, as articulated by Homi Bhabha:

[It] is a process of signification through which statements of culture or on culture differentiate, discriminate, and authorize the production of fields of force, reference, applicability, and capacity. [...] The concept of cultural difference focuses on the problem of the ambivalence of cultural authority; the attempt to dominate in the name of a cultural supremacy which is itself produced only in the moment of differentiation.[38]

In the Sino-Italian discourse, cultural difference is used to legitimize Italian superiority, as is clear from accounts produced by Italians in China. Indeed, the increasing presence of Italians in the PRC is reflected by a limited, yet still relevant, production of texts. For instance, the collection of blogposts *Te la do io la Cina* provides a suggestive portrayal of the expatriates' life in China. The volume collects all the posts that the author, TomcatUSA (the pseudonym of an Italian engineer who relocated to China), published in his blog from August 2006 to April 2008. TomcatUSA narrates his and his family's experience in Nanjing. The posts are written with the intention of being informative of the kind of difficulties that Italians have to overcome when moving to China. All posts are narrated with a questionable ironic tone, an irony that often originates from the use of well-known stereotypes and

---

38 Homi K. Bhabha, 'The Commitment to Theory', *New Formations*, 5 (1988), 5–23 (pp. 18–19).

relies on the depiction of Italians and Chinese as being too different to build an egalitarian relationship. One post in particular, from March 2007, is worth mentioning, as it clearly exemplifies Bhabha's definition of cultural difference. Entitled *Nel paese degli orbi chi ha un occhio è re* [In the country of blind people those with one eye are kings], the post describes the author's attempt to 'think positively' about his permanence in China:

> Per tirare avanti bisogna anche trovare i lati positivi di essere in Cina. Uno di questi è che ti senti molto intelligente. Questo non perché tu lo sia veramente in senso assoluto, ma tutto dipende da con chi ti confronti. Qui in Cina il livello culturale e professionale è mediamente basso perciò qualsiasi cosa tu dica o faccia risulta di una levatura eccezionale e tutti ti ascoltano a bocca aperta anche per concetti di una banalità disarmante.[39]

> [To carry on, one must find the positive aspects of being in China. One of these is that you feel very clever. Not because you are clever in general, but it all has to do with whom you compare yourself to. Here in China the cultural and professional level is usually low, so everything you say or do seems exceptionally intelligent and everyone listens to you in amazement even when you express disheartening ly banal ideas.]

This discriminatory portrayal of the Chinese population as culturally inferior echoes the allusions included in the report *Sulle orme di Marco Polo*, but it also recalls the attitude shown by the factory owner in Hu's novel and in Nesi's derogatory tone. It is a specific kind of racism that Étienne Balibar, drawing on Taguieff, describes as 'a racism without races [...] whose dominant theme is not biological heredity but the insurmountability of cultural differences'.[40] It is a racism that puts forward colonial ideas in a globalized world, as Ania Loomba affirms:

> Contemporary views of cultural difference mirror past and present geo-political tensions and rivalries. Thus, it is no accident that it is Muslims who are regarded as barbaric and given to acts of violence and Asians who are seen as diligent but attached to their own rules of business and family, both modes of being which are seen as differently incommensurate with

---

39 TomcatUSA, p. 58.
40 Étienne Balibar and Immanuel Maurice Wallerstein, *Race, Nation, Class: Ambiguous Identities* (London: Verso, 1991), p. 21.

the Western world. [...] These views not only reverberate with older colonial views [...] but speak to contemporary global economic and political rivalries.[41]

The ways in which China and Chinese people are represented in the Italian cultural discourse – a representation that increased after the PRC's entry into the WTO[42] – reflects the stereotypical representation suggested by Loomba: a one-dimensional category of people focused on working inside Chinese factories, the success of which relied on counterfeiting, labour exploitation and, ultimately, the production of lower-quality products.[43] This is also paralleled by one of the first counter-measures adopted by the US and EU after China's entry into the WTO, which entailed the obligation of declaring the origin of textile products from outside the EU. As Martinello pointed out in 2007, this measure was useless, yet is indicative of an underlying prejudice in which the indication of a 'not-Italian' origin becomes synonymous with lack of quality and suggestive of an unethical and unfair process of production.[44] Despite being inaccurate and meaningless for the consumer, this measure relies on an assumed perception of Italian products as being of superior quality, not on the basis of factual evidence but rather as a result of discriminatory preconceptions aimed at undermining rising Chinese power. This is evident, for instance, in one of TomcatUSA's posts: 'd'altro canto viene anche da pensare che sei finito in Cina perché in Europa eri al di sotto della media, per cui vieni retrocesso in B dove hai la possibilità di fare un campionato di vertice ...'[45] [On the other hand, you are tempted to think that you ended up in China because in Europe you were below average, thus you are moved back to second league where you can compete at the top].

Similar attitudes are described in the novel *Prezzemolo & cilantro*, whose protagonists – like the author herself – 'la Cina non l'avevano scelta ma subita' [did not choose China but endured it],[46] as they moved to China to follow their husbands' relocation. Following the success of her blog *cuCINAnto*,[47]

---

41   Ania Loomba, *Colonialism/Postcolonialism* (London: Routledge, 2005), pp. 217–18.
42   For the impact on literature see Zhang, 'Contemporary Italian Novels'.
43   See Simona Segre Reinach, 'China and Italy: Fast Fashion versus Prêt à Porter. Towards a New Culture of Fashion', *Fashion Theory*, 9 (2005), 43–56.
44   Martinello, p. 73.
45   TomcatUSA, p. 58.
46   Moretti, *Prezzemolo & cilantro*, p. 29.
47   Antonella Moretti, *CuCINAnto* <http://www.cucinanto.com/> [accessed 18 August 2017].

Antonella Moretti published her novel, inspired by her experience in China, in 2016. The story follows the three protagonists – Luisella (the alter-ego of the author), Emma and Astrid – and it covers a period of twelve months. It provides an insight into the lives of the Italian community in China but more specifically that of the expats' wives. This group of women spend most of their time in the expats' compound, attending yoga classes, chatting in a café, carefully keeping their life separate from the local population. This isolation resonates with analogous tendencies that have emerged in the discourse about the Chinese community in Italy, whose members are regularly accused of being closed and unwilling to integrate. As Raffaetà and others point out about Prato:

> In the Italian context, local Pratese discourses tend to define Chinese migrants and their children as segregated and 'closed', uninterested and unable to assimilate into Italian culture and society. This view is supported by the predominant essentialist and reductionist conceptions of identity (including both Chinese and Italian) as fixed and unchanging.[48]

If in Italy Chinese migrants are blamed for being 'segregated' and 'unable to assimilate into Italian culture', in China this seems to be the norm among Italians, who see this separation as the only possible way. As clearly stated by TomcatUSA: 'Qui in Cina gli expat rimangono un gruppo a sé stante. Vivono nei loro compound riservati, i bambini vanno alle scuole per expat, la sera a volte si va in qualche locale per expat e così via' [Here in China the expats stay among themselves. They live in their private compound, their children go to the schools for expats, and in the evening sometimes you go to some bars for expats and so on].[49]

Symptomatic of this situation is the opening of the *Scuola Italiana d'Ambasciata di Pechino* [Italian Embassy School in Beijing] in 2015, the only Italian school in Asia and Oceania.[50] According to the official webpage, the school will enable children of Italians to preserve their cultural identity.[51] As also suggested by this brief online description, the

---

48 Raffaetà et al., p. 423.
49 TomcatUSA, p. 296.
50 'Pechino: prima e unica scuola paritaria in Asia e Oceania', *Scuola italiana d'ambasciata di Pechino*, 2017 <http://www.scuolapechino.com/pechino-prima-e-unica-scuola-paritaria-asia-e-oceania/> [accessed 23 September 2017].
51 'Pechino: prima e unica scuola paritaria in Asia e Oceania'.

opening of the school is crucial in understanding the dynamics relating to the Italian community in China; on the one hand, it is indicative of the Italian expatriates' intention of planning a relatively long-term stay in China, but on the other hand the nature of the school, which is accessible only to the children of Italian and foreign diplomats, suggests a more complex issue related to Italians' attitude to separating themselves from the locals, something that noticeably recalls the stereotypical opinions on Italy's resident Chinese community mentioned above. Furthermore, the idea of the 'preservation of cultural identity' reflects the issue of cultural difference and the consequential self-confinement of the expat communities in compounds. In line with this behaviour, Chinese people are therefore almost totally absent from these texts. When they appear, they are drivers, shop assistants, cleaning ladies or yoga instructors with no agency and no ability to speak. As in Moretti's text:

> Il gruppetto di italiane quel giorno pareva avercela con la Cina e tutte si sfogavano a proposito delle piccole, grandi incomprensioni quotidiane che rendevano difficile il rapporto con i cinesi. C'era quella che si lamentava di quanto male pulisse la casa l'ayi, ce n'era un'altra che rideva della scarsa professionalità dell'idraulico o dell'operaio di turno.[52]
>
> [It seemed that that day the small group of Italian women was mad at China and they were venting about the small and big daily misunderstandings that undermine the relationship with the Chinese. There was one complaining about how how badly her ayi cleaned the house, another one mocking the lack of professional skills of the plumber or of any other workman.]

In the same novel, when Camilla, a young student in China for her university year abroad, joins the group, the other women are surprised about and sceptical of her passion for China and her inclination to experience what this country has to offer. She wants to live as the Chinese people live, do what they do and, ultimately, as she confesses to the other women, she would like to find a Chinese boyfriend.[53] Camilla belongs to the broader and more global community of international students. The Italian government and the Confucius Institute offer Italian students many opportunities to study in

---

52 Moretti, *Prezzemolo & cilantro*, p. 171. *Ayi* is Chinese for cleaning lady.
53 Moretti, *Prezzemolo & cilantro*, p. 29.

China.[54] Conversely, a key role is played by programmes such as 'Marco Polo' or 'Turandot', which allow Chinese students to enroll in Italian universities and to take language courses.[55] This phenomenon challenges the distinction between the Chinese community in Italy and Italians in China, which the majority of the sources analysed so far depicted as two clearly differentiated and separate entities, unable to communicate. In these contexts, cultural exchange and reciprocal knowledge are perceived, instead, as the starting point for a fruitful transnational dialogue. However, according to Brigadoi Cologna, international students in Italy 'tendono a fare gruppo a sé, sia perché la scarsa competenza linguistica ne limita le relazioni con i coetanei italiani, sia perché sono rare le iniziative promosse a livello di ateneo per rafforzarne le competenze sociali e culturali' [tend to stay among themselves, both because their scarce linguistic competence limits their relations with Italian peers and because there are not many events promoted by the university to reinforce their social and cultural awareness].[56] The latter point in particular, thinking back at Prodi's analysis mentioned at the beginning of this study, reiterates the scarce attention shown by Italian institutions towards diplomatic and cultural relations with China.[57] In line with this, even Camilla's enthusiasm is soon challenged by the difficulties she encounters when trying to relate to Chinese society, and, despite her disappointment, the rest of the group keeps pouring salt onto the wound:

> Camilla sarà pure stata un'appassionata della Cina, ma restava pur sempre una viziata ragazza italiana. Vivere negli odori forti, nella confusione e nella scarsa igiene non era attraente nemmeno per lei. [...] 'Dico che non sei costretta ad integrarti completamente in una società così diversa dalla

54   See, for instance, the information regarding the scholarships for the academic year 2017/18 'Borse di studio MAE Cina 2017', *Universita.it*, 2017 <http://www.universita.it/borse-di-studio-mae-cina-2017/> [accessed 12 July 2017].
55   For information on the Marco Polo project see 'Programma Marco Polo per Studenti Cinesi', *Università di Bologna* <http://www.unibo.it/it/internazionale/offerta-formativa-internazionale/programma-marco-polo> [accessed 12 July 2017].
56   Daniele Brigadoi Cologna, 'L'importanza crescente degli studenti universitari cinesi per la società italiana', *Orizzonte Cina*, 7 (2016) <https://www.twai.it/articles/cinesitaliani-limportanza-crescente-degli-studenti-universitari-cinesi-per-la-societa-italiana/> [accessed 24 July 2019].
57   Brigadoi Cologna, 'L'importanza'. For a fictional account about the Marco Polo project see Wen-Long Sun, 'Help Me, Brother!', in *Nuove lettere persiane*, ed. by Francesca Spinelli (Rome: Ediesse, 2010), pp. 43–48.

tua. [...] puoi continuare a mangiare la pizza e bere il caffè da Assunta. [...] Dopotutto tu sei italiana, no? Puoi conservare la tua identità pur continuando ad amare questo paese e la sua gente!'[58]

[Camilla was passionate about China, for sure, but at the end of the day, she was still a spoiled Italian girl. Living surrounded by strong smells, confusion and scarce hygiene wasn't appealing, not even for her. [...] 'I mean, you are not obliged to fully integrate in a society so different from your own. [...] you can carry on eating pizza and drinking coffee at Assunta's. [...] After all you are Italian, aren't you? You can keep your identity and carry on loving this country and its people!']

Beyond the superficial delineation of what constitutes Italian identity, this passage also reiterates the idea that, since these two cultures are so different, there is no need to fully understand one another – something that contrasts with the previously mentioned criticism about Prato's (as well as Italy's) Chinese community.[59] The only Chinese character who – to a certain extent – is included in the group is Assunta, the owner of the Italian bar. Assunta is a Chinese returnee migrant who, after living for fifteen years in Naples with her Italian ex-husband, decided to move back to China and to open the bar in the compound, 'uno dei pochi posti dove si poteva mangiare un vero toast all'italiana, una pasta al pomodoro ben fatta e il miglior caffè espresso, diceva Assunta, di tutta la Cina' [one of the few places where you could eat a real Italian toastie, a well-made pasta with tomato sauce and the best espresso, according to Assunta, in all of China].[60] Assunta's relative inclusion is granted by her experiences in Italy, where she learnt to speak the language, to cook Italian food and to make coffee. This mirrors the previous depthless elaboration of Italian identity, as well as the idea that integration is possible only when Chinese characters change in order to become more Italian, even when in China.

The analysis of these two texts shows how the effort to integrate has to be undertaken always and exclusively by the Chinese side, even when in China. By speaking Italian and making espresso, Assunta is included in the narrative, but not in the group of friends – going back to the limited and superficial representation of Chinese characters discussed above, she is merely their

---

58 Moretti, *Prezzemolo & cilantro*, p. 81.
59 Raffaetà et al., p. 89.
60 Moretti, *Prezzemolo & cilantro*, p. 20.

bartender. However, she is also symbolic of a portion of Chinese migrants, who after spending a period of time in Italy, return to China. According to Daniele Brigadoi Cologna, from 1994 to 2013 more than 12,000 Chinese migrants left Italy to go back to China, the majority between 2007 and 2013.[61] *Sulle orme di Marco Polo* devotes a section to the so-called 'cinesi di ritorno'[Chinese returnees]; interestingly, though, this mainly refers to Chinese Italians born or raised in Italy who decide to attempt a career in China and who are not necessarily 'returning' home. These are stories of success, yet the way this phenomenon is described by the authors of the analysis highlights a clear exclusionary attitude:

> Di certo un ruolo chiave nell'incontro delle differenti culture e abitudini nella gestione del lavoro e degli affari è ricoperto da coloro che fondono in sé entrambe le culture, quindi dai cinesi figli di immigrati di prima generazione, che sono cresciuti in Italia e si sentono integrati nel Paese, senza dimenticare la propria originaria appartenenza.[62]
>
> [Clearly, in the encounter of different cultures and customs of work and business, a key role is played by those who combine both cultures in themselves. They are Chinese, children of first-generation immigrant parents, born and raised in Italy, who feel they are integrated in Italy, but do not forget their original belonging.]

In the few pages dedicated to this topic, the two young men interviewed are never defined as *Italiani*, not even *Italo-Cinesi*; they are not 'integrati' [integrated] but 'si sentono integrati' [they feel they are integrated]. This is confirmed by the analysis carried out by Raffaetà, Baldassar and Harris on Chinese youth in Prato: 'These young people are constantly reminded that they are not Italian, both through everyday experiences in public spaces and through the formal legislation of the state, which does not assure them citizenship, even if born in Italy.'[63] According to the same analysis, as there is no space in the 'Italian national imaginary for hybridized belongings, young

---

61   Daniele Brigadoi Cologna, 'L'eterno mito del ritorno a casa: I cinesi d'oltremare che lasciano il "sogno italiano" per quello cinese', *Orizzonte Cina*, 5 (2014) <https://www.twai.it/articles/cinesitaliani-leterno-mito-del-ritorno-a-casa-i-cinesi-doltremare-che-lasciano-il-sogno-italiano-per-quello-cinese/> [accessed 24 July 2017].
62   Di Vincenzo et al., p. 89.
63   Raffaetà et al., pp. 426–31.

Chinese come to perceive themselves as "different" from Italians'.[64] Their mobility across the two countries and the advantage of embodying both cultures is often underestimated and ignored in the effort to reiterate the rhetoric of cultural differences.[65]

In conclusion, it is emblematic that, at times, the expression 'distretto parallelo' [parallel district] is used to refer to the industrial area in Prato that hosts Chinese-owned factories. It is a definition that to a certain extent can also be used to describe the relationship between the two countries. According to one of the protagonists of *Prezzemolo & cilantro*, the reason for this is to be found, once again, in cultural differences: 'L'espatriato medio non capirà mai la Cina' fece ad un certo punto Silvia 'né tantomeno cosa passa per la testa dei cinesi. È una società troppo diversa, hanno una storia troppo complicata!' ['"The average expat will never understand China", said Silvia at some point, "nor what is going on inside the Chinese mind. Their society is too different, their story too complicated!"'].[66]

If, on the one hand, the economic situation opens new opportunities for both countries, on the other the cultural representations of both communities suggest that both China and Italy's resident Chinese community are still perceived as unavoidably culturally distant. However, the sources analysed in this chapter also suggest that in reality it is not just a question of cultural distance, but rather of the reluctance to look at and understand that distance and, most importantly, to look beyond it.

In April 2017 the architect and blogger MartinoExpress published a book on his experience in China entitled *Lǎowài, un pratese in Cina. Diario di un expat da Chinatown all'estremo oriente*.[67] He describes how his life in China is marked by difficulties and wonders, which lead him to a better understanding of himself and of his home city, Prato. It is precisely his Pratese background that makes him question what it means to be a foreigner, creating a productive dialogue between him, as an Italian in China, and the Chinese community, those people that he had so far perceived as foreigners. His experience in China is full of encounters with other expats and with Chinese people, who

---

64   Raffaetà et al., p. 427.
65   For more information on the presence of second-generation Chinese Italians see the association Associna: 'Associna | Associazione Di Seconde Generazioni Italo-Cinesi' <http://www.associna.com/it/> [accessed 12 July 2017].
66   Moretti, *Prezzemolo & cilantro*, p. 57.
67   For his blog see MartinoExpress, *MartinoExpress – Un pratese in Cina (e dintorni)* <http://www.martinoexpress.it/> [accessed 18 September 2017].

often work with and for him, but who nonetheless are also behind 'inaspettati momenti di bellezza e a gesti di umanità'[unexpected moments of beauty and signs of humanity]. MartinoExpress's book ends with a collection of his favorite memories, which are not all positive (indeed, he struggled to adjust to the new society), but which, unlike the observations of TomcatUSA, include both other expats and his Chinese friends and colleagues. MartinoExpress's account, by looking at Chinese society with curiosity, provides an additional indication of how the emphasis on differences is hindering not only the two countries' economic exchanges but the human ones as well. As he points out:

> Al di là del fatto che c'è chi continua a dirmi che i cinesi agiscono sempre per un tornaconto e che dovrei essere più diffidente, scafato o disilluso, o banalmente che la mia stessa esperienza mi insegni come i rapporti di lavoro sono innanzitutto rapporti di lavoro [...] questi momenti hanno cominciato a servire a me, e soltanto a me, per capire che piuttosto che stare a guardare la differenza e a mettere sempre l'accento su quello che manca ci si può anche sorprendere inaspettatamente contenti o stranamente *completi* facendo la strada che si fa e perseguendola fino in fondo. [...] perché non si tratta di sforzarsi a guardare a ogni costo il positivo, quanto di sforzarsi a guardare punto e basta.[68]

[Beyond the fact that there are those who keep on telling me that the Chinese always act in their own interests and that I should be more sceptical, shrewd or disillusioned, or simply that my work experience should teach me that work relations are first and foremost work relations [...] these moments are helpful to me, and only to me, to understand that instead of continuing to focus on difference and emphasizing what's missing we could also be surprised by being unexpectedly happy or weirdly *complete* continuing on this path until the end. [...] because it is not about making the effort to look for the positive at all costs, but rather making the effort to look, that's it.]

---

68 MartinoExpress, *Lǎowài*, p. 62.

CHAPTER TWELVE

Writing the Neighbourhood: Literary Representations of Language, Space and Mobility

Rita Wilson

Introduction

In recent decades translingual and transcultural literary narratives have brought to the fore how the interplay of languages within superdiverse urban spaces[1] contributes to an individual's experience of the city. This has led, in turn, to a new engagement with the interrelated issues of linguistic and cultural diversity and the spatial construction of identity. Combining insights from cultural geography and translation studies, this chapter examines recent literary texts that focus on multi-ethnic urban scenarios in Italy. It will draw attention to the 'translation zones' – urban areas of intense interaction across languages[2] – produced by increased mobility and new settlements. In particular, it will explore the 'cultural edges' produced by transnational migration flows: transitional areas that 'are zones of social interaction, cross-fertilization, and synergy wherein people not only exchange material goods but also learn from one another'.[3]

---

1 Steven Vertovec, 'Super-diversity and Its Implications', *Ethnic and Racial Studies*, 30 (2007), 1024–54.
2 Sherry Simon, 'The Translation Zone', in *Handbook of Translation Studies*, ed. by Yves Gambier and Luc van Doorslaer (Amsterdam: John Benjamins Publishing Company, 2013), vol. 4, pp. 181–85.
3 Nancy J. Turner, Iain J. Davidson-Hunt and Michael O'Flaherty, 'Living on the Edge: Ecological and Cultural Edges as Sources of Diversity for Social-Ecological Resilience', *Human Ecology*, 31 (2003), 439–61 (p. 440).

J. Hillis Miller argues that fictional imaginings of real topography contribute to a reciprocal process of cultural signification, a back-and-forth crossing between fiction and reality that amplifies the meanings of place.[4] In this model, fiction and landscape are not in fixed hierarchical relation but work to augment each other, and literary discourse interacts with – and consequently modifies – the perception and production of place. In what follows, I will examine how fiction can inflect perceptions of 'real' translation zones by adopting the geocritical approach proposed by Bertrand Westphal, which assumes a literary referentiality between world and text: 'fiction is in the real; it contributes to fleshing out the real, which contributes to anchoring the aesthetic of representation in the ensemble of perceived contemporary society.'[5]

Geocriticism has a clear methodology built around four key concepts: multifocalization, polysensoriality, stratigraphy and intertextuality. The first, multifocalization, compares different cultural representations of a specific place, juxtaposing the endogenous perspective, that of the native city dweller, with an allogenous perspective, the in-between perspective of the migrant writer, for example. The second critical concept, polysensoriality, requires looking at the different sense perceptions described in the text, going beyond the visual aspect that is often the only focus of attention. The third concept, stratigraphy, refers to the detection of different historical strata in the representations of place and studies how different narratives about a place by different cultural communities construct temporalities of that place. Finally, Westphal expands the conventional meaning of the term 'intertextuality' and uses it to describe 'the intertextual chain that associates spatial "reality" with fiction. The writer is the author of his city, and a given representation, even – especially? – a fictional one, eventually acts upon the "realeme", affecting the way it is perceived.'[6]

Because geocriticism demands a polysensorial attention that takes into consideration all of the body's perceptual capabilities, without privileging the visual, it aligns well with the notion of translation as a 'sensory activity'. The latter arises from our relationship with the world around us, which is formed through sound, touch, taste and smell as much as sight. A combination of these two approaches offers a useful framework to investigate how literary

---

4 J. Hillis Miller, *Topographies* (Stanford, CA: Stanford University Press, 1995), pp. 9, 54.
5 Bertrand Westphal, 'A Geocritical Approach to Geocriticism', *American Book Review*, 37 (2016), 4–5 (p. 4).
6 Bertrand Westphal, *Geocriticism: Real and Fictional Spaces*, trans. by Robert T. Tally Jr. (Basingstoke: Palgrave Macmillan, 2011), p. 169.

representations of local linguistic practices in everyday transcultural encounters concretely contribute to understanding the construction of social and cultural identities in global multilingual landscapes.

Narrating Changing Places

In the last two decades a number of works written in Italian have focused on representations of multi-ethnic urban scenarios in which groups of people radically different from one another in lingua-cultural background, world view and power come together in new social formations. A significant group of writers has emerged from the last 30 years or so of immigration, including those who have been living in the country for several decades (Amara Lakhous, Tahar Lamri, Ornela Vorpsi, Laila Wadia) and those born in Italy either from non-Italian parents or from mixed couples (Cristina Ali Farah, Gabriella Ghermandi, Gabriella Kuruvilla, Igiaba Scego). Their increasingly flourishing literary production offers a critical portrayal of how transnational migrations have been affecting and transforming contemporary Italy and Italian identity as a whole. These stories of migration lend themselves well to geocritical analysis, not least because they are stories that unfold on specific local communities and are told through people's everyday life, practices, experiences and relationships, which are inevitably attached to particular places. By way of illustration, I have chosen four texts by four different authors for discussion in this chapter: *Scontro di civiltà per un ascensore a Piazza Vittorio* (2006) [Clash of Civilizations Over an Elevator in Piazza Vittorio, 2008] by Amara Lakhous; *Amiche per la pelle* [Best Friends] (2007) by Laila Wadia; *Milano, fin qui tutto bene* [Milan, so Far so Good] (2012) by Gabriella Kuruvilla and *Roma negata: Percorsi postcoloniali nella città* [Rome Denied: Postcolonial Paths in the City] (2014) by Igiaba Scego. While the texts selected belong to different genres, they have been chosen because each comprises a textual remapping of the authors' private relationship with the worlds they inhabit and each narrates the lived experience of migration in its two-fold dimension: emigration and immigration. Their intradiegetic narrators become the participants of intercultural communication and stress the interconnectedness of mobility, urban space and language choice in the construction of their complex identities.[7]

---

[7] Rita Wilson, 'Narrating the Polyphonic City: Translation and Identity in Translingual/Transcultural Writing', in *Multilingual Currents in Literature, Translation and Culture*, ed. by Rachael Gilmour and Tamar Steinitz (Abingdon: Routledge, 2017), pp. 55–80.

The first text, in chronological order of publication, is exemplary. Not only is Lakhous' novel simultaneously multifocal, polysensorial, stratigraphic and intertextual, but the text's linguistic history mirrors the author's migratory journey. In 2003 Amara Lakhous published an Arabic-language novel about his early years in Italy. Released in Algeria with the title *Kayfa tarḍa'u min al-dhi'ba dūna an ta'aḍḍaka* [How to be Suckled by the She-wolf without Getting Bitten],[8] it explores the relationship between memory, language and cultural belonging. The Italian version, published in 2006 with the title *Scontro di civiltà per un ascensore a Piazza Vittorio*, won him the prestigious Italian literary prizes Flaiano and Racalmare-Leonardo Sciascia. It also made the *Corriere della sera* bestseller list in the 'Italian fiction' category, which, as various critics have noted, launched Lakhous' career as a writer within the national literary system.

The plot of *Scontro* is shaped around a single apartment building located on Piazza Vittorio in Rome and revolves around the murder of one of the building's residents. The inhabitants of the building – five immigrant characters and five Italian characters – all give their views on the facts of the case, especially on the prime suspect, whose real name is Ahmed but who is universally known as Amedeo and thought to be Italian, although he is actually Algerian, and who mysteriously disappeared after the murder. Making the culturally hybrid Amedeo/Ahmed, a foreigner who seems to be more Italian than anybody else in the book, the protagonist enables Lakhous to explore and challenge exclusivist constructions of national identities. At the same time, *Scontro* also draws attention to the problematic relationship between language and the mainstream notion of nationality by presenting a critical reappraisal of the concept of 'mother tongue' and of its association to the notion of belonging to a single, unified nation, culture and ethnicity.

Published a year after *Scontro*, the plot of Wadia's novel, *Amiche per la pelle*, is also shaped around a condominium. This time the location is an imaginary street in Trieste, Via Ungaretti. The building is home to four migrant families from very diverse cultural backgrounds and ethnicities (Chinese, Albanian, Bosnian, Indian) and a single local man, Signor Rosso: a misanthrope who avoids any contact with anyone in or outside the building. The relationship between him and the four families is difficult and the cohabitation arduous. The specificity of Trieste as a setting for this story is significant. Because of its complicated history and its geographical position, Trieste has an unusually

---

8   Amara Lakhous, *Kayfa tarḍa'u min al-dhi'ba dūna an ta'aḍḍaka* (Algiers: Editions Al-ikhtilaf, 2003).

high number of widely spoken languages. Indeed, Sherry Simon considers Trieste to be exemplary of the 'translational city':[9] a space of heightened language awareness, of intensified intercultural exchanges.

Wadia and Lakhous' depiction of a transcultural building-community concentrates attention on the tensions of a multilayered local culture. The ways in which the fictional apartment blocks are used by their inhabitants, and the way people using them relate to one another, are largely dependent on language use: that is, the spoken interactions together with written texts that may give aesthetic or historical value to the building (e.g. the 'poetic geography' that overlays the geography of the urban planners in *Amiche*), or that impose and sanction power relations between its users (advising which spaces may be accessible to whom, such as the use of the elevator in *Scontro*), or that designate some spaces as 'communal' vs. 'private' (regulating patterns of behaviour in a neighbourhood, as depicted in *Milano* in a section on Corvetto, where the access of immigrants to the Bowling Centre is restricted to the first floor, where the slot machines are located, and Italians are not welcome at the Sherazad café, where all the clients speak Arabic or French). In short, these are sites (re)producing particular social values and relations (e.g. dominant power structures), and encouraging particular types of activity and social encounter.[10]

Kuruvilla and Scego employ a similar 'politics of microspection'[11] to investigate places and their inhabitants but widen the scope: moving from an exploration of the sociability patterns of a single building-community to focus on the processes of identity and otherness construction in relation to city neighbourhoods. Both *Milano, fin qui tutto bene* and *Roma negata: Percorsi postcoloniali nella città* are the result of collaborations with professional photographers. The stories in *Milano* emerge from a decision by Kuruvilla and photographer Silvia Azzari to explore the ghettoized districts affected by new by-laws limiting night-time opening hours for shops, introduced by the local administration as a measure to preserve public safety after a series of inter-ethnic riots erupted following the murder of a young Egyptian man in February 2010. Kuruvilla's aim was to gather first-hand accounts of the everyday life in these constantly

9   Sherry Simon, *Cities in Translation: Intersections of Language and Memory* (London, New York: Routledge, 2011).
10 Thomas A. Markus and Deborah Cameron, *The Words between the Spaces: Buildings and Language* (London: Routledge, 2002), p. 3.
11 Michael Cronin, *The Expanding World: Towards a Politics of Microspection* (Winchester, Washington: Zero Books, 2012).

transforming neigbourhoods. The result is a multifocal, polysensorial narrative structured around the distinctive topography of cultures found in four districts in Milan: Via Padova, Viale Monza, Via Sarpi and Piazzale Corvetto, each of which offers a glimpse of the complex pattern of socio-cultural interactions in these superdiverse communities. The accompanying photos by Silvia Azzari – one photo placed at the start of each chapter – visually reinforce the geometric distribution of the narrative. The four snapshots in black and white define the space of the word, anticipating the textual narrative and emphasizing the intertextual chain that links social life with fiction.

Like Kuruvilla, Scego organizes her narrative spatially: each chapter title references a monument or a neighbourhood that acts as a medium for colonial memories (e.g., 'Le cinquecento Afriche di un capolinea romano' [The Five Hundred Africas of a Roman Terminus]; 'L'obelisco della Discordia' [Obelisk of Discord]). Composed in collaboration with photographer Rino Bianchi, *Roma negata* is a work of creative nonfiction that chronicles the traces left by Italy's colonial past on the urban fabric. Together, Scego and Bianchi revisit some of the symbolic sites in Rome – monuments, buildings, streets and place-names – that bear traces of the Italian colonial enterprise in the Horn of Africa in the period following Italian unification and during Fascism. To counter the erasure of Italy's historical relation to Africa from Italian national memory, they re-vision Italian history through a creative and stratigraphic remapping of the urban space of Rome. They adopt the perspective defined by Glissant as a prophetic vision of the past, according to which the past has not only to be narrated by the historian but also to be imagined in a prophetic way for those communities and cultures whose past has been kept hidden or neglected.[12] The diasporic communities that have transformed the ethnic configuration of Rome and other Italian cities since the 1970s, as well as present-day migrants coming from the Italian former colonies of Eritrea, Somalia, Libya and Ethiopia, are a reminder of that past connecting Italy to Africa, and yet are still not, by and large, recognized as belonging to a common history.

Linguistic Landscapes: Visual and Aural

Research has shown that the forces of modernity, globalization and multiculturalism create new personal, social and professional identities and

---

12   Édouard Glissant, *Poetics of Relation*, trans. by Betsy Wing (Ann Arbor: University of Michigan Press, 1997), p. 86.

relations in neighbourhoods and cities, and between public authority and civil society, all of which contribute to the reshaping of urban linguistic landscapes.[13] Literary narratives such as the ones under discussion offer a new angle of approach to the multiform forces that create translational city spaces, by deploying narrative practices that accentuate the movement, complexity and texture of urban language interactions.

In urban neighbourhoods, physical proximity can create a sense of 'public familiarity', where people see each other as belonging to a local community, intended as a particular kind of social relation, warm and intimate.[14] However, the feeling of 'being at home' that we may get when we are close to home and start to see recognizable faces does not necessarily mean that we share any particular relation with these people that justifies the use of the term 'local community', intended as a spatialized sense of 'us', a cultural and symbolic local sense of belonging. Situations in which established residents are surprised by the rapid and deep transformations in their neighbourhood brought about by the arrival of newcomers can lead to defensive reactions rhetorically grounded in the existence of a more or less imagined community and the construction of socio-spatial boundaries that shape neighbourhood belonging and mark the exclusion or partial inclusion of those considered outsiders.

In *Milano*, Kuruvilla pays particular attention to the contrast between the established residents and the 'incomers' as manifested in everyday practices in public spaces. While, for the former, the streets, squares and parks have become mere spaces of transit, the new arrivals are making productive use of these as social spaces, particularly in the summer months, when North Africans, Chinese, Filipinos, South Americans, Romanians, Bangladeshi, Indians and Sri Lankans all go outdoors: 'i bambini giocano nei cortili, le donne chiacchierano sui ballatoi e gli uomini si incontrano per strada' [children play in the yards, women chat on the balconies and men meet on the street].[15]

A more detailed illustration of the dual nature of neighbourhoods characterized simultaneously by the dynamics of village life and by the dynamics

---

13 Elizier Ben-Rafael, Elana Shohamy, Muhammad Hasan Amara and Nira Trumper-Hecht, 'Linguistic Landscape as Symbolic Construction of the Public Space: The case of Israel', *International Journal of Multilingualism*, 3 (2006), 7–30.
14 Talja Blokland and Mike Savage, 'Social Capital and Networked Urbanism', in *Networked Urbanism*, ed. by Talja Blokland and Mike Savage (Aldershot: Ashgate, 2008), pp. 1–20.
15 Gabriella Kuruvilla, *Milano, fin qui tutto bene* (Rome-Bari: Laterza, 2012), p. 77. All translations from Italian are mine unless otherwise indicated.

of global relations, where the global flow of international goods and the daily routines of elderly people and families come together, is provided by the portrayal of the neighbourhood on Via Paolo Sarpi. Known as Milan's Chinatown, it consists of a 'dedalo di stradine in cui ci si perde [...], situato poco lontano dal Duomo [...] ma è come [essere] nel centro di Pechino' [maze of streets where you get lost [...], it is located not far from the Cathedral [...] but it is like [being] in the centre of Beijing].[16] Here, the endogenous point of view is provided by Stefania, a self-employed Milanese photographer and painter, whose photographs document the popular perception of the Chinese living in Milan as a closed, silent, introverted and isolated community: they rarely speak Italian with the locals and pass quickly through the streets 'come se fossero qui ma si trovassero altrove: ancora in Cina, forse. E in Cina probabilmente siamo' [as if they were here, but found themselves somewhere else: still in China, perhaps. And we probably are in China].[17] In a mixture of standard Italian and Milanese, Stefania reflects on how native Italians are excluded from the intimate, individual Asian topography of the neighbourhood:

> tu che sei italiano non ci capisci nulla, di quello che leggi e di quello che senti, degli ideogrammi e del mandarino: tanto che par che te set anda a scoeula de giuvedì. E un tempo le scuole, il giovedì, erano chiuse.[18]

> [you are Italian, and you can't understand anything you read or hear, the ideograms and Mandarin: so much so that it's as if you only attended school on Thursdays. And in the past, schools were closed on Thursdays.]

While Stefania's narrow viewpoint fails to consider that any non-Mandarin speaker is similarly excluded, her remark serves as a reminder that the linguistic landscape 'provides a unique perspective on the coexistence and competition of different languages and their scripts, and how they interact and interfere with each other in a given place'.[19] Indeed, public and commercial signs can be used to reinforce a collective identity, or, as Ben-Rafael puts it, they may be designed to assert 'their actors'

---

16 Kuruvilla, p. 97.
17 Kuruvilla, p. 87.
18 Kuruvilla, p. 106.
19 Peter Backhaus, *Linguistic Landscapes: A Comparative Study of Urban Multilingualism in Tokyo* (Clevedon: Multilingual Matters, 2007), p. 145.

particularistic identities, i.e. "who they are" in front of "who they are not", exhibiting thereby a priori commitment to a given group within the general public'.[20] It is commonly understood that, apart from indexing a particular linguistic community, the act of displaying a language, especially on official signage, carries the important symbolic function of increasing its value and status. Thus, the presence and dominance of one language over others (in frequency of occurrence or prominence of display) may indicate the relative demographic and institutional power of an ethnolinguistic group over others. The meaning and power of language is thus dependent on, and derived from, space. Via Paolo Sarpi is representative of a site of transculturation in which the power relations between, in this instance, Chinese and Italian residents are constantly renegotiated.

The use of Milanese in the above example shifts the emphasis from the 'transnational to the translocational'[21] and makes the links between language, place and personal identity even more explicit. Likewise, the forms of language used by Lakhous' characters in *Scontro* are strongly marked by their regional belonging: for example, the concierge constantly code switches to Neapolitan while the professor who moved to Rome to take up an academic post at La Sapienza University regularly lapses into Milanese. Similarly, Wadia uses Triestino to stress the regional contrasts and conflicts between Italians,[22] suggesting the fallacy of the notion of a world without borders: even as geographical borders may seem increasingly insignificant, linguistic boundaries may nevertheless remain intact. However, at the same time, she also uses the local idiom as an effective means of cementing her migrant protagonist's translational assimilation to Italian culture: 'Oramai il dialetto lo riesco a seguire. È essenziale per la sopravvivenza' [By now I can understand dialect. It's essential to survive].[23]

By using local accents and (forms of) languages, these writers effectively explore new directions in the challenge to linguistic normativeness. In these novels, the complex intersections of the 'local' and the 'global' that occur in this highly stratified multi-ethnic society are reflected in the characters' everyday language practices. In addition to traces of regional forms of Italian

---

20 Elizier Ben-Rafael, 'A Sociological Approach to the Study of Linguistic Landscapes', in *Linguistic Landscape: Expanding the Scenery*, ed. by Elana Shohamy and Durk Gorter (New York, London: Routledge, 2009), pp. 40–54 (p. 45).
21 Cronin, p. 39.
22 Laila Wadia, *Amiche per la pelle* (Rome: Edizioni e/o. 2007), pp. 89–92.
23 Wadia, p. 89.

that coexist with inflections and words from the immigrants' ethnic languages, their language use is influenced by varieties of English and global youth sub-cultures. A notable case in point is the character of Tony in *Milano*. His entire personality is characterized by his translanguaging practices: his speech is configured by Neapolitan, because his family is from Naples; by Milanese, learned in the suburban area of Corvetto, where there is still a strong sense of Milanese identity ('milanesità'); but also by English slang and Jamaican patois, reflecting the street language commonly used by youth in this district. The municipality has been promising for years that Tony and his family would be moved out of their tiny, overcrowded apartment to larger premises in a different area but, in Tony's colourful words, 'a promise is a comfort to a fool, una promessa è una comodità per uno sciocco. An wi nuh bawn back a cow: e noi non siamo stupidi, lo sappiamo che nisciuno c'aiuta' [a promise is a comfort to a fool. I wasn't born yesterday and we're not stupid; we know no-one will help us].[24] In order to convey the full extent of his disillusionment with local government, Tony uses all the linguistic codes at his disposal, from reggae lyrics and Jamaican patois to standard Italian and Neapolitan vernacular, in a form of translanguaging that, through the constant fragmenting and recombination of linguistic elements, points to how 'translating is a general part of language activities in multilingual societies. […] In a word, translation is working within our societies, on all levels, and not just between them.'[25]

The translanguaging practices deployed by these characters enable us to see how everyday practices and identities elucidate the notion of cities as translation zones. These are 'trans-spaces' in which 'new language practices, meaning-making multimodal practices, subjectivities and social structures are dynamically generated'.[26] In accounting for people's plurilingual behaviour in contemporary urban environments, it is useful to draw on Appadurai's notion of 'scapes', used to designate 'not objectively given relations that look the same from every angle of vision' but rather 'fluid irregular shapes' that are 'inflected by the historical, linguistic and political situatedness of different sorts of actors'.[27] These fictional characters

---

24 Kuruvilla, p. 159.
25 Anthony Pym, 'Response by Pym to "Invariance Orientation: Identifying an Object for Translation Studies"', *Translation Studies*, 10 (2017), 338–43.
26 Ofelia Garcia and Li Wei, *Translanguaging: Language, Bilingualism and Education* (New York: Palgrave Macmillan, 2013), p. 43.
27 Arjun Appadurai, *Modernity at Large: Cultural Dimensions of Globalization* (Minneapolis: University of Minnesota Press, 1996), p. 33.

reflect everyday practices in urban 'linguascapes':[28] from speakers deploying 'standard' linguistic resources in novel forms, styling self and other in new, often surprising ways, to playing with social norms and establishing new regimes of truth, and unexpectedly conflating instrumental and emotive uses of language (or moving between exchange-value and use-value). The movement through space of linguistic and communicative resources affects the function and value of the linguistic skills and repertoires of the speakers, which 'can change as the space of the language contact changes'[29] and may invoke different scales: local, national, public, private.

These literary representations of the ways in which languages converge within public space also provide insight into the translational dynamics that contribute to the redefinition of civic space and to the creation of communities across languages in the public sphere.[30] In this context, *Amiche per la pelle* offers an interesting perspective into how language learning can serve as a path toward community formation. Wadia's four female characters learn Italian primarily to communicate with one other, not having any other language in common. In other words, they learn Italian not to erase difference but to communicate despite, or across, alterity. Their language instructor is Laura, a retired school-teacher and a 'language activist': that is, someone who displays 'a languaging response to the phenomena that present themselves in the world' and, by engaging 'with the world-in-action', attempts 'to develop different, more relational ways of interacting with the people and phenomena that one encounters in everyday life'.[31] Laura engages with the 'world-in-action' by dividing her time between the 'Comitato per la salvaguardia dei fiori del Carso' [Committee for the preservation of the flowers of the Carso] and the 'Comitato per il bilinguismo a Trieste' [Committee for bilingualism in Trieste].[32] These fictional committees are an ironic allusion to the dominant negative discourse on migrants in Italy, particularly prevalent in the early 2000s with the blossoming of 'comitati di quartiere' [neighbourhood committees]: grass-roots residents' associations set up to 'safeguard' quality

---

28 Maria Lauret, *Wanderwords: Language Migration in American Literature* (London: Bloomsbury Academic, 2014), p. 20.
29 Jan Blommaert, James Collins and Stef Slembrouck, 'Spaces of Multilingualism', *Language & Communication*, 25 (2005), 197–216 (p. 211).
30 Sherry Simon, 'The City in Translation. Urban Cultures of Central Europe', *Target* 24 (2012), 126–40 (p. 127).
31 Alison Phipps, 'Travelling Languages? Land, Languaging and Translation', *Language and Intercultural Communication*, 11 (2011), 364–76 (pp. 368, 365).
32 Wadia, p. 53.

of life and security in their neighbourhoods and discursively constructed around issues of community and identity.[33] At the heart of this discourse is, of course, the question of national unity and the problematic myth of mono-culturalism. Wadia reproduces ideological linkages as rhetorical ones, and by so doing highlights how questions of national belonging, racial exclusion and cultural production are all equally tied up with issues of language. Further, in the parts of the narrative devoted to the language learning activities, Wadia draws attention to the audible surface of the city by emphasizing Laura's constant attempts to correct her students' idiosyncratic pronunciation.

Polyglot soundscapes form an integral part of everyday living experiences and complement visually perceivable textual multilingual communication. Linguistic actors within the soundscape display a wide variety of multilingual practices, ranging from 'pragmatic borrowings' such as the use of single 'transnational' expressions (e.g., greetings) to those for whom languages not only co-exist but form a new linguistic representation and identification: as Jørgensen puts it, a polylanguaging.[34] An extreme example of such polylanguaging is found in *Scontro*. The novel has a complex structure: 11 of the 22 chapters are narrated in the form of a monologue by different narrators. Each monologue is followed by a chapter written in diary form by the protagonist Amedeo/Ahmed. The chapters that contain the protagonist's diary are entitled 'Ululati' [Howls]: 'Primo Ululato', 'Secondo Ululato' [First Howl, Second Howl] and so on. Amedeo/Ahmed remarks that howling connects him to his adoptive 'mother', the Roman She-Wolf: 'Mi allatto della lupa insieme ai due orfanelli Romolo e Remo. Adoro la lupa, non posso fare a meno del suo latte'[35] ['I suckle on the wolf with the two orphans Romulus and Remus. I adore the wolf, I can't do without her milk'].[36] Bypassing both his languages – Italian and Arabic – the howls (representing both the she-wolf's language and the high-pitched ululations commonly practised by women in the Arab world to express celebration) allow Amedeo/Ahmed to remain bonded to both his cultures through the phonic representation of two mother tongues. In much

---

33   Antonello Petrillo, *La città delle paure: Per un'archeologia delle insicurezze urbane* (Avellino: Sellino Editore, 2003); Mariella Belluati, *L'in/sicurezza dei quartieri. Media, territorio e percezioni d'insicurezza* (Milan: Franco Angeli, 2004).
34   Jens Jørgensen et al., 'Polylanguaging in Superdiversity', *Diversities*, 13 (2011), <www.unesco.org/shs/diversities/vol13/issue2/art22011>.
35   Amara Lakhous, *Scontro di civiltà per un ascensore a Piazza Vittorio* (Rome: Edizioni e/o, 2006), p. 168.
36   Amara Lakhous, *Clash of Civilizations over an Elevator in Piazza Vittorio*, trans. by Anne Goldstein (New York: Europa Editions, 2008), p. 118.

of his work, Lakhous inscribes orality into his writing by privileging the phonic dimension of language. The result is a distinctive form of language, a multilingual idiom that not only consists of 'subtypes and varieties existing *within* the various officially recognised languages'[37] but, as in the case of the 'howls', is a new idiom that transforms the respective 'national' languages by transcending both the mother tongue and the adopted language.[38]

'Logics of Circulation': Language, Memory, Objects

In the 'trans-spaces' of multi-ethnic urban localities such as the fictional Via Ungaretti and the real Via Padova, the intersections between polyvocal perspectives demonstrate the power of language to recompose the difficult, but not impossible, coexistence of different worlds. The conduct of everyday life in the streets, squares, ethnic shops and community centres are constant reminders of the proximity of difference and of the diversity that finds expression in urban environments. The city is a place 'where people are drawn into all kinds of proximate relationships, often by chance, often fleetingly'.[39] These brief, chance encounters can evoke an array of emotions and memories that often create a defamiliarizing effect, as seen, for example, in several passages in Kuruvilla's text, in which Milan and India are merged within the narrator's personal geography: 'Strano negozio: mi ricorda i baracchini che vendono alcolici, sulle polverose strade di Kerala' [Strange shop: it reminds me of the kiosks selling spirits on Kerala's dusty roads]; 'Un traffico simile a quello indiano, nel caos stradale privo di regole: un gioco di prestigio regolato dalle urla e dai clacson' [Traffic similar to the Indian one, in its lawless street chaos: a conjuring trick executed by shouting and hooting]; 'la giovane zingara [...] mi ricorda le donne del Rajasthan che vendono per poche rupie argenti e tessuti sulle spiagge di Kovalam' [the young gipsy reminds me of the Rajasthani women selling silverware and fabric on the beaches of Kovalam for a few rupees].[40]

---

37 Dirk Delabastita and Rainier Grutman, 'Introduction. Fictional Representations of Multilingualism and Translation', *Linguistica Antverpiensia*, 4 (2005), 11–34 (p. 15).

38 See also Rita Wilson, 'Beyond Self-Translation: Amara Lakhous and Translingual Writing as Case Study', in *Self-Translation and Power: Negotiating Identities in Multilingual European Contexts*, ed. by Olga Castro, Sergi Mainer and Svetlana Page (Basingstoke: Palgrave Macmillan, 2017), pp. 241–64.

39 Diarmait Mac Giolla Chríost, *Language and the City* (Basingstoke: Palgrave Macmillan, 2007), p. 22.

40 Kuruvilla, pp. 20, 27, 32.

A similar defamiliarizing effect is evident in *Roma negata*, in which Scego and Bianchi take the reader on a guided tour of famous Roman landmarks with the aim of uncovering the hidden, silenced (his)stories of Italian colonialism. In an attempt to reappropriate and resignify those spaces denied to the Italian collective unconscious, Scego and Bianchi retrace the map of the city by following a route comprising monuments, other architectural traces and, crucially, people. The use of black and white photographs points to a temporal and spatial distance that nevertheless is brought closer by the physical presence of migrants from the former colonies inhabiting the present-day urban spaces of the Italian city. The composition of image and text is aimed at producing a sense of estrangement and disorientation in the spectator/reader as s/he is compelled to confront a common past that, while always there, had been hidden, and is currently resurfacing uncannily in the faces of the 'new Italians' occupying those public spaces. The first stratigraphic site the reader encounters is Piazza Porta Capena, now marked by the absence left by the 'Stele of Axum', an obelisk taken from Ethiopia in 1937 as part of the spoils of war following the Italian invasion of Ethiopia. The monument was erected in Piazza Porta Capena to celebrate the fifteenth anniversary of the March on Rome as a glorification of the 'new Roman empire'. It was returned to Ethiopia only in 2005, after long and painful negotiations. In 2009 two Roman columns were placed in the square as a memorial to those who died in the events of 9/11. The textual and visual multifocalization adopted by Scego and Bianchi implies negotiation between individual representations or recollections not only of the same space but also of their intersections. Here, the intersection of architecture and language forms an even more complex, multilayered cityscape in which we can discern the intertextual compound of succeeding layers of building or 'writing'. Focusing on the plaque at the base of the columns, inscribed with an aphorism by George Santayana: 'Coloro che non sanno ricordare il passato sono condannati a ripeterlo' [Those who cannot remember the past are condemned to repeat it], Bianchi and Scego highlight the extent to which previous strata of cultural coding underlie the present surface and each waits to be uncovered and 'read', like traces in a palimpsest. The square is viewed as a concrete entity participating in a precarious contemporaneity that hangs over in a 'present imperfect' temporality, a time in between a past that still lingers in the present.[41]

---

41 Giulia Grechi and Viviana Gravano, 'Immaginari (Post)coloniali. Memorie pubbliche e private del colonialismo italiano', in *Presente imperfetto. Eredità coloniali e*

A second, powerful example of how *Roma negata* functions as a reinsertion of Italy's multiple pasts into its present through the current inhabitants of 'national' places is constituted by Piazza dei Cinquecento. The square, named to commemorate the 430 Italian soldiers who died, defeated, at the 1887 Battle of Dogali in Eritrea, was the site of the Stele of Dogali until 1925 when the monument was moved to the Terme di Diocleziano. Nowadays, the Piazza dei Cinquecento, situated in front of Stazione Termini – location of the main train and bus stations – is also first and foremost a paradigmatic site of travel and exchange and deemed by Scego to be the 'true centre of Rome':

> quasi più del Colosseo, qui dove in una Babele folle le lingue si intrecciano e si contaminano con la lingua di Dante. E chi lo immaginava che proprio questa piazza babilonia fosse legata alla storia del colonialismo italiano? [...] E forse anche per questo, per un caso fortuito della vita, è diventata la piazza dei somali, degli eritrei, degli etiopi e anche di tutti gli altri migranti.[42]

> [almost more than the Colosseum, here, in a crazed Babel, languages are intertwined and contaminated with the language of Dante. And who would have imagined that this Babylonian square is linked to the history of Italian colonialism? [...] And perhaps because of a fortuitous circumstance, it has become the square of Somalis, Eritreans, Ethiopians, and of all the other migrants.]

This 'new Babel', a crossroads of migrants, cultures and languages, is both a translation zone and an instance of the 'regional urbanization' theorized by Edward Soja, which has led to 'the increasing erosion of the formerly relatively clear boundary between the urban and the suburban'.[43] In *Milano*, the dismantling of the binary construct centre–periphery is represented by Via Padova: a district that 'è ancora metropoli, ma sembra un paese' [is still part of a metropolis, but looks like a small town].[44] Since the 1980s, the

---

immaginari razziali contemporanei, ed. by Giulia Grechi and Viviana Gravano (Milan: Mimesis, 2016), pp. 23–37 (p. 34).
42 Igiaba Scego in Rino Bianchi and Igiaba Scego, *Roma negata: Percorsi postcoloniali nella città* (Rome: Ediesse, 2014), p. 68.
43 Edward Soja, 'Regional Urbanization and the End of the Metropolis Era', in *The New Blackwell Companion to the City*, ed. by Gary Bridge and Sophie Watson (Oxford: Blackwell, 2011), pp. 679–89 (p. 684).
44 Kuruvilla, p. 17.

many new multi-ethnic arrivals (Filipinos, Chinese, Egyptians, Peruvians, Senegalese, Romanians, Moroccans and Indians) have transformed its identity with their music, the colour and aroma of their spices and the 'gran vociare, in tutte le lingue' [prodigious clamour, in all languages].[45] It is depicted as a place characterized by a strong sense of community, currently lacking in other parts of the city: 'Mio è nostro: non è privato ma è sempre pubblico, in questo quartiere' [Mine means ours: it isn't private but it's always public, in this neighbourhood]; 'tutti si salutano, e si parlano' [people greet each other and everyone talks to each other];[46] and now this area seems to be more central in many ways than other streets located in the geographic centre of Milan.

To make sense of the circulation of languages through these culturally diverse neighbourhoods and the consequent creation of 'cultural edges', it is necessary to take account of the informal systems of knowledge arising from new social configurations as well as the shaping force of the 'logics of circulation' that determines 'the ways that knowledge is received and transmitted, shaped, developed, organized and passed on'.[47] By celebrating the multiplicity of endogenous and allogenous perspectives and by juxtaposing multiple voices that mutually enrich each other, the four authors under discussion demonstrate how the encounter with other cultures and languages creates a path to reciprocal knowledge. In effect, they propose a sensory geography of the city, in which the voices of new arrivals, their customs, the smells of their cuisines and even the variety of the ringtones of their mobile phones mingle with local sounds and smells, thereby constructing a new reality, a representation of a contemporary city with a fast-paced syncopated rhythm.

Together with sounds and smells, the circulation of material cultural objects contributes to the possibility of perceiving the global city in a multisensory way as a mobile, 'polyrhythmic', transcultural space. The 'reconfiguration of objects in foreign spaces' disrupts the established order of things, forces 'a reshuffle of the known' and 'the concomitant reorganization of the epistemological table of the receptor culture under the impact of those objects'.[48] In other words, transnational objects appear, and are interrogated, as spatial extensions of the self that connect translocated users and are

---

45 Kuruvilla, p. 6.
46 Kuruvilla, pp. 12–13, 6, 7–8.
47 Simon, 'The City in Translation', p. 129.
48 Spitta, p. 21.

fundamental to a rethinking of the 'sense of place', which Massey locates in the 'conjunction' of trajectories that form both a material and a socio-political crossroad.[49] In *Amiche*, for example, the interior of the building at number 25 Via Ungaretti exemplifies how, when objects leave their cultural frames, travel, reconfigure in new assemblages, they generate a chain of effects back and forth between the intersection of lingua-cultural formations and new social practices. A closer look at Wadia's detailed portrayal of the domestic interiors of the four migrant families reveals an idiosyncratic configuration of objects and furnishings that, in each case, reflect important elements of their migration stories. The home of the large Chinese family, the Fongs, is the most 'eccentrica e esotica' [eccentric and exotic], with red lacquered wardrobes and rice paper lamps. In the apartment of the Albanian couple, Lule and Besim Dardani, the blue and green neon lighting creates a 'Star Trek effect'.[50] The description of the lighting in these interiors alludes to the reframing of self-familiarizing cultural practices of migrant life, with the Fongs and the Dardanis representing two ends of the spectrum of migrant home-building: for the former, material objects function as cultural-memory portmanteaux, while, for the latter, the choice of furnishings implies they have chosen to cut ties with their (national) past in favour of new affiliations, which exist outside national time and space. In line with the quasi-autobiographical nature of the narrative and the author's own transcultural subjectivity, it is the décor of the Kumars' living room that exemplifies the 'micro-globalisation of the world city's everyday life and the globalisation of the biographies that are participating in it'.[51] Colourful cushions and silk screens of miniatures from the Mughal court are placed alongside gifts from the other residents: a brass plate from Durazzo, a Chinese vase, a framed handwritten copy of Umberto Saba's poem 'Trieste'.[52] Cultural material objects form part of the communicative activity of these transnational families, functioning as meaning-bearing elements (accentuated here by the addition of a linguistic dimension though the inclusion of the framed poem) and giving a vivid sense of a global space of cultural connection and dissolution, where local authenticities meet and merge in transient urban and suburban settings.

49 Doreen Massey, *For Space* (London: Sage, 2005).
50 Wadia, p. 39.
51 Jörg Durrschmidt, *Everyday Lives in the Global City: The Delinking of the Locale and the Milieu* (London: Routledge, 2000), p. 1.
52 Wadia, p. 39.

Concluding Remarks

The multi-sensory, multi-focal perspective adopted by these four authors is one that reflects the new strategies of interpersonal communication and intercultural competencies that are being developed in everyday life as people from a multitude of lingua-cultural backgrounds interact with each other in the 'cultural edges' of global cities. Close readings of their texts deepen our understanding of contemporary Italian literary production in several ways. Firstly, these plurilingual literary representations offer 'paradigms of plural societies that give insights into crucial questions of our time – questions concerning the preconditions for the fruitful interaction of peoples from different ethnic, religious, linguistic and cultural backgrounds'.[53] By emphasizing multilingual soundscapes and micro-histories of the everyday place-making of individuals, these texts show how changes to the political and economic macro level – the 'big issues' – are manifested in local language practices and experiences. The authors' 'highly personal detailed readings' of the diversified linguistic spectrum in multi-ethnic urban spaces provide insight into 'larger structures of coherence'[54] and offer a more nuanced understanding of the intricate relationship between language, mobility and space in transcultural urban societies. In short, these works are exemplary of how the subjective remapping of space from linguistic and aural perspectives – instead of only visual ones – can expose broader socio-political implications.

Second, the analysis of discursive spatial practices reveals how imagined spaces can have an impact on the construction of the urban spaces we encounter in our daily experiences; spaces in which the tensions between the globalizing and localizing displays of words and images reveal the competing voices of overlapping communities contending for visibility and for economic and political survival. It is not only what the fictional characters say that conveys certain understandings of self and environment. It is also how they mobilize 'the practice of translation as play' and are 'alert to the materiality of languages, beginning with their sounds'.[55] Semiotic artefacts, such as cultural

---

53 Marcel Cornis-Pope and John Neubauer, *History of the Literary Cultures of East-Central Europe. Junctures and Disjunctures in the 19th and 20th Centuries* (Amsterdam: John Benjamins, 2006), p. 11.
54 Westphal, *Geocriticism*, pp. 37–38.
55 Vicente Rafael, 'The War of Translation: Colonial Education, American English, and Tagalog Slang in the Philippines', *The Journal of Asian Studies*, 74 (2015), 283–302 (p. 302).

paraphernalia, can offer researchers a better understanding of how place descriptions are constructed, understood and interpreted as authentically multilingual and multi-ethnic, and may contribute to a greater understanding of language contact situations and the degree of multilingualism depicted in diasporic communities.

Third, transcultural public spaces are changeable, transient sites where place-making is often more a momentary performance than a planned strategy. Communication occurs across languages and cultures and, through the transmission of memory, across time. Thus, it becomes necessary to uncover the temporal rhythms and overlapping domains of in-group and out-group spaces, centres and peripheries, maintained by real, imaginary or experiential boundaries that sustain public spaces. Transcultural spaces are characterized by a relational visibility that, on the one hand, sustains multiple publics – the various subgroups within immigrant and 'native' communities – to communicate and become involved with each other. On the other hand, it allows each individual to interpret and recreate these spaces in different (personalized) ways. The discursive configurations of these spaces promote moving in, across and out of them in multiple ways. Such intertwined transcultural spaces change the way we describe multi-ethnic space in Italy. No longer is an ethnic space principally a site of difference. The depiction of the polylingualism characteristic of multi-ethnic neighbourhoods invites readers to reflect on how the translanguaging practices deployed by these fictional characters in response to their environment shape a perception of transcultural neighbourhoods as 'cultural edges': transitional zones that influence their cultures of origin by increasing diversity and flexibility, thus enhancing the resilience of the local societies as well.

By highlighting processes of linguistic as well as cultural translation, the work of these authors illustrates how the 'cultural' and the 'transcultural' cannot be studied in isolation but rather need to be seen as part of a complex system of circulation, which goes beyond national boundaries, canons or linguistic discreteness. The challenge placed on the reader is to attempt to make sense of the 'messy complexities' of these transcultural urban scenarios, knowing that any reading must always remain provisional. Perhaps one way of appraising the transformative potential of these narratives lies in the sense of 'interference' generated in the texts: they encourage a process of investigation into contemporary Italy and Italianness that cannot be tied up neatly. The ethnic differentiation of the characters and the juxtaposition of multiple viewpoints, together with the web of pluricultural intertextual references, lead us to the conclusion that their work is not only a textual manifestation of the wish to challenge the static notion of Italianness. It is also, and perhaps more importantly, an invitation to readers to imagine an inclusive, polyphonic literary tradition with the potential to redefine and diversify prevailing structures of meaning and knowledge.

CHAPTER THIRTEEN

From Substitution to Co-presence: Translation, Memory, Trace and the Visual Practices of Diasporic Italian Artists

Loredana Polezzi

Solo un pensiero mi fa sentire a mio agio: i tappeti. È nella tessitura dei tappeti che i nomadi depositano la loro sapienza: oggetti variegati e leggeri che si stendono sul nudo suolo dovunque ci si ferma a passare la notte e si arrotolano al mattino per portarli via con sé insieme a tutti i propri averi sulla gobba dei cammelli.

Just one thought makes me feel at ease: the carpets. It is in the weave of their carpets that the nomads deposit their wisdom: these variegated, light objects are spread on the bare ground wherever they stop to spend the night, and are rolled up again in the morning so they can carry them away with them along with all their other belongings on the humps of camels.

Italo Calvino[1]

---

1 Italo Calvino, 'Le sculture e i nomadi', in *Collezione di sabbia* (Turin: Einaudi, 1994), pp. 229–33 (pp. 232–33); English trans. by Martin McLaughlin, 'The Sculptures and the Nomads', in *Collection of Sand* (Boston, New York: Mariner Books, 2014), p. 210.

Introduction: Thick Weaving

Italo Calvino had a fascination for rugs and weaving. The image of intricately woven carpets providing a map of reality and of our experience of it recurs in his writing, perhaps most famously in the passage of Le città invisibili [Invisible Cities] devoted to Eudossia: a chaotic urban landscape that easily confuses the visitor but whose true shape and map are safely preserved in the form of a rug where 'un filo cremisi o indaco o amaranto' ['a crimson or indigo or magenta thread'] can help us find the way to our destination.[2] Elsewhere, in the closing essay of Collezione di sabbia [Collection of Sand] quoted above, Calvino describes a day trip to Persepolis during a visit to Iran. Caught between the permanence of stone and the incessant movement of natural life, he finds consolation and a sense of belonging in the image of the rugs that nomadic populations roll and unroll, fold and unfold, wherever they go: light, colourful objects that are the repository of collective wisdom and also of the ability to make home on the move.[3]

Calvino's exotic images, which I encountered as a reader decades ago, kept resurfacing later on as a way of figuring out the complex processes of production, circulation and reception of culture. As a researcher interested in travel, migration and translation, I returned to them looking for a way to hold together both the notions and the reality of transcultural communication and transnational spaces, but also as a helpful representation of how we study the intricate layering of such complex networks. I was reminded of rugs and their threads by Clifford Geertz's notion of thick description, Kwame Anthony Appiah's transposition of that idea into 'thick translation' and James Clifford's discussion of the crossing routes of translation and travel in the contemporary world.[4] Threads and their interweaving also make frequent appearances in contemporary memory studies, from Michael Rothberg's notion of multidirectional memory networks to Astrid Erll's definition of travelling memory.[5]

---

2   Italo Calvino, Le città invisibili (Turin: Einaudi, 1972), pp. 103–04; English trans. by William Weaver, Invisible Cities (San Diego, New York, London: Harvest, 1978).
3   Italo Calvino, 'Le sculture e i nomadi', pp. 232–33.
4   Clifford Geertz, The Interpretation of Cultures: Selected Essays (New York: Basic Books, 1973); Kwame Anthony Appiah, 'Thick Translation', Callaloo, special issue on 'Post-Colonial Discourse' (1993), 808–19; James Clifford, Routes: Travel Writing and Translation in the Late Twentieth Century (Cambridge, MA: Harvard University Press, 1997).
5   Michael Rothberg, Multidirectional Memory (Stanford, CA: Stanford University Press, 2009); Astrid Erll, Memory in Culture, trans. by Sara B. Young (Basingstoke: Palgrave Macmillan, 2011). On memory and translation see also Siobhan Brownlie,

Most of all, once I started looking for them, weaving, threads and their textures were everywhere in the work of artists who engage with the history of migration, its multiple demands for and offerings of translation, its regimes of (im)mobility and of labour, and its thick genealogies of gendered narratives of displacement, trauma and desire.

In this chapter I will try to weave together the notions and practices of migration, translation and memory, while, at the same time, unpicking some of the 'thicknesses' created by their connections. I will do so by focusing on a small set of key concepts: hospitality, substitution, trace and co-presence. I will approach these through a rereading of Ricoeur's foundational essay *On Translation* and through its own connections with Derrida's reflections on hospitality.[6] Equally important in my argument is the reflection on the work of three women artists: B. Amore, Luci Callipari-Marcuzzo and Filomena Coppola, whose visual and performance work explicitly references their families' history of migration from Italy to the United States (Amore) and to Australia (Callipari-Marcuzzo and Coppola). I encountered their work – and I encountered them – through my participation in the project 'Transnationalizing Modern Languages: Mobility, Identity and Translation in Modern Italian Cultures' (TML).[7] All three artists were involved, in more or less direct ways, in the TML initiative. Luci Callipari-Marcuzzo gave live performances at the opening events of two iterations of the project's exhibition, *Beyond Borders: Transnational Italy/Oltre i confini: Italia transnazionale*, held in Rome in the autumn of 2016 and in Melbourne the following year. B.'s contribution came in the form of the inclusion in the exhibition of one of her pieces, *Cracked Immigrant Mirror – Lo Specchio Spaccato dell'Immigrante*, a detail of which is also reproduced as the cover image of this volume.

Mapping Memory in Translation (Basingstoke: Palgrave Macmillan, 2016); Lieven D'Hulst and John Milton, eds, *Reconstructing Cultural Memory: Translation, Scripts, Literacy* (Amsterdam: Rodopi, 2000).

6 Paul Ricoeur, *On Translation*, trans. by Eileen Brennan (London, New York: Routledge, 2006); Jacques Derrida, *Of Hospitality: Anne Dufourmantelle Invites Jacques Derrida to Respond*, trans. by Rachel Bowlby (Stanford, CA: Stanford University Press, 2000).

7 For full details of this research initiative see <https://www.transnationalmodernlanguages.ac.uk/> [accessed 3 July 2020]. I am grateful to the AHRC and to all participants in the project for their support and collaboration – especially, of course, to B. Amore, Luci Callipari-Marcuzzo and Filomena Coppola for their willingness to share and discuss their work with me, for their permission to reproduce images of their art in this article, and, most of all, for their friendship.

Filomena's presence, finally, was first felt through the work of researchers connected to the TML group, such as Eliana Maestri and Rita Wilson, and then directly, through her own self-reflective contributions to a number of workshops and conference panels linked to the project.

The production of these three artists, who work in the context of Italian American and Italian Australian communities, directly engages with a personal and collective history of migration, its travelling memory and its transnational legacy. It is important to note here, however, that I will not just use their work to illustrate my reflections on these themes. On the contrary, it is through dialogue with the artists, through research carried out in the form of conversation, that I have made some progress in my own attempts to reformulate the link between migration and translation and to understand how and why rethinking that link also means rethinking migration's memory and its narratives. Discussing their work and discussing it with them has allowed me to examine how these female artists from the Italian diaspora use gendered practices, images and objects to construct a visual genealogy of migration that reminds us of its roots not just in trauma but also in desire. Their work embraces metaphorical as well as material forms of translation to invoke the double-edged nature of migration and of its memory: the ability to look towards the future while maintaining the threads that link us to our past. For me, their creative practices have come to substantiate a vision of translation that emerges as much from my engagement with theoretical reflection as from my own personal, biographical experience. This is a reinterpretation of the concept and the practices of translation that refutes fixed binary models based on notions of substitution and replacement, pointing instead towards the dynamic processes that allow us to travel, migrate (self-)translate, while actively constructing individual and collective narratives that – though they do not eliminate tension or fragmentation – insist on narrative continuity and co-presence. As I will argue below, translation can then be seen not as a form of erasure but as a trace,[8] testifying to and making visible the tension between continuity and discontinuity that lies at the heart of transnational experiences and transcultural narratives.

---

8   It should be noted here that, while acknowledging the role of these terms in a philosophical debate mostly associated with Derrida and with deconstruction, my use of these words does not directly reference that context. Another important point of reference for the reflections presented in this article is to be found in the photography of Fazal Sheikh and especially his *Erasure Trilogy*, one of whose volumes is entitled *Memory Trace*; see Fazal Sheikh, *The Erasure Trilogy* (Göttingen: Steidl, 2015).

Using visual art to talk about translation also underscores the importance of images in the construction and circulation of meaning – and sends me back to weaving, to Calvino and his rugs. In recent years, there has been growing interest in the link between art and translation and Birgit Mersmann has even proposed a reframing of 'cultural visual studies as translation research'.[9] If we reverse this perspective, we can also note that art can both visualize and operationalize translation, freeing it, in the process, from its inevitable meta-linguistic and meta-discursive nature (talking about translation is talking about language that already talks about other languages) and from a paradoxical condition that always invites us to choose one idiom in order to discuss an operation between multiple and often co-existing tongues. Finally, thinking visually and thinking about visual representations reminds us of the complex, difficult and often biased metaphorics of translation.[10] If the Western tradition favours the images of transfer and transportation inscribed in the Latin roots *translatio* and *traductio*, different metaphors can take us in different directions. Maria Tymoczko noted how 'the most common Chinese phrase for translation, *fan yi*, ... means "turning over"'. This concept, she says:

> is linked to the image of embroidery: thus, if the source text is the front side of an embroidered work, the target text can be thought of as the back side of the same piece. Like the reverse of an embroidery ... a translation in this conceptualization is not expected to be equivalent in all respects. At the same time, of course, the 'working side' of an embroidery teaches us much about its construction.[11]

---

9 On this topic, see Genevieve Warwick, 'Crying *Laocoon*: The Visual Arts of Translation', *The Translator*, special issue on 'Translating Cultures: Thematic Approaches to Translation', ed. by Charles Forsdick and Barbara Spadaro, 24 (2019), 311–34; and Birgit Mersmann, 'Bildkulturwissenschaft als Kulturbildwissenschaft? Von der Notwendigkeit eines inter- und transkulturellen Iconic Turn', *Zeitschrift für Ästhetik und allgemeine Kunstwissenschaft*, 49 (2004), 91–109 (p. 107); the English translation is by Doris Bachmann-Medick, who cites it in 'Introduction: The Translational Turn', *Translation Studies*, special issue on 'The Translation Turn', ed. by D. Bachmann-Medick, 2 (2008), 2–16 (p. 11).
10 James St. André, ed., *Thinking through Translation with Metaphors* (Manchester: St Jerome, 2010).
11 Maria Tymoczko, 'Reconceptualizing Translation Theory: Integrating Non-Western Thought about Translation', in *Translating Others*, ed. by Theo Hermans, 2 vols (Manchester: St. Jerome, 2006), vol. 1, pp. 13–32 (p. 22).

Translation, in this interpretation, is not just a copy or a poor reproduction. Like the working side of an embroidery, it makes visible the painstaking architecture that underpins the thick weave of communication, culture, creativity and memory. It also reminds us of the hidden labour and complex skills of the people who make those processes possible. There will be much in what follows about women's (and men's) labour as well as about the labour of translation.

Translation, Migration and the Question of Hospitality

Like translation, hospitality is a multidirectional word, a word constructed on a constant and irresolvable tension. The Latin *hospes* is both host and guest, local and stranger. Both meanings, as Derrida noted in commenting on the French word *hôte*, have an affinity with 'hostage'. Here is Derrida (in Rachel Bowlby's translation):

> So it is indeed the master, the one who invites, the inviting host, who becomes the hostage—and who really always has been. And the guest, the invited hostage, becomes the one who invites the one who invites, the master of the host. The guest becomes the host's host. The guest (hôte) becomes the host (hôte) of the host (hôte).[12]

In a similar vein, in his *Vocabulaire des institutions indo-européenes*, Émile Benveniste remarked that the word *hospes* sits in close proximity to *hostis*, which is, in turn, both stranger and enemy.[13]

Translation too is an act, a practice, built on the tension between sameness and difference, between what appear as irreconcilable opposites, between the foreign and what is 'peculiar to us'. Hence, following Antoine Berman's *L'Épreuve de l'étranger* [The Experience of the Foreign], the test and trial of translation is in receiving the foreign *as* foreign.[14] The traditional,

---

12 Derrida, *Of Hospitality*, pp. 123–25.
13 Émile Benveniste, *Vocabulaire des institutions indo-européenes* (Paris: Minuit, 1969), vol. 1, pp. 88–101.
14 Antoine Berman's *L'Épreuve de l'étranger: Culture et traduction dans l'Allemagne romantique: Herder, Goethe, Schlegel, Novalis, Humboldt, Schleiermacher, Hölderlin* (Paris: Gallimard, 1984); English trans. by Stefan Heyvaert, *The Experience of the Foreign: Culture and Translation in Romantic Germany* (New York: SUNY Press, 1992).

binary, dichotomous formulation of translation – which opposes neatly self-contained source text and target text, source language and target language, source culture and target culture – by insisting on equivalence and on substitution, on the replacement of one text and one language with another, constantly reinstates the opposition between foreign and same and demands the erasure of the first in order to produce the latter. Just as the Western tradition of hospitality relies on a clear demarcation of self and other, same and foreign, so a binary model of translation relies on the assumed self-contained nature of languages, cultures, texts. Yet that same assumption makes both translation and hospitality impossible: there can be no perfect translation, no perfect hospitality, because there is no perfect equivalence and substitution.

This epistemological model has important ethical and political consequences, which impact the nature not just of translation but of community, society and citizenship, and which make the question of translation and hospitality particularly poignant in relation to migration and to the condition of being a migrant. When in 2016 the then British prime minister, Theresa May, quipped that 'If you believe you are a citizen of the world, you are a citizen of nowhere', she was invoking similarly dichotomous and self-contained world views which divide reality into local and global, centre and periphery, national and foreign, admitting only one possibility of belonging, asking us to take a side and stick to it, or, if we move, to erase who we were in order to acquire a new, more fitting, identity. Similar assumptions are associated with the recurrent calls for everyone in the UK to speak English and are implicit in the strong association between language proficiency and citizenship rights, all of which rely on a normalized and normative model of the monolingual state and view multilingualism as an obstacle to social cohesion and integration.[15] Language

---

15   Theresa May made her speech at the Conservative Party conference on 5 October 2016, in the aftermath of the UK's Brexit vote; for the full text see <https://www.independent.co.uk/news/uk/politics/theresa-may-speech-tory-conference-2016-in-full-transcript-a7346171.html>; for an example of public recommendations associating citizenship, integration and the English language see *The Casey Review*, published in December 2016, available at <https://assets.publishing.service.gov.uk/government/uploads/system/uploads/attachment_data/file/575973/The_Casey_Review_Report.pdf> [both accessed 8 July 2020]; on these topics see also Anne-Marie Fortier, 'On (Not) Speaking English: Colonial Legacies in Language Requirements for British Citizenship', *Sociology*, 52 (2018), 1254–69; David Gramling, *The Invention of Monolingualism* (London: Bloomsbury, 2016).

and translation, in their classic formulations based on containment and substitution, are complicit in this kind of ideology and political discourse, which are closely connected with the nationalist and imperialist imprint of Western modernity. As observed by Sheldon Pollock, in fact, it is only in that era that the notion of a mother tongue to be loved and never betrayed, in all exclusivity, imposed itself. And, as Naoki Sakai has eminently demonstrated, translation can be the gatekeeper of fictions of self-sufficiency and monolingualism, when, in fact, what he calls 'the heterolingual address', the ability to approach the other as other, is at the heart of all communication and cultural production.[16]

So, what happens if we change that model? In *On Translation* Paul Ricoeur explicitly links translation and hospitality, coupling them in the notion of 'linguistic hospitality'. He likens the work of translation to the work of memory on the one hand and to that of mourning on the other, as it carries within itself the need for 'some salvaging and some acceptance of loss'.[17] The loss we have to accept to make translation possible is that of perfection or even of the wish for perfection.[18] We have to 'give up the ideal of the perfect translation',[19] with its 'nostalgia for the original language or the will for control over language by means of the universal language'.[20] Instead, we need to acknowledge our language as one among many[21] and also as one that already always includes the foreign: we as well as the foreigner always have more than one language. It is this renunciation, 'this mourning for the absolute translation, that produces the happiness associated with translating'.[22] Untied from the double imperatives of equivalence and adequacy, from the impossible task of perfect and definitive substitution, the translator finds happiness in 'the recognition of the impassable status of the dialogicality of the act of translating as the reasonable horizon of the desire to translate'.[23] This is 'linguistic hospitality, then, where the pleasure

---

16 Sheldon Pollock, 'Cosmopolitan and Vernacular in History', in *Cosmopolitanism*, ed. by C. A. Breckenridge, S. Pollock, H. K. Bhabha and D. Chakrabarty (London: Duke University Press, 2002), pp. 15–53; Naoki Sakai, *Translation and Subjectivity: On "Japan" and Cultural Nationalism* (Minneapolis: University of Minnesota Press, 1997).
17 Ricoeur, p. 3.
18 Ricoeur, p. 16.
19 Ricoeur, p. 8.
20 Ricoeur, p. 23.
21 Ricoeur, p. 13.
22 Ricoeur, p. 10.
23 Ricoeur, p. 10.

of dwelling in the other's language is balanced by the pleasure of receiving the foreign word at home, in one's own welcoming house'.[24]

Together with the pleasure and desire associated with translating as the hospitable welcoming of difference, this dialogical and imperfect notion of translation also ushers in ethics. The work of linguistic hospitality remains fraught with difficulty, but, precisely because of this, it is inherently, foundationally ethical and also constitutes a worthy foundation for our ethics. Translation – imperfect translation, translation that does not aspire to substitution – is part of 'the long litany of "despite everything". Despite fratricides, we campaign for universal fraternity. Despite the heterogeneity of idioms, there are bilinguals, polyglots, interpreters and translators.'[25] Here, in joining together translation and the birth of ethics, Ricoeur also juxtaposes two of the core myths of the Western Judeo-Christian tradition: the fall of the Tower of Babel and the story of Cain and Abel. It is 'the fratricide, the murder of Abel, which makes fraternity itself an ethical project and not a simple fact of nature'.[26] Similarly, in a post-Babel world defined by the translator's task, 'the scattering and the confounding of languages',[27] far from being an evil to be repaired, sits at 'the heart of the exercise of language. This is how we are, this is how we exist, scattered and confounded, and called to what? Well ... to translation!'[28] Both ethics and happiness are tied to translation, as we have been 'set in motion by the fact of human plurality and by the double enigma of incommunicability between idioms and of translation in spite of everything'. Without that test, we would risk 'shutting ourselves away in the sourness of a monologue' and also losing all sense of 'the strangeness of our own language'.[29] It is through translation (and not in spite of it) that we come to appreciate 'the *textures* which *weave* the discourse into longer or shorter sequences', starting from narratives and the discovery that 'we can always tell a story in another way'.[30] An ethics of translation (and a translational ethics) thus returns us to the thick weave of languages and narratives that make up our daily life and to the labour, but also the pleasure and the desire, that come with difference and with translation.

---

24 Ricoeur, p. 10.
25 Ricoeur, p. 18.
26 Ricoeur, p. 18.
27 Ricoeur, p. 18.
28 Ricoeur, p. 19.
29 Ricoeur, p. 29.
30 Ricoeur, p. 27. Emphasis in the original.

B. Amore and Luci Callipari-Marcuzzo: The Red Thread of Migration and of Translation

In 2001, one of the most iconic spaces in the history of migration, the Ellis Island Museum, became the location for B. Amore's exhibition *Life Line – Filo della vita*. I did not see the site-specific installation, but Joseph Sciorra and Edvige Giunta describe it as:

> an overwhelming ensemble of objects, images, texts, media, and exhibition styles culled from seven generations of the artist's family, artfully arranged in [six] rooms for visitors to behold. A delicate red thread ran through the exhibition, making its way across time and space, connecting visitors to the past and propelling them into the future. This thread evoked the unravelling yarn immigrants used to temporarily remain connected to relatives standing on the docks as they sailed away to an unknown world.[31]

The exhibit, which further travelled in the United States and in Italy, was documented in a volume, *An Italian American Odyssey: Life line – filo della vita. Through Ellis Island and Beyond*.[32] The book, which is fully bilingual, tells a story that is at once collective and personal. B. herself calls this work 'a visual memoir, which sets the destinies of two families from Italy's *Mezzogiorno* (Midday or South) in the historical context of emigration from Italy and assimilation in America in the one hundred years of the twentieth century'.[33]

In the exhibition and in the book, each individual visual story 'is set against the fabric of the general history of immigration since one family exists not as a solitary entity but within the sociological context of its times'.[34]

---

31   Edvige Giunta and Joseph Sciorra, 'Introduction', in *Embroidered Stories: Interpreting Women's Domestic Needlework from the Italian Diaspora*, ed. by E. Giunta and J. Sciorra (Jackson: University Press of Mississippi, 2014), pp. 2–24 (p. 6). I can think of no better document on the history and meaning of Ellis Island than Robert Viscusi's poem *ellis island* (New York: Bordighera Press, 2012).
32   B. Amore, *An Italian American Odyssey: Life line – filo della vita. Through Ellis Island and Beyond*, Italian trans. by Franco Bagnolini (New York: Center for Migration Studies & Fordham University Press, 2006). B.'s work can also be seen on her website <http://bamore.com/> [accessed 8 July 2020].
33   Amore, *An Italian American Odyssey*, pp. x–xi.
34   Amore, *An Italian American Odyssey*, p. xv.

The interwoven story of the De Iorios and the D'Amores is narrated by B., a third-generation Italian American, through unfolding family triptychs and life-size ancestor scrolls, both made from inherited photographs and from words that maintain their idiosyncratic spelling or grammatical features. Other narratives take the form of columns of history, made of quotes and images from Italian migrants and inspired by the graffiti left by immigrants on the walls of the Ellis Island building. Yet others are told through reliquaries where 'transitional objects' are encased in glass or in the *Odyssey* installation of stark, hand-worked monoliths of black Italian Trentino marble. The *Odyssey* pieces are partially wrapped in transparent black silk (fabric used 'to bind things together – pieces of experience – to make it whole') and surrounded by neatly folded cloth bundles inherited from a grandmother's dressmaking business. The result is 'a story that spans two countries, told in a non-traditional way, across the boundaries of class, gender, race and identity'. The display creates 'a huge shrine with smaller sub-chapels', where 'the sense of the sacred' allows art 'to transform material so that it has the possibility of expressing the inexpressible'.[35] Gradually, as if in a series of concentric circles, in the installation 'the immigrant experience is extended to become a metaphor for the journey of the whole human race'.[36]

While B. took the image of the red thread from the Neapolitan writer Luciano De Crescenzo,[37] the idea of art and its narrative as 'the red thread of memory, the life line, the death line, stretching back to the past and into the future' is inscribed deeply into all of her work and into our conversations. I met B. in Toronto in 2014, at a conference where I was trying to articulate my efforts to reformulate translation through the image of weaving or as the 'translational fabric' of our daily lives. The dialogue that started there has continued through a *conversazione a distanza*, punctuated by email exchanges, occasional phone calls and a few more meetings – including a video interview recorded in New York in the winter of 2019, in the middle of a snow storm, through sheer ingenuity, resourcefulness and serendipity, which allowed us to 'borrow' a friend's apartment and locate a cameraman while the whole city was placed in unexpected (but, in hindsight, very

---

35 Amore, *An Italian American Odyssey*, p. xi.
36 Amore, *An Italian American Odyssey*, p. xv.
37 De Crescenzo repeatedly returned to this image. See, for instance, *Sembra ieri* (Milan: Mondadori, 1997), p. 48; a version of the story is quoted in *An American Odyssey*, p. xix.

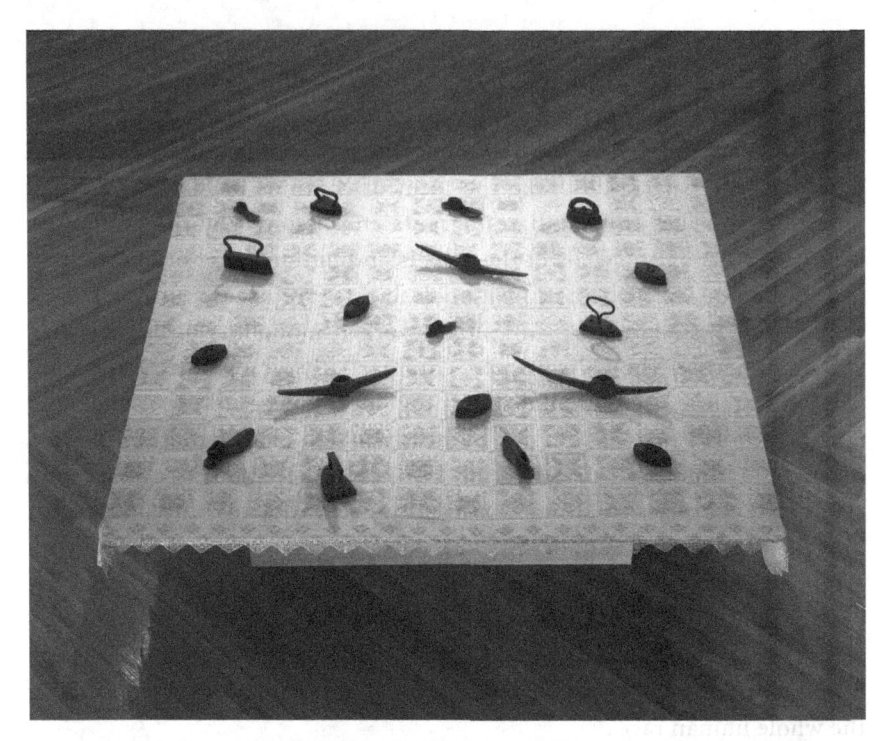

Fig. 13.1: B. Amore, *Great Grandmother's Ocean*. Dowry bedspread made by Giovannina Forte. Antique linen weaving, iron artefacts, fabric, Plexiglas, wood. 2' × 8' × 8', 2004. Image courtesy of the artist; photograph by Christopher Burke.

short) lockdown.[38] Our conversations often return to cloth, as in B.'s great-grandmother Giovannina's beautiful linen, with her bright red initials stitched in the corner, part of a trousseau of belongings that has followed the routes of female family genealogy; or, on my side, the gift of colourful fabric, a marker of new female friendships, with which I came back from Zambia not long after that New York interview with B. Our exchanges also always linger on migration, its threads, its often invisible routes, its labour, which are a constant through B.'s work and through mine.

38   The interview was shown at the international conference 'Diaspore Italiane – Italy in Movement: Between Immigration and Historical Amnesia', held in Genoa at Galata – Museo del Mare in June 2019. It was part of a panel that also included contributions by the other two artists discussed here, Luci Callipari-Marcuzzo and Filomena Coppola. I would like to thank Teresa Fiore for the hospitality she extended to B. and to me on a cold New York day.

One of the most striking pieces in *Life Line – Filo della vita* is *Great-Grandmother's Ocean* (Figure 13.1). In this installation, the dowry bedspread brought to the US from Lapio, in Campania, by the artist's great-grandmother as she crossed the Atlantic in 1901 is laid over frosted blue-green plexiglass symbolizing the ocean of immigration. On the spread, 'antique irons and pick-axes float like boats, traversing the vast space, stretching from Giovannina's Irpinian hill town to *L'America*. The installation evokes the labour of both men and women.' That work could be equally backbreaking and took migrant men to construction sites and railway lines, while it led women to sweatshops, but also made 'the immigrant kitchen a de facto extension of the factory floor'. In this exhibit, familial memory and collective history, intimate spaces and intercontinental routes, visible and invisible labour materialize in a striking visual image that captures the tension of migration, its *fatica* (labour and fatigue) and its beauty, the lightness of the desire for a new and better life and the weight of daily reality. The intricate weaving of the filet technique, of '*punto tela* (linen stitch), *punto rammendo* (darning stitch), and *punto spirito*, a delicate and decorative stitch in which the threads are wound around the corners of the net', contrast with the stylized forms of the superimposed objects, echoing the apparent improbability of boats floating over ocean waves and the difficult balancing act at the heart of migration.[39] Through that contrast of light and heavy, we can see how:

> the stories of Italian immigrants are sewn into the stitches of the women and preserved in the constructions of the men. From the mundane to the extraordinary, the objects themselves tell the story of immigration. The traces of people mark the remains of their handwork. The past does not feel so far away when I touch the fine linen thread of the bedspread that my great-grandmother wove one hundred and fifty years ago. Her fingers touch mine and my grandmother's voice whispers in my ear – '*filo*' – the thread that sews history into one delicate, open piece.[40]

That tension also resurfaces in later work that focuses even more closely on the notion of trace, such as the 2010 project *Invisible Odysseys: Art by Mexican Farmworkers in Vermont/Odiseas invisibles: Arte de trabajadores mexicanos en Vermont*, in which B. worked with mostly undocumented Mexican migrants.

---

39 B. Amore, 'Great-Grandmother's Ocean', in Giunta and Sciorra, *Embroidered Stories*, pp. 103–05 (p. 104).
40 Amore, 'Great-Grandmother's Ocean', p. 104.

Pieces such as *Walk in My Footsteps ... / Camina en mis zapatos ...* (B. Amore and participants, 2010) and *Worker's Mandala / Tracing the Journeys – Mandala de los trabajadores / Siguiendo los viajes* (B. Amore, 2011) return, in different ways, to the themes of weaving and stitching as well as to labour and its visible or invisible traces. In the first, a map of the United States and Mexico is created on burlap coffee sacks by Mexican workers who actually walked their journeys with inked feet, thereby making themselves and their labour visible through the physical imprints. In the second, that same, iconic map is traced by intricate red stitching following the migrants' journeys, while the whole image is surrounded by a heavy frame made of found worker's gloves and ex votos.[41] In this as much or even more than in all her other projects, B. is also alert to and careful to foreground the labour of translation. As a speaker of both English and Italian, she is meticulous in ensuring that her work is accessible in both languages. Her sensitivity to the inter-traffic between verbal and visual codes also means that she often incorporates the written word in her installations – carefully maintaining difference and its markers of class, education, gender and regional as much as national belonging. When working with Mexican migrants, the translational dimension of visual art became all the more explicit: artisan skills and shared manual knowledge became strategies of communication, routes to common understanding via connected practices.[42] It is precisely through these practices that visual art can help us to perceive and to experience the deep translational fabric of our lives, the way in which a continuum of translation activities (across languages and media as well as within each of them) forms the weft and the warp of our experience.

The materiality of thread and the translational texture of its weave are also central to the work of Luci Callipari Marcuzzo. A performance and visual artist of Calabrian descent, Luci is based in Mildura, north-west Victoria, a town that is home to a well-established Italian Australian community. It was Luci who found me, rather than vice versa, spotting our common interest in translation and migration. The first I saw of her work was a video in which she talks about one of her performances, entitled *Tracing the Threads of the Past – Tracciando fili del passato*.[43] There is an

---

41 See *Invisible Odysseys: Art by Mexican Farmworkers in Vermont/Odiseas invisibles: Arte de trabajadores mexicanos en Vermont*, ed. by B. Amore (Benson, VT: Kokoro Press, 2012), p. 17 and p. 80.
42 B. discusses this point in the interview I recorded with her in 2019.
43 The video is available at <https://vimeo.com/160694827> [accessed 8 July 2020]. I am also grateful to Luci for sharing with me her dissertation, 'Tracing the threads of the

immediately striking similarity between that title and B. Amore's work, and while that similarity is at least partly linked to the importance of crafts such as sewing, weaving or embroidery in gendered traditions of popular art,[44] the commonalities between B.'s and Luci's work run much deeper. Both use familiar (and familial) as well as 'noble' materials, the latter including paint on canvas for Luci and marble for B. Both firmly highlight the importance of labour, especially the often invisible labour of migrant women, and both are interested in the materiality of culture, using the language of cloth and thread to visualize the work of memory. Both also follow personal itineraries that trace networks of knowledge and affect, mixing personal and intergenerational memory not to speak of their own experiences of migration (in fact, neither of them did migrate) but rather to stitch together individual and collective memory. Both, also, connect to and make visible their own genealogies. In B.'s case, family history is usually displayed through objects and text, but it can also be visualized more directly, as in a memorable photo that depicts her standing by one of her own works, which incorporates a photographic portrait of her grandmother, Concettina, evidencing their striking family resemblance.[45] In Luci's work, genealogy is foregrounded through conspicuous performances of gender as she 'transforms' herself before every event through the use of inherited articles of clothing and traditional hairstyles. Her performative approach to gendered behaviour is also notable in the choice she makes, in each individual case, between silence and intimate conversation. That choice allows her to distance herself or to invite participation from her audience, as she often does during multi-generational embroidery workshops and collective crochet sessions, where members of the public (mostly, though unintentionally, women) are invited to sit, pick up a piece of cloth and join in both craft and dialogue.

Calabrian diaspora to North-West Victoria: Explorations through performance, video and relational art', which she submitted for her Master of Visual Arts by Research at La Trobe University in November 2017.
44   See Giunta and Sciorra, *Embroidered Stories*, as well as the by now classic Jane Schneider, 'Trousseau as Treasure', in *Beyond the Myths of Culture: Essays in Cultural Materialism*, ed. by Eric B. Ross (New York: Academic Press, 1980). On weaving and migration see also Maria Pallotta-Chiarolli, *Tapestry: Interweaving Lives* (Sydney: Random House, 1999). On the links between crafts and contemporary art see also the emblematic case of Maria Lai: Maria Elvira Ciusa, *Maria Lai: Il filo dell'esistere/The Thread of Existence* (Sassari: Carlo Delfino Editore, 2017).
45   The image is included in *An Italian American Odyssey* (p. xiii).

In Luci's work, the interweaving of visual and verbal language, of art and translation, and their centrality in tracing the narrative memory of migration through transnational spaces is, if anything, even more visible and audible than in B.'s. The video that served as my introduction to her performance art starts with the sentence: 'With every stitch, I am re-tracing threads of the past. I am re-exploring, re-tracing the threads that my family created when they emigrated to Australia in the 1950s.' Luci, who is sitting at her mother's 1960s vintage treadle powered sewing machine, wearing traditional-style clothing and an elaborate hairstyle inspired by those worn by both her grandmothers, then goes on to describe sewing as primarily 'tactile' and to explain that she has had to 'work out what language my sewing machine is speaking to me. I've translated, in a way, how its stitches and those threads have been a form of language.' In her work, Luci makes repeated use of and constantly returns to variations on the theme of threads and traces, and to their links to visual and verbal language. These are evident in a series of embroidered pieces that incorporate traditional proverbs in Calabrian dialect and translate them into visual images (2018); or in the stitched reproduction of postcards sent by women across the ocean that bears the title *Traces: to all the women ...* (2020). Paintings such as *Traces of Settlement: Migratory Objects* (2019) capture everyday items transported across the world by members of her family. The inter-generational memory of migration is not only inscribed in objects, however, but is also assumed and presented as a constitutive part of her self-identification processes. This is evident in Luci's performances as well as in a number of self-portraits, such as the series of two artworks entitled *Tracing the thread of memory I* (2019) and *Tracing the thread of memory II* (2020): both display Luci in her performance dress, the first through the medium of painting and the second in a combination of embroidery and drawing that plays with permanence and impermanence by using a mix of thread, human hair, graphite and domestic pigments such as coffee or pomegranate tea.

Crucially, in Luci's retracings and in her performances of the multigenerational memory of migration, there is space not only for loss but also for desire. The trauma of migration is there, but so is the resilience of affects and material practices, the pleasure of making, sharing and enjoying – and the aspiration to a better future.[46] In reminding us that what she is doing

---

46 On these topics see Marianne Hirsch, 'The Generation of Postmemory', *Poetics Today*, 29 (2008), 103–28; and also Luci Callipari Marcuzzo, 'Tracing Threads of the Past', in *Diaspore Italiane – Italy in Movement: Between Immigration and Historical*

Fig. 13.2: Luci Callipari-Marcuzzo, *Tracing Threads of the Past: Apron [Tracciando fili del passato: grembiule]*, live art performance, 27 October, *La Soffitta*, in *Beyond Borders: Transnational Italy/Oltre i confini: Italia transnazionale*, curated by Viviana Gravano and Giulia Grechi. The British School at Rome, Italy, 2016. Image courtesy of the artist; photograph by Carolina Farina (Routes Agency).

is creating items that the women in her family could only dream of but could not afford to buy, Luci is highlighting how migration and its processes of translation look as much towards the future as towards the past. This narrative continuity, which does not deny pain and fragmentation but refuses to let them descend into schizophrenia, offers a viable model for a different type of translation and of migration: a model that is based not on substitution but on co-presence, and which does not ask us to delete what and who we were, nor to erase our links to our own past and to the past of those who came before us. Rather, this model invites us to follow the traces of change along thickly woven maps marked by multiple translations.

My conversations with Luci and with B. have certainly changed the way in which I think about – and visualize – this non-binary reconceptualization

Amnesia, conference proceedings (Genova: Galata, 2020), pp. 45–49, available at <https://www.diasporeitaliane.com/images/files/20200319_Diaspore_Italiane_conference_proceedings.pdf> [accessed 8 July 2020].

of translation. At the same time, our exchanges have also created new networks and traced new journeys. Although we have not yet managed to be in the same place at the same time, a distant dialogue has been established between Luci and B., if nothing else because of their mutual awareness of each other's work. In a more material sense, B.'s visual art and Luci's performances came together, in October 2016, at the opening of the TML exhibition *Beyond Borders: Transnational Italy/Oltre i confini: Italia transnazionale*, curated by Viviana Gravano and Giulia Grechi and hosted by the British School at Rome.[47] In the exhibition, which took the visitor through a sequence of 'public' and 'private' spaces, B.'s *Cracked Immigrant Mirror – Lo Specchio Spaccato dell'Immigrante* occupied an enclosed, intimate area that represented the *soffitta*: the attic where memory and reflection find their home. On the day of the opening, Luci sat at a locally sourced old sewing machine, wearing her grandmother's green dress (the same dress she wears in many of her portraits and performances), and made an apron out of vintage fabric and red thread, following a template passed down from mother to daughter and grand-daughter (Figure 13.2). It is one of the paradoxes of migration and of diasporic culture that both phenomena often continue to reference the point of origin even as ties with it become increasingly faint. In the case of B. and Luci, while they have both maintained strong links with Italy, their work speaks of it from afar, at once as centre and as periphery of the diasporic experience. As a physical connection was created in Rome between their artistic practices and their production, Italy, the space of memory, of pain and of desire in both B.'s and Luci's work, also became a material place where an audience (national and international) could reposition their work in the context of an exhibition that aimed to materialize, perform and translate into a set of embodied experiences both the history of Italian mobility and the equally embodied practices of research.

Filomena Coppola: Translation as Trace

The work of Filomena Coppola also makes frequent use of thread and fabric, either in their material form or as decorative motifs and often out-of-scale details. In 2001 she took part in the exhibition *Stitches – Fare il punto*, which

---

47 For a detailed discussion of the exhibition see Gravano and Grechi, in this volume.

gathered the work of eight Italian Australian women around the theme of textiles.[48] Her recent production includes a contribution to the collaborative global project *@covid19quilt* (2020),[49] which is constituted by an embroidered spiral representing continuity in the face of the unexpected: 'Shadowed by the spiral is the earth (our hemisphere) as seen from space. Graduating tonally from blood red to indigo – the colours of a bruise – a marker acknowledging the grief, restrictions and isolation that we are enduring.'[50] The two images of this piece, its front and its back, or working, side, are strongly remindful of the Chinese expression for translation, *fan yi*, which I discussed in my opening section. The similarity sparked a conversation between Filomena and me on her own response to that metaphor. For her, the attractiveness of embroidery comes from its decorative as well as functional nature, but also from its connection with time, through 'the use of, changes to and deterioration which occur during its lifetime'. It is precisely this sensitivity to use, change and deterioration that I want to concentrate on here to unpick further the notion of trace, its connection with translation and its implications for migration and for an ethics of hospitality. I will do this with the help of Filomena's own words and through our shared analysis of another of her works, the installation *Wallflower – Mirror, rorriM*, which was exhibited in the Rio Vista Cellar Basement, Mildura Arts Centre, in 2011. The installation occupied an entire room in an old colonial house (the original Chaffey Home) and consisted of two elements: a wall-mounted pastel-on-paper drawing combining the image of a native orchid with the luxuriant motif from a William Morris wallpaper; and an intricate 'rug' made of layers of Mildura dirt and Murray River sand, also reproducing the wallpaper motif, which covered the entire floor of the room (Figures 13.3 and 13.4).

The choice of materials and their layering underscored the ecological theme of the installation, as did the choice of depicting the blown-up

---

48 See Ilaria Vanni et al., *Stitches – Fare il punto* (Darling Harbour: Australian National Maritime Museum, 2001); the bilingual catalogue includes essays by Ilaria Vanni, 'Cross-Stitching Objects, Memory and Cultural Difference/Intessendo oggetti, ricordi e differenza culturale', pp. 6–13, and by Maria Pallotta-Chiarolli, 'Writing about Tapestries, Weaving Tapestries through Writing/Scrivere sugli arazzi, intessere arazzi di scrittura', pp. 14–19.
49 See *@covid19quilt*. The project is described as 'An online (Instagram) global quilt project started by artists Kate Just and Tal Fitzpatrick to gather, narrate and share experiences of Covid 19 via craft'.
50 This and the following quotations are from personal communication during June 2020; I am grateful to Filomena for her permission to quote from her email messages.

Fig. 13.3 and Fig. 13.4: Filomena Coppola, *Wallflower – Mirror, rorriM*. Pastel on paper, H 108 cm × W 216 cm. Mildura dirt and Murray River sand (approx 300 × 300 cm). Exhibited in Rio Vista Cellar Basement (original Chaffey home), Mildura Arts Centre (Australia), 2011. Images (before and after viewings) courtesy of the artist.

image of a native Australian flower. At the same time, the contrast between the indigenous plant and the iconic Morris wallpaper pattern (with its imperial associations), together with the fact that the installation was located within a colonial building, added a historical and cultural dimension to the work. Once we consider use, change and deterioration, the reading of the work becomes even more complex, throwing into relief the ecological as well as the ethical dimension attached to the notions of trace and translation (and of translation as trace). In order to see the drawing hanging on the far wall of the room, visitors had to enter it, cross its floor and, in doing so, both leave their trace on the 'carpet' that covered it and destroy its delicate image. Though the materials that made up the floor covering (river sand and dirt) were not precious, many hesitated before stepping into the room.[51] Eventually,

---

51 In fact, Filomena also remembers that she 'had to fight for this work to be walked over as the gallery was concerned about Health and Safety and it was only allowed to be walked over on the opening night whilst I was in the space'.

however, the tracing began and the flower pattern was replaced by a multitude of footprints, until a few traces of the initial pattern remained visible only at the edges of the floor.

Significantly, Filomena noted that the installation was 'the beginning of major changes in the way I made work and my awareness of how the viewer interacts with' it and also of 'a really personal exploration into cultural loss'. In its interaction with and interrogation of its audience, the installation materializes in front of our eyes (or, for the visitors, under their feet) the fact that no act, not even the act of viewing, is neutral and innocuous. Our presence leaves traces and those traces alter their environment in ways that both change and deteriorate it. Yet traces also work backwards: they tell the story and hold the memory (in this case, in the form of physical imprints) of an event, a series of acts, and testify to their consequences. Filomena recognized this dimension of her work, remarking that she, most of all, wanted it 'to evoke a sense of emotion and response' and, therefore, 'the most integral part of this work ... was the act of it being walked across'. Weaving makes a new appearance in this context, this time in relation to its materiality and the way it is affected by time:

> In the same way that embroidery and fabrics are worn by constant use, the floor was worn away by a similar movement but there are always fragments that maintain the integrity of the original. This occurred around the edges of the wall whilst the centre was returned from a beautiful carpet feel to flat powdery dirt, and the Murray River sand merged into the red dirt. Yet it carried the markings, the journeys and the conversations of all who had walked across it, from the first hesitant steps to those more confident as the pattern disappeared. Culturally for me it was also a physical mapping of how we change, accept and retain our own cultural histories.
>
> As much as I have documented what was left behind I feel that everyone who walked across that floor carried something away with them. I feel we all carry those traces of conversation and actions, which living makes us a part of, and it is how we carry this that defines us.

We can thus read *Wallflower – Mirror, rorriM* in relation to the rethinking of translation I have been outlining throughout my argument. Like Filomena's work, translation does involve forms of loss, but also demands response, engagement, however difficult or ambivalent this might be, as in the experience the viewers of her work must have had while they walked over the pattern on the floor to reach the flower on the wall, and by so doing partly destroyed that pattern but also left their trace on it. That action speaks of how all intervention leaves a trace, both altering, overlaying one reality with another and also building on it and still containing it, as does the trace of what was there or the memory of our actions.

I see this as a model of translation based not on perfect equivalence, substitution and erasure (a model doomed to fail, as Ricoeur observed) but on trace and co-presence, on the connectedness between present and past, between foreign and same. This kind of translation does not aim to erase difference but rather to keep its trace and to keep it *as* trace. Like memory, it is not necessarily harmonious nor neatly linear, but it leaves a trace of our existence and a testimony of our being and intervening in the world. It forms a piece of our narrative rather than imposing an erasure that requires us to abandon who and what we were, becoming something and someone else. In this sense, translation, while not neatly 'traceable' back to any presumed origin,[52] is a guarantor of narrative continuity, however hidden or fragmented that might be.[53] Or, as the translingual writer Aleksander Hemon recently phrased it when describing his personal experience, translation becomes 'the narrative of how I have changed'.[54] Translation is a trace: of what was there before, of what I was before. It is also engraved, woven through with traces: of our individual and collective past, of our histories and our stories, of our memories and of the tales we tell about who we were and how we came to be who we are. This has important consequences for the social and historical functions of translation. Translation as trace is both an ethical and an ecological notion. Its practice is rooted in change and imperfection and its engagement is not with relics and their conservation but with dynamic ecologies and their

---

52   In this respect I am at least partly aligning my use of 'trace' with Derrida's interpretation; see, for instance, Jacques Derrida, *Of Grammatology*, trans. by Gayatri C. Spivak (Baltimore, MD: Johns Hopkins University Press, 1976), p. 66 and elsewhere. On trace and origin see also, in the same volume, Spivak's 'Translator's Preface', pp. ix–lxxxvii.
53   This hidden, fragmented continuity has points of contact with the 'archeologic' approach to translation traces (rather than translation as trace) described in Hephzibah Israel and Matthias Frenz, 'Translation Traces in the Archive: Unfixing Documents, Destabilising Evidence', *The Translator* (2020), 335–48 [accessed 26 August 2020].
54   The comment was made during a panel on 'Migration and Narration' chaired by Sandra Bermann at the MLA International Symposium 'Remembering Voices Lost', Lisbon, July 2019.

preservation.[55] Its hospitality, however imperfect, extends well beyond the human to encompass how change, use and deterioration affect our world.

Conclusion: Threads, Traces and Promises

In a plenary address she gave at the 2014 American Comparative Literature Association conference in New York, a version of which has since been published as an essay 'On Cruelty', Judith Butler spoke of the promise as an act that carries within itself the implicit possibility of failure ('I promise' is not the same as 'I state') and therefore also, in a relationship of reciprocity, the possibility of pardon.[56] Butler was talking about the death penalty and the way in which we can defend our opposition to it, beyond a logics of violence. But the promise is also an apt figure for a notion of translation based on hospitality and co-presence: translation as an opening, a gift, perhaps, in the sense in which anthropology, starting with Marcel Mauss, understands the gift as a gesture that is both gratuitous and indispensable, both highly codified and superfluous.[57]

Like any real promise, like the gift, like hospitality, translation – as a multidirectional word – requires reciprocity. Like Luci's performances, Filomena's sand and dirt carpet, B.'s travelling objects, with their familial traces and gendered genealogies of labour, it demands a response, an engagement – and, in implying the possibility of failure, it also commits us to the possibility of pardon. It is the potential for failure, the imminence of conflict or destruction, the shadow of fratricide, but also the equally powerful

---

55 In this respect, Michael Cronin aptly notes that 'the constant regeneration of materials, peoples, life forms, ideas, the endless translation, that generates multiple forms of language, textual and cultural practice is the ultimate form of resistance to the extractivist lockdown of toxic uniformity': *Eco-Translation: Translation and Ecology in the Age of the Anthropocene* (Abingdon: Routledge, 2017), p. 153.

56 Judith Butler, 'On Cruelty', *London Review of Books*, 36 (2014); available at <http://www.lrb.co.uk/v36/n14/judith-butler/on-cruelty> [accessed 8 July 2020]. On these themes see also Judith Butler, *The Force of Non-Violence: An Ethico-Political Bind* (London and New York: Verso, 2020).

57 Marcel Mauss, *The Gift*, trans. by W. D. Halls (London: Routledge, 1990); it is worth noting here that Umberto Eco's *The Search for the Perfect Language* – a book devoted to the failed search for a universal language in European culture, which is among Ricoeur's main sources of inspiration for *On Translation* – closes with a chapter made up of two sections: 'Translation' and 'The Gift to Adam'. See Umberto Eco, *The Search for the Perfect Language*, trans. by James Fentress (Oxford: Blackwell, 1995).

demand for pardon that make translation 'hospitable': that is, an ethical act and not 'a simple fact of nature'. In its ethical engagement, its commitment to being hostage to our hosts and guests, it is that promise that keeps us human. Our promise, the unrelenting commitment to what Homi Bhabha recently called 'disappointed hope',[58] the promise we don't know we will be able to keep and therefore the promise on which we can found our ethics, is to continue to be hospitable to other lives and other narratives, to their languages, their figurations and their memory threads, as they cross and interweave with our own.

Translation – translation as trace, as co-presence, as the negotiation and renegotiation, the mediation and remediation of sameness and diversity – is at the core of that ethics, at the core of our ability to recognize ourselves through the thread of change, to see ourselves in others and others in ourselves, and to acknowledge that home is always made on the move but also that someone can always remove our homes from us. An ethics of translation as co-presence allows us to remain hospitable and to recognize the reciprocity always inscribed in hospitality, without exacting the price of erasure or imposing it upon ourselves.

---

58   Homi K. Bhabha, 'Human Rights and Human Deaths: On Migration and Dignity', keynote address, MLA International Symposium 'Remembering Voices Lost', Lisbon, July 2019.

Index

Note: locators in italics indicate images

accents 30, 44, 140, 152–53, 305
ACLI office, Clerkenwell, London 28
Addis Ababa 10, 103, 208, 220n22
Ahmed, Sara, et al. 268
Alfieri, Cesare 106
alienation, sense of *see* marginality and Italianness
Allatson, Paul 254
Americas, colonization of 54, 55
Amore, B. 319–20, 326–30, 331, 333–34
    Cracked Immigrant Mirror 319, 334
    Great Grandmother's Ocean 328, 329
    Life Line: Filo della vita 326–29
anti-Semitism 17, 228, 237–38, 240–42, 243–52
apartment buildings and community 300–01, 306, 313
Appadurai, Arjun 136, 306
    The Social Life of Things: Commodities in Cultural Perspective 168
Appiah, Kwame Anthony 318
Arabic language 232, 249, 250, 251, 300, 301, 308–09
archaeology projects, Rhodes 81
architecture
    Asmara 113, 116, 117, 118
    impact of migration on cities 185
    'Little Italy', London 14, 25–28, 27, 45
    Rhodes 76, 78–79, 80–84, 82, 85–88, 93–94
    Rome 302, 310–11

Argentina 16, 158–67, 170–77
art
    Amore 319–20, 326–30, 328, 331, 333–34
    Callipari-Marcuzzo 319–20, 328n38, 330–34, 333
    Coppola 319–20, 328n38, 334–38
    and translation 19, 183–84, 186–87, 188, 190–206, 321
    see also Cattapan, Jon; Paolozzi, Eduardo
art-based language research projects 129–51
Asmara 78–79, 110, 113, 114–18, 117, 123–24
assimilation/integration of migrants
    Argentina 160–64
    Australia 180–81, 203–04, 254
    Chile 49–50, 63, 66, 73
    China-Italy relations 289–95, 304–05
    United Kingdom 323–24
    United States 326
    and uses of language 304–05, 323–24
    see also Italianness/italianidad/italianità; Jews
associations of Italians
    Argentina 159–64, 165, 166–67, 166, 171–76, 177
    La piccola Gerusalemme 234–35, 236, 237–38
    neighbourhood committees 307–08

Australia 16
  Callipari-Marcuzzo 330
  Cattapan 179–206
  diasporic gardens 17–18, 253–74, 254, 257, 261, 264, 267, 269, 272
  Melbourne 179, 186–88, 194, 198, 208, 319
  Queensland 261, 262, 265, 266
  Sydney 253–74
  textile arts 334–38
  Wollongong 258
Azzari, Silvia 301–02

Babel, Tower of 162, 311, 325
Backhill (newspaper) 38
Badagliacca, Mario 207, 215
Baily, Samuel L. 159
Bal, Mieke 127, 137
Balducci, Hermes, *Architettura turca in Rodi* 82–83
Balibar, Étienne 287
Ballinger, Pamela 50–51, 71
Balzola, Andrea, *L'arte fuori da sé* 215–16
Baratti, Marisa 106, 109–12
Barnet, Rachel 133
Bastia, Tanja 161, 162, 176–77
Baths of Kalithea, Rhodes 86–87, 94
BBC Radio 4, *Great Lives* 152–53
Becker, Elisabeth 28n9, 38n24
Ben-Rafael, Elizier 304–05
Benghazi 231–22, 247–49, 250
Bennett, Bruce, *Teaching Transnational Cinema* 137
Benveniste, Émile 322
Berlinische Galerie, Berlin 127–28
Berman, Antoine 322
Bernasconi, Alicia 163, 177
Bertella Farnetti, Paolo 209
Besagni, Olive, *A Better Life* and *Changing Lives* 32n15, 35–42, 44
Beyond Borders exhibition 10–11, 16–17, 103n5, 207–24, 212, 215, 219, 221, 334
Bhabha, Homi 216n13, 218, 218n18, 286, 287, 340
Bhatt, Sujata, *The House of Fiction* 216–17
Bianchi, Rino 302, 310
Billig, Michael 61

biographies of things 167–68
biomimicry 148
bitter greens 257, 261
BOLT! art project 138–41, 152
Bond, Emma 4–5
Brigadoi Cologna, Daniele 291, 293
British government
  administration in East Africa 110, 111n28, 116
  Aegean population exchange 95
Buenos Aires 16, 158–67, 170–77
Burdett, Charles 15, 101–24
Burns, Jennifer 14, 23–46
Butler, Judith 164–65, 339
Byrne, Denis 29

Callipari-Marcuzzo, Luci 319–20, 328n38, 330–34, 333
  Tracing Threads of the Past 330–31, 333
Calvino, Italo 188–89, 317–18
Capitoline wolf statue, Valparaíso 52–53, 53
carpets 317–18, 335–38
  see also weaving
Carrera Airola, Leonardo 48n7, 57n34, 59, 66
Casa Italiana San Vincenzo Pallotti, Clerkenwell, London 28
Castlebrae High School, Edinburgh 15
  Castlebrae in the World art project 141–44, 151
Cattapan, Jon 16, 180, 182–83, 185–90, 191–98, 199, 200, 201–06
  The Bookbuilder 193, 194
  The City Submerged 189
  Documentary: Melbourne as Rome 186–88
  Study after Endless 200
  Travel Suite 191, 191, 197
  Under New York 189, 191
  Untitled 191–92, 191
Ceccagno, Antonella 278
ceramics 133, 141–44
Certeau, Michel de 71, 211n7
childhood
  becoming 'part of the world' 150–51
  Object Workshops, Argentina 172–73, 175–76

Index

O'Brien's photographic collections 40–42, 43–44
Paolozzi's 152
in the Second World War 110
in Valparaíso 59–60, 63–64
see also memory
Chile 14, 47–73
China-Italy relations 18, 275–95, 304–05
Chinese language 304–05
fan yi (translation) 321–22
Chow, Rey 153
Ciarlantini, Franco 77–78
cities
in Cattapan's work 185–200, 203–04, 205–06
as 'translational' spaces 18–19, 297–98, 300–09, 311–12, 314–15
see also individual cities
citizenship
and Italianness 293–94
and language 60–61, 153, 323–24
Clerkenwell, London ('Little Italy') 14, 23–46
Clifford, James 47, 73, 318
Collins, Judith 128, 144n32
Colombini, Jacopo 145, 147
colonial history, Italian
Beyond Borders exhibition 209
East Africa 15, 101–24
institutional discourses on 52–57, 71–73, 162
la più grande Italia 36–37, 42
Libya 228–29, 239–40
Rhodes 76–99
Roma negata (Scego) 302, 310–11
Valparaíso's monuments 52–56
Colpi, Terri 152n45
Columbus, Christopher 53–54
statue, Valparaíso 55
commodification 168–69
Consiglio, Giuseppe 238
contact zones, Italian Australian gardens as 255–57, 263, 267
cookery *see* food and Italianness
Cooley, Charles Horton 157
Coppola, Filomena 319–20, 328n38, 334–38
Wallflower - Mirror, rorriM 335–38, 336

Corradini, Enrico 80
Cracked Immigrant Mirror (Amore) 319, 334
Craik, Jennifer 180
Cronin, Michael 182, 185, 188, 200, 204, 339n55
Crusader legacy, Rhodes 80–84
cultural capital project, Rhodes 75–76, 78
cultural conflicts, China-Italy 281–95, 304–05
'Curriculum for Excellence', Scotland 129–30

Da Vinci, Leonardo 144–48
dancing, Italian traditional 165, 166–67, 166
data visualization, in Cattapan's work 192–24, 196–67, 199, 200–01
De Cesari, Chiara 6
De Crescenzo, Luciano 327
De Felice, Renzo 231
De Vecchi, Cesare 83–84, 97
Del Boca, Angelo 123
Deleuze, Gilles 213
Dell'Oro, Erminia 106, 107n18
L'abbandono 120–22
Demonte, Matteo, and Rocchi, Ciaj, *Chinamen. Un secolo di cinesi a Milano* 275
Derrida, Jacques 319, 320n8, 322, 338n52
desire and migration 329, 332–33
and translation 319, 324–25
in visual art 19, 180–81, 185, 187–88, 320
Deumert, Ana 51
Di Meglio, Rita 120
Di Paolo, Nicky 106, 107n18, 120–21, 123–24
dialects, use of 50, 59, 63–64, 77, 250–51, 304–07, 332
Didi-Huberman, Georges 209n5
Diet, Emmanuel 171
Djuderia 97–98
Dolce & Gabbana 281–82
Donald, James 139
dots, in Cattapan's work 191–93, 194, 196, 201, 202, 203–04

Drummond, Philippa 130–31, 132, 135, 144–45, 147–48
Drummond Community High School, Edinburgh 15, 130, 132–41, 144–48
Duilio (ship) 110, 111–12
Duncan, Derek 15, 127–54
Durkheim, Émile 168
Durrell, Lawrence 84

economic relations, China-Italy 18, 275–80
   cultural conflicts in 281–95, 304–05
Edinburgh 15–16
education
   art-based language research projects 129–51, 153
   Giannetto Paggi's school, Tripoli 239–40, 243, 244, 246, 247
   illiteracy levels under Fascism 172
   international students 290–92
   Scottish education system 129–30, 143
   see also language teaching, current approaches to; Scuole Italiana
Ekathimerini (Greek newspaper) 94
Ellis Island Museum 326–27
embroidery 335, 337
'emigrant colonialism' 53, 54–56, 58
empire-building *see* colonial history, Italian
emporios, Valparaíso 64–68, 65, 69–70, 69, 70, 72
equivalence and substitution in translation 322–23, 324–25, 338
Eritrea 102–24, 113, 117, 302
Erll, Astrid 5–6, 51, 318
ESOL students 141–44, 153
ethics and translation 323–25, 335, 336, 338–40
Ethiopia 102–04, 108, 116, 124, 302, 310
   Beyond Borders exhibition 10, 208, 220n22
ethnographic research approaches 16, 51–52, 131–32, 158, 230, 236, 260
   self-ethnography 135–37
European Union, relations with Rhodes 75–76, 79
exhibitions, conceptualizations of 210–24
expats in China 289–95
Expo 2010, Shanghai 276

Expo 2015, Milan 275–76

Fabian, Johannes 131–32
fan yi (translation) 321–22
Farringdon Road, Clerkenwell, London 31n14, 34
Fascism 17
   and education 172
   in Libya 228, 240–42, 243–52
   in Rhodes 77, 78–79, 84, 85–89
   summer camps 152
   Valparaíso's monuments 52–56
Favero, Luigi V. 163
Fazel, Shirin Ramzanali 11
Federation style, Australia 253, 254, 265–66
Fellini, Federico 187–88
fence relations 271–72
'Feria de Colectividades', Morón 165, 166–67, 166
Festa della Repubblica, Valparaíso 57
finta pietra sandstone 81, 84
Fiore, Teresa 59
First World War 37, 95, 132n13, 245
first-generation migrants 181, 203, 258, 262, 263–65, 273
Fo, Dario, *Non si paga, non si paga* 130
Fondazione Italia Cina 279–80
food and Italianness 63–64, 67–69
   gardening in Australia 257–58, 261, 263–65, 266, 270–71, 273
   Jewish cookery 233–34, 237
For Leonardo (sculpture, Paolozzi) 144–45
Fort, Matthew 34n18
Foster, Hal 152
Fox, Alan 50
fruit flies 265, 268–69
Fuller, Mia 78–79, 84n14

Gabaccia, Donna R. 36, 71
Galata, Constantinople 88
Gallinaro, Angelina 253, 265–67, 268, 272
Gandolfo, Romolo 160
gardens and diasporic cultures 17–18, 253–74, 254, 257, 261, 264, 267, 269, 272
Gazzano, Joe 34n18

Index

Gazzano café and delicatessen, Clerkenwell, London 34, 35, 45
Geertz, Clifford 222, 318
gender and migration 19, 320, 328–29, 331–33
generational issues *see* transgenerational Italianness
Genovese 49–50, 63–66
geocriticism 298, 299
Germany 90–91
    Berlinische Galerie, Berlin 127–28
Ghermandi, Gabriella 103–04
Giard, Luce 68
Ginzburg, Natalia, *Lessico famigliare* 243
Giuili, Miriam and Elia 248, 249
Giuili, Nella 243–45, 246–47
Giuili, Paola 240–42, 243–52, 246
Giuliani, Chiara 18, 275–95
Giulio Cesare (ship) 110, 111–12
Giunta, Edvige 326
Glissant, Édouard 302
globalization 13, 202–04, 279–80, 287–88, 302–03, 314
Governor's Palace, Rhodes 87
Grassby, Al 179
Gravano, Viviana 16–17, 207–16
Great Grandmother's Ocean (Amore) 328, 329
'greater Italy' 36–37, 42
Grechi, Giulia 16–17, 216–24
Greece 15, 75–99
Gruber, Ruth Ellen 235
guidebooks, Rhodes 85, 99

Haberfield, Sydney 253, 265–67, 267
hara (Jewish quarter of Tripoli) 250–51
harbour, Rhodes 87–88
Head, Lesley 259
Hemon, Aleksander 338
Henare, Amira 174
Henderson, Nigel 39
heritage, cultural
    Jewish heritage tourism 234, 235–36, 237
    multivocality of 51, 71
    on Rhodes 75–76, 79–84, 94–95, 97
    of Scottish pupils 133–34

UNESCO world heritage sites 75, 94, 118
    in Valparaíso 66, 69–72, 73
'heritage corridors' 29, 32
Herrmann, Daniel 128, 152
heterogenous migrant communities
    in 'Little Italy', London 26, 37–39, 41, 44–45
    in Rhodes' history 76–78, 92
    in Valparaíso 48–49
    see also multiculturalism
Hicks, Dan 157
Higgins, Christina 184
High Season (film) 75
Hills de Zárate, Margaret 16, 155–77
history, constructing narratives of
    in *Beyond Borders* exhibition 208–09, 217–24
    in *Mai Taclì* 107–12, 115–16, 123–24
    oral histories of diasporic gardens 261–67
    Paggi family 228–30
    in Valparaíso 52–57, 71–73
    see also colonial history, Italian
Holocaust memories 237–38, 245–46
home
    in *Beyond Borders* exhibition 216–23
    and diasporic gardening 17–18, 253–74
    language use in 63–64, 143n26
    objects' roles in 313
Hoskins, Janet 157
hospitality and translation 322–26, 339–40

I want to be a machine exhibition (Paolozzi/Warhol) 127–28
identity *see* Italianness/italianidad/italianità
Il reduce d'Africa (journal) 105n12, 116
illiteracy levels under Fascism 172
Impact, in TML projects 130, 136–38
imperialism *see* colonial history, Italian
India 309
institutional discourses
    in China-Italy relations 281–82, 285–86, 288, 291
    on Italian colonial history 52–57, 71–73, 162
    on Italian nationalism 85n16

on Italianness 59–62
on language studies 8
integration of migrants *see* assimilation/
    integration of migrants
intercultural translation *see* translation,
    linguistic and intercultural
Irish migrants, London 26, 37, 38, 44
Italian Hospital, Queen Square Gardens,
    London 32–34, 33
Italian Schools *see* Scuole italiane
Italianness/italianidad/italianità
    Beyond Borders exhibition 208,
        218–20n22
    'brava gente' 78, 93
    in China 289–94
    and Italian associations 163–67, 307–08
    of Jewish families 229, 233–34, 240,
        243–45, 247, 249–50, 251–52
    in literature of migration experiences
        300, 315–16
    in Valparaíso 47–48, 50–52, 54–56,
        59–73
    see also food and Italianness; transgenerational Italianness

Jewish Institute of Pitigliano (JIPI) 228,
    231, 235–37, 252
Jews
    in Clerkenwell, London 39
    and Libya 231–32, 233, 239–42, 243–52
    in Pitigliano 17, 227–52
    in Rhodes 84, 97–98
    in the US 232–34, 235
Jørgensen, Jens 308
Joseph, Galen 176–77
journals for Italians in East Africa
    105–15
journeys of migrants 110–12, 172–73, 195,
    227, 228, 231–32
Judeo-Arabic language 232, 250, 251

Kermode, Frank 43n38
Kibble, A. W. 38–39
Klein, Oliver, et al. 164
Kopytoff, Igor, 'The Cultural Biography of
    Things' 167–69
Kos 95, 97
Kress, Gunther 192–93

Kuruvilla, Gabriella, *Milano, fin qui tutto
    bene* 299, 301–02, 303–05, 306–07,
    309, 311–12
Kuusisto-Arponen, Anna-Kaisa 175

La piccola Gerusalemme (association)
    234–35, 236, 237–38
'La piccola Gerusalemme' (Pitigliano) 17,
    227–52
labour, migrant 329, 330, 331
Lago, Mario 83, 91n28
Lakhous, Amara, *Scontro di civiltà per un
    ascensore a Piazza Vittorio* 299, 300,
    301, 305, 308–09, 312
Lanbo, Hu, *Petali d'orchidea* 277, 283–84
language
    in Cattapan's work 189–95
    and citizenship 59–62, 300, 323–24
    and power 137, 301, 305, 309
    see also multilingualism; translanguaging; translation, linguistic and intercultural
language learning
    in art-based language research projects
        133, 137, 141–44
    and community formation 307–08,
        312
    ESOL students 141–44, 153
    see also Scuole italiane
language teaching, current approaches to
    8–9, 11–12, 128–29, 233
    see also TML project
Latin root words 187, 217–18, 222, 321,
    322
Law, John 270
layering 189
    in literature of migration experiences
        300–01, 304–06, 310
    in translation 318, 321–22
    in translational visual art 186–87, 188,
        194–95, 197, 198–205
Leeuwen, Theo van 192–93
Lefebvre, Henri 183–84, 185, 187, 190,
    195, 198–99
Leite, Naomi 17, 230, 238
Leonardo art project 144–48
Leros 93
Levi, Carlo 172

Index

Libya 77, 79, 81, 302
  Jews in 17, 227, 228, 229, 231–32, 239–40, 247–50
Life Line: Filo della vita exhibition (Amore) 326–29
Ligurian, or 'Genovese dialect' 49–50, 63–66
Lionnet, Françoise 141, 148
literature
  of migration experiences 18–19, 297–316
  as postcolonial legacy in East Africa 103–04
'Little Italy', London 14, 23–46
local and global intersections
  in art-based language research projects 141–44
  artists in Australia 182
  Italian associations in Buenos Aires 159
  in migrants' homes 313
  in Rhodes 78–80, 86–92
  in urban spaces 303–07, 314
Lombardi-Diop, Cristina 93–94
Lombroso, Cesare 161
London, 'Little Italy' 14, 23–46
Londra Sera (newspaper) 25
Lonely Planet 99
Loomba, Ania 287–88

Made in China 284, 288
Made in Italy 276, 278–80, 284, 285, 288
Maestri, Eliana 16, 179–206
Mai Taclì (journal) 15, 105–24
Mancosu, Gianmarco 103n5
Manuscript of Monte Cassino, The (Paolozzi) 132–33
Marciniak, Katarzyna, *Teaching Transnational Cinema* 137
marginality and Italianness 61, 150–53, 163, 229
Marrickville, Sydney 263–65, 264
Martin, Simon 153
Martinello, Paolo 278, 288
MartinoExpress, *Lǎowài, un pratese in Cina. Diario di un expat da Chinatown all'estremo oriente* 277, 294–95
Marzaroli, Oscar 139
Mason, Raymond 152
masseria 263, 265, 269

Massey, Doreen 313
material culture studies 155–58
Mauss, Marcel 167, 217, 339
May, Theresa 323
Mayne, Roger 39
McAuliffe, Chris 187–90, 191–92, 194, 197–98, 204
McDonnell, Terence E., et al. 170–71
McGuire, Valerie 15, 75–99
medieval Rhodes 80–84, 82, 94–95
Melandri, Francesca 104
Melani, Marcello 105–06, 108
Melbourne 179, 186–88, 194, 198, 208, 319
Meltzer, David 145
memory
  in art 331–34
  in *Beyond Borders* exhibition 209, 217, 220, 223
  in diasporic gardening 263–67
  and food 63–64, 67–69, 233–34
  in *Mai Taclì* 106–24
  mobility of 5–6, 17, 227–52, 318–20
  and objects 172–76
  and translation 19, 324, 338
  in Valparaíso 50–52, 63–68
  see also childhood; colonial history, Italian; history, constructing narratives of
Mengiste, Maaza 104
Mercouri, Melina 76
Mersmann, Birgit 321
Mexican migrants 329–30
Mezzadra, Sandro 144
migration statistics 3, 177, 276, 285, 293
Milan 275–76, 301–02, 303–06, 309, 311–12
Miller, Daniel 155, 156
Miller, J. Hillis 298
Minonne, Francesca 176, 177
misplacement, in migrant gardens 253–74
mixed ethnicity 119–22
mobility
  in Cattapan's work 16, 179–206
  of memory 5–6, 17, 227–52, 318–20
  'moving objects' 16, 167–68, 312–13
modern languages *see* language teaching, current approaches to
'moments of truth' 230, 243, 245, 252

monolingualism 129, 233, 323–24
monuments
    Rhodes 75–76
    Rome 310
    Valparaíso 52–56
Moran, Joe 39–40
Moretti, Antonella, *Prezzemolo & cilantro. Storie di donne italiane in Cina* 277, 288–89, 290–92, 294
Morón 165, 166, *166*, 171, 173–74
Morris wallpaper 335–36, *336*
Morrison, Toni, *Home* 222–23
mosaics, Tottenham Court Road tube station (Paolozzi) 133, 141–42, *143*, 153
Mosque of Solimon *hammam*, Rhodes 83, 94
mother tongue, notions of 217, 300, 308–09, 324
'moving objects' 16, 167–68, 312–13
multiculturalism
    in Australia 179–82, 185, 204, 254, 259, 263
    in Italian cities 302–03, 311–12
    in Rhodes' history 76–78, 92
multilingualism
    and citizenship 323–24
    and intercultural translation 128–29
    in Lakhous's novel 308–09
    in urban spaces 300–01, 303, 311–12, 314–15
    see also translanguaging
Munck, Ronaldo 160
Munley, Thomas 133
museums *see* exhibitions, conceptualizations of
Mussolini 77, 79, 85–86, 243
mutual aid associations, Argentina 159–64, *165*, 166–67, *166*
    and Object Workshops 167, 171–76, 177
My Backyard, Your Backyard (documentary) 258
My Father's Backyard 269–70, 271, 273

Namibia 12
Nanjing 286–87
Nascia, Gaetano 249

'national' languages 54, 60, 61, 72, 129, 133, 309, 323–24
    see also language teaching, current approaches to
nationalism
    Greek 78, 79
    Italian 36–37, 54–57, 61, 80, 85n16, 88–89, 96, 98
Nazism 97
Neilson, Brett 144
Nesi, Edoardo, *Storia della mia gente* 277, 279–80, 283
New York 28n9
    and Cattapan's work 186–87, 194
Nuovo, Fiorella 119
Nuzzaci, Daniela 285–86

O Jerusalem (film) 98
objects
    commodification of 168–69
    in material culture studies 155–58
    and misplacement 255–56
    Object Workshops, Argentina 158, 167, 170–75, 173
    Paolozzi's *objets trouvés* 138–39, 151
    singularization of 169–70
    see also Beyond Borders exhibition
O'Brien, Colin 39, 40–42, 43–44
oral histories of diasporic gardens 261–67
orality in literature 309
Orientalism, Rhodes 83, 84, 87–89, 95, 99
Ortelli, Giovanni 32
orti 265, 266, 269, 273
Otsuji, Emi 195
Ottoman legacy, Rhodes 76, 79, 80–84, 85–87, 94–95

Paggi, Ariel 238
Paggi, Clelia 240–42, 243, 246, 247
Paggi, Giannetto 17, 228–29, 238–40, 243
Paggi, Ida 240, 242
Paolozzi, Eduardo 15–16, 141–42, *143*, 144, 148, 151–53
    I want to be a machine 127–28, *127*–29
    For Leonardo 144–45
    The Manuscript of Monte Cassino 132–33
    Vulcan 138–39, *141*

Pariani, Laura, *Dio non ama i bambini* 162–63
Parque Italia, Valparaíso 52–53
Pascali's Island (film) 98
Passerini, Luisa 17, 229–30
Pastene, Giovanni Battista 56
  bust of, Valparaíso 53, *53*, 54
'path that leads me home, the' (art piece, *Castlebrae in the World*) 149, *150*
Pauluzzo, Rubens 281
peach trees 265, 268–69
Pennycook, Alastair 65, 195
Philip, Julie 130–31, 141–42, 144
photography
  gardens in Australia 254, 257, *261*, *264*, 267, *269*, 272
  Holocaust memories 237–38
  in literature of migration experiences 301–02
  of 'Little Italy', London 27, *31*, 33, *35*, 36, 39–42, 43–44
  in *Mai Taclì* 107, 108, 112–14, *113*, 115–16, *117*
  North African Jewish portraits 249
  of objects 173–74
  of Pitigliano 234, 237
Piazza dei Cinquecento, Rome 311
Pink, Sarah 51
Pitigliano 17, 227–52
Pivetti, Irene 280
plants and place-making 256–73, *257*, 270–71
Polezzi, Loredana 19, 187, 237, 317–40
Pollock, Sheldon 324
polylanguaging 308–09
Pop Paolozzi! art project 132–33, *134*, *135*
Portelli, Alessandro 261–62
porteña/o, definition of 47n1
power and language 137, 301, 305, 309
Prato 278–80, 283, 289, 294–95
Pratt, Mary Louise 105
  Imperial Eyes: Writing and Transculturation 255
Prentice, Norma 130
prickly pears 266–67, 272, 273
Print Generation art project 133–36, *136*

printing processes 133, 135–36, *136*, 144–48, *146*
Prodi, Giorgio 280–81, 291
promise, as metaphor for translation 339–40
Pym, Anthony 205

Qiankui, Wu 275–76
Queensland 261, 262, 265, 266
Quijada, Monica 163, 176

race issues
  anti-Semitism, Libya 17, 228, 240–42, 243–52
  in Argentina 161–63, 176–77
  in Australia 185, 203
  in Eritrea 120–22
  experiences of mixed ethnicity 119–22
  and Fascism 79, 84, 88n24, 93n31, 96–97
  Greek and Turkish population exchange 95
  in Italo-Chinese relations 281–83, 285–95
Raffaetà, Roberta, et al. 289, 293
Rampone, Oscar 106, 121–22
'repatriation'
  from Eritrea 110–12
  from Libya 228, 240, 241–42
resonance, in Object Workshops 170–71
Rhodes 15, 75–99, *82*, *86*
Ricatti, Francesco 5, 17, 230, 254
Ricoeur, Paul 319, 324–25, 339n57
Rigney, Ann 6
Risorgimento 159
Rocchi, Ciaj, and Demonte, Matteo, *Chinamen. Un secolo di cinesi a Milano* 275
Roma (film) 187–88
Rome
  Beyond Borders exhibition 212–13, *212*, *215*, *219*, *221*
  and Cattapan's work 186–88
  Paggi family in 240, 242
  in Scego's novel 300, 302, 310–11
Romeo, Caterina 93–94
Romiti, Cesare 279–80

Rosa, Paolo 223
  L'arte fuori da sé 215–16
Rose, Marcia 130
Ross, Silvia 279
Rothberg, Michael 318
Roumani, Jacques 232
Roumani, Judith 231–38, 240
rugs 317–18, 335–38

Sakai, Naoki 324
Samata, Susan 50
Santayana, George 310
Sarmiento, Domingo Faustino 161–62
Savolainen, Ulla 175
Scego, Igiaba 103–04
  Roma negata: Percorsi postcoloniali nella città 299, 301, 302, 310–11, 312
Schneider, Arnd 160
Schostal (clothing shop) 243
Sciorra, Joseph 326
Scotland
  art-based language research projects 129–51
  historic Italian community 152
Scuole italiane
  Beijing 289–90
  Buenos Aires 162, 239–40
  Tripoli 239–40, 246, 247
  Valparaíso 49, 52, 58–62, 58, 63
Second World War
  Holocaust memories 237–38
  impact on Italian colonies 83, 91–93, 94, 97, 98, 110–12
  impact on Italians in the UK 37, 41
  Paolozzi's experiences during 152
second-generation migrants 37, 262, 265–67, 272–73, 293–94
  see also Cattapan, Jon; Paolozzi, Eduardo
Sedgwick, Eve 151, 154
Selva, Gustavo 120
sensory experiences
  and cultural memory 63, 66, 68
  in diasporic gardening 259–61, 273–74
  in literature of migration 300, 302, 312, 314
  and translation 298, 308
  see also Beyond Borders exhibition

Sephardic culture *see* 'La piccola Gerusalemme' (Pitigliano)
Sephardic Horizons (journal) 231, 235–36, 238–39
Servi, Elena 234, 238, 252
Servi Machlin, Edda, *The Classic Cuisine of the Italian Jews* 233–34, 237
sewing 331–32, 333, 334–35
Shan, Hongxia 259
Shanghai 276, 282
Sheikh, Fazal 320n8
Shih, Shu-mei 141, 148
Simon, Sherry 182, 185, 188, 203, 301
singularization of objects 169–70
societies of Italians *see* associations of Italians
Soja, Edward 311
Somalia 302
Sommer, Doris 127, 143, 149, 153
Spackman, Barbara 88
Spadaro, Barbara 17, 227–52
Spadoni, Gianfranco 111–12
Spain 53–54
spatiality
  in *Beyond Borders* exhibition 209, 210–13, 216–24, 334
  in Cattapan's work 179–206
  in literature of migration 297–316
Spencer, Robin 128n3, 151
Spitta, Silvia 268
  Misplaced Objects 255–56
SS *Arandora Star* 25, 41, 152
St Peter's Italian Church, Clerkenwell, London 25–28, 27, 37, 38
statues, Valparaíso 52–56
Steedman, Carolyn 150
Stieber, Nancy 23–24n2
stories
  in *Beyond Borders* exhibition 209–10, 216–18, 220–23
  oral histories of Italian Australian gardens 261–67
  see also literature
Strathern, Marilyn 158, 175
students, international 290–92
Studio Azzurro 213–14, 223
substitution and equivalence in translation 322–23, 324–25, 338

Sulle orme di Marco Polo report 285, 287, 293
superdiverse urban spaces as 'translation zones' 18–19, 297–98, 300–09, 311–12, 314–15
Sydney 253–74, 264, 267
Szeeman, Harald, *When Attitudes Become Form* 211–12

Taddia, Irma 102
Taha, Amin 45
Taylor, Diana 68
technology, and Cattapan's work 191–94, 196, 198, 199–201, 203, 205, 206
Terroni's Italian delicatessen and café, Clerkenwell, London 28, 30, 31, 37
textiles 133–36, 326–38
  see also weaving
thick translation 184, 201–04, 318, 322
  see also layering
Thomas, Elly 144n32
threads and migration 318–19, 326–37
  see also weaving
Tilley, Christopher 156, 177
TML project 4, 9–12, 16–17, 129–32, 207–08, 319
TomcatUSA *Te la do io la Cina* blogposts 277, 286–87, 288, 289, 295
Tottenham Court Road tube station, London 133, 141–42, 143, 153
Touring Club Italiano 85
tourism
  Jewish heritage tourism 234, 235–36, 237
  Rhodes 75, 79–80, 85–92, 90, 93, 97, 99
trace, notion of 320, 329–30, 332–39, 340
transculturation and place-making 253–55, 259, 262–74
transformation as translation, in *Leonardo* project 145, 148
transgenerational Italianness
  in art 180–81
  in gardening 259, 263–64, 272–73
  role of objects in 16
  through textiles 328, 329–34, 333
  in Valparaíso 16, 62–69

translanguaging 231, 232–33, 304, 305–06, 308–09, 315
translation, linguistic and intercultural 270, 321–22
  in art-based language research projects 128–51
  in *Beyond Borders* exhibition 210, 214
  in Cattapan's work 183–84, 187–88, 190–206
  in diasporic gardening 269–70
  and hospitality 322–26, 339–40
  in *Leonardo* project 144–48
  in superdiverse urban spaces 18–19, 297–98, 300–09, 311–12, 314–15
  thick translation 184, 201–04, 318, 322
  as trace 320, 330, 332–39
  transformative impact of 6–8, 237
  and visual art 19, 183–84, 186–87, 188, 190–206, 321–22
  and weaving 318–22, 325, 327, 330, 332, 333
'travelling' memories 5–6, 227–52, 318–20
trees, in diasporic gardening 257, 261, 263, 264–65, 266–67, 268–69, 269, 271, 272, 273
Trieste 243, 300–01, 307–08
Tripoli 17, 227, 228, 229
Tunis 220n22
Tunisia 80n8
Turkish bathhouses, Rhodes 83, 94
Turkish community, Rhodes 83, 84, 95–97
  see also Ottoman legacy, Rhodes
Turner, Victor, *Antropologia dell'esperienza* 222
Tymoczko, Maria 205, 321

UNESCO world heritage sites 75, 94, 118
United Kingdom 14, 23–46, 127–28
United States 28n9
  Ellis Island Museum 326–27
  New York 186–87, 194
  Roumani family 232–34, 235
Universal Exhibitions (World Expos) 275–76
University College London (UCL)
  Bloomsbury Project 34

university programmes for international students 290–92
'uprooting and regrounding' 268, 270
  see also gardens and diasporic cultures
urban spaces
  in Cattapan's work 184–206
  intercultural translation in 18–19, 297–98, 300–09, 311–12, 314–15
  'Little Italy', London 14, 23–46
Urry, John 2–3, 23

Valparaíso 14, 47–73
Van Holstein, Ellen 259
Vanni, Ilaria 18, 253–74
Vannini, Aldo 114–15
Venice 188–89
Vertovec, Steven 5
Vigili, Sergio 106
Vom Hau, Matthias 161, 162, 176–77
Vulcan (Paolozzi) 138–39

Wadia, Laila, *Amiche per la pelle* 299, 300–01, 305, 307–08, 312, 313
Wallflower - Mirror, rorriM (Coppola) 335–38, 336
Walter, Pierre 259
Warhol, Andy, *I want to be a machine* 127–28

Warton, Michael 143–44n26
weaving
  Great Grandmother's Ocean (Amore) 328, 329
  and translation 318–22, 325, 327, 330, 332, 333
Weise, Kyle 196, 201, 205
Wells, Naomi 14, 47–73
Westphal, Bertrand 298
When Attitudes Become Form (Szeeman) 211
'White Australia' policy 180, 203, 204
Whitechapel Gallery, London 127–28
Whitford, Frank 128n3
Whitlam government, Australia 179–80
Wilson, Rita 19, 182, 297–316
Wittgenstein, Ludwig 132n13
Wollongong 258
World Expos (Universal Exhibitions) 275–76
World Trade Organization 277–78, 279, 288

Young Achievers, Castlebrae Community High School 139–41

Zhang, Gaoheng 283

9 781789 622553

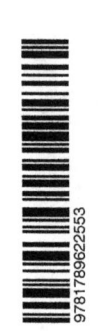